ANCIENT MONUMENTS
AND THEIR
INTERPRETATION

Arnold Taylor   *Bassano*

ANCIENT MONUMENTS AND THEIR INTERPRETATION

ESSAYS PRESENTED TO A. J. TAYLOR

Edited by

M. R. APTED, R. GILYARD-BEER and A. D. SAUNDERS

PHILLIMORE

1977

Published by
PHILLIMORE & CO. LTD.

London and Chichester

Head Office: Shopwyke Hall, Chichester,
Sussex, England

ISBN 0 85033 239 7

Printed in Great Britain by
UNWIN BROTHERS LIMITED
at the Gresham Press, Old Woking, Surrey

CONTENTS

List of Plates   vii

List of Figures   x

Foreword   xiii

Introduction   xv

1   New light on Neolithic habitation sites and early Iron Age Settlements in Southern Britain: 1963-73
G. J. WAINWRIGHT   1

2   The Turrets on Hadrian's Wall
D. CHARLESWORTH   13

3   Witcombe Roman villa: a reconstruction
DAVID S. NEAL   27

4   Enamels from Roman Britain
S. A. BUTCHER   41

5   The developing role of the natural sciences in archaeological interpretation
JOHN MUSTY   71

6   The cathedral and relics of St. Magnus, Kirkwall
STEWART CRUDEN   85

7   Romanesque bases in and south-east of the limestone belt
S. E. RIGOLD   99

8   Usk Castle and its affinities
J. K. KNIGHT   139

9   The Wakefield Tower, Tower of London
P. E. CURNOW   155

10   De Ireby's Tower in Carlisle Castle
R. GILYARD-BEER   191

11   Three stages in the construction of the hall at Kenilworth Castle
M. W. THOMPSON   211

12   Langerwehe stoneware of the fourteenth and fifteenth centuries
J. G. HURST   219

13   Craignethan Castle, Lanarkshire: an experiment in artillery fortification
IAIN MACIVOR   239

14   The building of Upnor Castle, Kent, 1559-1601
A. D. SAUNDERS   263

15   Heath Old Hall, Yorkshire
O. J. WEAVER   285

16   The Lady Anne Clifford (1590-1676)
JOHN CHARLTON   303

17   The seventeenth-century buildings at Tredegar House, Newport
M. R. APTED   315

18   Stott Park bobbin mill, Colton, Cumbria: an historical outline, 1835-1971
P. R. WHITE   335

19   Bibliography of the published works of Dr. A. J. Taylor   349

Index   357

LIST OF PLATES

Frontispiece   Arnold Taylor

Between pages 348 and 349

I a   Hadrian's Wall: Turret 26b (Low Brunton)
  b   The Rudge Cup

II a   St. Magnus Cathedral: the north side
  b   Plan

III   St. Magnus Cathedral: the Romanesque choir

IV a   St. Magnus Cathedral: polychrome masonry
  b   Choir pier, north aisle
  c   East arch of Romanesque choir
  d   Romanesque window

V   Usk Castle in 1732

VI a   Usk Castle: the twelfth-century keep
  b   The Garrison Tower

VII a   Usk Castle: the gate to the inner ward
  b   The fourteenth-century outer gatehouse

VIII a   The Wakefield Tower and Old Treasure House, 1801
  b   The same, 1886
  c   The nineteenth-century Jewel House office
  d   The Bloody and Wakefield Towers today

IX a   Wakefield Tower: excavation of postern, Stage 1
  b   The same, Stage 2
  c   The twelfth-century plinth with seven offsets
  d   Junction of 'c' with plinth below Bloody Tower

X a   Wakefield Tower: excavation of interior, Stage 1
  b   Stage 2
  c   Stage 3

XI a   Wakefield Tower: exterior as excavated, 1975
  b   Excavation of curtain wall, 1957
  c   Wakefield Tower: lower chamber restored
  d   Upper chamber restored

XII   Carlisle Castle: indenture of 1378

XIII	a	Carlisle Castle: De Ireby's Tower from the north
	b	The Tower from the south
XIV	a	Kenilworth Castle: the Hall from outside
	b	The same, interior
XV	a	Kenilworth Castle: inner face of east side of Hall
	b	The Hall: springing of vault; column bases
XVI		Craignethan Castle: aerial view from the north east
XVII		Craignethan Castle: aerial view from the north west
XVIII	a	Craignethan Castle: tower-house from the west
	b	Tower-house: angle round
	c	Tower-house: platform of west parapet
XIX	a	Craignethan Castle: caponier
	b	West towers and curtain of the outer courtyard
XX	a	Upnor Castle: aerial view from the east
	b	Bastion with heightened parapet
XXI		Upnor Castle: early eighteenth-century plan of magazine/original barrack range
XXII	a	Heath Old Hall: from the east
	b	View from the south
XXIII	a	Barlborough Hall, Derbyshire: front elevation
	b	Heath Old Hall: front elevation
XXIV		Heath Old Hall: the 'Jezebel' chimney piece
XXV	a	Heath Old Hall: ceiling in chamber 'B'
	b	Ceiling in the long gallery
	c	Ceiling in the great chamber
XXVI	a	Heath Old Hall: plasterwork in the hall
	b	The same
XXVII	a	Brough Castle in 1739
	b	The castle today
XXVIII	a	Tredegar House: the north-west range
	b	The Gilt Room
XXIX	a	Tredegar House: painted ceiling in Gilt Room
	b	Engraving (1647) of part of ceiling, Barberini Palace, Rome
XXX	a	Tredegar House: entrance to stable yard
	b	Front door
	c	Side gates and stable block

XXXI a	Tredegar House: front (north west) elevation
b	Clarendon House, Piccadilly (demolished 1683): front elevation
XXXII a	Stott Park bobbin mill: exterior
b	The new lathe shop: interior

COPYRIGHT ACKNOWLEDGMENTS

LIST OF FIGURES

Chapter 1   page
1   Plans of buildings constructed c.2000 b.c.   2
2   Distribution of causewayed enclosures in Wessex   5
3   Iron age settlement at Gussage All Saints, Dorset   8
4   Balksbury Camp, Hampshire   10

Chapter 2
1   Turret 29a (Blackcarts)   15
2   Turret 51a (Piper Sike)   17

Chapter 3
1   Plan of Witcombe Roman villa   28
2   Diagram of different levels of the villa   30
3   Overall reconstruction   32
4   Reconstruction of north-west wing   33
5   Reconstruction of north-east wing   35
6   Reconstruction of south-east wing   37

Chapter 4
1   Handle from Kirkby Lathorpe, Lincs.   46
2   Bowl from Brougham, Cumbria   47
3   Bowl from Beadlam, Yorks.   48
4   Miniature stands from Water Newton, Cambs.   50
5   Brooches from Wanborough, Wilts., Leicester and St. Albans   52
6   Disc brooches from Thistleton, Leics.   53
7   Plate brooches from Hockwold, Norfolk, Water Newton and
    Wanborough   55
8   Brooches from Nornour, Isles of Scilly   57
9   Trumpet brooches from Rudston, Humberside and Hockwold   61
10 Bow brooches from Thistleton, Old Winteringham and
    Winterton, Humberside   63

Chapter 6
1   St. Magnus, Kirkwall, end of Phase 1, c.1137-42   89
2   End of first period style c.1145   90
3   North arcade of the nave, after c.1142   92
4   The first completed church c.1150   93
5   Conjectural east end, 1137-c.1142   94

Chapter 7

1	Generalised Romanesque bases to show terminology	105
2	Classes A, I-IV	109
3	Classes A, V-VIII and BI	112
4	Classes BI, 1-2	115
5	Classes BI, 2-5, BII and BIII	118
6	Classes BIII, 1-4	121
7	Classes BIII, 4, D and E	125

Chapter 8

1	Usk Castle, general plan	141
2	Plan of inner ward	143
3	Plans of twelfth-century keep	145
4	Plans of Garrison Tower	152

Chapter 9

1	Environs of the Wakefield Tower	156
2	Ground floor plans	160
3	Ground floor 1867-1970	164
4	Ground floor, sections	166
5	Plan of first floor joists and ring-beam	167
6	Axonometric view, details	169
7	Table of masons' marks	172
8	Papal bull of Innocent IV	174
9	Excavated sections	178
10	Coarse pottery associated with postern	180
11	Coarse pottery from basement in-fill	182
12	Coarse pottery from basement in-fill and south-west loop	186

Chapter 10

1	Carlisle Castle, plan	193
2	De Ireby's Tower, plan in 1962	194
3	De Ireby's Tower, plan in fourteenth century	201
4	De Ireby's Tower, planning diagram	206

Chapter 11

1	Inner bailey of Kenilworth Castle	212

Chapter 12

1	Map showing Längerwehe and stoneware centres	219
2	Type I jugs	227
3	Type II jugs	228
4	Type III jugs	230
5	Type IV jugs	232
6	Costrels, cups, horns, pipkins and tripod jugs	235

Chapter 13

1	Map of area of Craignethan castle	240
2	Ground floor plan of courtyards	242
3	Tower house and east range	246
4	West rampart and ditch, section	248
5	West rampart and ditch, plans	249
6	Caponier	252

Chapter 14

1	Defences of the Medway estuary, sixteenth-nineteenth century	264
2	Upnor Castle, ground floor plan	267
3	Basement plan	268
4	Barrack building	274
5	South Tower	275
6	Section and conjectural reconstruction	278

Chapter 15

1	Plan of Heath village	285
2	Sections across Heath Old Hall	287
3	Plans of basement and principal floor	290
4	Plans of top floor and roof	291

Chapter 17

1	Plans of medieval and seventeenth-century Tredegar compared	316
2	Tredegar House, ground floor	318
3	First floor	319
4	The attics	321
5	The stables	330

Chapter 18

1	Map and plan of Stott Park bobbin mill	337
2	Sections through mill buildings	338
3	Ground floor plan	339
4	First and second floor plans	341

FOREWORD

ARNOLD TAYLOR joined H.M. Office of Works in 1935 as Assistant Inspector of Ancient Monuments for Wales. In those days, not so long after the passage of the 1931 Act, Assistant Inspectors were still relatively new phenomena: how different — and gratifyingly different — the picture is now. Those who complain of the inadequate complement of the Inspectorate should look back and then realise how much is owed to Arnold Taylor for the size and status of the Inspectorate today. It is the case that his years as Chief Inspector were seminal in the development of today's Inspectorate, including not least the development of the Ancient Monuments laboratory. Furthermore it fell to him to lead the Inspectorate into the new world of amalgamation with the Historic Buildings organisation of the former Ministry of Housing: an amalgamation which for years had proclaimed itself as a necessary development in the administration of these matters, but which was always frustrated by the curious doctrine that Historic Buildings belonged in essence to planning. It was not until the invention of the Department of the Environment that this could be broken down: and it is enormously to the credit of those responsible at the time that it was in fact broken down, and that quite soon. Of these, Arnold Taylor was not the least effective (I, as Permanent Secretary of the Ministry of Works, had never been able to make any headway in this direction, though I did my inadequate best).

Arnold Taylor was among the more distinguished of the line of Chief Inspectors of Ancient Monuments: and the fact that he is the first since Charles Peers, who started the whole thing off, to be elected President of the Society of Antiquaries is a fitting tribute by the archaeological community to his service as Chief Inspector, and also to his distinction as a scholar, not least as the historian of medieval fortification, notably the Edwardian castles in Wales.

This work signifies in a notable way all he has done for the growth of what I suppose must be called 'official' archaeology in Great Britain and reflects not least the quality of the Inspectorate with the development of which he has had so much to do.

Sir Edward Muir, K.C.B.

Kirkwall

Craignethan

Hadrian's Wall
51A   29A
Carlisle

Stott Park

Heath

Kenilworth

Usk   Witcombe
Tredegar   Wakefield
Upnor

INTRODUCTION

THE Inspectorate of Ancient Monuments was created more than ninety years ago with the appointment of Gen. Pitt Rivers in 1882 as the first Inspector. Apart from a steady expansion of the number of the sites and monuments in care or given legal protection by scheduling there were no major changes in the pattern of work for many years thereafter. The years which followed the end of the Second World War however presented radical changes for the Inspectorate; the range of responsibilities increased dramatically as the frontiers of archaeology expanded. Whereas before the war preservation of standing buildings was the principal task, now, with intensive arable farming, urban renewal and .the increase in the amount of land required for road making and the extractive industries, the preservation of monuments had also come to mean the recognition of new classes of monument requiring protection and the preservation of archaeological data from sites threatened by destruction. Arnold Taylor's career encompassed this period of rapid archaeological expansion and enlargement of duties and function, and in his last ten years of service he was himself responsible for leading the Inspectorate into this wider role. In these radically changing years he succeeded in maintaining the traditional identity of the Inspectorate; its professional standards, philosophy and its corporate sense remained unaltered.

The role of the Inspectorate is defined in the Ancient Monuments Act of 1882: 'the Commissioners of Her Majesty's Treasury shall appoint one or more inspectors of ancient monuments whose duty it shall be to report to the Commissioners of Works on the condition of such monuments and on the best mode of preserving the same'. The key is in the final phrase. Although the present Directorate is a team in which the inspectors are in partnership with their architect colleagues who are responsible for carrying out the work of preservation and with its secretariat who are interpreters of policy and keepers of the purse, it is the inspector who identifies the monuments for preservation and recommends the course of action which will be most beneficial for the monument and limits the loss of its archaeological evidential quality. It follows that the Inspectorate acts as adviser in all archaeological and historical matters to the Secretary of State and other departments of government.

The preservation of monuments is perhaps taken for granted today, particularly at a time when the conservation of our heritage of sites, buildings and environment has such wide, vociferous and sometimes uncritical support. Yet the questions have still to be asked: which monuments should be preserved and why?

In the 1930s and before the chief concern was for the standing ruins of Roman Britain and of the Middle Ages. The great abbeys and castles were deteriorating fast through the neglect of the effects of weather and vegetation. Since the last war when the threat to the heritage has become more acute, the emphasis has changed to include wider classes of monument: the remnants of our industrial historic past, redundant churches, the country house and a brave sweep of buildings architecturally much less grand, if not to say vernacular. We have also come to realise that preservation may also mean the recording of sites which cannot be preserved in their own right and the conservation of the resulting products of excavation.

We have moved a long way from the cult of ruins, attractive though this can be, to something a good deal more scientific. The decision to preserve arises not only from desire to save objects which are visually attractive and ancient but from the belief in the value of a site or monument for the way it can advance our knowledge of mankind in general through the study of the creation, use and alteration of its material remains. This is an unashamedly archaeological approach which sees in the sites and monuments essential data for the study of man through the remnants of his material culture, the equivalent of the historian's documents. This is as true of the standing buildings as it is of the site now contained within the soil. All the more so since excavation itself is an unrepeatable experiment while the standing structure has a peculiar value since it can be critically examined time and again to the increasing benefit of posterity so long as it continues to exist. We do not depend for our knowledge of the monument on the written record of a single examination at a given point in time.

It is increasingly realised that preservation should not be confined to the narrow limits of the monument itself. Any monument is part of a wide continually changing environment and must be related to its natural setting as well as to other man-made features. This leads to the selection and sampling of sites within as wide a framework as possible, to the ultimate creation of a national bank of sites and the need for its management as a cultural resource.

An unnecessary and specious argument has unfortunately developed in recent years between those wishing to conserve the environment as a living and developing entity and those who preserve 'dead' monuments. In some quarters this has led to the view that 'conservation is good, preservation is bad'. The 'static' ruin policy is criticised for fossilising a monument at a particular point in its history and maintaining it in a clinical and didactic manner. There are still those who see virtue in the 'progressive' ruin; who value monuments more for their 'atmosphere' and the aesthetic appeal of decay and creeper. It is however a selfish view which tolerates the rapid destruction of the object which is admired. A balance has to be struck between the romantic approach which can at least be catered for at monuments of little archaeological importance and the identification of those monuments to be kept for their evidential quality. It is also stressed that monuments need to be brought back into use, and this too can be a dangerous generalisation. It begs the question of why a monument is being kept and does not take into account the degree to which adaptation to modern use may impinge on the archaeological features within the monument.

The truth is that there is room for both concepts, conservation and preservation, one complements the other. There is a clear need for conservation in terms of maintaining appearances, character and atmosphere, in keeping and enhancing the visual appeal of landscape and townscape, breathing life into the old buildings by retaining their original functions or finding new uses in order to keep the historic fabric about us. Preservation on the other hand implies a selective process whereby archaeologically valuable sites, buildings or objects, are identified and maintained by virtue of the information they contain and of what they can tell our successors, unhampered as far as possible from compromise with the present.

If preservation is the foundation of the Inspectorate's purpose its practical expression is a belief that a monument should be preserved without imaginative embellishment and restoration of what might have been. The most well intentioned and scholarly restoration inevitably makes assumptions and rests on hypothesis. Once started the restorer is on a slippery slope as the restoration of churches in the last century demonstrates all too well. The construction of full scale models can be extremely instructive to the specialist when carried out away from the original site but using the monument itself for such experiments usually leads to permanent accretion expressing the extent of knowledge at a particular point in time and presuming that future scholars will not produce alternative interpretations, By its nature restoration makes suspect the original fabric. Remove decay, stitch fractures, make wall tops waterproof but in all essentials 'treat as found'. This is the traditional philosophy which has governed site policy by the Ancient Monuments branch as a whole, architects as well as inspectors. The 'works' element under the architect's control which carries out the bulk of the practical preservation has had this attitude engrained within it since the 1920s. It is a philosophy which belongs to the teachings of William Morris but is expressed as a modification of the Morris doctrine that it was enough 'to prop a perilous wall or mend a leaky roof by such means as are obviously meant for support or covering and to show no pretence of other art'. Inspectors have encouraged their architect colleagues to strengthen and support by hidden means whenever possible and to repair ancient fabric with materials matching the original as closely as one can today. In the joint operation which is necessary for most preservation work it is the Inspector's task to safe-guard the archaeological features contained in a monument to no less a degree than the monument itself. Respect for the evidence is the first criterion.

Apart from the mechanics of physical repair and the preservation of evidence through excavation there is another element in the Inspectorate's duties which has developed almost entirely since the war. This is the technical advice and more particularly financial help for preservation work given to owners of sites and monuments. Since 1953 inspectors have assisted the Historic Buildings Councils in recommending aid for individual buildings, groups of buildings and historic quarters. From the more limited Ancient Monuments funds it has also been possible to encourage the efforts of independent trusts engaged, for, example in salvaging early industrial monuments.

These are the main practical considerations of preservation but this is not enough. There are also the academic problems of interpreting the evidence so carefully preserved and, by no means least, of the diffusion of knowledge to a wider public. The Inspectors may sometimes feel that growing pressures involved in preserving the monuments and the increasing demands for popular explanation and interpretation of such sites within the Department's care mean less and less time for scholarly study and advancement of knowledge. Nevertheless, this is a factor of the Inspectorate's role which must not be and is not ignored and the essays in this volume demonstrate that the concomitant of preservation is understanding what is preserved and making this knowledge available for our successors.

As well as contributing to the understanding of particular monuments this collection demonstrates the many facets of the Inspectorate's work not only in range and date of sites but in the employment of excavation in conjunction with observations on standing buildings, historical research, the study of objects resulting from excavations and the scientific processes which support and contribute to archaeology today. It was for this reason that its contributors were limited to the Inspectorate, unlike the *festschrift* to another former Chief Inspector, Bryan O'Neil which took building history as its theme.[1] It is not perhaps surprising in a volume dedicated to Arnold Taylor, that castle studies figure uppermost. However, the time scale covered by the essays ranges from a synthesis of recent excavation of Neolithic and Iron Age settlements and a study of the Hadrian's Wall turrets to a description and history of a bobbin mill of the latter part of the nineteenth century. Not only is excavation a factor but also the product of excavation whether small finds or pottery. The survey of enamelling in Roman Britain depended to a considerable extent on the conservation and scientific examination carried out in the Ancient Monuments laboratory and it is wholly appropriate that there should be an account of the role of the natural sciences as an aid to archaeological interpretation. But Arnold Taylor is first and foremost an historian who applies his skill to the study of buildings. It is therefore particularly happy that several contributions involve the correlation of documentary evidence with the fabric of the buildings and that the buildings concerned extend beyond medieval military architecture to the great cathedral of St. Magnus, Kirkwall, to a corpus of Romanesque bases and so to the more decorative architecture of the seventeenth and eighteenth centuries.

The editors acknowledge the help they have received from many colleagues by no means confined to the Inspectorate. Particular thanks are due to David Neal and his illustrator colleagues, James Thorn, Frank Gardiner, Diane Miller, Susan Heaser, and Christine Boddington, for their work in producing the line drawings and designing the jacket, to Margaret Fletcher for the index, to the Department of the Environment for permission to publish and to the publishers for their enthusiasm to produce such a work in difficult times.

Not all inspectors could share in this offering for reasons of space, and by and large the contributors have been those who knew Arnold Taylor longest. Nevertheless this volume is presented to our former colleague in the name of the Inspectorate as a whole in recognition of his love of the Monuments, the leadership and friendship he gave to their servants and for his encouragement of scholarship in their service.

ANDREW SAUNDERS

1. *Studies in Building History, essays in recognition of the work of B. H. St. J. O'Neil* ed. E. M. Jope 1961.

New Light on Neolithic Habitation Sites
and Early Iron Age Settlements
in Southern Britain: 1963-73

by

G. J. WAINWRIGHT

A MAJOR PROBLEM confronting a student of prehistoric Britain is high-lighted by a passage from a guide to field archaeology, published by the Ordnance Survey in 1963:

> The great company of round barrows implying population and the frequent finds of pottery, bronze weapons and tools of high quality belonging to the Bronze Age suggest that Bronze Age dwellings should be found. So far they have been very elusive.

The gaps in our knowledge of settlement types and patterns in the early second millennium BC were emphasized in papers published in 1971 by Dr. I. McInnes and Dr. Derek Simpson which are both characterised by the unavailability of concrete data.[1] For the whole of later Neolithic Britain, house plans which carry conviction could be portrayed as two figures (17 and 18) and similarly for houses of the Beaker people only two figures (23 and 24) were necessary. Henge monuments and related structures have for long been claimed as temples or observatories, but we may fairly ask what sort of a society constructed imposing public works of this character and no domestic structures. No clearly defined domestic areas were obviously associated with the barrow groups and ceremonial centres, yet a large population must have contributed to the operation and maintenance of a single economic system and the centre around which it functioned. Ceremonial or cult centres appear to be a normal step in the development of human cultures. They appear at, or shortly after, the development of economically efficient agriculture which brings with it the need for full-time professional manipulation of the system of supernatural controls required by an agricultural economic base. This suggests the need to reconsider the whole range of structures which were built for this purpose in the late third and early second millennia BC with special attention to those for which a more secular use might be argued, and this in the light of new information provided by excavations undertaken in recent years.

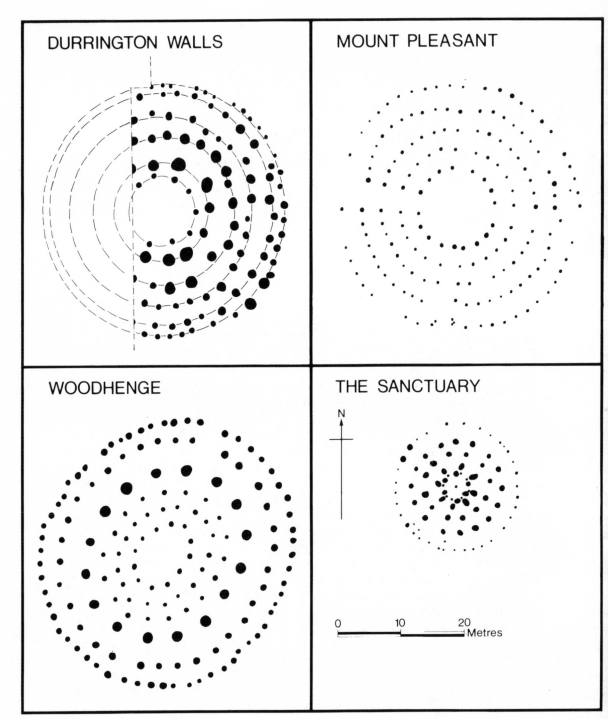

Fig. 1 Comparative plans of buildings constructed *c*.2000 bc in mid-southern England.

The first such structure was excavated by Mrs. Cunnington at Woodhenge near Amesbury in 1926–8.[2]

A timber structure comprising six egg-shaped rings of post-holes with a maximum diameter of 44.00m was sited within a small enclosure which was oval in plan with a single entrance facing north-east and an external bank. In 1939 Professor Piggott interpreted Woodhenge as a roofed building of one period.[3] More recently, Mr. Musson has made an alternative suggestion that Woodhenge represents two separate buildings, both with an outward sloping roof and a central court.[4] The predominant ceramic association is with Grooved Ware and when Dr. John Evans and the author excavated a single cutting across the bank and ditch in 1970, radiocarbon dates of 1867± 74 bc (BM–677) and 1805 ± 54 bc (BM–678) were obtained from the primary silts.[5]

In 1930 Mrs. Cunnington excavated The Sanctuary on Overton Hill in North Wiltshire.[6] The complex history of the monument was initially elucidated by Professor Piggott[7] and has since been discussed in some detail by Mr. Musson.[8] The earliest building was a circular hut 4.50m in diameter which was succeeded by multi-ring buildings 11.50 and 20.00m in diameter respectively. The final timber building was eventually replaced by two concentric stone circles which were linked with the West Kennet Avenue and Avebury. Grooved Ware formed part of the late neolithic ceramic series from the site but no radiocarbon dates are available.

In 1967 a road improvement scheme south of the village of Durrington Walls (Wilts) provided an opportunity to examine a wide strip across a large externally embanked enclosure immediately north of Woodhenge. Little was known of this enclosure and even its plan was uncertain. Earlier excavations had produced Grooved Ware from the fossil soil beneath the enclosure bank which at least provided a tenuous link with the buildings described above. The Ministry of Public Buildings and Works commited what was for that time a substantial sum of money to excavate totally the route of the new road where it crossed the enclosure and its environs.[9] These excavations led to the recognition of large externally embanked enclosures as a class and to the subsequent series of planned rescue excavations at Marden and Mount Pleasant. Among other things, the Durrington excavations revealed the remains of two multi-ring-post structures of which the larger was called the Southern Circle.[10] Like Woodhenge, this was a six-ring structure in its final form, 38.00m in diameter with a single entrance. It produced a great quantity of Grooved Ware and three radiocarbon dates which group between 2000 and 1900 bc. The structure was reconstructed by Mr. Musson as having an open court with a free-standing ring of timber uprights. The second timber structure at Durrington is the Northern Circle which has been interpreted as a roofed building about 14.50m in diameter, the four central posts perhaps supporting a raised lantern. This building was approached up an incline from the south by means of an irregular avenue of timber uprights through a facade of closely-set posts. Again associated with Grooved Ware this structure has a radiocarbon date of 1950 ± 110 bc (NPL–240).

These excavations led to the identification of a category of large externally embanked enclosures which include Marden in the Vale of Pewsey, Mount Pleasant to the east of Dorchester and the well-known site at Avebury. The first two enclosures were under plough and therefore were the subjects for a planned series of rescue excavations from 1969 to 1971. In 1969 the post-holes of a simple timber structure were excavated at Marden.[11] It consisted of a ring of post-holes 10.50m in diameter. A radiocarbon date of 1988 ± 110 bc (BM–557) in association with Grooved Ware was recorded from the base of the ditch of the large enclosure within which the structure was sited.

In 1970 and 1971 extensive excavations were undertaken within a comparable enclosure on Mount Pleasant Hill in the eastern outskirts of Dorchester. These revealed the plan of a building which like The Sanctuary was a multi-period building commencing with a timber phase later replaced by a stone structure. Site IV as it has been called—comprises five concentric rings of post-holes with an overall diameter of 38.00m surrounded by a ditch 1.70m deep and 3.50m wide which enclosed a circular area 42.00m. in diameter with a single entrance 7.00m. wide facing north. Associated pottery from the base of the ditch and from the post-holes was of the Grooved Ware ceramic tradition and three radiocarbon dates from the base of the ditch indicated a date for its construction around 2000 bc.[12]

Clearly there are many points of similarity between these buildings and their associated earthworks. A comparative diagram of the ground plans of the largest buildings indicates that they are closely similar and that The Sanctuary, although of similar design, is on a much smaller scale (Fig. 1). With each structure is associated pottery of the Grooved Ware ceramic tradition in some quantity, along with flint artifacts, antler picks and animal bones. Not only is this distinctive pottery associated with the structures themselves, it also occurs with the earthworks which surround them. The radiocarbon chronology of the structures is also fairly consistent. The chronological range from Durrington, Marden and Mount Pleasant indicates a potential genesis for these structures around or slightly before 2000 bc, with Wood-henge being built a century or so later if the ditch is indeed contemporary with the building. In the case of the Durrington, Marden and Mount Pleasant structures the buildings occur within large earthworks with external banks which form a restricted class in mid-southern England. Marden encompasses some 35 acres, Durrington 30 acres and Mount Pleasant 12 acres. Their siting is variable and there is no particular order in the number and orientation of their entrances. In every case the enclosures are associated with great quantities of Grooved Ware and other artifacts in their primary silts and they are all assigned to the period around 2000 bc.

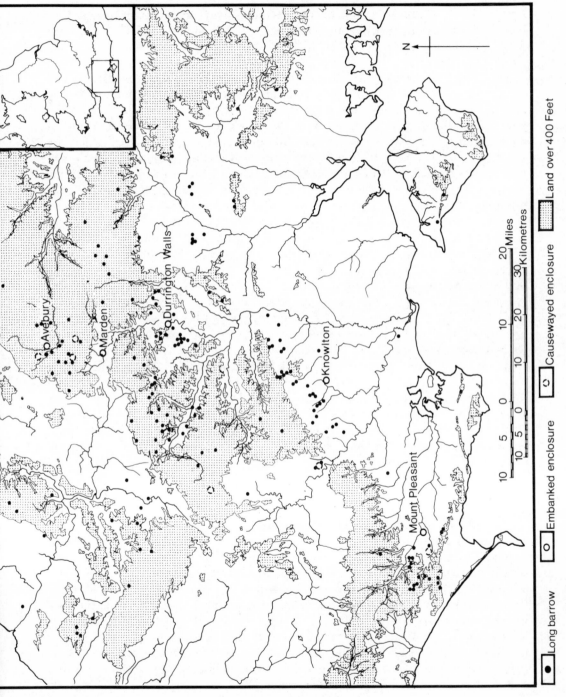

Fig. 2 Distribution of causewayed enclosures, long barrows and large embanked enclosures in Wessex.

The distribution of round barrows in the vicinity of these earthworks emphasizes their importance as centres and their origin lies in the causewayed enclosures of southern England, which themselves occur at centres of long barrow distributions and are therefore ancestral in many senses to the large Late Neolithic enclosures (Fig. 2).

This series of rescue excavations therefore demonstrated the presence in Wessex of a series of large circular buildings which were constructed basically to the same plan at about the same time and which were associated with the same very distinctive ceramic style. It is clear from the distribution of contemporary earthworks that these buildings and the enclosures which are sometimes associated with them were centres of regional groupings which may have corresponded to tribal units. On the basis of our present understanding of the problems the buildings and earthworks should be regarded as the product of indigenous traditions, developed under social conditions which permitted and encouraged the employment of manpower on a relatively large scale under the direction of a centralised authority, either to affirm the personal status of individuals or to display the power of a political unit. They are perhaps best regarded as secular centres dominated by large public buildings, which were accompanied as at Durrington and Marden by less massive structures for which a more purely domestic use might be deduced. At Mount Pleasant in 1700 bc, ten acres of the hill-top was fortified by a palisade 6.00m high—a development which must have relevance in terms of what Trigger has called the archaeology of government.[13] Indeed, in the focal area around Mount Pleasant, which includes the Maiden Castle hill-fort, it is possible to discern the evolution of an embanked or otherwise fortified settlement focus which persisted on one hill or the other for 3,000 years and which eventually descended into the valley to become Roman Dorchester. This persistence of territorial and focal patterns can be paralleled elsewhere in Wessex and has been brought into focus by the excavation programme which terminated at Mount Pleasant in 1971.

A second major theme which can be appropriately reconsidered in the light of recent excavation is also concerned with settlement, in this instance in the first millennium BC. This emerged with the total excavation in 1965 of a small one-acre settlement in Cranborne Chase above the village of Tollard Royal. Initial trial excavations showed that it was a small enclosed farmstead which typified a basic unit of settlement throughout the Late pre-Roman Iron Age and it was totally stripped of plough soil by machinery— the first time that such a technique was used so extensively for this purpose on chalk downland.[14] Its value as a type site is enhanced as the farm was in use for a relatively short time and was devoid of later alterations. The farmhouse itself was a circular hut 5.00m in diameter set within a kite-shaped enclosure less than one acre in extent delineated by a shallow ditch and provided with a single ungated entrance.

In 1968 a similar operation was carried out on a comparable enclosure at Walesland Rath in Pembrokeshire. It is well known that the area of south-west Wales is densely covered with small embanked settlements which are normally one acre or less in extent. This distribution contrasts with the character of the settlements to the east which are more dominated by the large *oppida*. The same situation appertains in south-west England where the small earthworks are termed 'rounds'. Nothing was known of the date or internal arrangements of a single such enclosure in south-west Wales and the opportunity was taken at Walesland Rath of uncovering the entire interior and obtaining the complete structural sequence. It was shown that the settlement was founded in the third century bc and continued in use into the third century AD.[15] So far Walesland Rath is alone in having produced dating evidence and evidence for internal arrangements.

In the spring and summer of 1972 the Department attempted the most ambitious operation yet performed on chalk downland in the Wessex region by the total excavation in one season of a three-acre settlement near Gussage All Saints in Dorset. This was a problem-orientated piece of research within a rescue framework which was deliberately organised with the intention of looking back at the excavation by Dr. Bersu of the Iron Age farmstead of Little Woodbury near Salisbury in 1938–9. For the last thirty-five years Little Woodbury has seemed to many people to provide the pattern for Iron Age life in southern Britain—what Dr. Dennis Harding has called 'this slavish reiteration of the typicality of Little Woodbury'.[16] The influence which Bersu's excavations and his interpretation of them have had on Iron Age studies in Britain is all-pervading and yet the evidence was obtained from a partial excavation. The site has given its name to a Woodbury-type economy for the Iron Age, to what Professor Hodson has called a Woodbury Culture and also to a settlement type characterised by a roughly circular enclosure of 3–6 acres, a single entrance gap which is normally in the east and sometimes flanked by antennae ditches and a siting which is frequently off-set from the crest of a ridge.

For years it has been apparent that the total excavation of a Little Woodbury-type enclosure was a prime necessity for the advancement of socio-economic theory in Iron Age studies. Such enclosures were visited and assessed over a period of some two years before various factors indicated that Gussage All Saints was the most suitable candidate for total excavation. It was an enclosure of Little Woodbury type with antennae ditches at the east-facing entrance, it was of just manageable size for a single operation and it was threatened by plough erosion—indeed in passing one may remark that nowhere does any similar enclosure survive as an earthwork.

This is not the place to attempt a description and discussion of what was found in the course of this excavation. The three-acre enclosure was totally stripped and as an act of deliberate policy all the deposits were excavated

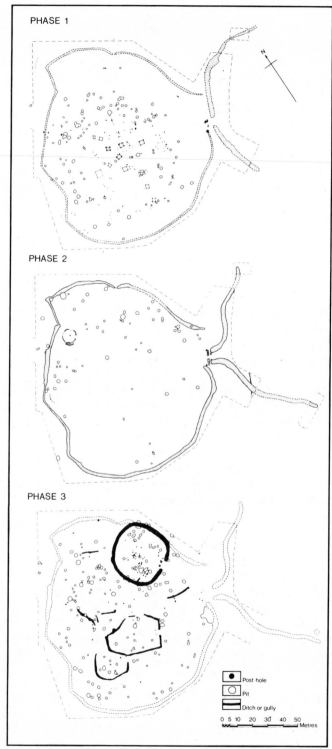

Fig. 3 The development of the Iron Age settlement at Gussage
All Saints, Dorset.

so that the first time one would have a totality of evidence on which to base socio-economic arguments.[17]

As expected, the enclosure produced a maze of pits, gullies and post-holes, representing settlement from about 500 bc to a generation or so after the Roman conquest of the area. In brief, three phases of settlement were represented which have been portrayed as a series of period plans (Fig. 3):

(i) The Early Iron Age settlement is essentially a central setting of four-post structures surrounded by pits and a shallow boundary ditch. The single entrance in the east had a timber gateway and was flanked by antennae ditches.

(ii) What has been termed the Middle Iron Age settlement saw an extension of the pit distribution north from the earlier nucleus, the enlargement of the boundary ditch and the re-modelling of the entrance. Small round houses appear in this phase.

(iii) The Durotrigian settlement from about 50 bc to AD 80 saw an expansion of the settlement with many pits, post-hole settings and internal enclosures, including a very late circular defensive work.

The excavations produced a wealth of evidence regarding the material culture, economy, human types and industrial processes of the settlement. Among the last should be mentioned the debris from a bronze-smith's work-shop which specialised in the manufacture of equestrian fittings in the second and early first centuries bc. The debris includes many thousands of investment mould fragments together with the tools and raw materials necessary for such a specialised craft.

Further east in Hampshire at Owslebury a smaller enclosure of Little Woodbury type was partially excavated by Mr. Collis between 1965 and 1972 as a rescue project. The settlement began comparatively late in the first millennium and continued for some 600 years. The interest of the site derives from the development of the settlement, its association with an Iron Age cemetery and its eventual demise in the fourth century AD. Other large-scale investigations of single sites have recently occurred at Basingstoke and at the Portway near Andover, which will eventually add appreciably to our knowledge of settlements of the period.

The investigation of settlements of the first millennium bc has also included hill-forts. In this field the ideal has been to record the entire settle-ment pattern within the defences of a given hill-fort. This is an objective which is generally considered to be essential for the furtherance of hill-fort studies, but which requires considerable resources. An attempt to meet this need is being made at Danebury in Hampshire where it is proposed that the entire thirteen acres of the Iron Age settlement area should be excavated as a programme in advance of a tree-planting scheme. A similar opportunity has arisen in recent years at Balksbury Camp near Andover where it was necessary

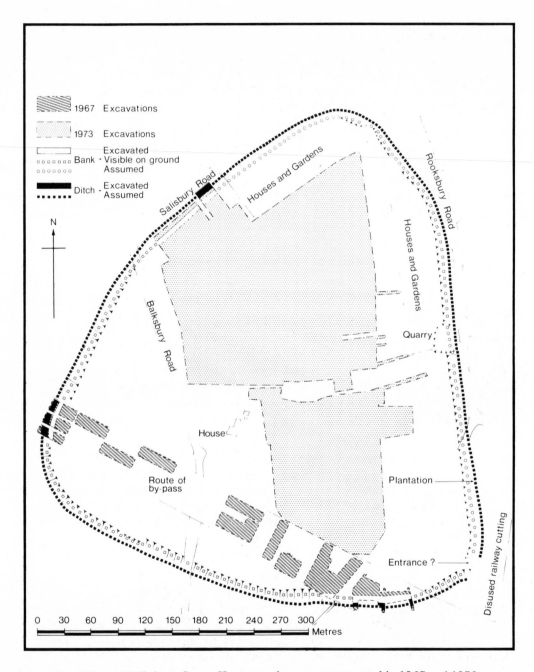

Fig. 4 Plan of Balksbury Camp, Hants., to show areas excavated in 1967 and 1973.

in 1967 to conduct extensive excavations in advance of the Andover By-Pass which now cuts through the southern half of the hill-fort.[18] These investigations sorted out the sequence of the single rampart fairly thoroughly but very few internal structures were recorded despite extensive stripping. In 1973 at Balksbury, an additional opportunity presented itself when planning proposals were approved which would cover some 20 acres of the hill-fort interior with housing development. In advance of this development it was decided to strip the entire area so that a substantial part of the hill-fort interior could be examined. It was taken into consideration that Balksbury is a weakly defended univallate hill-fort which differs from Danebury with its multiplication of earthworks and could therefore be considered to have been less intensively settled than the latter. As a result of this large-scale exercise nearly three-quarters of the hill-fort interior has been investigated (Fig. 4). Settlement contemporary with the hill-fort defences consisted of a linear arrangement of four-post structures across the centre of the enclosed area, with sporadic settings of such structures in the shelter of the ramparts. No pits were contemporary with this settlement but these appear with a change of pottery style at about 200 bc along with a single isolated round house. After this the hill-top was abandoned until the third century AD, there was no Late pre-Roman Iron Age settlement on the hill, and the focus of settlement appears to have moved to Bury Hill about one mile away, which is defended by the multiple rampart system characteristic of the period.

The two major themes under discussion have been concerned with settlement in the second and first millennia bc. The policy has been the large-scale or total excavation of selected settlement sites—what has been called the single site approach which has been advocated by a C.B.A. research and policy document issued in 1948. This, however, is only one element in a conceptual framework which views the landscape as an ever-changing whole. Any future excavation policy for the countryside should pursue this single site approach in conjunction with a broadly-based study of developing ancient landscapes.

This account of two aspects of archaeology in southern Britain considered in the light of discoveries during the period 1963–73 is essentially a personal view, but it illustrates how academic themes can be pursued within the rescue framework. Most excavation in southern Britain during the period concerned was inevitably motivated by the need to rescue as many sites as possible from destruction, but none the less such exigencies did not inhibit a planned approach which made archaeological sense in a situation where the money available could never be sufficient for all the work and which assured an academic return in published form commensurate with the effort involved.

REFERENCES

1. I. J. McInnes, 'Settlements in Later Neolithic Britain', pp. 113–130, and D. D. A. Simpson, 'Beaker houses and settlements in Britain', pp. 131–152; in D. D. A. Simpson (ed.), *Economy and Settlement in Neolithic and Early Bronze Age Britain and Europe* (1971).

2. M. E. Cunnington, *Woodhenge* (1929).

3. S. Piggott, 'Timber circles: A re-examination', in *Archaeol. J.*, vol. 96 (1940), pp. 192–222.

4. C. Musson, 'A study of possible building forms at Durrington Walls, Woodhenge, and The Sanctuary', pp. 363–377, in G. J. Wainwright and I. H. Longworth, *Durrington Walls: Excavations 1966–1968*, Reports Research Comm. Soc. Ants. London, No. 20 (1971).

5. J. G. Evans and G. J. Wainwright, 'Woodhenge: the 1970 Excavation', in G. J. Wainwright, *Mount Pleasant: Excavations 1970–1971*, Reports Research Comm. Soc. Ants. London, in the press.

6. M. E. Cunnington, 'The Sanctuary on Overton Hill, near Avebury', in *Wiltshire Archaeol. Natur. Hist. Soc.*, vol. 45 (1931), pp. 300–335.

7. S. Piggott, *ibid.* (1940).

8. C. Musson, *ibid.* (1971).

9. Some retrospective criticism was expressed concerning the decision to excavate rather than attempt to preserve the enclosure intact. At the time it was necessary to balance the bad accident record of the old road and the considerable expenditure involved in diverting the road because of local geological and topographical problems, against the potential interest of the enclosure, which was entirely speculative. The Department's substantial commitment of funds to this excavation would undoubtedly have been criticised had the results been disappointing.

10. G. Wainwright and I. H. Longworth, *Durrington Walls: Excavations 1966–1968* (1971).

11. G. J. Wainwright, 'The excavation of a Late Neolithic enclosure at Marden, Wiltshire', in *Antiquaries J.*, vol 51 (1971), pp. 177–239.

12. G. J. Wainwright, *Mount Pleasant: Excavations 1970–1971*, in the press.

13. B. Trigger, 'The archaeology of government', in *World Archaeology*, vol. 6 (1974), pp. 95–106.

14. G. J. Wainwright, 'The excavation of a Durotrigian farmstead near Tollard Royal in Cranborne Chase, Southern England', in *Proc. Prehistoric Soc.*, vol. 34 (1968), pp. 102–147.

15. G. J. Wainwright, 'The excavation of a fortified settlement at Walesland Rath, Pembrokeshire', in *Britannia*, vol. 2 (1971), pp. 48–108.

16. D. W. Harding, *The Iron Age in Lowland Britain* (1974), p. 21.

17. G. J. Wainwright and M. Spratling, 'The Iron Age settlement of Gussage All Saints', in *Antiquity*, vol. 47 (1973), pp. 109–130.

18. G. J. Wainwright, 'The excavation of Balksbury Camp, Andover, Hants', in *Proc. Hants. Field Club*, vol. 26 (1969), pp. 21–55.

The Turrets on Hadrian's Wall

by

DOROTHY CHARLESWORTH

THE one hundred and fifty-eight turrets, two per Roman mile, from *Segedunum* (Wallsend-on-Tyne) to *Maia* (Bowness-on-Solway) were vital links in the original plan of organisation of Hadrian's Wall.[2] Planned as an integral part of the broad wall (stone) and of the turf wall, they were built before the curtain wall, consequently the turrets of the stone wall, with wing walls ready for bonding with the curtain wall, show a point of reduction in the stretch from the North Tyne to the Irthing, turrets 27b and 49b (its east wall only),[3] where the wall constructed to the narrow gauge meets them. There is one exception, an early turret built as a free-standing unit on Walltown crags but incorporated into the system as turret 45a.[4] Pike Hill tower, built at the same time, never became part of the turret system, although incorporated in the curtain wall.[5] Turrets 49a to 79b are free-standing stone towers incorporated into the turf wall, a point which indicates how early was the decision to build the west sector of the curtain wall in turf instead of stone. At the east end it is assumed that turrets were included in the Hadrianic extension, narrow gauge wall, from *Pons Aelius* (Newcastle-upon-Tyne) to *Segedunum*, although none has been recorded. The structure thought to be a turret, 800 yards from the west wall of *Segedunum*, has subsequently been accepted as milecastle 1.[6] There should be six turrets 1a–3b on this stretch.

Four turrets were demolished almost immediately, indeed they may never have been completed, when the decision to site forts on Hadrian's Wall was implemented. Turret 27a was submerged under *Cilurnum* (Chesters), 36b under *Vercovicium* (Housesteads), 49a (of the turf wall series) under *Camboglanna* (Birdoswald), and 66b must be under *Petriana* (Stanwix)' Turret 71b may be under the east side of *Aballava* (Burgh-by-Sands), but its position has not been proved by excavation.[7] The original turf wall turrets 49a, 50b, and 59b had a short life. In this sector the turf wall was replaced by a stone wall on a new alignment, not long after AD 130. The turrets were demolished and re-sited on the new line. Hadrianic material found in both lots of turrets proves the early date of the stone wall here.[8] The rebuilding of turf wall turret 54a (Garthside)[9] as a free-standing unit, after the original turret had seen considerable use and collapsed into the wall ditch, immediately to the south of its original site, shows that a longer period elapsed before the stone wall replaced the turf in this sector.

At one time it was thought that the free-standing turret on Walltown Crags, 45a, and the Pike Hill tower between 51b and 52a were part of the Trajanic frontier scheme, but the pottery found in them indicates a Hadrianic date[10] and it is early in the Hadrianic scheme that their position makes sense. Turret 45a provided a look-out for the forts of *Magna* (Carvoran) and Haltwhistle Burn, neither of which has any view to the north. Pike Hill could communicate with 45a and, in good weather, via Gillalees Beacon, with *Banna* (Bewcastle) on the north and Nether Denton, Throp and Mains Rigg signal tower on the south. Once the forts had been established on the wall itself the field of view was greatly improved, but in the first stages with the forts on the Stanegate line, most of them blind on the north side, these two towers were vital in a vulnerable area. At that stage of planning also the spacing of turrets as signalling-cum-watch towers seems reasonable, although the rigidity of spacing gives some of them a very limited outlook. Turret 52a, at the west foot of Pike Hill, seems particularly useless (and the Pike Hill tower could have done the signalling work of 51b also) unless it is assumed that the turrets' primary importance was to meet the need of a messroom for the patrols who were obviously based on them for a period of duty, although not resident in them. It is difficult to see why the system persisted after the forts were put on the wall line, with the result that turrets were built on the 'new' lengths of wall, both the eastern extension and the western sector alterations from turf to stone. It was not until the end of the second century[11] that so many were dispensed with (see p. 24) and their obliteration must have been the result of an entirely new system of watch-keeping on the wall.

The appearance of the turrets has never been satisfactorily established.[12] The best evidence must be the Rudge Cup[13] (Pl. 1b), and the Amiens patera,[14] contemporary 'documents', which show a castellated outline to towers which rise above wall height, and no sign of a roof. Possibly supporting evidence is the merlon coping stone, if correctly identified, from 51b.[15] The alternative is the pyramidal or gabled roof, on the lines of the watch-towers on Trajan's Danube frontier, depicted on his Column, a near-contemporary illustration. The essential, surely, is a viewpoint higher than the parapet walk and this could be achieved by either roof type but only the flat or very low-pitched roof, sheltered behind a castellated parapet, would give an unrestricted all-round view. For such a roof stone slabs are the obvious material, but the slabs found among debris in 29b, 34a, and 44b, for instance, cannot be identified with certainty as part of the roof. A tile roof would not be strong enough, but in 18b a fragment of roof tile (imbrex) was found.[16] Possibly the centre of the roof was tiled with a low pitch and the sentry walk ran round the edge. Most of the turrets excavated so far are those deliberately dismantled at the end of the second century and therefore most unlikely to produce evidence of the construction of the upper storey. Even in those with a longer occupation, such as 7b, 51b and 52a, no collapsed roof was found. In 48a, in the upper level, rectangular fragments of bevelled stone were interpreted as possible parts of a cornice, projecting inwards and indicating a flagged rampart walk.[17] A square, chamfered stone, used as a hearth stone, was found in 54a, but here, as on many turrets of the turf wall sector, there was a plinth and the stone could have been cut for that. In plan the turrets are about 20 ft. externally and 14 ft. or less internally. It seems reasonable to suggest 30 ft., twice the presumed height of the curtain wall rampart walk,

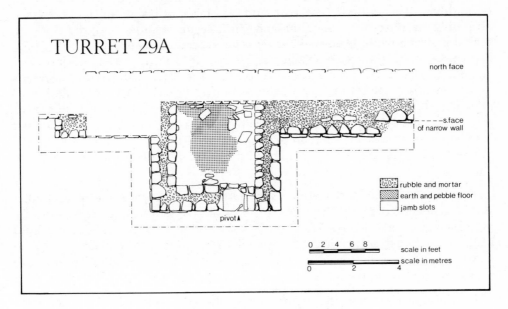

Fig. 1 Turret 29a (Blackcarts)

as the height of the turret roof with a 5 ft. parapet. The only archaeological evidence is negative, the absence of deep foundations, such as were put in for the signalling tower at Pike Hill. This must indicate that the turrets were not massive structures. The thickness of the walls varies from about 3 ft. to 4 ft.

Some constructional details are worth noting. The use of clay in the walls of 19b is exceptional.[18] Normally mortar is used and the core of the turret wall is small stone and mortar, the construction of the wing walls being the same. At 34a the small stone and mortar core of the turret walls contrasted sharply with the almost dry core of large whin blocks not only in the adjoining section of curtain wall but also in the wing wall of the turret, which raises the question of how far any wing wall was constructed before the curtain builders joined up with it. Here the wing walls are exceptionally short, only 3 ft. 3 in., instead of about 12 ft., standing on the broad foundation. At 29a (Fig. 1) the narrow wall can be seen riding up over the east wing wall, its south face resting, somewhat insecurely, on the core.[19] Turret 25b was built with mortar, the curtain wall on either side of it, with clay.[20] Here the wall is broad gauge and so there is no projecting wing wall distinguishable, but the wall and turret were bonded and some wall must, one would think, have been built out from the turret and again the different building technique offers the same problem as the core difference at 34a. It is generally assumed that the legion responsible for the length of curtain was responsible also for the structures on it. This can be demonstrated at the milecastles by a number of legionary building records, but of the turrets only 33b, 44b, and 50a have produced legionary stones. However, the legions had slightly different styles of building. The door at the east end of the south wall of the turrets is invariably in turrets on the 2nd and 20th legion sectors and the door on the west in the 6th legion sectors.[21] The recent discovery of a 6th legion inscription in turret 33b,[22] which has an east door in no way invalidates this argument. The inscription may be Antonine, the style of lettering suggests a date later than the initial construction of Hadrian's Wall. The additional argument that narrow turret walls can be associated with the 6th and 20th legions and broad with the 2nd is less convincing as the walls vary considerably from turret to turret rather than present a standard thin or thick, 3 ft. or 4 ft. but the offset at the level of the third course is generally associated with a thin wall.

The turrets of the turf wall are generally of poor quality masonry, smaller stones generally than those of the stone wall. Probably there was a shortage of skilled stonemasons. At 51a (Fig. 2) the corners were very insecurely built and its north-east corner had been rebuilt from ground level. Turret 51b had its walls pointed with mortar but the core was of clay. Turrets 53b, 54, and 57a are of red sandstone, the local stone of that area.

The internal arrangements of the turrets are only known with any certainty at ground level. At the level of the rampart-walk of the curtain wall there must have been at least a walk-way or a floor with a trap door to give access from the ground floor, two doors, one to the east and one to the west giving on to the rampart-walk and enough windows to light it. Several threshold stones remain, massive slabs with dressed slots for stone jambs and a pivot-hole with a run-in on the outer edge of the stone, where the door would be exposed to the weather (Pl. 1a). A door jamb was found in the blocking wall of 19a.[23] The threshold is generally a step above ground level outside and inside may be level with the offset course, which might be assumed to carry the original floor were it not for the quantity of occupation material below that level. The number and placing of the windows is entirely conjectural. No masonry fragments of these have been recorded and window glass only in 7b,[24] 33b, 50a, 50b[25] and 51b.[26] If all the windows were glazed the interior would be extremely dark and almost uninhabitable with smoke from the cooking-hearths. There is nowhere evidence that Roman glazed windows could be opened, or even that the glass was fixed in a wood frame which could be taken out. Probably some of the windows were fitted only with shutters.

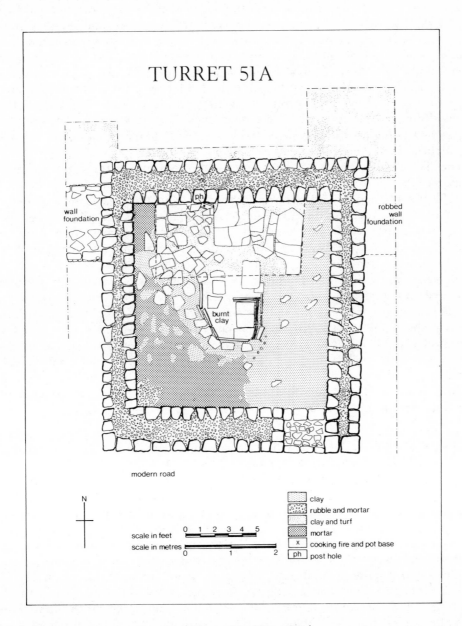

Fig. 2 Turret 51a (Piper Sike)

A ladder must have given access to the upper floor, presumably a vertical wooden ladder fixed to the wall as space is very restricted. It was generally placed on a stone platform against the south wall at the opposite end from the door. The platforms are not of any standard dimension and this invalidates Parker Brewis' argument[27] for a ladder which could be drawn up to the roof and which would require a platform, as its length could not equal the height from floor to ceiling. Probably the main function of the platform was to provide a solid, clean and dry base for the ladder on a floor otherwise mainly clay or earth and mortar. Turret 18a, which provided the evidence for Parker Brewis' theory, has proved exceptional. Nowhere else has a platform with six steps leading up to it been recorded. Generally platforms are only a matter of inches above the floor and most have occupation material under or in them. Turrets 19a and b, for example, had a narrow platform, three courses high in 19b in the south-east corner with occupation material under it.[28] In 29b pottery was recorded in the rubble of which the platform was built.[29] In 33b the platform stood four courses high (1.36m). The platform of 48a, in its south-east corner, was not built until the third successive floor level was formed, identified as Wall Period II by its excavators, i.e. Severan.[30] No platform was found in 26a, nor in 34a, but the south-west corner of the turret was noticeably free from occupation debris and a quantity of mortar had been put in around an upstanding piece of whin. The whin also outcrops in the north-west corner and had been similarly treated, to give a raised floor over it above the level of the early occupation. No platforms were noted by Simpson in the stone wall turrets 49b, 50a and 50b. Turret 51a had the remains of the core of a platform in its south-west corner. The Vindolanda Trust's turret reconstruction shows that a staircase could be accommodated, but the existence of scattered hearths in most turrets would make such a staircase a serious fire hazard and the vertical ladder seems the better solution.

In some turrets another raised flagged area or platform has been recorded against the north wall. In 51a this was a secondary feature, the front part of the platform having partially collapsed into the original central sunk hearth. In 52a (Banks East) the platform in the north-west corner was thought of as 'a bench or bed'.[31] A similar platform was found more-or-less centrally against the north wall of turret 51b.[32] In turret 26a the platform against the north wall was secondary, with a cache of butchered ox-bones stuffed in between the edge of it and the east wall to tidy the place up.[33] Turret 17a had a rectangular platform in the north-west corner.[34] The purpose, where such platforms occur, is clearly to provide a clean dry area away from the hearth, presumably for meals, a bench rather than a bed. No detachment could have lived in a turret; there is not space. Those temporarily off-watch could sleep on the first floor, and the ground floor was obviously the messroom. The patrols or signallers on duty brought their rations with them.

There is no standard arrangement. Some turrets, 7b, 33b, and 51a. (Fig. 2) for example, have a well-built sunken central hearth in the first period. Turret

26a had a hearth in the south-west corner where the ladder platform might
be expected.[35] Turret 25b had three hearths, a floor of clay and mortar with
a 'working area' limited by clay and boulders in the south-west corner, where
the ladder platform was later built.[36] Turret 29b had an amphora without a
top set in clay packed round with cobbles against the east wall.[37] This was
a secondary feature and is the only case of an amphora being found *in situ,*
but they are a normal feature among turret finds. A large part of one was
found broken in behind the blocking wall of 34a. At turret 35a, 90 sherds of
amphorae were found.[38] The amphora in the north-east corner of turret 44b[39]
had two holes deliberately made near its base, so it at least could only be
intended for storage of dry goods, and there are other fragments from various
turrets with holes drilled for rivets. An amphora, or large part of one, is such
a common find that it may be regarded as part of a turret's normal fittings,
but not necessarily in its primary use as a wine-jar. Turret 26a produced
evidence of bronze-working in an upper level, a crucible and cut bronze, and
at 18b possible iron-working, but these are exceptional.[40] Normally the finds
are all appropriate to a messroom, cooking pots, pie-dishes and flagons with
some mortaria often repaired with rivets and beakers. Samian is rare. Querns
are occasionally found but most turrets give the impression that the principal
diet was meat-stews. Both 34a and 51a produced a large quantity of animal
bone, mainly cattle, sheep and pigs, both inside and out. The ox-bones in 26a
have already been mentioned. A few items of equipment have been found,
shield boss and spearhead in 29b[41] javelin head and arrowhead in 34a, which
also produced, inexplicably, five ballista balls. One ballista ball each was
found in 8a and 18b.[42] Brooches and coins are rare finds.

The early floor is generally clay. This was later found unsuitable and flagging
was introduced, but in most cases it would appear to be patching rather than
a total re-flooring and thereafter ashes were spread, broken pottery and bones
interred under spreads of clay, mortar or new flagging. Very often the earliest
occupation must be associated with the period of construction, first of the
turret and then the turret providing shelter for nearly curtain-building gangs.
In 7b, 12a, 12b, 13a, and 35a, mason's chippings were noted on the first clay
floors.[43] At 25b evidence of lime burning was found for the construction of
the turret, not the Wall itself which is bonded with clay.

It is doubtful that period Ia (122-139) can be distinguished from Ib,
starting probably 158, after the first occupation of the Antonine Wall. In
the milecastles the dismantling of the doors is clear evidence for disuse, but
the turret doors and windows must have been locked up when the troops
moved north. Where the threshold survives it is normally the only one. That
in 34a is cracked but shows little signs of wear. The same threshold was said
to serve two floor levels in 29b[44] and in 7b[45] the new threshold is associated
with the Severan reoccupation and there is no distinction between periods Ia
and Ib. Turret 29a which also had a long occupation, if the coin of Constantine
the Great[46] is really to be associated with the turret, has an almost unworn

threshold. Clayton gave no details of his excavation and he cleared the turret so thoroughly that an attempt to gain information in 1971 before its consolidation, proved useless. No material was left in or around it. Turret 26b, on the other hand, has a heavily worn threshold. Here again there are no details, except that Clayton seems to have been responsible for some re-building. The continued use of the same threshold was possible because the door opened outwards and the early occupiers would have to step down inside the turret, the later step up. The raised threshold and its subsequent blocking in 33b is exceptional in a turret with only second-century occupation, which was obliterated.[47] In the six turrets dug by Mrs. Woodfield she remarked a definite re-flooring in 18b, which could be associated with period Ib, but at 26a and 51b 'the Ia occupation seems to slide into the Ib'.[48] Recent work at turrets 34a and 51a,[49] both producing only second-century pottery, also showed a close succession of floors or patches to floors with no clear break. Turret 29b, with only second-century pottery, had two occupation levels each marked by about 6 in. of burnt rubbish, the lower floor clay, the second flags and this also had burning on it, 'the conflagration which marked the end of the occupation'.[50] With the frequent cooking fires on the ground floor it is surprising that more turrets did not go up in flames more often, enemy action need not seriously be considered. In 48a, which had a longer occupation, four distinct periods were noted. The first two were equated with Wall periods Ia and Ib, the second, 8 in. above the first, which had a floor of gravelly clay on which burnt material but no masonry had accumulated. The major break was between periods Ib and II (Severan) when a build-up of 1 ft. 8in. of ash and masonry debris underlay the new flagged floor. At this period the platform was introduced. Period III is marked by a floor 2 ft. above this, with mainly fallen masonry intervening and little burning, which suggests a period of abandonment and decay. Turret 48b likewise contained four floors.[51]

The study of the turrets throws no light on the question of what was happening in the northern part of the province in the later second and early third century, since there are no dated inscriptions, few stratified coins (none significant in this context), and the dating of the not very great quantity of coarse pottery depends on the interpretation of other sites where positive dating is equally absent.[52] But it is at this time that a great number of turrets go out of commission and, possibly after a lapse of time, are demolished systematically, the recess at the back being filled up so that the rampart-walk continues uninterrupted across them and the south face of the curtain wall being rebuilt from such a low level that there is no straight joint to mark the alteration. In the central sector where one can see several miles of standing south face of the curtain wall, the sites of the turrets cannot be identified. There is no trace of a turret between 35a (Sewingshields), which stands consolidated a few courses high with a blocking wall in it, and 41a just east of Cawfields, the next consolidated turret, reduced to its foundations.[53]

The Wall is visible for most of this stretch and in fact two turrets, 39a (Peel Crag) and 39b (Steelrigg) have been dug and found to be obliterated.[54] Others have been located but not dug. Turret 41b west of Thorney Doors, on Cawfields, examined by F. G. Simpson in 1912 (Dr. Grace Simpson kindly informed me) has vanished without trace. At its measured position the whin outcrop is immediately below the turf and there has been no foundation. Enough work has now been done between *Cilurnum* and *Aesica* to suggest that the turrets there normally went out of use at the end of the second century and that 29a is exceptional. There is no obvious reason why it should be spared. Milecastle 29 at the top of Walwick Bank would have still been in use to provide a link west of *Cilurnum,* and 29b on the top of Limestone Bank would seem the more useful to retain for its outlook. An early and careful excavation shows clearly that, although it was not obliterated by the blocking of the recess, no pottery later than the end of the second century was found. One curious feature here deserves note, the road linking the turret to the Military Way.[55] A similar feature, leading south-east from turret 37a can be seen on an air photograph.[56] There is no doubt that the Military Way must be, at latest, Antonine. At 34a a pathway of flags was found leading out of the turret, but this does not compare with the road described at 29b, where the curb where it joined the Military Way was found. Although repaired, the 34a path seemed designed only for casual foot traffic.

East of the North Tyne no generalisation is possible. Some turrets are known to have been retained: 7a, 12a[57] and 26b. Turret 19b was still standing six courses high and had no blocking wall[58] and 13a had a blocking in its doorway, but its recess was not filled in.[59] Turret 19a was obliterated[60] but the fate of a great number is unknown and the fact that several sites have produced only second-century pottery is not a reliable guide in this area where modern activity, stone robbing and agriculture, has denuded the possible upper levels. Probably here as in the *Aesica* to *Camboglanna* length the fate of the turrets was variable.

West of *Aesica* there is a fair amount of information. Gibson reported[61] very little masonry at 44a, so probably it was obliterated. Turret 44b was occupied until the mid-fourth century. Turret 45a (Walltown) produced no pottery later than the end of the second century, but it was not destroyed.[62] It is unfortunate that nothing is known of 46a and b, on either side of the hamlet of Gap, a weak point about halfway between *Magna* and *Camboglanna.* The fort of *Magna* is sited to cover the valley of the Tipalt and this is an area of extensive rebuilding indicated by the building record of the tribal levy of the *Dumnonii,* so it probable that the turrets were demolished, or fell down. Turrets 48a and b had a long occupation. The Irthing and its steep escarpment separate them from *Camboglanna,* but the river running across their front makes this a strong point.

West of *Camboglanna* only 50a and 54a are known to have been obliterated.[63] Turret 50a was demolished uniformly to the first course and the recess filled in. Turret 51a showed no evidence of use after the end of the second century. There is no pottery later than this, but it was not demolished. The coin of Victorinus found in the doorway is not evidence of occupation. Any passer-by could have dropped it. Turret 53a produced an unstratified coin of Constantine I, but otherwise no evidence of late occupation.[64] Turret 55a[65] was found in ruinous condition, but this could be late robbing and at 57a[66] there is mention of only second-century material.

Only eleven turrets were certainly used after the end of the second century and in some this seems to have been only by people seeking temporary shelter. At 51b the door was blocked and a hut was built within the walls of the turret in the fourth century.[67] At 52a the upper level was thought to be a pent-house within the turret.[68] Fragments of a third-century mortarium were sealed beneath it and fourth-century pottery, including a piece of Huntcliff, was found in the topsoil. At 12a the evidence for third-century occupation is very slight.[69] At 13a there is the blocking of the door to suggest third- or fourth-century use. Clayton's excavations at 26b (Brunton) and 29a (Black-carts) have removed evidence of any upper floors, but both are exceptionally well preserved. Only 48a and b (Willowford), where four periods of occupation were found, or 7a (Denton), where three periods (123–95, 205–95, 300–67) were identified in 1929,[70] are comparable. At 44b (Mucklebank) there were three levels of occupation with a coin of Valens (364–78) in the upper level.[71] That is four, or at most seven, turrets with what appears to be regular military occupation in the third and fourth centuries. The coin of Valens is the latest stratified coin.

It has been estimated that a minimum of 1,300 men would be required as a patrolling garrison (a separate establishment from the fort units) based on the milecastles and manning the turrets.[72] With 154 or 153 turrets in use (four or five have disappeared under forts) this would only allow eight men to each turret, which does not seem excessive, but leaves no one to hold the milecastle, which is their base and could, if provided with two barrack-blocks, as at 48 (Poltross Burn),[73] hold 32 men. Milecastle 37 (Housesteads) on the other hand had only one barrack-block and only half of that was thought to serve as living accommodation, presumably for eight men.[74] Turret 36b did not have to be manned as it was under the fort, but 37a had to draw its men from milecastle 37. Turrets 42b and 43a would, on the normal plan, depend on milecastle 43, but this was removed when *Aesica* was built. Some provision for the turret patrols must have been made in the fort, or else the fort garrison must itself have patrolled this stretch, which seems an unlikely exception. Even in its initial stages the system must have proved difficult to work. Properly manned it would prove a heavy drain on military resources, a thin dispersal of manpower, provisioning problems and a weakening of discipline, suggested by the unhygienic state of the turrets.

As signalling towers some were always unnecessary, for example 52a, near Pike Hill tower, 13b, very close to *Vindovala* (Rudchester), and 21a and b, on either side of *Onnum* (Haltonchesters), and it is difficult to judge whether any would have operated efficiently. The smoke from the cooking hearths would cause confusion, if smoke-signals were used. A heliograph is unlikely in the north British climate. Flares are possible, the speaking-tube of the early antiquaries a charming idea, but untenable. No remains of signalling equipment have ever been found. Perhaps no signals were sent. The only reliable means of communication would be by runner. There is no evidence of a horse being stabled for the use of a mounted messenger.

As watch-towers and messrooms the turrets have an obvious use, but the scheme has all the hallmarks of something thought up in an office—it looks efficient on paper. The wonder is that it was used so long and that the re-thinking of the organisation of the Wall did not come when the forces first returned there in 158. It is, however, clear that the full use of the turrets continued until the end of the second century and there may then have been a period of disuse before some were demolished and the whole scheme abandoned possibly *c.* 205–8.

TURRETS IN THE CARE OF THE DEPARTMENT OF THE ENVIRONMENT

7b (Denton)   36b (Housesteads)   49b (Birdoswald West)
26b (Low Brunton)   41a, b (Cawfields)   51a, b, (Piper Sike and Leahill)
27a (Chesters)   45a (Walltown)   52a (Banks East)
29a (Blackcarts)   48a, b (Willowford)   (19 altogether)
33b–35b (Sewingshields sector)

SCHEDULE OF TURRETS

No information	Located*	Second century occupation only	Occupied in third/fourth century
1a–6a	0b	12b	†7b (third/fourth cent.)
7a	6b	13a obliterated	12a (third cent.)
9a	8a, b	17a?	†26b
10b–11a	9b	17b?	†29a
13b	10a	18a?	44b (third/fourth cent.)
14b–16b	11b	18b	†48a, b (third/fourth cent.)
20a–21b	14a	19a obliterated	†49b (fourth cent.)
23a, b	22a, b	19b?	50b (third cent.)
27b–28b	24a, b	25b	†51b
31a–33a	25a	26a	†52a (fourth cent.)
†34b	30a, b	†27a (Chesters)	53a (fourth cent.)?
42a–43b	†35b	29b	
47a, b	36a	†33b	
52b	40a	†34b	
55b	40b	†35a obliterated	
56a	44a		
57b–58a		†36b (Housesteads)	
59a–66a	45b	37a obliterated	
67a–70a	53b		
71a		37b obliterated	
73a–75b	54b	38a, b obliterated	
	55a		
76b–77b	56b	39a obliterated	
	58b		
78b–79a	(doubtful) 70b	39b obliterated	
	(doubtful) 71b	†41a, b obliterated	
	(doubtful) 72a	†45a	
	(doubtful) 72b	46a obliterated	
	76a	46b obliterated	
	78a	49a (Birdoswald)	
	79b	50a obliterated	
		†51a	
		54a obliterated	
		57a	
		66b (Stanwix)	

*Located—in these cases there is no information about the interior.
†In care of the Department of the Environment.

REFERENCES

1. A shortened version of this paper was given to the Hadrian's Wall conference at Newcastle-upon-Tyne in January 1974.

2. J. C. Bruce, *Handbook to the Roman Wall*, 12th edition by I. A. Richmond (1965) for a summary of the structures and building sequence. (Hereafter *Handbook*).

3. *Transactions of the Cumberland and Westmorland Antiquarian and Archaeological Society*[2], xxvi (1926), 432-6 (hereafter *CW*). Note 26b (Brunton) east of the N. Tyne appears to have a wing wall jointed to a narrow wall on its east side. This is not the original Wall but a rebuilding.

4. *Archaeologia Aeliana*[4], xliii (1965), 162-7 (hereafter *AA*).

5. *CW*[2], xxxii (1932), 145f; xxxiii (1933), 271f.

6. *Northumberland County History*,xiii (1930), 494 (hereafter *NCH*) *Handbook* 43. *AA*[5], iii (1975), 104-115. M. G. Simpson *The moving milecastle*.

7. *CW*[2], lxi (1961), 38. No structure was found. The pottery could be from the fort.

8. *CW*[2], xxv (1935), 232f.

9. *CW*[2], xxxiv (1934), 138f.

10. *AA*[4], xliii (1965), 165-7.

11. The exact date is an open question. AD 197 is no longer acceptable. Early in the third century may be more accurate. The turrets, however, may have been out of use for some time before they were demolished.

12. D. J. Smith, *Hadrian's Wall in Models* (1969); *AA*[4], ix (1932), 198f; *CW*[2], lxix (1969), 83-93.

13. *AA*[4], xii (1934), 310f.

14. *Journal of Roman Studies*, xli (1951), 22-4.

15. *AA*[4], liii (1965), 171.

16. *Ibid.*, 89.

17. *CW*[2], xxvi (1926), 442.

18. *AA*[4], x (1933), 99.

19. *AA*[5], i (1973), 98.

20. *AA*[4], xliii (1965), 109.

21. C. E. Stevens, *The building of Hadrian's Wall* (1966), 11; *AA*[4], xvi, 227; *AA*[4], xlvi, 97f. R. G. Collingwood and R. P. Wright, *Roman Inscriptions of Britain* (1965), 1443 (2nd legion) attributed to 26a by Stevens, 1504 (centurial stone) 28b, 1512 (centurial stone) in 29a, 1762 (20th legion) in 44b, 1763 (centurial stone) *in situ* 44b, 1938, 1939 (6th legion) in 50a.

22. *Britannia* ii (1971), 291, No. 11. *AA*[4], 1 (1972).

23. *AA*[4], x (1932), 98.

24. *AA*[4], vii (1930), 148, in the post-Roman structure 'X' but this contained Roman material.

25. *CW*[2], xiii (1913), 311.

26. *AA*[4], xliii (1965), 171.

27. *AA*[4], ix (1932), 202-4. He assumes a fixed ladder for the first period only.

28. *AA*[4], x (1933), 98-9, pl. V.

29. *AA*[3], ix (1913), 61.

30. *CW*[2], xxvi (1926), 441.

31. *CW*[2], xxiv (1934), 150.

32. *AA*[4], xliii (1965), 171.

33. *Ibid.*, 133.

34. *AA*[4], ix (1932), 257.

35. *AA*[4], xliii (1965), 129.

36. *Ibid.*, 110.

37. *AA*[3], ix (1913), 61.

38. *AA*[4], xliii (1965), 156.

39. AA^2, xxiv (1903), 16.

40. AA^4, xliii (1965), 133, 100.

41. AA^3, ix (1913), 61.

42. AA^4, ix (1932), 200.

43. AA^4, viii (1931), 326; AA^4, xliii (1965), 110.

44. AA^3, ix (1913), 58.

45. AA^4, vii (1930), 148 and 174 'as general renovation' in period Ia/b.

46. AA^2, vii (1876), 256.

47. AA^4, 1 (1972), 149, 159 mention of third-century pottery must be treated with caution.

48. AA^4, xliii (1965), 100.

49. AA^5 (197?); CW^2, lxxiii (1973), 67–78.

50. AA^3, ix (1913), 60.

51. CW^2, xxvi (1926), 439ff and 435f.

52. AA^4, xlvii (1970), 1–45.

53. AA^4, xlvi (1968), 69–73.

54. CW^2, xiii (1913), pl. IV following p. 306. Peel Crag turret standing six courses in places. At Steelrigg 'the wall itself was entirely rebuilt above ground level' (AA^4, viii [1931], 316).

55. AA^3, ix (1913), 63f.

56. *Journal of Roman Studies*, xli (1951), pl. V (no comment in text) and AA^4, xlvii (1970), 16.

57. AA^4, viii (1931), 326.

58. AA^4, x (1933); AA^5, iii (1975), 222–226.

59. AA^4, x (1933), 98.

60. AA^4, x (1933), 98.

61. AA^2, xxiv (1903), 17.

62. AA^4, xliii (1965), 162f.

63. CW^2, xiii (1913), 307, pl. II; CW^2, xxxiv, 138f, Figs. 5 and 6.

64. CW^2, xxxviii(1933), 265.

65. CW^2, xxxiv (1934), 131.

66. CW^2, xxxiv (1934), 132.

67. AA^4, xliii (1965), 175.

68. CW^2, xxxiv (1934), 149, Fig. 14.

69. I am indebted to the Department of Archaeology, Durham University for the loan of an M.A. Thesis by J. R. Dockerill, *Pottery from the milecastles and turrets on Hadrian's Wall* (1969).

70. AA^4, vii (1930), 169.

71. AA^2, xxiv (1903), 15.

72. *Handbook*, 241.

73. *Handbook*, 159.

74. *Handbook*, 126.

Witcombe Roman Villa:
a Reconstruction

by

DAVID S. NEAL

In the course of making a reconstruction drawing of this building many details emerged which are not documented elsewhere. This paper attempts to explain the reconstruction in order that a fuller understanding of the villa building may be possible.

INTRODUCTION

WITCOMBE ROMAN VILLA, Glos., was discovered in February 1818 by labourers engaged on uprooting an old ash tree. They came upon a large stone, 6ft. long, resting on two upright stones 6ft. 2in. high and forming a doorway. Excavations were then carried out by Samuel Lysons who communicated an account of the work to the Society of Antiquaries of London on 30 April 1818 and 4 February 1819.[1] In 1919 the monument was taken into guardianship by the then H.M. Office of Works, who in 1938 undertook an excavation of the bath houses under the direction of Mrs. E. M. Clifford.[2] Since 1960 further excavations have been directed by Mr. Ernest Greenfield to whom the writer is indebted for his help.[3]

DESCRIPTION

The Site

The location of the villa (G.R. SO 899144) is one of great beauty. It is situated on a hillside overlooking a wide combe, but from the start it must have presented very difficult structural problems, not only because the villa had to be planned to be built on the hillside, but because the house was to be constructed on unstable sub-soil prone to earth slip. In an attempt to overcome these problems the villa was constructed on terraces either cut into the hillside, or artificially raised. Apart from the splendid views obtainable from the site, another factor which may have governed the choice of position was the availability of water. Springs are abundant in the area, and were tapped by the Roman engineers to provide water for the villa. This water may not have been solely for domestic use, but perhaps was also used for ornamental pools or fountains (cf. Discussion of the feature against the south wall of the corridor, p. 36).

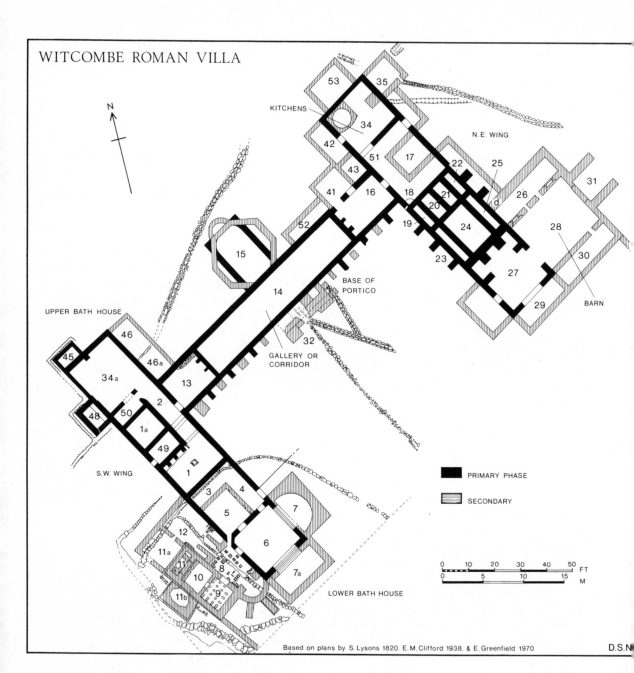

Fig. 1 General plan of Witcombe Roman villa.

General Plan

The Villa is difficult to describe in detail because its relatively complex building history involved more than one period of construction and because it was built on a terraced slope with consequent changes of level. In outline, however, the plan takes the form of an H, with two parallel ranges (referred to below as the south-west and north-east wings) running downhill and linked by a corridor.[4]

The lower, south end of the south-west wing contains a complex bath house with heated rooms and a plunge bath. The upper north end was also a bath suite: it originally had a hypocaust and hot and cold plunge baths.

Midway along the corridor connecting the two wings was an octagonal room and along the south side were a number of buttresses and a feature shown on the plan (Fig. 1) as the base of a portico.

In the northern end of the north-east wing was a kitchen which was connected to a number of smaller rooms and a latrine. Further south was a raised terrace reinforced on its east, west and south sides by buttresses. The southern end of this wing was on a lower level and appears to have been an aisled barn entered through a door on the eastern side.

Throughout the account that follows the room numbers used are those adopted in the past by successive generations of excavators.

The Terracing

A full understanding of the plan of the villa is only possible after considering levels in different parts of the house; therefore before a detailed description is made of the reconstruction a brief explanation of the levels will be given (Fig. 2).

The South-west Wing

The floor level in the lower bath house is known; mosaic pavements and supported floors still survive. The floor in Room 1 also survives (it is approximately 12in. higher than the floors in the bath house) although its surface falls 6in. from the north side of the room to the south probably as the result of subsidence. This room was originally about 13ft. lower than the level of Room 34a, and was connected to it by means of a ramp with steps (2). The present floor in Room 34a corresponds approximately to the lower floor level of a hypocaust that once existed here; therefore the original floor must have been approximately 3ft. higher. The floors in Rooms 50 and 1a would probably have been on the same level as the upper hypocaust floor in Room 34a, although the floor in Room 49 was about 7ft. lower.

The Corridor

Room 13 at the west end of the corridor was situated half-way along the ramp in the south-west wing, about 5ft. 6in. above Room 1 and about

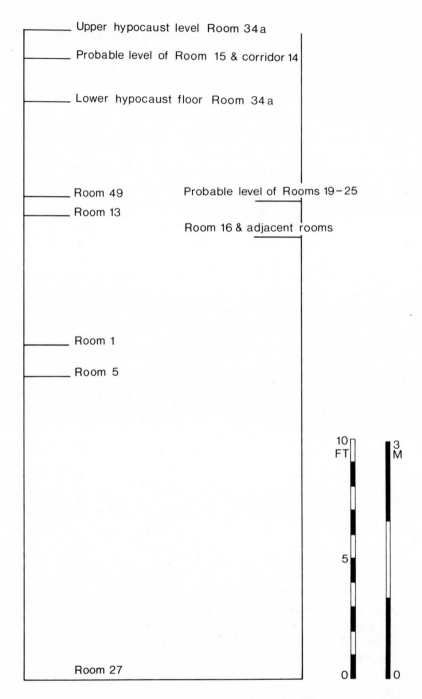

Fig. 2 Diagram showing the relationship of levels in different parts of the
villa.

7ft. 6in. below Room 34a. The corridor floor is lost (14), but according to Greenfield was on the same plane as the floor in the octagonal room (15). Here no floor survives, but its surface is unlikely to have been much more than 6in. above the present surviving walls. It appears to have been covered with an *opus sectile* pavement—this was recorded by Lysons:[5] 'it had a chequered pavement, of which a small fragment remains, formed of squares of 5in. and some triangles of a white calcareous stone and blue lyas'. The level of this room and the corridor would have been about 6ft. 6in. above Room 13.

The North-east Wing

The floors in Rooms 16, 17, 18, 34, 41, 42, 43 and 53 survive, and were roughly on the same level as one another, about 12in. lower than Room 13, and about 7ft. 6in. below the corridor (14) and Rooms 15 and 52. No floors survive in Rooms 19-25,[6] but they may have been as much as 18in. higher than the floors to the north. Room 27 was almost 20ft. lower than Rooms 19-25.

The floors in Rooms 26-30 are not level; Room 27 was approximately 12-18in. lower than the west side of Room 28, the floor of which sloped up towards the entrance (31). Room 26, and possibly also 30 were on the same level as Room 28.

Conclusion

The separate levels of the rooms in the villa were very complex, and a casual visitor to the site may wonder how occupants of the house gained access from one side of the villa to the other when the levels differed so much. However, when comparing these it will be found that Rooms 34a, 50 and perhaps 1a in the south-west wing were approximately the same level as the corridor 14 and Room 15, and that Room 16 and adjacent rooms at the east end of the corridor would have been roughly on the same level as Room 13 at the west. The similarity of planes on separate areas of the site therefore would suggest that they were in some way connected.

THE RECONSTRUCTION (Fig. 3)

The South-west Wing

The South (lower) Bath House

The complexity of the lower bath house plan (Rooms 3-12) suggests that it was of more than two phases; the complicated roof levels shown on the reconstruction also imply a sequence of rebuilding of more than two periods. The plan of the three-roomed structure (Rooms 9-11), incorporating a *caldarium*, *tepidarium* and *frigidarium* appears to be the simple lay-out adopted in many early bath houses, i.e., those at Chedworth,[7] Gadebridge Park,[8], High Wycombe,[9] and Park Street.[10] The different alignment of these rooms to those elsewhere would also indicate that it was an independent structure originally.

The plan of the bath house in its latest phase is not in question, but during the course of making the reconstruction the problem arose as to how bathers

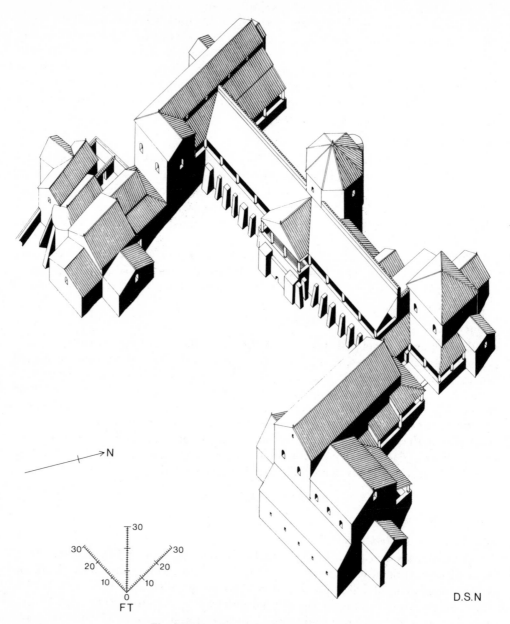

Fig. 3 Witcombe: overall reconstruction.

entered the baths. The entrance into the bath house was situated in the north
corner of Room 6; another was located close by in the east wall of Room 4.
There does not seem to have been a direct route from the upper baths or the
main house itself as no entrance was provided in the south wall of Room 1.

Lysons only refers to one door into this room and states, 'it did not appear that the room . . . communicated with any other'. Bathers wishing to use the lower bath suite, therefore, had to walk across the courtyard, and presumably had to make their way either from the north-east wing (as a revetment wall shown on Lysons's plan running east of the entrance into Room 4 might suggest) or possibly down steps situated against the south wall of the corridor 14[11] (see p. 36).

The fact that there were two bath houses may indicate two separate periods, although there is a possibility that the lower baths were intended for use by estate workers. The separation of the lower baths could have been designed to prevent bathers, when using these facilities, from passing through the main house—an hypothesis suggested for the isolated bath house at High Wycombe.[12] The possibility of the lower baths being for villa workers is perhaps further supported by the presence of the revetment wall leading from Room 4 towards the barn-like building in the eastern wing. The close proximity of the lower baths to the villa and the fact that the main villa was equipped with an integral bath house, rules out its isolation being designed to avoid the risk of fire.

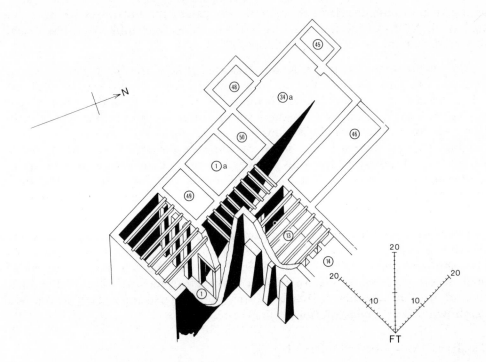

Fig. 4 Witcombe: reconstruction of north-west wing.

The North (upper) Bath House (Fig. 4)

The supports on the east side of Room 13 and on the west side of 16 (Fig. 5) were generally considered to have marked the position of a staircase up to the raised level of the corridor (14). These rooms may have had staircases in them, but a better explanation (bearing in mind that 6ft. 6in.–7ft. 6in. once separated the levels of these rooms and the corridor) is that they were merely buttresses and that the corridor floor originally ran over the lower rooms. The rooms therefore were cellars and presumably intended for storage. The corridor probably provided direct access into the upper baths, by means of a short return passage on the east side of Room 49, leading directly into an upper storey over Room 1. The corridor did not turn north. Sufficient headroom had to be provided beneath this corridor to get from the upper bath suite down the ramp into Rooms 13 and 1. The purpose of Rooms 46 and 46a (probably not two rooms, but one; the presence of the drain causing misinterpretation by Lysons) is uncertain, but it was probably a passage leading from the main corridor (over Room 13) to the ramp—a route designed to by-pass the upper baths.

This hypothesis is further supported by the presence of buttresses on the south side of Room 13. The floor in this room was almost on the same level as the ground outside. Had no upper floor existed, the buttresses would seem to have had little function. Such massive supports are unlikely to have been necessary to reinforce a dwarf corridor wall.

The height of the ceiling in Room 1 is doubtful. If the floor level in Room 34a was the same as over Room 1 the ceiling height would have been about 12ft., which appears excessive. However, if the height of the floor above corresponded approximately to the level of Room 49, the ceiling would only have been about 5ft. high. This seems low, especially as the room was probably, judging from its decoration, a room of some importance.[13] Lysons describes Room 1 as follows:[14] 'the walls of which remained in a very perfect state, to the height of from five feet four inches to six feet. When first opened they were covered with a coat of stucco, two inches thick, painted in pannels of different colours'. He thought it had a religious function.

The reason for the change of level and the purpose of Room 49 is unknown: the floor surface may have been the lower floor of a hypocaust (Mrs. Clifford's plan shows a gap in its west wall which may have been a flue) or the room may have been a water cistern. Room 1 therefore had a ceiling higher than around 5ft., but whether the height of the room reached the level of Room 34a (as shown on the reconstruction) is uncertain.

The Raised Corridor or Gallery (Fig. 3)

The level of the corridor (14) in relation to Rooms 13 and 16 has already been explained, but that it was a raised terrace is further demonstrated by the many buttresses built against its south wall. The idea of the gallery was probably to provide occupants of the house with the maximum view of the surrounding countryside. This may also have been the intention when Room 17 (Fig. 5) was demolished, since its removal would have allowed an uninterrupted view along the corridor to the scenery on the east. The later corridor, built around the three sides of Room 17 and along the east side of the house, was at a lower level than the main gallery and therefore its height would not have impaired the view.

On the north side of the corridor (which is shown on the reconstruction drawing as having had a pentice roof supported on its south side by columns set on a low wall) was an octagonal room, possibly a *triclinium*, the height of which is shown to be greater than that of the corridor roof in the belief that the builder would have desired its octagonal shape to be seen from both sides

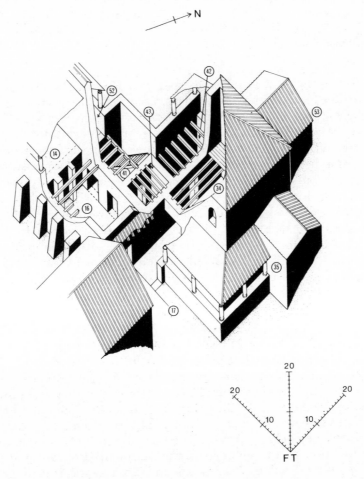

Fig. 5 Witcombe: reconstruction of north-east wing.

of the house. However, the height of the room may have been less, and may have been only visible from the north.

On the south side, and running parallel to the corridor, was a feature shown on Greenfield's plans as a portico. Leading from this were three drains,[15] two from the centre of the structure and another from its eastern side. The situation of the drains would suggest that the feature was associated with water, and therefore the possibility arises of it having been a *nymphaeum* or possibly an ornamental water cistern. This theory is supported by the way the structure has been reinforced, not merely by buttresses, but also by narrow retaining walls which could have been strong enough for a water proofing, but which were totally inadequate to withstand pressure from the raised gallery. There is an alternative suggestion as to its purpose—it could have combined both a staircase (leading from the courtyard) and an ornamental pool.

The North-east Wing

North End (Fig. 5)

An upper storey probably also existed over Rooms 16, 41, 42, 43, 53 and 34. The reason for assuming this is that these rooms had been terraced into the side of the hill, so much so that the floors of Rooms 34, 41, 42, 43 and 53 were once between 7–8ft. lower than the ground level to the north, and originally would have been about 8ft. 6in. lower than the gallery (14). Entry to the villa from its northern side was probably via an upper storey corridor (level with the outside surface) situated over Room 42, a corridor matching Rooms 46 and 46a on the west side of the villa. This corridor led directly into the main gallery (14). To descend into the lower rooms (which were level with the ground surface to the east) or to leave the premises from its eastern side (via the door in the east wall of Room 16), a staircase probably existed in Room 41. Room 52 was probably a continuation of the corridor adjacent to the staircase well, as it had no upper storey; its floor was level with the outside ground surface.

South End (Fig. 6)

The north wall of Room 27 (which is likely to have been part of a barn) was reinforced by two massive buttresses which probably stood almost 20ft. to the floor level of the living room in the upper terrace (Rooms 19–25). It is probable that the level of the upper terrace continued southwards over Room 27, up to the wall dividing Rooms 27 from 29. The function of the two internal buttresses on the east and west sides of Room 27 is problematical, but it is likely they held an arch designed to support a wall in the upper storey; a similar function to the supports in the basement (Room 20) at Gadebridge Park.[16] The floor level in Rooms 26 and 28 was 12–18in. higher than in Room 27. These rooms were first excavated by Samuel Lysons who observed that Room 28 appeared to be subterraneous and that the doorway of the

passage 18 at (d) was 6ft. 8in. above the level of 26.[17] These differences in
levels therefore suggest that the corridor (18) which falls steeply from the
north side of Rooms 19–22, led directly into a floor above 26, 28 and 30.
However, a number of points emerged whilst making the reconstruction
drawing which suggest that only Room 26 had another storey.

The width of the entrance (31) in the east wall of Room 28 was 7ft. 6in.
wide. The door was flanked by two walls which probably supported a pitched

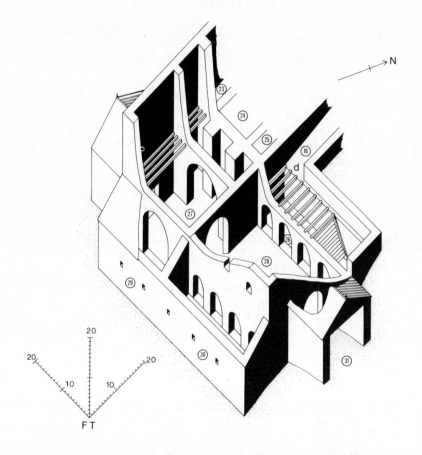

Fig. 6 Witcombe: reconstruction of south-east wing.

roof intended to keep the area around the entrance dry, and may have been
designed to enable vehicles to enter the room particularly if this was used as
a barn as its overall aisled plan would suggest. The reconstruction shows this
entrance arched; it is unlikely to have been spanned by a horizontal wooden
beam as this would have been insufficiently strong for the weight above. It

was also reconstructed as an arch in an attempt to harmonise with one which probably once existed between Rooms 27 and 28, an arch which was probably the original entrance into this lower entrance and which was designed to support upstairs walls. Bearing in mind the width of the entrance, a reasonable height to the soffit would have been about 11ft., and yet the height of the room, allowing for ceiling timbers would have only been about 6ft. if its ceiling corresponded to the ceiling in Room 26. It is probable, that a corridor existed over Room 26 from which a staircase descended to the lower level, and that no upper storey existed in Rooms 28 or 30.

Since Rooms 26, 28 and 30 were interconnected, the dividing walls probably had openings. Lysons plan shows two doors about 5ft. wide, and two smaller gaps (probably drains) some 18in. wide. Greenfield's plan also shows these features, but shows the doorways blocked.

An inspection of the wall between Rooms 26 and 28 shows three massive stone blocks that were probably piers. Lysons also described similar piers in the wall between Rooms 28 and 30. He writes:[18] 'In the wall between No. 28 and 30 are several large upright stones, some of them 4 feet high, resting on plinths'. It would seem from a visual inspection and Lysons' description that these walls once comprised a series of arches or openings separated by piers formed by massive stone blocks, and this is what the reconstruction drawing shows. No attempt has been made in the reconstruction to represent the blocking of the openings.

DISCUSSION

The construction of a building on such steep and unstable sub-soil must have been an expensive undertaking and this suggests that cost was no object. It may be that the unstable nature of the terrain and problems of construction were not realised, but the many buttresses erected against the first house suggest that the hazards were understood even though attempts at overcoming them (judging from later buttresses) were not always successful.

The slope of the hillside made it necessary to construct the villa on terraces, but Witcombe (although built on a steeper slope than many other villas) should not be considered unique in this respect. Many villas had rooms constructed on raised levels, or had rooms terraced into the hill slope.[19] Nor should it be regarded as unusual in having had upper storeys. Room 27 was similar to Room 20 at Gadebridge Park;[20] the north side of this room was terraced into the hill slope, but its south side was level with the outside ground surface. In this room were three piers which originally supported upper walls. The Deep Room at Lullingstone[21] was also open on one side and almost certainly supported a room above. Room 8 at Lockleys[22] may also be cited. Unfortunately evidence for double storeyed rooms is rarely found on villas situated on even ground. The only evidence available is foundations of unusual thickness or small rooms (which appear to have had little function as passages) possibly used as staircase wells. Also some internal buttresses may have been designed to support walls upstairs, e.g., the internal walls in Room 27.

The main entrance into the villa is uncertain. The building seems to have had two approaches, one from the north side, and the other from the east. The north entrance was probably the most commonly used since visitors would have been able to enter the raised gallery and living rooms without having to use the staircase possibly situated in Room 41. The eastern entrance, adjacent to the kitchen (34) is more likely to have been used by staff. It is unlikely that, had a staircase existed on the south side of the corridor, it was used as public access. The situation of entrances into a villa on the opposite sides from the courtyard is not without parallel. Even though the courtyard at Gadebridge Park in the second century was on the south side, no obvious public entrance was provided in the outer courtyard wall; more stylish entrances were provided on its north side where two porches were situated. In the fourth century when the courtyard was transferred to the north, a gatehouse was built on the opposite side of the villa. It should not be assumed therefore that the approach into the house was always through the courtyard.

The number of living rooms in the villa is unusually small. Most of the southeast wing was taken up with the bathing suites. Room 1, although probably not forming part of the bath house, is unlikely to have been used for living quarters owing to its semi-basement nature and possible religious function. Room 15, midway along the gallery, could have been the *triclinium*. Room 34 appears to have been a kitchen, Rooms 41–43 an entrance complex, and 53 and 35 service quarters. Room 35 was a latrine. The massive sub-structure forming Rooms 19–25 was probably two rooms, perhaps both living quarters. It is unlikely that any of the rooms in the barn (Rooms 26–30) would have been suitable for accommodation except possibly for servants or slaves.

Accepting double storeys on the basis of the reconstruction, however, the number of rooms suitable for living quarters can be increased from three to seven. This allows for an additional living room over Rooms 1 and 34 and two rooms over 27. There could even have been an additional storey over Rooms 19–25, but as this is doubtful it is not shown on the reconstruction. Room 34a could also have been used as a heated apartment as well as being part of the upper bath suite.

CONCLUSION

The reconstruction of Witcombe was undertaken in the hope that the results obtained from the drawings might explain the various levels on the site and be a contribution towards the understanding of the architecture. This proved to be the case, so that time spent on further such reconstructions of other villas might well be justified.

REFERENCES

1. *Archaeologia*, Vol. 19, p. 178.

2.*Transactions of the Bristol and Gloucester Archaeological Society*, Vol. 73 (1954), p.5.

3. Any misinterpretation of the excavators' plans is solely the responsibility of the writer; in the light of further excavation the suggested reconstruction may have to be amended.

4. For convenience of description within this report it will be assumed that wings of the villa run north-south. They do in fact run north-west to south-east.

5. *Archaeologia*, Vol. 19, p. 182.

6. The walls separating Rooms 19–25 were underfloor walls designed to support a terrace, and do not reflect the plans of the rooms. It is probable that 19–22 was one room and 23–25 another.

7. R. G. Collingwood and I. Richmond, *The Archaeology of Roman Britain*, revised edition (1969), Fig. 46, p. 145.

8. D. S. Neal, *The Roman Villa in Gadebridge Park, Hemel Hempstead*, Society of Antiquaries Research Report, No. XXXI, p. 8.

9. *Records of Buckinghamshire*, Vol. 16 (1953–60), 237.

10. *Archaeological Journal*, Vol. 118 (1961), p. 116.

11. There is possibly one other route the bathers took: this was via a staircase descending into Room 4 from the storey over Room 1.

12. *Records of Buckinghamshire*, Vol. 16 (1953–60), p. 242.

13. The room may be compared to the deep room at Lullingstone (G. W. Meates, *Lullingstone Roman Villa* [1955], pp. 61–64) since both rooms had a box-like water basin set into the floor. The Lullingstone room almost certainly had some religious function as it had a niche painted with three water nymphs—perhaps local water deities.

14. *Archaeologia*, Vol. 19, p. 178.

15. Whether these drains were contemporary with one another is uncertain.

16. D. S. Neal, *Gadebridge Park*, *op. cit.*, p. 19.

17. *Archaeologia*, Vol. 19, p. 183.

18. *Ibid.*

19. This was a relatively common building technique in Italy where rooms were often raised above *crypto-portici*. This also raises the question as to whether such a feature once ran between Rooms 13 and 16.

20. *Op cit.*, p. 19.

21. G. W. Meates, *Lullingstone Roman Villa* (1955), pp. 61–64.

22. *Antiquaries Journal*, Vol. 18 (1938), plan f., p. 376.

Enamels from Roman Britain

by

SARNIA A. BUTCHER

THE USE of enamelled decoration is common on bronze objects of the Roman period found in Britain, yet little is known of the location and dating of the industry. It is proposed to review the evidence on the subject in relation to a number of recent finds with which the Inspectorate of Ancient Monuments has been associated and to publish objects from several sites in advance of the full excavation reports.

The term 'enamel' is used here to cover coloured vitreous material applied as decoration to bronze objects (Maryon 1954). No general study has yet been made of the composition of Romano-British enamels and the present discussion is based upon visual examination only.[1] The technique generally used is that known as *champlevé,* in which cells ('fields') cut or cast in the bronze were filled with frit (powdered glassy substance) or pieces of coloured glass, and the object fired to fuse the two materials.

In most Romano-British objects the individual cells remain small, so that the pattern itself is carried out in reserved bronze (e.g., Fig. 5, 5; Fig. 9, 24). However, a style developed, possibly in the Rhineland, in which objects were covered in enamel of different colours with few metal divisions. Colour was the main element, and it was often enriched by the insertion of plaques of mosaic or millefiore glass. Several objects decorated in this way have been found in Britain, but there is little to suggest that any were made here.

The fundamental study of the subject remains that of Mlle Françoise Henry: *Émailleurs d'Occident,* published in 1933, with minor modifications in her paper of 1936 on Hanging Bowls. (Full reference to works mentioned here will be found under authors' names in the Bibliography.) Mlle Henry discussed the principal enamelled objects of the western Roman Empire and showed that a number of different schools could be distinguished on stylistic grounds, and that some of these could be ascribed to the British Isles. R. G. Collingwood's study of some enamelled brooches (1930) and Cowen and Richmond's of the Rudge and other bowls (1935) further distinguished the source and distribution of particular classes of object (although both require modification in the light of more recent discoveries).[2] Detailed studies of enamelled brooches found in the Rhineland and of all classes of enamelled objects from Pannonia have been published by K. Exner (1939) and I. Sellye (1939).

As Collingwood and other writers have remarked, in the second century AD the individuality went out of minor craftsmanship in bronze under what is usually seen as the deadening influence of Roman provincial art. The Rhineland appeared to be the main source of a flood of trinkets which were exported throughout the western provinces and even beyond (e.g., to Dura-Europos), and it might be thought that, as with some classes of pottery, mass production in relatively large workshops had replaced the individual craftsman working for a small market. The ascription of a manufactory to the villa at Anthée (Béquet, 1900) provided the substance for this idea, but as Dr. Spitaels has recently shown (1970) the grounds for supposing that the manufacture of enamels took place there are very slight. No other centre of production is known and the British evidence suggests that the objects made here emanate from a number of small workshops rather than one large factory.

However, so far no example of an enameller's workshop of the period of the Roman Empire has been adequately recorded. From finds of the periods immediately before and after the Empire we know what the distinguishing features are likely to be. Mt. Beuvray in the first century BC (Bulliot, 1899) and Garranes from perhaps the mid-fifth century AD onwards (O'Riordain 1942) both provide evidence. At each there were abundant fragments both of the raw material and of waste pieces from the process, together with tools such as the tongs which held crucibles or objects in the heat of the hearth or furnace, punches and gravers for preparing the cells in the metal, and stones for polishing the surface to bring out the colour after firing. Because of the presence of metal-working proper in the same area it is not completely certain that the furnaces described in houses 18 and 20 at Mt. Beuvray were specifically designed for firing the enamels, and no very distinctive hearth was found at Garranes. Possibly the object bearing the prepared frit or glass was protected by a simple baffle and plunged into charcoal in an ordinary bowl hearth. The temperature could be raised sufficiently by the use of bellows.

Some of these items have occurred in Romano-British contexts, but never as a complete assemblage and the individual objects may often have a different explanation. What appear to be crucibles with traces of glassy substance are sometimes reported, but this effect can be produced on pottery which has been burnt in contact with wood-ash at a high temperature. Copper melting slags can give the impression of red enamel.[3] May (1904) describes the finds at Wilderspool as including an enameller's workshop, but unfortunately the details given are not sufficiently precise for certainty. Fragments of coloured glass, crucibles with bronze adhering and a few enamelled objects were found in rubbish layers near a furnace, but direct association is not established.

In the Iron Age and Early Christian sites already described the enamelling process was carried out in the same workshops as the fabrication of the bronze objects themselves, and it is likely that this would be the case in Roman times as well, since enamelling appears as a minor part of the decoration on objects such as brooches, studs and rings (e.g., Fig. 7, No. 14, Fig. 8, Nos. 21 and 22). At Traprain Law, where moulds for casting small bronzes have been found, an untrimmed enamelled fastener has been recognised (Burley, 1956, p. 194). The production of brooches has been suggested at several sites,[4] and it is likely that some of these workshops included enamelling in their repertoire of decoration.

The distribution of some classes of object points to a multiplicity of origins, and the notion that all enamels found in Britain came from the Rhineland does not survive an examination of the brooches of the period. In many cases those bearing enamel have close parallels in non-enamelled brooches of purely local distribution. The well-known 'dragonesque' brooches are found mainly in the northern half of Britain (Feachem, 1951 and 1968); they share details of decoration with the trumpet and head-stud brooches (Fig. 9, Nos. 24, 25, and Fig. 10, Nos. 27, 28) and it is probable that all originated in that area.

The enamelled vessels are probably too rare a class of object for distribution within the province to be very significant. The presence in Britain of several of the Braughing type and the scarcity of the Pyrmont type (Forsyth, 1950, and see p. 45 below) provides reasonable grounds for ascribing manufacture to Britain and the continent respectively, while the naming of forts on Hadrian's Wall on two of the Rudge type suggests a British origin for those.

The mainly northern origin of many of the best-known classes of enamels can be counter-balanced by the group from Nornour in the Isles of Scilly. Most of these have been published by Mr. M. R. Hull (1968). Since then a few more have been found, which are illustrated here (Fig. 8). The distribution of some of the main types of enamelled bow brooch found at Nornour falls within a clearly defined area of southern England: from both sides of the Bristol Channel (Somerset, Gloucestershire and Monmouthshire) eastwards and southwards into Wiltshire, Berkshire and Oxfordshire. Examples do occur at Nornour of types of bow brooch common all over Britain while some of the plate brooches have a much wider distribution, chiefly on the Continent.

In the original publication of the site on Nornour it was suggested that this was one of the elusive Romano-British enameller's workshops (Dudley, 1968, pp. 17 and 28). More than 400 bronze trinkets (mostly brooches) have been found there, of which some two-thirds were enamelled, and the layout of Room I with its central hearth and 'table' surrounded by stone benches appeared suitable for a finishing shop. Mr. Hull pointed out that most of the brooches showed a fair homogeneity of technique and could have been manufactured on the site. However, no actual trace of manufacture was found in the excavations of 1962-6 and further work in 1969–73 has not produced the desired evidence (Butcher, 1970-1972). The central hearth area of Room I has now been completely excavated and no scrap of metal, slag or enamel, nor any object associated with manufacture, has been found in any of the features associated with the hearths. The brooches and other metal objects all came from higher levels, mainly from amongst the rubble filling the house. The Ancient Monuments Laboratory has examined samples of all materials from the features described and found no trace of metallurgical or enamelling processes, nor any evidence that temperatures high enough for bronze-working or enamelling had been reached.

Even a finishing shop might be expected to contain some waste materials such as trimmings and scraps of surplus metal and enamel, if not broken and discarded objects. In spite of careful search nothing of the sort has been found anywhere on the site. It appears that Nornour is basically a prehistoric habitation site with some secondary occupation of one of the houses in the Roman period. If manufacture is ruled out it is necessary to account for the presence of such a large number of bronze objects. They cannot be the result of shipwreck or plunder in view of the diversity of origins and the wide range of date displayed by the collection (the main group of brooches dates from the later first to the early third centuries). Nor is the site likely to be a shop serving a local market: the population of Scilly in Roman times would not have been large enough to support a specialised trade, and very few similar objects have been found elsewhere in the islands. The strongest alternative possibility is that they were votive offerings at a shrine (of which it must be acknowledged that there is no structural indication) and the presence of clay figurines and numerous coins rather supports this.

In the absence of direct evidence for centres of production it is necessary to study the objects themselves for indications of their provenance. The following groups, from various sites, will help to show the range of enamelled products of the Roman period found in Britain. The designs vary from ambitious all-over patterns such as those on vessels (e.g., Figs. 1 and 2) which were no doubt the work of specialist craftsmen, down to the crude patches of colour added to simple forms of brooch (Figs. 6, No. 10, and 8, No. 22).

The dating of the objects presents considerable problems. They are durable and quite likely to be kept for long periods, and the typological developments are of the sort which does not necessarily imply any wide span of time (see Nos. 27 and 28, pp. 62-64). There are, however, a few points in the time scale which are fixed by site evidence. The best-known British enamelled brooches: the trumpet (e.g., Nos. 24 and 25), the head-stud (Nos. 27–28), and the dragonesque, must all have been in production well before the end of the first century somewhere in the northern part of the country. In the south the equally fine scale-patterned disc-brooches (Nos. 5, 6 and 7) seem to date to the late first and early second centuries. The second century sees the main development of the plate and disc brooches which are so well represented at Antonine Newstead (Curle, 1911). Many of these were products of the continental industry, which continued into the third century (Exner, 1939,

p. 64) but beyond this there is little to fill the gap until enamelling reappears in the post-Roman period.[5] Some of the objects listed below which were found in late contexts must have been survivals (e.g., No. 24), but the tiered stand from Brigstock (No. 4) was probably a late product and the crudest horseman brooches (No. 11) now seem reasonably well dated to the fourth century (p. 54).

Vessels

Fig. 1.* Handle of skillet from Kirkby Lathorpe, near Sleaford, Lincs. Nat. Grid TF 078458. Recovered from a builder's trench and recorded by Mrs. M. U. Jones. Length 9.5cm.

The handle is a flat bronze plate, one end of which is shaped to fit the curve of a bowl 11.8cm. in diameter. Most of the upper surface is cut away and filled with enamel, leaving only thin lines of reserved bronze to form the design. Three of the edges of the panel are serrated to key the enamel. The design has three main elements: two leaf shapes and a roundel. The interior of the leaves is divided into three lobes and they end in tendrils which fill the spaces of the panel. The roundel contains a pair of leaves; where the handle broadens there are scrolls. There seem to be only two enamel colours: that shown red in Fig. 1, which appears under the microscope to be entirely a brownish-green, and blue, which only survives in small areas.

There is a very close parallel in the handle of the skillet from Linlithgow[6] which bears two similar leaves but has a ribbon-like motif in a semi-circle in place of the roundel. The body of the Linlithgow vessel is closely similar to the Braughing bowl[7] and another from Maltbroek.[8]

None of these vessels is from closely dated contexts and they have usually been ascribed to the early second century by analogy with non-enamelled skillets and with samian bowls which bear scroll and wreath decoration. The style of decoration is similar to that on the vessel found at Bartlow, where an accompanying burial contained a coin of Hadrian.[9]

Fig. 2. Bowl from Brougham, Cumbria.[10] Miss D. Charlesworth's excavation. From Burial 12. Diameter 9.2cm. Handle: length 8cm.

The plain bronze handle is an addition. There are signs of wear and a patch on the foot of the bowl. The decoration takes the form of a scroll with stylised leaves. It is outlined in reserved bronze and filled with enamel: red for the scroll, red and green for the leaves, and blue for the background. Some edges are serrated as in No. 1 above.

The general scheme of decoration is obviously related to the scrolls of the Linlithgow and Braughing bowls but is much more stylised and lacks the finer details of stalk and tendril. The long pointed leaves with asymmetrical inset have a parallel on the Pyrmont bowl[11] and the lobed design in the alternating panels is somewhat like the motif on that from Rochefort (Forsyth, 1950, p. 302). These resemblances are not close enough to place the Brougham bowl in their type: the scheme of decoration is freer flowing and the motifs less geometrical in effect. Whatever the exact relation of these pieces the similarities are, however, probably sufficient to place the Brougham cup within the second century, though possibly towards its end. This would accord with the accompanying pottery, which is likely to date from after AD 200 and would probably have had a shorter life than the bronze vessel.

*See Note 1, p. 68.

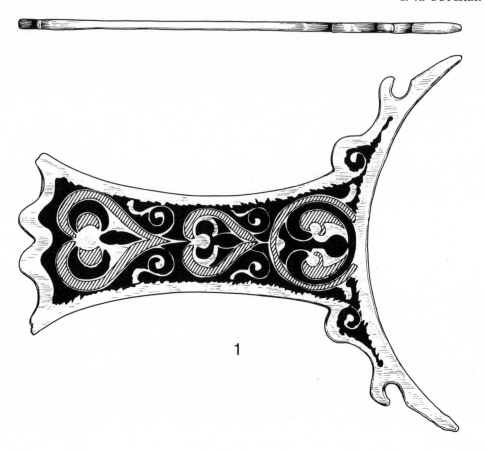

1

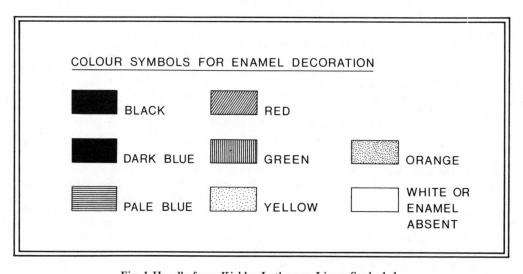

COLOUR SYMBOLS FOR ENAMEL DECORATION

■ BLACK	▨ RED	
■ DARK BLUE	▥ GREEN	⣿ ORANGE
▤ PALE BLUE	⣿ YELLOW	□ WHITE OR ENAMEL ABSENT

Fig. 1 Handle from Kirkby Lathorpe, Lincs. Scale 1:1.

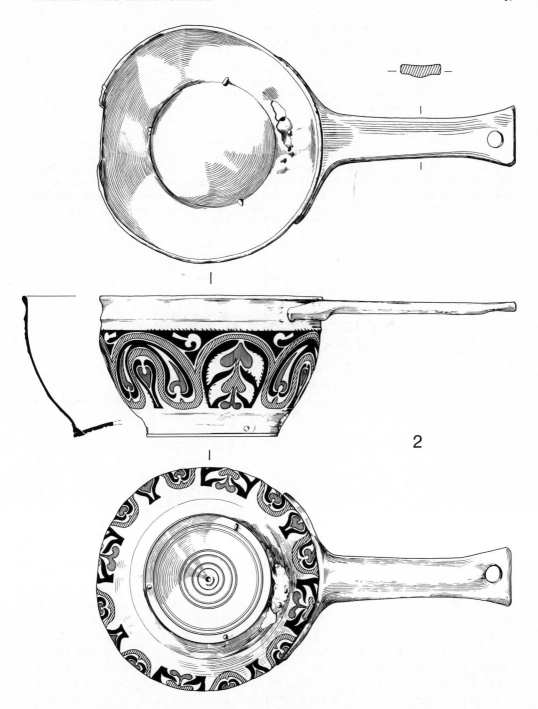

Fig. 2 Bowl from Brougham, Cumbria. Diameter 9·2 cm.

Fig. 3.* Fragment of bowl from Beadlam, Yorks. Dr. I. M. Stead's excavation.[12] LB/NZ, AM 705837.

The decoration, in relief bronze, shows part of an inscription] CITR followed by a zig-zag line. Below this there is a continuous double scroll, again formed by lines of reserved bronze. The cavities were filled with enamel, of which only fragments survive; blue within the scroll and turquoise in the outer field. The upper edges of the panels are serrated in a similar manner to Nos. 1 and 2 above.

The position of the inscription and the style of lettering place this in the same group as the Rudge cup (Cowen and Richmond, 1935), and this is reinforced by the scroll, which appears to be very like that on the handle of the Amiens vessel (Heurgon, 1951), which also bore an inscription below its rim. Both of these vessels showed the names of forts on the northern frontier of Britain; the Beadlam inscription may refer to Tarraconensis. By analogy with the other two it should date from the mid or later second century, but it was found on a floor with numerous fourth-century coins.

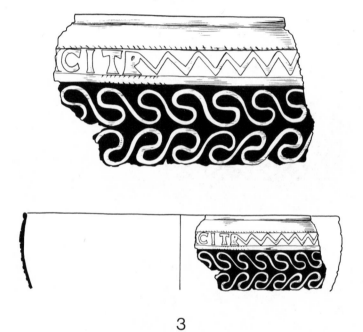

3

Fig. 3 Bowl from Beadlam, Yorks. Fragment shown 1:1.
Outline 1:2.

The three vessels represented here form a considerable addition to the small group already known from Britain, most of which have been quoted in the foregoing account. That from Kirkby Lathorpe adds another example to the well-known Braughing group, but the other two show some new features. It seems possible that they are British products: the parallels to the Beadlam cup and the curvilinear style of the Brougham bowl both suggest this attribution. The enamel colours (red, blue and turquoise/green) and method (used as filling for a design carried out in bronze) are familiar on British brooches. The absence of precise dating evidence makes it difficult to decide whether the variations of style are due solely to typological development or to the existence of different workshops within the province. There is a general similarity amongst all the enamelled bowls in shape and the placing of decoration which suggests that they are all part of the same tradition and that a date within the period *c.* AD 100 to 200 might cover whole series.

They have been described as bowls, cups, skillets and paterae according to the presence or absence of a handle, but it seems likely that a handle might easily become detached and leave no trace since it was not rivetted. The plain handle on the Brougham example may be a replacement for one which matched the design, and the Braughing, Maltbroek, and Rudge bowls may originally have had handles similar to those on the Linlithgow, Amiens, and Pyrmont examples.

Miniature Tables or Stands

Fig. 4. Water Newton, Mr. E. Greenfield's excavation.[13] From a rubble spread near building 2, site 3, in the extra-mural settlement. Combined height 7.5cm.

Two small bronze objects in the form of a table, one of which is smaller and is pegged into the top of the other. Each side is decorated with enamel: on the larger stand two sides have a row of tall narrow triangles, two blue and two red alternately (one side has an extra blue triangle in the centre) and the opposite sides have a curved strip with tendrils, rather like half a scroll. The centre is red, the field above turquoise and that below blue. On the smaller stand the 'half-scroll' is repeated, but with the colours reversed, and the other two sides are divided into three triangles of which the central one is red and the other two turquoise; each has a ring of reserved bronze in the centre. There is a large round opening in the top of each stand, and a small hole near each corner. The legs of the smaller stand fit into these holes in the larger, and as found they are tightly fixed, projecting about 3mm. through the metal.

Several similar objects have been found, most of them having exactly similar decoration (e.g., a pair from Silchester in Reading Museum which is a complete parallel). That in the British Museum from (?) Farley Heath[14] has a crenellated pattern instead of the triangles. The stand from Brigstock[15] has the same decoration but is smaller and its legs would fit into the holes of the upper of the two Water Newton objects. Since the Brigstock example also has holes in the top it would seem that sometimes there were four tiers. However, the British Museum has one of the same size as Brigstock (i.e., the third tier) which does not have holes for attachment but does have a collar of bronze, 7mm. high and 1cm. in diameter, which is fixed over the central opening as if to form a funnel. This stand has the same pattern on each of the four sides: two curved lines of bronze divide the enamel field into three equal areas, two green and one white except for one side which has two white and one green.

The Water Newton example is undated but that from Brigstock was on the floor of a shrine built in the mid-third century and in use until the late fourth century. The object probably had a religious or ritual use and so can be regarded as contemporary with the building. Few enamelled objects can be dated so late (pp. 44-45 above) and these stands do not display the characteristics of the latest continental enamels. (Exner, 1939, p. 63). On the other hand their uniformity of decoration is unlike most groups of first and second century British enamels.

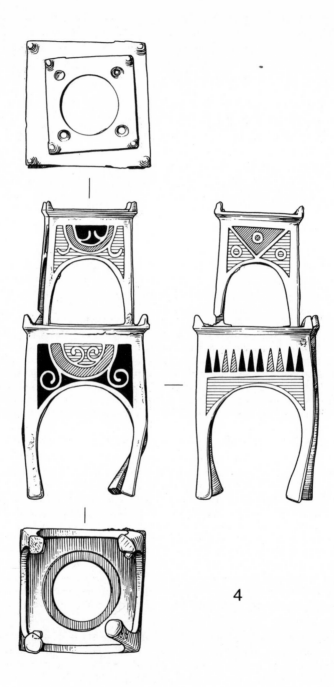

Fig. 4 Miniature stands from Water Newton,
Cambs. Scale 1:1.

The purpose of these stands is obscure. The fact that the central hole diminishes in size with each tier rules out many suggestions: as a unit they would not make an effective support for anything taller than themselves. It is possible that they were used separately but if this was their main function they would surely have been made all the same size, or nearly so. The stacking principle may be the clue to function since either a single 'tower' or a set of separate stands would be more effective if made as such. A suggestion which would cover this is that the sections were removed one at a time to mark the stages of a ritual. (In view of their small size this might have been a personal ritual: rather like the use of a rosary.) If a candle burned down inside the tier (which the enlargement of the central opening towards the bottom would permit) the passage of time would also be measured. The funnel on the British Museum example has a functional look and might perhaps be a wind-shield for a newly-lit candle.

Scale-patterned Châtelaine and Disc Brooches

Fig. 5, 5. Châtelaine brooch from Wanborough, Wilts. Mr. E. Greenfield's excavation of 1967[16] (WANX 1) unstratified. Width 30mm.

Bronze brooch with two loops which probably carried a set of toilet instruments, as on complete examples from Baldock and Canterbury (see p. 52). The design, carried out in two colours of enamel and outlined by reserve bronze, consists of a ring of scales round a central six-rayed floret. The ring is broken for a row of interlocking triangular scales on the straight lower edge, and there is a large lug at the top with a quatrefoil. All the motifs are in red, with light blue or green in the surrounding cells. There are two smaller lugs at the sides which probably once contained enamel. The pin is sprung round a central lug. The back is flat apart from a depression corresponding to the projection in front.

Fig. 5, 6. Disc brooch from Leicester (Redcross Street, No. 316, 1962, 193). Mr. M. G. Hebditch's excavation of 1962.[17] Diameter 30mm.

A bronze disc brooch bearing a ring of crescent-shaped scales surrounding a central boss with cinquefoil design similar to that on the Wanborough brooch, No. 5 above. The scales are alternately yellow and turquoise on a green ground. It has six small plain and two larger lugs round the circumference. One of the larger lugs is a loop (a similar brooch at Richborough, Bushe Fox, 1932, Pl. X, 14, had a length of chain attached to this) and the other has recessed concentric circles which may have contained enamel. The pin is hinged between the two lugs at the back, which is concave. The brooch was found on the floor of a period 3a timber building, with Hadrianic samian.

Fig. 5, 7. Disc brooch from St. Albans. Dr. I. M. Stead's excavation of 1966[18] S F 418. Diameter 26mm.

A bronze disc brooch with a very similar scheme of decoration to that from Leicester (No. 6 above) except that the cells are triangular rather than crescent-shaped. The colour scheme is also similar with yellow, turquoise and blue in the outward-pointing triangles and green in those between. The arrangement of lugs on the circumference is also the same as on the Leicester brooch and the pin is hinged between two lugs at the back. The closest parallel is a brooch in the Ashmolean Museum from East Garston Warren, Berks, which is the same size, has the same arrangement of lugs and the same triangular cells. The only colour which remains on this is red.

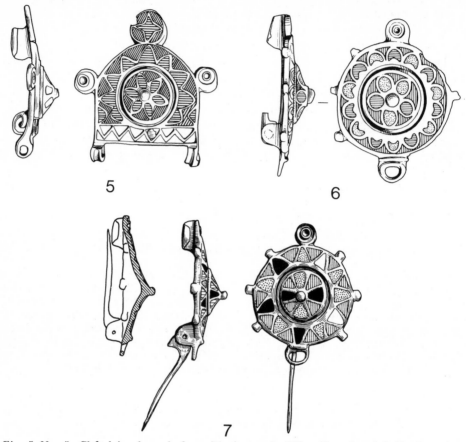

Fig. 5 No. 5, Châtelaine brooch from Wanborough, Wilts. Nos. 6 and 7 disc-brooches from Leicester and St. Albans. Scale 1:1.

A number of brooches, both disc and châtelaine, share the main features of those illustrated here:

Châtelaine

Baldock, Herts. Letchworth Museum.[19]
Canterbury Museum.[20]
Charterhouse, Somerset, in Bristol Museum (F 1969).
Gloucester (City Museum, A 1297).
London, Guildhall Museum.

Disc

Canterbury (Ashmolean Museum, 1927, 291).
Charterhouse (Bristol Museum, F 1968).

Richborough, Kent, three examples:

Third Report (Bushe Fox, 1932, p. 78, Pl. X, 14).
Fifth Report (Cunliffe, 1968, p. 88, Pl. XXI, 66).
Fragment in site museum: No. 2414.

Others from Caerleon, South Ferriby and Peterborough are quoted by Mr. Hull in the fifth Richborough report (Cunliffe, 1968, p. 88).

From their distribution it seems likely that the source of these brooches was in the Midlands or south of Britain; with their wide range of colours and symmetrical, carefully executed design, these are some of the best of British products. That from Baldock was in a burial with late first century samian and glass, the Leicester brooch, No. 6, was in a Hadrianic context, and brooches which seem to be a variation of this type (see No. 8 below) are current by *c*. AD 100.

Disc Brooches from Thistleton, Leicestershire (Mr. E. Greenfield's excavations).[21]

**Fig. 6, 8.* BH 1694 Bz 127. From surface exterior to Building 3.
Diameter 26mm.**

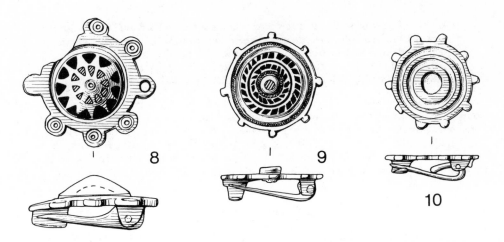

Fig. 6 Nos. 8-10 disc-brooches from Thistleton, Leics. Scale 1:1.

Umbonate brooch. The boss has two rings of triangular cells cut into the metal; the inner containing red enamel, the outer blue. It has a broad flat edge with eight lugs: that over the catch-plate is plain, the opposite one is pierced and the other six have concentric circular depressions which contain a pinkish substance, possibly enamel. The pin is hinged between two lugs and the back is concave.

Very many brooches of this general type are known, although most have only four lugs and there are variations in the details of the enamelled triangles. (Nearly all are in blue and red.) Others with broad rim and numerous lugs include Newstead (Curle, 1911,

Pl. LXXXIX, 20), Kingsholm (Ashmolean Museum, 1927, 343), and Malton. One of the standard type from Wroxeter (Bushe Fox, 1913, Fig. 10, 9) was in a deposit dated to *c.* AD 100. It seems likely that these are influenced by the design of the scale-patterned disc brooches already discussed; they are perhaps a 'cheaper version' since they would be much simpler to make. A few occur in the Rhineland (Exner, 1939, Taf. 17) but many more in Britain.

Fig. 6, 9.* Bz 37/15 THZ 1752. Unstratified. Diameter 24mm.

Thin flat disc brooch with iron central stud containing red enamel, which is set in a ring of pale green glass. The surface shows white metal and bears a wreath in niello. It has eight small plain lugs round the circumference and an outer ring of fine beading. This is an early type of brooch: niello is usually a first century feature and the enamel is of the texture seen on La Tène objects.

Fig. 6, 10. THZ 2213. Unstratified. Diameter 21mm.

Small flat disc brooch with two incised concentric rings containing traces of red enamel. There are ten small plain lugs round the outer edge, and the pin is sprung between two lugs.

Representational Plate Brooches.

Fig. 7, 11. Six brooches in the form of a horse and rider from Hockwold-cum-Wilton, Norfolk. Mr. Charles Green's excavation of the area where the ritual crowns had been found.[22] One was on the chalk floor, associated with fourth century coins, the others in upper layers, Norwich Museum. Small find Nos. 18, 19, 47, 81, 82, 84; length of each *c.* 30mm.

All virtually identical except for the enamel insets which vary slightly in shape and colour, and the crude engraving of eyes, mane and tail. The pin is sprung on a single lug at the back. Similar brooches have been found at Nornour (Hull, 1968, catalogue 132), Cold Kitchen Hill, Wilts,[23] Near Woodyates, Dorset,[24] Brettenham, Norfolk,[25] and at Woodeaton, Oxon.[26] Recently Mr. R. H. Leech has recorded four from a temple on Lamyatt Beacon in Somerset which was not built until *c.* AD 300.[27]

Fig. 7, 12.* Brooch in the form of a horse from Water Newton, Cambs. From Mr. E. Greenfield's excavation of the defences[28]: in a pit cut into the rampart, containing pottery of third and fourth century date. WN 285. Length 32mm.

Generally similar to the Hockwold brooches but less crude; the horse has no rider and there are two long bars of enamel on the body broken into a series of squares on the forequarter. There are similar brooches from York[29] and Painswick (Ashmolean Museum R160. 1900).

The general style of these brooches is common. Some much more carefully modelled examples are known: Charterhouse (Bristol Museum F 1981), one unprovenanced in the British Museum, and many on the continent: e.g., two from Besançon (Lerat 1956, Nos. 299 and 300). These, of horses without riders, show the animal's head in relief on both sides. They have a row of

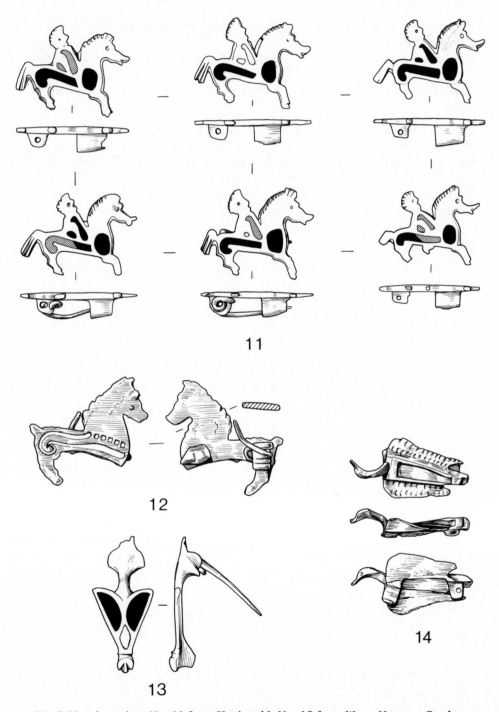

Fig. 7 Plate-brooches. No. 11 from Hockwold, No. 12 from Water Newton, Cambs., and Nos. 13 and 14 from Wanborough, Wilts. Scale 1:1.

spots of enamel along the body and five spots on the rump. There is a horse and rider brooch in the British Museum and another from Corbridge[30] much closer to the Hockwold examples but still rather more carefully modelled. The subject does appear on continental brooches but they are not usually enamelled (e.g., one from the Pyrmont spring deposit and another from Osterburken).[31]

The well-modelled horse brooches belong to a group of representational plate brooches which is common on the continent; it includes dogs, hares, fishes, birds, and mythical beasts. Exner (1939, pp. 68–9) dated these to the second century; it is possible that, as he suggests, they have an apotropaic significance, but representational brooches are worn today for no other reason than that the subjects are attractive, and a similar bestiary appears on mosaics and pottery of the Roman period.

The British horse and rider brooches do, however, seem likely to have been the badge or at least the souvenir of a cult. The Lamyatt brooches are from a temple and the Hockwold group comes from a site which has yielded religious objects; Cold Kitchen Hill and Nornour may also be religious sites. They are quite crudely made and reminiscent of the pilgrim badges of later periods.

Fig. 7, 13. Brooch in the form of a moth or fly from Wanborough (Wilts),
Mr. E. Greenfield's excavation of 1967.[32] WANX 3. Length 36mm.

The wings are flat with two lunettes of dark blue enamel and there is a lozenge of greenish enamel on the thorax. The insect's head is represented by a small moulding with two gashes for the eyes and there is a completely unnaturalistic trumpet shape at the other end. This covers two lugs holding the bar on which the pin is sprung.

Similar brooches are known from London,[33] Lincoln,[34] Kennet,[35] Caistor,[36] and Brough (Ashmolean Museum, 1836. 62). These vary mainly in the colour and position of the enamel. One from Vitrinef[37] is similar but lacks the trumpet. The type seems likely to be British and no date is known.

Fig. 7, 14. Brooch in the form of a duck from Wanborough. Site as Nos. 5
and 13 above. WAN 2045. Length excluding head and neck 23mm.

The wing feathers are represented by engraving and there is a recess for enamel on the bird's back. The head and neck are crudely formed from a square bar of metal. The two lugs and catchplate for the pin are squashed against the back. A similar brooch is known from Zugmantel.[38] Fontaines Salées[39] has one with rounded body from a second century bath-building, and at Besançon there is another in the same style (Lerat, 1956, No. 311). These may derive from first century brooches in the form of a dove: e.g., *Camulodunun*, No. 180 (Hawkes and Hull, 1947, p. 326).

Enamelled Brooches from Recent Excavations at Nornour, Isles of Scilly

For the main series of Nornour brooches the reader is referred to Mr. Hull's catalogue (1968, p. 30 ff). Those illustrated here are additional, having been found in recent excavations;[40] they do serve to emphasise certain features

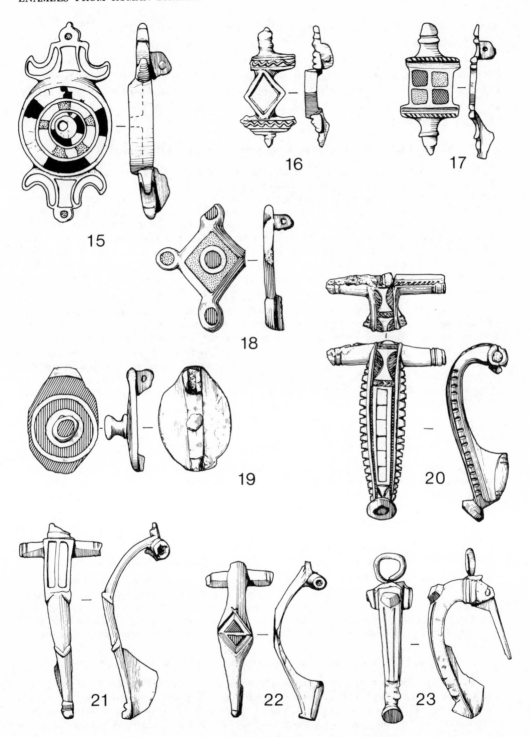

Fig. 8 Brooches from Nornour, Isles of Scilly. Scale 1:1.

already seen. First there is the fine composite plate brooch, No. 15, a continental import. In contrast there is No. 22, another representative of Mr. Hull's type 12, of which ten have already been found: these are simple bow brooches, only differing in small details, with enamel used for a touch of colour. They demonstrate that enamelling was a technique which came easily to a bronze-worker whose standards of craftsmanship were not very high; they are plain and poorly made.

Fig. 8, 15.* (NN 69.24). From the beach over House III. Length 52mm.

Heavy bronze brooch with large central disc set between two projections bearing pairs of crescent-shaped panels. The disc is cast, with a circular hollow at the back and the pin (hinged between two lugs) and catch-plate are attached to the flat backs of the projections. On the disc are three concentric rings hollowed to receive enamel which is set in blocks of different colours without any dividing lines of bronze. Black occurs in the outer ring and orange alternates with green in the next, and with black in the inner ring. The centre is flat and pierced, probably to take the shank of a moulded projection such as is seen on others of the type (e.g., examples from Namur, Richborough and Pannonia quoted below). There are spots of orange in the small round lugs at either end, remains of black in the crescents and green in the intervening fields.

There are several parallels to this very distinctive brooch. In Britain there is one from Richborough,[41] and another from East Anglia in the British Museum which is very similar to our example. Most parallels are from the continent, the best known being that from Namur, illustrated by Béquet (1900, Pl. II, 4). There are several from Pannonia[42]: one from a Sarmatian grave of c. AD 200; and from the Rhineland, including one from a burial of c. AD 150 at Wollstein (Exner, 1939, p. 94). They occur also in France (e.g. Henry, 1933, Fig. 37). From the much greater frequency abroad of these brooches and others of similar style No. 15 seems most likely to be an import.

Fig. 8, 16.* (NN 69.30). From beach south of House I. Length 31mm.

Equal-ended brooch having a lozenge-shaped plate between two wide bars bearing an undulating line in relief. The lozenge has traces of pale green enamel. There are projecting mouldings at top and bottom which cover the lugs for the pin and the catch-plate. This type has already been found at Nornour (Hull, 1968, Catalogue, 157). Parallels are quoted there from London, and it also occurs abroad; in the Rhineland,[43] France,[44] and Belgium.[45]

Fig. 8, 17.* (NN 69.35). From beach south of House I. Length 34mm.

Equal-ended brooch with a square plate between two knurled bars, with mouldings top and bottom. The plate is divided into four squares enamelled in green and blue alternately. This type is also represented in the main Nornour catalogue (Hull, 1968, Nos. 161 and 162), and the general form is common abroad: e.g., Mandeure,[46] Trier,[47] and Osterburken;[48] Exner (1939, p. 58) dates equal-ended brooches to the latter half of the second century.

Fig. 8, 18.* (NN 69.22). From beach south of House I. Length c. 35mm.

Lozenge-shaped plate brooch with round lugs at each corner. Enamel fills the field and there is a central roundel of it outlined in bronze. Each lug also contains enamel. The pin is hinged between two lugs at the back. Out of twenty-five lozenge-shaped brooches from Nornour this is the only one to have enamelled lugs and only three of the disc brooches show this feature, though many have lugs. Parallels which have enamelled lugs include Alesia,[49] and an unprovenanced brooch from Pannonia (Sellye, 1939, Pl. XII, 10).

Fig. 8, 19.* (NN 69.26). From beach, over House III. Diameter *c*. 30mm.

A bronze disc brooch which has been deliberately trimmed to the shape shown. Originally it had two rings of enamel separated by a raised bronze ring, and with an outer rim of bronze. The inner ring is turquoise or light blue and the outer probably red. There are traces of enamel in the attached central stud. The pin was hinged between two lugs; almost all of the catch-plate is missing. This represents a large class of disc brooches of unambitious design (cp. No. 10). They are usually flat, with one or two rings of enamel, sometimes they have a central stud or peripheral lugs. Nornour has several and they turn up in ones and twos on many sites.

Fig. 8, 20.* (NN 69.2). From recent sand-filling of passage in House II.
Length 47mm.

Heavy bow brooch with deeply cut square teeth down each side. The pin is hinged in a long narrow head tube. There is fine engraving on the head and beading alongside a band of enamelling which runs down the rest of the bow. This is in rectangles of two alternating colours (of which one was green) with no divisions between them. There is a 'V' engraved immediately above the forward pointing toe-knob which also has a socket for enamel. The catch-plate is central and has two grooves at top and bottom, similar to those on the head.

This unusual brooch has several points in common with some of Mr. Hull's 'saw-fish' brooches:[50] the toothed edge, the forward facing toe-knob and the zone of enamelled decoration. However, its upper part is very different, lacking any trace of discs or appendages and recalling the Nornour brooches of his Type 16 (Hull, 1968, p. 38). There is another unusual brooch at Nornour with similar enamelling (*op. cit.* catalogue 261) which also occurs on head-stud brooches from Newstead. There is no site dating, but one of the Wroxeter saw-fish brooches was found in association with objects from the last quarter of the first century.[51]

Fig. 8, 21* (NN 69.23). From beach, over House III. Length 50mm.
(incomplete).

Bronze brooch with two panels of enamel at top of bow. Very little remains but from faint traces it appears that each panel had four rectangles of alternating light and dark colours (cp. No. 20). It is Type 8 of Mr. Hull's catalogue (1968, p. 32) and very similar to his Nos. 12 and 14, except for a slightly different moulding at the toe. The pin is hinged on a bar enclosed in the head tube. There is a very similar brooch in the Charterhouse collection (Bristol Museum) and others from Stockton, Wilts (Salisbury Museum) and from Woodeaton.[52]

Fig. 8, 22.* (NN 69.50). From beach south of House I. Length 41mm.
(incomplete).

Plain brooch with lozenge in the centre of the bow outlined by grooves. This encloses two opposed triangular cells, one of which contains orange enamel, the other turquoise. The pin is hinged on a bar enclosed in the head tube and the catch-plate springs from one side of the foot. A projection at the head is broken off. There are ten similar brooches in the main collection (Hull, 1968, Fig. 13) and most of these have a plain tab at the head; sometimes there is a weak circular stamp, but only one is perforated (this is one of the details suggesting poor workmanship). Mr. Hull (*op. cit.*) quotes parallels; since then one has been found at Gadebridge, Herts.[53] There are also nine examples in the Charterhouse collection at Bristol, another from the Chew Valley, Somerset, and one in Wells Museum from Cheddar.

Fig. 8, 23.* (NN 69.38). From wall of House I. Length 37mm. (without loop).

A head-stud brooch which is included here for comparison with Nos. 27 and 28. It has a hinged pin and fixed head-loop, the stud is solid and there are two grooves down the bow where enamel usually occurs. There are only roughly-formed mouldings at the foot. It might be suggested that this is an unfinished brooch except that the pin is already fitted, and there is another head-stud brooch from Nornour (Hull, 1968, Fig. 24, 235) with only grooves down the bow. This has well-formed mouldings at the foot, settings for some form of decorative insert, and traces of blue enamel in a spot on the head, showing that this one at least is not unfinished.

Enamelled Bow Brooches from the North and Midlands of Britain

Fig. 9, 24. Trumpet brooch from Rudston, Humberside. Dr. I. M. Stead's excavation of the well.[54] SF 68. Length 52mm. (without loop).

Bronze trumpet brooch of Collingwood's class *Rii.*[55] The central moulding is continuous round the back of the bow, the pin is hinged in a tube from which issues a wire loop passed through a rectangular clip which is attached to a tab on the trumpet head. The foot has a hollow for a decorative inset and a hole for the rivet remains.

The enamel decoration on the head is in the form of a three-legged scroll and a simpler version of the same scroll appears on the loop clip. It is light blue with yellow spots, all outlined by reserved bronze, and there is enamel, probably green, in the surrounding field. All enamel is missing from the triangular cells down the upper part of the bow, but below the central moulding similar triangles are filled with light blue, with an indeterminate colour in the outer zone.

The well contained pottery and coins of the late fourth century.

Fig. 9, 25. Trumpet brooch from Hockwold, Norfolk. Mr. Charles Green's excavation of 1957 on the site where a deposit of ritual head-dress had been found (cp. No. 11 above) SF 15. From topsoil. Norwich Museum. Length 60mm. (without loop).

Similar to No. 24, except that the central moulding almost fades out at the back of the bow, the pin is sprung and the clip of the head-loop is not continuous at the back. The head bears a blue crescent on a white field and below the central moulding is a row of reserved bronze lozenges once flanked by enamel. The toe is solid.

Both these brooches come from a fourth-century context, but they conform so completely to the normal type that this can hardly be their actual date. A brooch from Baginton[56] has most of the essential features and it is dated 'hardly later than AD 75' by site evidence. At Newstead similar brooches have been found in deposits earlier than AD 100,[57] and many are found in early second century contexts.

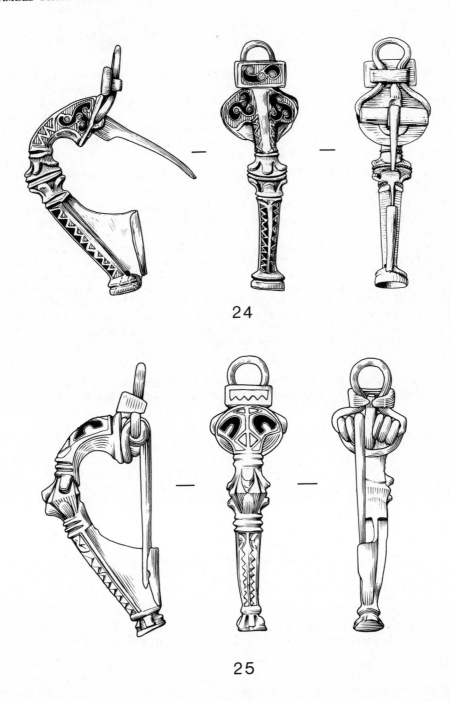

24

25

Fig. 9 Trumpet brooches. No. 24 from Rudston, Humberside. No. 25 from
Hockwold, Norfolk. Scale 1:1.

Fig. 10, 26.* Thistleton, Leicestershire. Mr. E. Greenfield's excavation (see Nos. 8-10. p. 53-54) (THV Bz. 14). Length 50mm. (without loop).

Heavy bronze brooch with enamel in double lattice pattern on the bow. There is Celtic-style relief decoration surrounding the sockets for decorative studs on the cross-bar and at the top of the bow. These and a plain socket on the foot have holes where a rivet has held the missing stud. A spring of sixteen turns is held by a bar passing through the head tube and the chord is also held by a hook which is part of the head of the brooch. The head loop is formed by a separate piece of wire now attached only to the ends of the bar, but probably once clipped as in Nos. 24, 25 and 27. There is a central groove at the back where the catch-plate was slotted in: it is now missing.

The enamel shows as dark and light yellowish green; it is held in deep cells separated by bronze and the enamelled zone is flanked by lines of beading.

This is the finest example so far discovered of a small group of brooches with a mainly Midland distribution. One from a nearby site (Great Casterton)[58] has discs on the bar, head and foot, but they are filled with enamel. It has only slight traces of plastic decoration and two rows of separate triangles enamelled in orange, white and black, instead of the double lattice. The pin is hinged and the head-loop fixed. It also has a toothed edge to the bow (cp. No. 20) as has one from Caistor in Norwich Castle Museum which is smaller, but does have the four discs and a single panel of lattice in green, white and red. Another at Norwich, from Threxton, has fine plastic decoration (raised trumpet scrolls surrounding the settings for separate discs) and a broad lattice panel in red and white. The form of the head and loop in some examples, the forward pointing toe knob and the plastic decoration, all suggest a date in the first century AD for the origin of this type.

Fig. 10, 27. Head-stud brooch from Old Winteringham, Humberside (Dr. I. M. Stead's excavation of 1965,[59] SF 61). Length 50mm (without loop).

Bronze bow brooch with enamel decoration in the interstices of a design carried out in reserved bronze. Down the foot there is a spine of bronze lozenges flanked by panels of enamel. The head-stud, which is solid, contains four spots of enamel and there is also enamel on the head bar and the separate strip which clasps the loop (cp. Nos. 24 and 25). The colour is not visible in any of these and the enamel has bubbled out in places. The pin is hinged on a bar through the head-tube which may be continuous with the loop. The catch-plate is plain and central.

Mr. K. S. Painter has recently discussed head-stud brooches;[60] the present example belongs to his type with hinged pin and loose head-loop. One of these was found at Richborough in a pit of c. AD 75–90,[61] and another in the same report (No. 34) has plastic decoration which also supports a first century date. Others have appeared in later contexts: e.g., Stanwix,[62] from a mid-second century deposit.

Fig. 10, 28. Head-stud brooch from Winterton, Humberside. Dr. I. M. Stead's excavation of 1963.[63] SF 124. Unstratified. Length 42mm.

Bronze brooch with panel of enamel on either side of the bow. There is no certain trace of enamel in the head-stud, which bears a quatrefoil in relief bronze. This is obviously a simplified (devolved or merely cheaper?) version of No. 27. The head loop is cast solid with the bow, there is no enamel on the cross-bar and the lozenges have degenerated to a toothed spine on the bow. The pin is hinged in a tube behind the head and there is a central catch-plate.

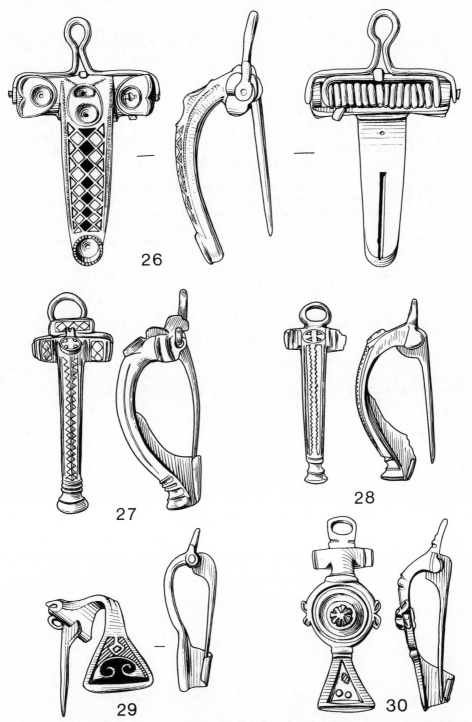

Fig. 10 Bow-brooches. Nos. 26, 29 and 30 from Thistleton, Leics. No. 27 from Old Winteringham, and No. 28 from Winterton, Humberside. Scale 1:1.

Brooches of this sort are common (they and other head-stud brooches are often referred to as the 'Lamberton Moor' type after a well-known find).[64] Many have a panel of lattice decoration instead of the toothed spine and it is uncertain whether this indicates a different maker.A few are found abroad, but they are usually accepted as being of British origin. Some have been found in Antonine contexts, but Mr. P. J. Drury has shown me one (with lattice pattern on the bow but otherwise similar to No. 28) from the temple site at Chelmsford which comes from a surface sealed soon after *c.* AD 80.

Fig. 10, 29.* Fan-tailed brooch from Thistleton. Mr. E. Greenfield's excavations in Black Wong (see Nos. 8–10, p. 53) THZ 326 Bz. 7; in filling of fourth century grave. Length 38mm.

On the triangular-shaped foot is the only decoration: a design in reserved bronze with traces of red and blue enamel in the field. The main motif is a double trumpet scroll and there is also a lozenge outline very like that on some Dragonesque and trumpet brooches (cp. No. 25). A very similar brooch was found at Kirkby Lathorpe[65] and others are known from Richborough[66] and Corbridge.[67] The Richborough example was with pottery of the early second century.

There is a slightly angular head-loop and the pin is hinged in a head tube; the catch-plate is central.

Fig. 10, 30.* Thistleton. From same site as No. 29. No dating. THZ 274. Length 44mm. (without loop).

A bronze brooch with fan-tail and disc on bow. The head, pin and catch-plate arrangements are similar to No. 29 and the foot has a triangular field for enamel, of which some green remains, with two small knobs of bronze. In addition it has a disc in the centre of the bow which once bore a ring of enamel surrounding a central knurled knob. Another was found at Leicester.[68] They are presumably to be dated to the Antonine period by analogy with the trumpet and disc type.[69]

ACKNOWLEDGEMENTS

Thanks are due to the excavators who have allowed me to study their finds: Miss D. Charlesworth, Messrs. C. Green, E. Greenfield, M. G. Hebditch, Mrs. M. U. Jones, and Dr. I. M. Stead; and also to Mr. L. Biek and Mr. J. W. G. Musty of the Ancient Monuments Laboratory for discussion of technical aspects of the subject; to the Museum officials who have allowed access to comparative material; to Mr. D. S. Neal and his colleagues for the line drawings; to Mrs. E. C. Palmer for assistance with research; and to Miss J. Smalley for her meticulous excavation of the crucial area at Nornour. Dr. P. Spitaels of the University of Ghent has generously given me information from her unpublished work on the enamelled fibulae of Belgium, Luxembourg and the Netherlands.

BIBLIOGRAPHY

D. Atkinson, *Excavations at Wroxeter 1923-1927* (Oxford, 1942).

A Béquet, 'La Bijouterie chez les Belges sous l'Empire Romain', *Annales de la Société Archéologique de Namur,* XXIV (1900), p. 1 ff.

G. C. Boon, 'The latest objects from Silchester, *Med. Archaeol.,* III (1959).

British Museum Guide to the Antiquities of Roman Britain (London, 1958).

J. G. Bulliot, *Fouilles de Mont Beuvray 1867-1895,* II (Autun, 1899).

E. Burley, 'A Catalogue and Survey of the metal-work from Traprain Law', *P.S.A.S.,* LXXXIX (1955-6), p. 118 ff.

J. P. Bushe Fox, First, second and third reports on *Excavations at Wroxeter,* 1913, 1914, 1916.

J. P. Bushe Fox, First to fourth Reports on *Excavations at Richborough,* 1926, 1928, 1932, 1949.

S. A. Butcher, 'Excavations at Nornour, Isles of Scilly'; interim reports: *Cornish Archaeol.,* 9 (1970), p. 77 ff; 10 (1971), p. 94; 11 (1972), p. 59.

S. A. Butcher, 'Enamelling', in *Roman Craftsmen,* ed. P. D. C. Brown and D. E. Strong (1976).

R. G. Collingwood, 'Romano-Celtic Art in Northumbria', *Archaeologia,* LXXX (1930), p. 37 ff.

R. G. Collingwood, 'The Roman Objects from Stanwix', *Trans. Cumberland and Westmorland Antiquarian and Archaeological Society,* XXXI (1931), p. 69 ff.

R. G. Collingwood, 'Objects from Brough-under-Stainmore in the Craven Museum, Skipton', *Trans. Cumberland and Westmorland Antiquarian and Archaeological Society*, XXXI (1931), p. 81 ff.

R. G. Collingwood and I. A. Richmond, *The Archaeology of Roman Britain* (London, 1969).

J. D. Cowen and I. A. Richmond, 'The Rudge Cup', *Arch. Aeliana,* 4 Ser., XII, 1935.

B. W. Cunliffe, *Fifth Report on Excavations at Richborough* (1968).

J. Curle, *A Roman Frontier Post and its people. The fort of Newstead . . .* (Glasgow, 1911).

D. Dudley, 'Excavations on Nornour in the Isles of Scilly 1962-1966', *Archaeol. Journ.,* CXXIV (1968).

An Inventory of the Historical Monuments in the City of York, Vol. I., Eburacum (R.C.H.M., 1962).

K. Exner, 'Die provinzialrömischen Emailfibeln der Rheinlande', 29 *Bericht der Römisch-Germanischen Kommission,* 1939, p. 119 ff.

R. W. Feachem, 'Dragonesque Fibulae', *Antiq. Journ.,* XXXI (1951), 33 ff: XLVIII (1968), p. 100 ff.

W. H. Forsyth, 'Provincial Roman Enamels recently acquired by the Metropolitan Museum of Art, *Art Bulletin,* XXXII, p. 298 ff.

S. S. Frere, Mould . . . from Gestingthorpe, *Britannia,* I, pp. 266-7.

T. G. Frisch and N. P. Toll, Enamelled bronzes of Dura-Europos. Final Report IV, pt. IV, fasc. I, 1949.

C. F. C. Hawkes and M. R. Hull, *Camulodunum. First Report on the Excavations at Colchester 1930-39.* (1947).

F. Henry, 'Emailleurs d'Occident', *Préhistoire,* II (1933), fasc. I, p. 65 ff.

F. Henry, 'Hanging Bowls, *J. Roy. Soc. Antiq. Ireland,* LXVI (1936), p. 209 ff.

F. Henry, 'Irish Enamels of the Dark Ages and their relation to the Cloisonné techniques, *Dark Age Britain,* ed. D. B. Harden (London, 1956).

J. Heurgon, 'The Amiens Patera', *J. R. S.,* XLI (1951), p. 22 ff.

H. Hodges, *Artifacts* (London, 1964).

M. R. Hull, 'The Nornour Brooches', *Archaeol. Journ.,* CXXIV (1968), p. 28 ff.

M. J. Hughes, 'A technical study of opaque red glass of the Iron Age in Britain', *P.P.S.,* Vol. 38 (1972), pp. 98–107.

J.R.S. . . . *Journal of Roman Studies.*

E. M. Jope, in 'A Souterrain identified in Angus', F. T. Wainwright, *Antiq. Journ.,* XXXIII (1953), p. 68 ff.

J. R. Kirk, 'Bronzes from Woodeaton', *Oxoniensia,* XIV (1949).

L. Lerat, 'Catalogue des Fibules Gallo-Romaines', *Annales Litteraires de l'Université de Besançon,* III (1956), fasc. I.

L. Lerat, 'Les Fibules Gallo-Romaines de Mandeure', *Annales Litteraires de l'Université de Besançon,* Vol. 16 (1957).

H. Maryon, *Metal-work and Enamelling* (London, 1954).

T. May, *Warrington's Roman Remains* (1904).

S. P. O'Riordain, 'The excavation of a large earthen ring-fort at Garranes, Co. Cork', *Proc. Royal Irish Acad.,* XLVII (1942), p. 77 ff.

O. R. L. 40, *Der Obergermanisch-raetische Limes des Römerreiches.* Abt. B. Band IV Nr. 40 Kastell Osterburken (Berlin, 1929).

P.S.A.S. . . .*Proceedings of the Society of Antiquaries of Scotland.*

K. S. Painter and M. Sax, 'The British Museum collection of Roman head-stud brooches', *British Museum Quarterly,* XXXIV (1970), 153 ff.

K. M. Richardson, 'A Roman brooch from the Outer Hebrides with notes on others of its type', *Antiq. Journ.,* XL (1960), p. 200 ff.

I. G. Sellye, 'Les Bronzes Emaillés de la Pannonie Romaine', *Dissertationes Pannonicae,* Ser. 2, No. 8 (Budapest, 1939).

P. Spitaels, 'La villa gallo-romaine d'Anthée; centre d'émaillerie légendaire', *Helinium,* X (1970), p. 209 ff.

J. M. C. Toynbee, *Art in Roman Britain* (London, 1962).

J. S. Wacher, *Excavations at Brough-on-Humber 1958–1961* (Metal working: p. 227 ff) (London, 1969).

R. E. M. Wheeler, *London in Roman Times* (London Museum, 1930).

R. E. M. and T. V. Wheeler, *Report on the excavation of the Roman site in Lydney Park* (1932).

REFERENCES

1. Recently microscopic study of some of the objects in the Ancient Monuments Laboratory has shown that the present appearance of the enamel can be misleading as colours have been altered by decay and corrosion. The objects examined are marked with an asterisk (*) in the catalogue and it will be found that in some cases the colours described differ from those shown in the drawings. Technical reports on other groups and individual specimens will be found in: Hughes 1972, Painter and Sax 1970, Jope 1953 and *Trans. Lichfield and S. Staffs A.S.*V., p. 45. A group from the Ashmolean Museum has been analysed by Mr. D. Bateson and Dr.R. Hedges, who have published their results in *Archaeometry* 17, 2, 1975, 177–190.

2. Trumpet brooches: see p. 60; Rudge: *J.R.S.*, XLI, p. 22 ff.

3. See Appendix, p. 70. Recently a genuine glass or enamel has been found on a crucible fragment from Chapel Street, Chichester, and it appears that production may have taken place there in the late first century AD. I am grateful to Mr. L. Biek and to the excavator, Mr. A. Down, for this information.

4. Eg. Brough (Cumbria): Collingwood 1931; Stanwix: Collingwood 1931; Gestingthorpe: Frere 1970, pp. 266–7; Lydney: Wheeler 1932, pp. 15 ff; Richborough: Cunliffe 1968, p. 239; Wroxeter: Bushe Fox 1916, p. 65; Woodeaton: Taylor 1917, p. 99; Brough (Humberside): Wacher 1969, p. 228.

5. Boon (1959) suggests that some enamelled disc-brooches with central intaglio are of fourth century manufacture, and a bracelet of fourth century type from Frocester has enamel decoration (*Trans. Bristol and Glos. A.S.* 89 (1970), p. 63, No. 110.

6. Toynbee, *Art in Roman Britain*, 1962, catalogue No. 113; *P.S.A.S.*, LXVI (1931), p. 303 ff.

7. *B.M. Guide to the Antiquities of Roman Britain*, 1958, pl. xxi, 2.

8. *P.S.A.S.*, LXVI (1931), p. 303 ff.

9. *B.M. Guide*, 1958, pl. XXI, 1; *V.C.H. Essex*, III (1963), p.39 ff; Exner in *Marburger Studien* (Darmstadt, 1938), 49 ff. (Miss Charlesworth informs me that the glass vessels accompanying the enamelled bowl in Bartlow Barrow IV can be earlier than the late second century date ascribed to them by Exner.)

10. *Antiq. Journ.*, XLVIII (1968), p. 306, pl. LXXVIII B.

11. Lindenschmit, *Alterthümer unserer heidnischen Vorzeit*, Band III, Heft XI, 1881, Taf III: *Bonner Jahrbuch* 38, 1865, 47 ff. From a spring deposit which seems to have been sealed after *c.* AD 218.

12. *Britannia* I (1970), p. 277; the inscription: *Britannia* IV (1973), p. 334.

13. *J.R.S.*, XLVIII (1958), p. 140.

14. *B.M. Guide*, 1958, Fig. 37, 3.

15. *Antiq. Journ.*, XLIII (1963), pp. 243, 268.

16. *J.R.S.*, LVIII (1968), p. 201.

17. *J.R.S.*, LIII (1963), p. 134.

18. *J.R.S.*, LVII (1967), p. 188.

19. *Archaeol. Journ.*, LXXXVIII (1931), p. 261.

20. *Proc. Soc. Ant. London*, Ser. 2, VI (1875), p. 375.

21. *J.R.S.*, XLVIII (1958), pp. 137–8.

22. *J.R.S.*, XLVII (1957), p. 211 and XLVIII (1958), p. 142; Toynbee, *Art in Roman Britain* (1962), p. 178.

23. *Catalogue of Antiquities in the Museum . . . at Devizes*, Part II, 1934, Pl. XXXIVa, 6.

24. *B.M. Guide*, 1958, Fig. 11, 41.

25. Ashmolean Mus., 1927, 440.

26. *Oxoniensia*, XIV, p. 14, Fig. 3, 6.

27. *Archaeological Excavations 1973*, H.M.S.O., p. 57.

28. *J.R.S.*, XLVIII (1958), p. 139.

29. R.C.H.M., *Eburacum*, Pl. 34.

30. *Arch. Aeliana*, 3 Ser., VII, 1911, p. 186, No. 27.

31. *Bonner Jahrbuch* 38 (1865), Taf. 1, 5; *O.R.L.*, No. 40, Taf. VI, 18.

32. *J.R.S.*, LVIII (1968), p. 201.

33. Wheeler, *London in Roman Times*, Fig. 29, 32.

34. *B.M. Guide*, 1958, Fig. 11, 23.

35. *Catalogue of Antiquities in the Museum . . . at Devizes*, Part II, 1934, Pl. LXXII, 7.

36. Myres and Green, *The Anglo-Saxon cemeteries of Caistor-by-Norwich . . .*, Fig. 63, 2.

37. 's-Hertogenbosch Museum. Information from Mr. D. S. Neal.

38. *Saalburg Jahrbuch*, V (1913), Fig. 9, 10.

39. *Gallia*, I, fasc. 2, p. 38, No. 11.

40. Butcher, 1970–1972.

41. Bushe Fox, 1926, Pl. XII, 8.

42. Sellye, 1939, p. 58, Pl. VIII, 5 and 6, Pl. XVII, 22.

43. Exner, 1939, Type II, 18.

44. *Gallia*, 23, p. 431.

45. Information from Dr. P. Spitaels.

46. Lerat, 1957, Nos. 131 and 132.

47. Hettner, *Drei Tempelbezirke im Treverlande* (1910), Fig. 5, 52.

48. *O.R.L.*, 40, Fig. 6, 6.

49. *Gallia*, II (1945), p. 126–7, Fig. 5.

50. In Cunliffe, 1968, p. 82.

51. Atkinson, *Excavations at Wroxeter 1923–1927* (Oxford, 1942), p. 203.

52. *Antiq. Journ.*, XV (1935), p. 200, D.

53. Neal, *Roman Villa in Gadebridge Park, Hemel Hempstead* (1974), Fig. 54, 18.

54. *J.R.S.*, LVII (1967), 179.

55. Collingwood and Richmond (1969), p. 297.

56. *Trans. Birmingham Arch. Soc.*, Vol. 83, p. 110 ff, Fig. 19, 9.

57. Curle, 1911, Pl. LXXXV, 11 and 12, p. 322.

58. Miss C. M. Mahany's excavations of 1966 (report forthcoming).

59. *J.R.S.*, LVI (1966), p. 202.

60. *British Museum Quarterly* XXXIV (1970), p. 153 ff.

61. Bushe Fox, 1949, Pl. XXVIII, 35, p. 114.

62. Collingwood, 1931, p. 72, Fig. 3.

63. *J.R.S.*, LIV (1964), p. 159; *Antiquity* XLVI (1966), p. 72 ff.

64. *P.S.A.S.*, XXXIX, p. 367.

65. *Lincs. Archit. and Arch. Soc. Reports and Papers*, 10 (1964), p. 67.

66. Bushe Fox, 1926, Pl. XII, 4, p. 43.

67. *Arch. Aeliana*, Ser. 3, VII, p. 45.

68. *Britannia* IV (1973), pp. 45–46.

69. Richardson, 1960. Another is thought to be of this period at Newstead (Curle, 1911, Pl. LXXXVI, 24, p. 324).

APPENDIX

ENAMEL RESIDUES AND SIMILAR MATERIALS
by
L. BIEK

Pottery sherds and other fragments of refractory material are sometimes found coated with a glaze, or glost material, which superficially resembles residues due to enamelling processes. Most commonly such 'false enamel' is fuel slag, but it has also been found on self-fluxing stones, in lead and copper melting waste, and, of course, associated with various aspects of glass making.

All these materials (including enamels) are essentially silicates fluxed and coloured by metal oxides, so that they are very closely related to each other and may be difficult to distinguish in certain cases. Sometimes analysis can be useful, in conjunction with internal evidence, in making a firm interpretation possible.[1] In other cases the decision rests on circumstantial evidence[2] and must remain to some extent ambiguous. In all cases analytical results need to be seen in relation to the colour, texture, gloss, thickness and distribution of the vitreous deposit, and where possible also to the typology, fabric and thermal history of any crucible remains. Fuel slags[3] can result from the fluxing of siliceous materials, such as pottery (but also clay or sand), by wood ash at elevated temperatures. They are thus in effect (colourless) alkaline and alkaline earth glasses, but they will clearly pick up colour even from traces of associated chromogens and are normally greenish or brown (from iron compounds present in the soil); when linked with specific industrial activities they can be coloured deceptively red, yellow[4] or black from contact with copper, lead or iron in quantity. The presence of tin can give an opaque white 'enamel' or confer opacity to other colours.

The whole range of such vitreous materials from archaeological contexts is at present under investigation at the Ancient Monuments Laboratory with a view to illumining their nature and suitable criteria for distinguishing them. Work on material from Lincoln[5] has shown, for example, that 'sealing-wax' red enamel clearly differs from copper-bearing slag in its far higher ratio of lead to copper.

1. R. G. Newton, in Rahtz and Greenfield, *Excavations at Chew Valley Lake* (H.M.S.O., forthcoming).

2. e.g., H. P. Rooksby, in report submitted to A. Down on specimens from Chichester. See Note 3, p. 68.

3. L. Biek, 1970; *Bull. Hist. Metallurgy Gp.*, 81-2.

4. e.g., H. P. Rooksby and L. Biek in P. A. Rahtz, *The Saxon Palace at Cheddar* (forthcoming).

5. From nine–tenth century AD levels, evidently containing jewellers' waste, excavated in Flaxengate by Miss C. Colyer for the Lincoln Archaeological Trust.

The Developing Role of the Natural Sciences in Archaeological Interpretation

by

JOHN MUSTY

GENERAL PITT RIVERS, the first Inspector of Ancient Monuments, was appointed to that post on 1 January 1883.[1] As he has been rightly described as the founder of modern techniques in archaeology[2] it seemed appropriate on this special occasion to examine the development of the application of scientific techniques in archaeology from the time of his Inspectorship to that of Arnold Taylor, whose term of office as Chief Inspector has coincided with an increasing impact of the natural sciences on archaeological work.

In such an enquiry it is also necessary to consider the use of scientific aids in the pre-Pitt Rivers era in order to seek the origins of the development. Pitt Rivers, himself, in an address to a joint meeting of the Wiltshire Archaeological Society and the Royal Archaeological Institute in 1887[3] gives us his views of the developing role of the natural sciences and suggests that 'an entirely new era in prehistoric archaeology was to be inaugurated by methods imported from the other sciences'. He names these as geology, anthropology, and ethnology. In the course of his address he also considers the shortcomings of his archaeological predecessors, in particular Sir Richard Colt Hoare (1758–1838).

Of Hoare he says 'when we consider the time that he devoted to his excavations, and the number of them that must have passed under his eyes, we may well ask what evidence we ourselves are failing to notice, through ignorance of its bearing upon our investigations'. Having listed some of the strengths and weaknesses of Hoare's work he concludes, 'But where he failed totally was in neglecting to take any notice of the skeletons found in the graves. The scientific study of human osteology had not commenced in his time, and his mind was a blank upon all anthropological subjects. He thought it right to re-inter them quickly without measuring them. Here and there we find them spoken of only as the skeleton of a stout person or a tall person, and in only one instance he describes a skeleton, saying that 'it grinned horribly a ghastly smile, a singularity that I have never before noticed'.

In these remarks, Pitt Rivers is both demonstrating his own strong anthropological leanings and confirming that the main scientific influences at the time of his address were geological and anthropological. Thus thirty years earlier, in 1859, there had been the double event of the publication of Darwin's *Origin of the Species* and the visit of John Evans (archaeologist) and Joseph Prestwich (geologist) to Amiens to test the value of the discovery of the association of flint implements with animal remains. Following their acceptance of the findings, Prestwich on 26 May reported the matter to the scientists in a paper delivered to the Royal Society; Evans likewise reported to the Society of Antiquaries of London on 2 June. Prestwich was already a fellow of the Royal Society; Evans was subsequently given that honour in 1864 (it should be noted that Pitt Rivers himself was elected F.R.S. in 1876).

A degree of ecological interpretation was added in 1862 by the work of Ruetimeyer and Heer on the flora and fauna from the Swiss Lake dwellings.[4] General Pitt Rivers was also to make a very positive contribution to this aspect by killing test animals to provide date for the evaluation of animal bones found during his own excavations.[5] In his reports he also describes his methods of measurement and considers the experimental errors involved in dealing with human bones. It is also clear from the *Excavation in Cranborne Chase* volumes that he took account of pathological evidence (such as rheumatoid arthritis) and that he had his charcoals and stone indentified (by Mr. Carruthers, F.R.S., and the Geological Museum respectively). He also compared wheat obtained from his excavations with modern wheat grown in the same areas. If one also takes into account his tabulated recording of data one must conclude that he was, by and large, making a very full use of the natural sciences as far as these were available to make a contribution at that time. He might have gone further, but possibly did not feel the need.

Thus he does not seem to have taken any account of the potential evidence from the soil itself. Ironically, the initiative for obtaining the first soil analysis, at least from a Wessex site, rests with Sir Richard Colt Hoare (although prompted by the curiosity of a friend), who in discussing the black earth found on the floor of long barrows, writes in 1812,[6] 'A friend of mine was so convinced that it arose from the decomposition of numerous human bodies by means of fire, that he sent some of the soil to two of the most able chymists of the day, Mr. Hatchett and Dr. Gibbes, to be properly analysed . . . They both reject the idea . . . Dr. Gibbes is of the opinion that it arises from the decomposition of vegetable matter'. It is of some interest to note that in the year Hoare died Charles Darwin published his first thoughts on the formation of vegetable mould through the agency of earthworms although he was not to develop the subject fully until the year before his own death in 1882.

Neither does Pitt Rivers seem to have felt the need to obtain analyses of the artifacts he discovered, although he must have taken account of the various analyses which had been carried out at intervals during the previous hundred years.[7] This period roughly equates with that covered by E. R. Caley in his *Early History and Literature of Archaeological Chemistry*[8] who concluded that scarcely any scientific relationship could exist between chemistry and archaeology before about 1875 (the date of the excavation at Olympia which Caley considered to be the first to be conducted on correct scientific principles). Nevertheless, Caley was able to locate one hundred publications prior to 1875 involving the results of chemical analysis, the earliest being that of Dr. Pearson in 1796. Clearly, chemistry must be joined with geology and given early priority as a scientific aid to archaeology.

Many of the contributions by chemists at this time were in the form of single investigations possibly to satisfy some particular curiosity. However, these contributions do include some notable 'firsts' as Caley points out. Thus in 1810 we have the first analysis of Roman mortar; in 1815 Sir Humphrey Davy published a paper on ancient pigments and in 1826 his brother, John, published the first study of the process of corrosion in metals. Surprisingly, the credit for the first analysis of an ancient lead glaze rests with Michael Faraday, who examined Roman glazed pottery from Ewell, Surrey.

To what extent this scientific curiosity also reflected a related archaeological interest is hard to judge. Evidently that of Sir Humphrey Davy's might seem to be such as his work on pigments followed a visit to Rome and Pompeii. Later, he was also to report on wall plaster from the Bignor Roman villa. Davy's visit to Rome was in a sense a singular event. Despite the fact that France and England were at war, he travelled in 1813 first to France with his wife and Michael Faraday (then his assistant), having obtained Napoleon's permission for the visit, carrying with him a small box of chemical apparatus (possibly the first field laboratory). During his travels through France hearing of a substance which released a violet-coloured gas he set to work with his box of apparatus and was able to establish the properties of this gas and demonstrate that it was a new element similar to chlorine, which he named iodine. From France he travelled on to Italy where he was to have his interest aroused by the Roman wall paintings. Immediately on his return to England he was invited to investigate the problem of mine explosions. The result was his invention of what was to be known as the Davy lamp, an invention which coincided with the publication of his work on ancient pigments.

So various individual scientists had their curiosity aroused from time to time by antiquities and used their scientific skills to satisfy it. However, one institution, the Royal Agricultural College at Cirencester, was to carry on its staff three scientists whose interest was to be more sustained and who clearly had a strong archaeological bent, doubtless developed by an interest in Roman Cirencester. Thus in 1850 (eight years after the college was founded) appeared *Illustrations of Roman Art in Cirencester. The Site of Ancient Corinium* under the authorship of C. H. Newmarch and James Buckman. Buckman was a geologist and professor at the college. Professor Buckman also drew on the help of John Voelker, the Professor of Chemistry, for glass analysis, the results of which are published in the *Illustrations of Roman*

Art. But there is more. Voelker's successor, A. H. Church, was to publish in 1867 a *Catalogue of finds in the Corinium Museum*. He later became professor of Chemistry in the Royal Academy of Arts and was ultimately knighted. Church also published (in 1865) analyses of bronze artifacts found in Great Britain.

One archaeological/chemical event of the 1850s, as pointed out by Caley, was the publication (in 1853) of Layard's *Discoveries in the Ruins of Nineveh and Babylon* with an appendix describing the results of the chemical examination of objects recovered in the investigation. It was the first occasion on which a specialist chemical report appeared as an appendix in an archaeological publication and perhaps it started the tradition of the specialist scientific appendix in such publications.

Apart from the application of chemical examination there were other potential techniques available in the pre-Pitt Rivers era, some not to be exploited until long after his death. For example, the use of tree rings for dating archaeological sites had been suggested by de Witt Clinton as early as 1811 and again in 1837 by Babbage (the inventor of the calculating engine) in the Ninth Bridgewater Treatise. In 1842, Sir Charles Lyell visited Marietta, Ohio, with Dr. Wildreth and it was demonstrated to him that the Ohio mounds must be at least 800 years old because a tree with that number of rings was growing on one of them.[9] Archaeology had to wait until 1901 before the full potential of dendrochronology was to be recognised. A little later (1877) Nevil Story Maskelyne was publishing in a county archaeological journal[10] a paper on the petrology of the stones of Stonehenge and illustrating it with 'microscope sections', although it was not until 1923 that H. H. Thomas was to provide the classic paper which positively identified the provenance of the blue stones. At about the same time (1878) Baron G. de Geer provided the concept of dating by counting annual layers of sediments (varve analysis).

One piece of scientific work of the early 1880s whose archaeological worth remained unrecognised until comparatively recently was Charles Darwin's study of earthworms published in 1881 under the title *The Formation of Vegetable Mould through the Action of Worms with Observations on their Habits*. Not only is this book of considerable interest to archaeology; it is also the first quantitative ecological study of an animal's role in nature and through it Huxley and Kettlewell[11] claim Darwin may be seen as one of the founding fathers of ecology. As Darwin remarks: 'archaeologists ought to be grateful to worms, as they protect and preserve for an indefinitely long period every object, not liable to decay, which is dropped on the surface of the land, by burying it beneath their castings'. He achieved two notable firsts in this work: by demonstrating that worms would cast up in a period of ten years a layer of soil over an inch thick (or several tons per acre each year) and by measuring the rates at which objects sink into the soil—including an observation at Stonehenge which demonstrated that the undersurfaces of some of the fallen sarsens were now ten inches below the present ground surface. Other sites discussed by him include the Roman villas at Abinger, Chedworth and Brading; the Roman towns of Silchester and Wroxeter and Beaulieu Abbey. Strangely, Darwin did not anticipate a great sale of the earthworm book and he remarks in his autobiography[12] that, 'this is a subject of but small importance, and I know not whether it will interest any readers, but it has interested me. It is the completion of a short paper read before the Geological Society more than forty years ago, and has revived old geological thoughts'. In fact, 8,500 copies were sold between November 1881 and February 1884.

The further recognition of the importance of Darwin's work in relation to archaeology is due to Professor R. J. C. Atkinson who, writing in 1957,[13] 'remarked that Darwin's book is largely unknown to archaeologists and that since his death little new information on the subject has been assembled—and indeed that little attention has been paid by practical excavators to the process of formation of the sites which they dig. One excavator who did give some attention to this subject was Pitt Rivers. In his address to the Archaeological Institute (published in *Excavations in Cranborne Chase*, Vol. IV, 1898) he described his re-excavation of previously excavated sections of the ditches of Wor Barrow and suggested a mechanism for the silting of these.

The General died in 1900 at the start of a new century which has already seen considerable developments in interpretive techniques applied to archaeology. Strangely, many of these are only just gaining ground towards wider acceptance. Possibly the last new technique he himself adopted was that of photography, and Dr. Thompson has observed[14] that Pitt Rivers's field books mention the use of photography in recording monuments on the tours he made in 1889. Significantly also, the final volume (Vol. IV) of *Excavations in Cranborne Chase,* in contrast with the earlier volumes, contains photographic illustrations both of sites and finds—including photographs of skulls and of his craniometer.

Up until the First World War, the work continued to be the contribution of individuals; institutional activities were to be more commonplace after World War I and more especially after World War II. Thus in 1901 we find astronomers turning their attention to Stonehenge with a paper in the scientific journal *Nature* by the editor, J. N. Lockyer, and F. C. Penrose.[15] In the same year another astronomer, Douglas, conceived the scientific method of dendrochronology, although it was not until 1929 that he obtained his first dated tree ring record. Also during these years, culminating in 1918, Professor William Gowland had been engaged in what Coghlan[16] has described as the first phase of a systematic metallurgical analysis of archaeological material (he sets the start of the second and third phases at the end of World Wars I and II respectively), and in 1918 appears Gowland's last paper, *Silver in Roman and Earlier Times.*[17] It is interesting to note an echo from the Royal Agricultural College, Cirencester, with a quotation by Gowland in his paper of a series of determinations of sodium chloride in rain, by Professor E. Kinch of the college. Gowland, himself, was another of the select band during the period of our review to have been admitted to the fellowships of both the Royal Society and the Society of Antiquaries of London.[18] A product of the Royal School of Mines he was admitted to the Antiquaries in 1895, and in 1897 contributed to its *Proceedings* a paper on the chemical analysis of the bronze and copper hoards from Grays Thurrock in Essex and Southall in Middlesex. From then on he continued to pioneer the metallurgical field, although in 1901 he showed versatility in other directions by conducting an excavation at Stonehenge with the object of restoring Stone 56 to an upright position.

Abroad, in the Near East, the excavations at Anau in 1904 have some significance in respect of our theme in demonstrating how, at this comparatively early date, a group of scientific specialists could be drawn together to help in the interpretation by analysis of the human and animal skeletal remains, the cultivated grains and the metal implements.[19] Such an effort was, however, before its time, and many years were to elapse before the ecological approach was to become more generally adopted.

During these pre-World War I years there was also a number of purely scientific events which were to be of considerable importance in latter years in their application to archaeological interpretation. Thus in 1895 X-rays had been discovered by Röntgen, and a year later Becquerel discovered the effect which he called 'radio-activity' following the observation that a photographic plate wrapped in black paper was affected by uranium compounds. Development then rapidly followed development in this field, and the years up to 1914 saw the establishment of the concepts of isotopes, atomic numbers and a general build-up of a precise picture of the structure of the atom. Many of the methods of non-destructive examination of antiquities, and of course C14 dating, which have been the feature of the post-World War II developments in the application of science to archaeology depend critically on these events.

Also, in 1906, the first archaeological aerial photograph had been taken (of Stonehenge, using a balloon) laying the foundation for a method of archaeological prospecting which surely would have been welcomed by the General if it had been available to him. (It should not be overlooked that the first aerial photograph from a balloon had been taken as early as 1858 by the French portrait photographer, Nadar, who also happened to be an enthusiastic balloonist.) As a method of archaeological prospecting, air photography was to remain unchallenged until 1946, when Professor R. J. C. Atkinson introduced resistivity measurements—although to General Pitt Rivers rests the credit for a primitive form of acoustic geophysics with his use of 'bosing' ('It [the Angle Ditch, Handly Down] was on the grass-covered down, and was only discovered by hammering with the flat side of the pick on the grass. The sound of a blow on a grass-grown surface is hollow over an excavated and filled-up excavation, and this sometimes affords the only means of tracing such works on the downs').[20]

One scientific body, The British Association for the Advancement of Science (founded 1831), had taken early note of archaeology through its Anthropological Section (established in 1884), for example, by setting up committees to deal with the 'Age of Stone Circles' (1899), the 'Distribution of Bronze Age Implements' (1913), and the 'Classification and Distribution of Rude Stone Monuments' (1919). Possibly this interest might be seen to be at that time more archaeological than in the employment of scientific aids, although in its persistence to the present day with the establishment of committees to undertake field experiments (concerned with the construction of earthworks and with ancient agriculture) it has now certainly provided such encouragement.[21]

Both Sir John Evans and Sir Arthur Evans had the distinction as archaeologists of being in their time (1897 and 1916 respectively) presidents of the British Association and Fellows of the Royal Society. Sir John Evans was also in 1892-3 president of the Society of Chemical Industry, a reminder that although distinguished for his work in archaeology, his earliest connections had been with paper making, and he carried out explorations of water-bearing strata in his locality in connection with scientific researches into water supply.

Institutions were also beginning to take note of the need to provide facilities for the conservation of antiquities, the earliest possibly in Berlin in 1888. By 1895, the Victoria and Albert Museum had in its employ twenty-one repairers and can lay claim, as pointed out by Thomson,[22] to the credit of having the earliest established conservation facilities in the United Kingdom. Only four other museums had established such facilities up until World War II.

The institutional laboratory approach to the scientific study of antiquities was not, however, to gain momentum until after World War I. Thus a laboratory was set up in 1922 under the direction of Dr. Alexander Scott, F.R.S., as an out-station of the Department of Scientific Industrial Research to deal with problems arising from the incorrect storage of British Museum material during the War. Three reports on the *Cleaning and Restoration of Museum Objects* described the investigations carried out (the last report appeared in 1926) and although intended as a short-term experiment, the laboratory continued to flourish and in 1931 it was transferred to the Trustees of the British Museum to become the British Museum Research Laboratory. With the initial establishment of this Laboratory we see the beginning of an institutional approach to the study of antiquities—both in scientific conservation and examination.

About the same time (1923) a *Conservation Manual* published under the authority of the Government of India used the term 'archaeological chemist'. This is possibly the earliest recognition, by title, of the emergence of persons trained in science and professionally engaged to employ their knowledge in the study of antiquity.

By the early 1930s environmental studies of the type pioneered at the beginning of the century at Anau, but not developed, received new life. Notably,
the Fenland Research Committee provided in 1932 much of the impetus. In
the words of C. W. Phillips, 'so far as the actual founding of the Committee
was concerned, however, the over-riding factor was the realisation that little
could be effected save by co-operative effort in which every resource of
modern science could be brought to bear on each problem in turn and this
resulted in the ultimate association of 42 specialists for the purpose'.[23] At
the same time individual workers such as the Curwens excavating in Sussex,
and Dr. J. F. S. Stone in Wiltshire, were also bringing a scientific precision to
their work not only in its purely archaeological content but also in the utilisa-
tion of scientific evidence. Thus Dr. J. Wilfrid Jackson (animal bones), A. S.
Kennard (mollusca), and J. C. Maby (charcoal) figure very prominently as
specialist contributors to the excavation reports of the 1930s produced by
the Curwens and Stone as well as contributing to the work of the Fenland
Research Committee. It is also to be noted that Kennard and Jackson combined in 1935 to publish[24] a report on the mollusca and animal remains from
Colonel Hawley's excavations at Stonehenge of the early 1920s (1920–26).
The fact is noteworthy, not only in that a report on environmental evidence
was added to the earlier archaeological reports produced at the time of the
excavation—and in a sense 'updating' these in keeping with the new environmental trend—but also that such a report should have been published on its
own merits as a piece of scientific evidence in an archaeological journal. A
valuable aspect of Dr. Jackson's work was the retention by him of the animal
remains he examined and in 1946 he presented the material from English
sites to the British Museum (Natural History), thus providing the basis for a
national reference collection.[25]

The report on the pottery from one Curwen excavation, that of Thundersbarrow Hill dug in 1932, written by Kenneth Oakley[26] was also forward
looking both in the description of the wares and in the use of heavy mineral
analysis to relate the fabric of a hand-made jar to the local clays. Although as
early as 1883 Anatole Bamps had presented a paper in the New World in which
he recognised the value of the microscope for the examination of pottery,
the adoption of petrological techniques in the systematic study of pottery
has been a slow developer and, in Britain, has only recently become standard
practice.

The 1930s, however, saw the inception of a systematic programme of
petrological work on stone implements, with the appointment in 1936 of a
sub-Committee of the South-Western Group of Museums and Art Galleries
to look to the correct petrological identification of stone implements, primarily
in the south-west. The following year saw the foundation of the Institute of
Archaeology, the brainchild of Sir (then Dr.) Mortimer Wheeler, and amongst
the speeches at the opening ceremony that of Sir Charles Peers, who had
succeeded Pitt Rivers as Chief Inspector of Ancient Monuments, contained the

following important sentence, 'if the essential character of the Institute may be expressed in a word, it is this, that it is a laboratory: a laboratory of archaeological science . . .'.[27] In its subsequent development the Institute has lived up to this charge placed upon it with the establishment of Departments which are playing a considerable role in the developing impact of natural science and archaeology. In particular that of Environmental Archaeology (under Professor Zeuner), subsequently to become in recent years under Professor Dimbleby's direction the Department of Human Environment, has done much to make environmental studies an essential feature of any well regulated archaeological excavation. The Institute was also to provide through its Conservation Department both practical training and a professional qualification in the conservation of antiquities.

Within a few years of the foundation of the Institute of Archaeology the war clouds again descended upon Europe. When these receded not only was there to be a more widespread professional approach to archaeology in Britain, born to some extent of the necessity for widespread excavation arising from the rebuilding of post-war Britain, it was also an approach which recognised the value of scientific evidence. Science, itself, because of war-time developments was also in a position to make a greater contribution. The prime example being of course that of C14 dating which represented a by-product of the intense activity in atomic physics associated with the development of the nuclear bomb.

Before World War II ended plans were already being made to organise the necessary archaeological effort to deal with the situation which had arisen as a result of the demolition of large areas of ancient towns and in anticipation of an increased need for archaeological excavation. Sir Alfred Clapham announced in the Anniversary Address to the Society of Antiquaries on 15 April 1943[28] that its Council had decided to invite all the archaeological societies directly concerned in the matter to a conference. In his Anniversary Address the following year[29] he was able to announce the formation of the Council for British Archaeology, the setting up of which involved the undertaking of some of the functions of the Congress of Archaeological Societies—the latter, which had been founded in 1888, was dissolved at the Forty-Eighth Congress on 30 November 1945.[30]

At the first meeting of the Executive Committee of the new body it was agreed to set up a Committee 'to report on questions concerning co-operation between archaeologists and those natural scientists whose work is related to or has a bearing on, various branches of British Archaeology'.[31] This Committee met on six occasions during the period 1944-1946.[32]

In its general recommendation it welcomed a proposal to establish a Committee or Institute for Quaternary Research at Cambridge; recognised the need for more workers in the field of pollen analysis, for an archaeologically-minded botanist in Britain to specialise in the study of cereal grains from their impressions in pottery and for research students to make palaeo-ecological studies of mollusca and mineralogical studies of pottery clays. It also took the practical step of setting up two Committees: one to extend the work being undertaken by the South-Western Group of Museums and Art Galleries so as to organise the petrological study of stone implements throughout the country. The other was to organise a metallurgical survey of early copper and bronze axes and daggers in Britain. Another action was to prepare 'Notes for the Guidance of Archaeologists in regard to Expert Evidence', which was published in 1947. A reconstituted Scientific Research Committee of the C B.A. brought out a new publication, a *Handbook of Scientific Aids and Evidence for Archaeologists* in 1970. This replaced the earlier *Notes* which by then had long been out of print.

The new emphasis on excavation in the immediate post-World War II period which led to the growth of a considerable State involvement in such work under the auspices of the Inspectorate of Ancient Monuments also led (in 1950) to the establishment of the Ancient Monuments Laboratory to deal with the finds and scientific interpretation of evidence from the Inspectorate's excavations. Previously, a small amount of work had been undertaken on finds from monuments in the care of the Ministry of Works (formerly the Office of Works and now the Department of the Environment), but with the sudden increase in excavations there was realised the need for improved facilities to deal with the excavated evidence. From its inception, the Laboratory had been sited in the headquarters building of the Ministry, but in 1972 it moved to new and more spacious premises at Fortress House, Savile Row.

Many of the advances that have been made since World War II can be attributed to the technical progress, especially of an instrumental kind, made during the war-time years and to continuing post-war development. Of special significance has been the establishment of the Oxford Research Laboratory for Archaeology and the History of Art. Very much concerned with the development of instruments, the Oxford Laboratory has pioneered magnetic surveying and palaeomagnetic and thermoluminescent dating as well as undertaking work on the analysis of artifacts using the various non-destructive methods of recent origin, especially X-ray fluorescence spectroscopy. The influence of this Laboratory has been considerable and the rapid spread of its influence has been ensured through the periodical, *Archaeometry,* launched by the Laboratory in 1958. Initially intended as a Laboratory bulletin which would provide a medium for the rapid publication of the investigations carried out within the Laboratory, this periodical soon developed into a national journal reporting scientific developments of application to archaeology. It also, incidentally, provided by its title a label 'archaeometry' for this branch of study.

The rapid post-war growth of archaeometry or archaeological science has also been reflected in the publication of a large number of books covering various aspects of the developing subject, and as these (notably, for example, *Science in Archaeology*) provide a comprehensive survey of the subject, I do not propose to attempt a review of individual developments here.

One development, that of C14 dating, must, however, be mentioned, not only because of its special importance but also because it further illustrates the increasing dependence of archaeology upon the institutional laboratory. Thus, following the realisation of the first clue pointing the way towards the possibility of C14 dating in 1939, and the putting of theory to test during the years 1945–1950 by Professor Willard Libby at the University of Chicago, a number of C14 dating installations were established in this country—the first initiative being taken by the British Museum Research Laboratory in an approach to the Atomic Energy Research Establishment, Harwell, for help and advice in 1949. Subsequently, close collaboration between these bodies and the Royal Institution (each looking at different aspects of the problem) led to the establishment of a dating service at the British Museum by the early 1950s.[33] Equipment was also to be set up at the National Physical Laboratory and the Universities of Cambridge, Birmingham and Belfast. The results of the activities of these various institutions is that up to December 1970 approximately 500 British dates have been accumulated[34] and it is likely that new dates will be added at a rate approaching several hundreds a year. The consequences have been quite major in that not only has a new element of scientific precision been added to archaeological interpretation, but also the method has brought with it an inflexible sampling discipline which has inevitably led to a strengthening of the relationship between the field archaeologist and his professional scientific colleagues in the laboratory. There is in fact already a growing recognition of the need to include a specialist in an excavation team to deal with environmental problems on the spot, especially on waterlogged sites and often in an urban context. Thus the increasing tendency to instal 'flotation machines' at excavation sites enables a variety of biological debris (seeds, insect remains, etc.) to be separated from the bulk deposits in the course of excavation for subsequent identification and evaluation in a laboratory.

Possibly the most intensive scientific activity carried out in the field at the present time is that of geophysical surveying and the Ancient Monuments Laboratory has teams operating all the year round mapping buried deposits in advance of excavation. Indeed the geophysical survey associated with intensive fieldwork provides a method of archaeological interpretation of field monuments which can enable the deployment of excavation resources to be made on a more cost-effective basis or, alternatively, may prevent the need (in a rescue-type situation) for excavation by providing information upon which planning decisions can be based to enable development areas to be re-sited. Interpretation of the results of geophysical surveys are now heavily dependent on automated methods of date collection and subsequent recourse to the computer for help in 'filtering' data and the more widespread use of the computer in archaeological work as a whole is a current trait.

It is evident that the study of archaeology, in both its language and method, continues to merge with that of the natural sciences. At the least it could be said that the growth of archaeological science has been matched with a corresponding development of scientific archaeology. Indeed, in recent years there has been much debate as to whether archaeology itself must now be seen as a science. Professor C. F. C. Hawkes considered the question in his presidential address to the British Association, Section H, in 1957, and in his opening remarks said: 'Archaeologists often insist that their subject is a science'. Later he went on to express the opinion that, 'Its distinctively scientific character seems to be that it excavates its sites according to the principles of stratigraphy and association which it has borrowed from geology, that it makes exact measurements wherever necessary, and the exactest possible comparisons where it has to classify its material, and then it hands over everything to a natural scientist of which identifications or analysis by him will have anything to reveal that may aid archaeological interpretation'.[35]

It is often objected that archaeology, itself, cannot be judged a science as archaeological results are not determined by repeatable experiment. However, another post-war development has been the establishment of experimental methods to check the validity of hypotheses which have been advanced in explanation of certain observed facts. Some of these have been conducted within the laboratory to check manufacturing techniques, etc.; others have been in the form of field experiments, mainly under the auspices of research committees of the British Association for the Advancement of Science. Thus in 1958 a committee was set up to make an experimental investigation of the denudation and burial of archaeological structures and the first 'artificial earthwork' was constructed on Overton Down, Wiltshire, in 1960. Between 1964 and 1966 the Ancient Fields Research Committee (later to become the Ancient Agriculture Committee) carried out ploughing experiments with a replica of a Donnerupland ard, pulled by humans and small cattle at Broadchalke, Wiltshire. The underground storage of grain in pits was also studied at the same time in a parallel series of experiments. Another aspect of early technology which has been examined is that of pottery manufacture and five experiments with replica Roman or medieval kilns have been carried out between 1958 and 1967 by excavators anxious to obtain a fuller understanding of the kiln structures they have uncovered. All these experiments have been co-operative ventures between archaeologists and scientists.

Whatever the status of archaeology—whether it be an art or a science or a convenient bridge between the two—it is evident that, since World War II, the resources of the natural sciences have been successfully marshalled into an inter-disciplinary approach to the problems of archaeological interpretation. This approach is aimed at a total study of man in his environment and the only limitations to the attainment of this aim are, apart from the differential survival of evidence, those imposed by national priorities in the allocation of manpower and resources. Equally, it is often only by recourse to the natural sciences that the limitations imposed by the differential survival of evidence (in the archaeological sense) can be overcome as a layer sterile in conventional archaeological evidence may still yield chemical, biological or other relevant data.

What of the future? With the growth of scientific archaeology it is to be anticipated that the questions posed by archaeologists for answer by scientific enquiry will be increasingly refined. Thus, although on the one hand both archaeologists and scientists alike must continue to ask the question posed by Pitt Rivers as to what 'evidence we ourselves are failing to notice through ignorance of its bearing upon our investigations', there is, on the other, an increasing need to establish the relative degrees of importance of the different sorts of potential evidence. Archaeological science is thus entering a new phase, that of consolidation and definition of purpose having already moved from the pioneer days of individual effort to that of an institutionalised activity. With the new phase comes the opportunity to establish the types of academic enquiry needed and to match these with the scale of resources required.

REFERENCES

1. M. W. Thompson, *J.B.A.A.*, XXIII (1960), p. 103.
2. Dr. Glyn Daniel, *A Hundred Years of Archaeology* (1950), p. 173.
3. *Wilts. Arch. Mag.*, XXIV (1889), pp. 7-23.
4. K. W. Butzer, *Environment and Archaeology* (1964), p. 5.
5. A. Pitt Rivers, *Excavations in Cranborne Chase*, II, pp. 217-228.
6. R. Colt Hoare, *Ancient Wiltshire, South*, p. 92, footnote.
7. He does for example observe (*Excavations in Cranborne Chase*, Vol. III, Appendix B) in discussing samian ware, 'It would be easy to split hairs over the term glazed, as any other that is applied to this pottery, for a scientific examination of its surface has shown it is rather a polish than a glaze'.
8. Earle R. Caley, *J. Chem. Educ.*, XXVIII (1951), pp. 64-66.
9. Sir Charles Lyell, *The Antiquity of Man* (1883), p. 41.
10. *Wilts. Arch. Mag.*, XVII (1877), pp. 147-60.
11. Sir Julian Huxley and H. B. D. Kettlewell, *Charles Darwin and his World* (1965).
12. Ed. by Nora Barlow. *The Autobiography of Charles Darwin 1809-1882* (1958), p. 136.
13. *Antiquity*, XXXI (1957), pp. 219-233.
14. M. W. Thompson, *ibid.*, p. 118.
15. *Nature*, LXV (1901), pp. 55-7.
16. In R. F. Heizer and S. F. Cook, *The Application of Quantitative Methods in Archaeology* (1960), p. 1.
17. *Archaeologia*, LXIX (1917-18), p. 120.
18. See Obituary Notice, *Antiq. J.*, II (1922), pp. 390-91.
19. Dr. Glyn Daniel, *ibid.*, pp. 290-91 (1950).
20. A. Pitt Rivers, *ibid.*, IV, p. 14.
21. One should not overlook, however, that these committees led to unexpected side effects. Thus when the bronze implements in the Manx Museum were listed for the B.A. Committee on the Distribution of Bronze Age Implements the opportunity was taken to secure elemental analyses of each and these were published in 1923. (*Antiq. J.*, III [1923], pp. 228-230). It is also of interest to note that the British Association's Council found it necessary in 1902-3 to direct the attention of the Office of Works and the Local Government Board to the desirability of appointing an Inspector of Ancient Monuments as the post had been in abeyance since General Pitt Rivers' death. A new appointment was made in 1910.
22. Garry Thompson, *Museum* XXIII (1970/71), pp. 134-39.
23. C. W. Phillips in *Aspects of Archaeology in Britain and Beyond* (1951), pp. 258-277.
24. *Antiq. J.*, XV (1935), pp. 432-440.
25. This gift is recorded in a note in *Antiq. J.*, XXVI (1946), pp. 77-78, with a list of the sites concerned.
26. *Antiq. J.*, XIII (1933), pp. 134-151.
27. Sir Mortimer Wheeler, *Still Digging* (1956), p. 88.
28. *Antiq. J.*, XXIII (1943), p. 95.
29. *Ibid.*, XXIV (1944), p. 90.
30. B. H. St. J. O'Neil, *Antiq. J.*, SSVI (1946), pp. 61-66.
31. The members of this Committee were Dr. W. J. Arkell, Mr. D. F. W. Baden Powell, Prof. A. J. E. Cave, Dr. J. G. D. Clark, Dr. F. C. Fraser, Dr. H. Godwin, Mr. W. F. Grimes, Mr. C. F. C. Hawkes, Mr. A. D. Lacaille, Dr. G. M. Morant, Dr. F. J. North, Dr. K. P. Oakley, Dr. F. S. Wallis, and Prof. F. E. Zeuner.
32. See typescript reports in the records of C.B.A.
33. H. Barker, *Nature*, 172 (1953), p. 631.
34. Archaeological Site Index to Radiocarbon Dates for Great Britain and Ireland. Council for British Archaeology, 1971.
35. *Archaeological News Letter*, VI (1957), pp. 93-100.

The Cathedral and Relics
of St. Magnus, Kirkwall

by

STEWART CRUDEN

THE *Orkneyinga Saga* relates how after an unsuccessful attempt to recover his Orkney heritage from earl Paul of Birsay, the earl Ronald Kolson, in Norway, makes a long and eloquent speech in which he proclaims his intention to do or die in a second attempt. His speech is applauded heartily and he is promised more faithful help for another expedition. Then up stood Kol (his father) and said, 'We have heard from the Orkneys that all men there wish to rise against thee, and defend thy realm against thee along with Earl Paul; they will be slow to give over their enmity when once they have taken up arms against thee, kinsman. Now my advice is to seek for help where it is abundant, for I think that he may grant thee thy realm who had it by right—I mean St. Magnus the Earl, thy uncle. I desire that, to provide for his granting thee the ancestral lands that are thine and were his, thou make a vow to have a church of stone built in Kirkwall in the Orkneys, when thou gainest thy realm, so that there be not a more magnificent in the land; and let it be dedicated to St. Magnus the Earl thy kinsman. And let it be endowed so that the foundation may increase and that to it may be brought his relics and with them the Episcopal seat'.[1]

This passage has been quoted or paraphrased in histories of the cathedral which say it was founded in memory or in honour of St. Magnus. That is true enough, but does not get to the heart of the matter. The foundation was much more than a pious gesture of remembrance. It was the fulfilment of a contract. Seek help where it is abundant, said Kol, for I think that *he* may grant thee thy realm who had it by right. I mean St. Magnus the Earl, thy uncle.

That was said in 1136, and earl Magnus had been dead for more than twenty years, yet he is spoken of as though alive and effective still. This last-minute advice of the shrewd and practical Kol is a striking illustration of that medieval belief in the power of relics and the continuing presence of the saints which is so difficult for us to understand today. The dead saints were among those present still, to give counsel, lend their aid, receive presents, even to sign documents, and in their relics resided their awful power. Every church was eager to possess them, and every king. They authenticated possession, vindicated action and ensured success, however secular, and about them miracles were to be expected which spoke more powerfully than any argument, as we shall see. They influenced the very design of churches, and the influential part they played in the founding and building of St. Magnus Cathedral in Kirkwall is of great significance in the interpretation of its architecture.

Earl Magnus was slain by earl Hakon in 1116 (or 1117) on the island of Egilsay. Soon afterwards his remains were interred on the off-shore island of Birsay, in Christ Church, which was the first cathedral in Orkney. It stood within the precincts of the island palace of Hakon's son Paul who 'laid heavy burdens on the friends of Earl Magnus'. The resident Bishop William was prudently in the anti-Magnus party.

But the sanctity of Magnus was soon manifest. Stories began to circulate, of heavenly lights and fragrance about his tomb, and miracles of healing. They were strenuously denied by Bishop William, who even declared it heretical to believe such tales. 'He took the edge off what men said', says the saga tersely, and we may add, how could he do otherwise?

The miracles which are related in the *Orkneyinga Saga,* either in the main narrative or an interpolated catalogue from the *Book of Miracles,* are of two sorts, or rather, seem to have had two purposes: to establish the sanctity of Magnus, and to urge the translation of his relics to Kirkwall. And, we may surmise, because the saga was compiled a hundred years afterwards, retrospectively to justify the subsequent actions of Bishop William.

First, they urge recognition of Magnus's sanctity; 'men besought Bishop William for Magnus's tomb to be opened and the relics taken up. And the Bishop was much troubled at this proposal'. He himself experienced two persuasive manifestations however. In one, returning from Norway where he had been on 'needful business', and troubled by storm, he is asked by the ship's steersman if for a fair wind he would vow no longer to oppose the taking up of the relics of earl Magnus. This was an unseamanlike thing for a steersman to say in a storm, but nonetheless the bishop agreed, provided the improvement in the weather was sufficient for him to sing Mass on Birsay the following Sunday. It was; he sang his Mass, but he failed to keep his word. In a later experience the bishop is stricken blind in his church. He gropes his way to the grave of Magnus and vows to have the relics lifted whatever earl Paul might say. His sight being restored he now fulfils his vow, and with the help of learned clerics elevates the relics in a shrine over the altar and recognises Magnus as a saint.

This object having been achieved, papal approval not yet being required, the other series of miracles immediately follows, with the vision of a farmer who dreamed that St. Magnus came to him and told him to tell the bishop that he wished to go to Kirkwall. This was an embarrassing request, which if granted would displease the resident earl greatly, as indeed it did. But the farmer said nothing when he awoke 'for he feared that Earl Paul would take offence at him'. On the following night earl Magnus again appeared to him in a dream, and it was he who had taken offence, and he was very wroth, and said to the farmer 'if thou goest not, thou shalt pay for it in this world, and more so in the next'.

Immediately after that crisp observation, which shows that Vikings were Vikings in the next world as well as in this, the saga relates that the farmer hastened to Birsay and related his dream to all the worshippers there, among whom was earl Paul; 'and men now besought the Bishop to take the holy relics east to Kirkwall as the Earl Magnus had signified. And Earl Paul kept silence as if he had water in his mouth, and turned red as blood'. And there we seem to hear the authentic voice of an eye-witness.

'And after that Bishop William went east to Kirkwall with a worthy retinue and carried thither the holy relics of Earl Magnus and they set the shrine over the high altar in the church that was there. At that time the market town in Kirkwall had few houses', adds the saga inconsequentially.

The worthy retinue which fared east with the shrine of the saint from Birsay to Kirkwall, a distance of some seventeen miles overland, must have been a great and splendid procession and we would imagine it was making for the new cathedral. But this could not have been so. When Bishop William admitted the sanctity of earl Magnus it 'was on St. Lucia's Day', and Magnus had then 'lain in the earth 21 years'. That is to say, this was in 1137, the very year in which the cathedral was founded by Ronald after he had regained his earldom. Consider too the statement, that when they arrived in Kirkwall with the shrine 'they set it over the high altar of the church which was there'. That is no way to refer to a cathedral, and one dedicated to the saint moreover. Clearly they made for an existing church.

In their laconic and detached style the saga-writers give nothing away. What was this remarkable conversion of Bishop William the Old, forced by divine chastisements to be as zealous an adherent of Magnus as he had been of Paul? He held office for over sixty-six years, and at this time had yet another thirty to go. Why the haste, after twenty years of scepticism? Why did he remove the relics and his episcopal seat from renowned Birsay to Kirkwall which had but a few houses and an unnamed church, when he must have known that a great new cathedral in honour of the saint was promised, which in a year or two would be sufficiently far advanced to receive them worthily? Not just because the saint wanted it in a farmer's dream.

Reading between the lines we may surmise political reason for his abandoning Birsay. It is not unlikely that he had broken with earl Paul and transferred his allegiance to the more promising future of earl Ronald who was then about to embark upon his second attempt to overcome Paul and regain his heritage from him. It was not before his first attempt that Ronald vowed to build a magnificent stone church but, at the last minute apparently, before his second, and in between the two attempts Bishop William had been to Norway 'on needful business', as the saga says. Was this the needful business, to discuss a new cathedral as reward for support? It was an undertaking which could not possibly have commenced without considerable discussion before foundations were marked out and builders procured.

'The work on it went on faster for the first three years than during the four or five years following', continues the narrative, and we are reminded of the building of Canterbury in the early twelfth century. 'You do not know which to admire the most', wrote William of Malmesbury about it, 'the beauty or the speed'. Praise of a good start was probably literary convention, but it proclaims a virtue in speed and indicates a real possibility that initial impetus could raise the choir of a church a great deal faster than average building progress of other parts. At Kirkwall they did indeed run quickly out of funds. Ambition outran resources, and the interruption was so severe that it was rectified only by legislation permitting the outright sale of odal land rights to the people, with a building tax deducted from the proceeds, 'and thenceforward there was no lack of money for the building of the church and it became a magnificent structure'.

Like so many another notable ancient monument in this remarkable country it is more than a good example of its kind, it is absolutely outstanding. (Pl. II.) The choir, which is the earliest part, is the finest romanesque work north of Durham which inspired it. (Pl. III.) It owes nothing to size for its effect, but derives it from sound proportion and bold scale. Contrasting red and white ashlars in alternate courses, voussoirs and archrings must have invested the building with an almost eastern splendour. This is not so fanciful as it sounds. In sunshine Orkney sea and sky have an extraordinary brilliance.

The later twelfth-century nave and the thirteenth-century extension of the choir are also notable, but it is the original choir which distinguishes the church. It stands as a lasting memorial to the Norse dominions west-over-seas, to remind us that they were not the cultural backwaters they are too often assumed to be, but in the full stream of European cultural and artistic development. Founded by a Norseman, named after a Norseman, for the veneration of Norsemen, it seems nonetheless to have been built by masters and masons of the great Durham school coming perhaps by way of Dunfermline.

No dedication date is known, but in 1151 the founder and his bishop departed from Orkney on a two-year crusade to the Holy Land and back, an adventure which had been discussed with the king of Norway in 1148. It is unlikely that they would leave before the choir was completed and the relics of St. Magnus enshrined within it. With the work advancing as rapidly as the saga says it did, 'and the work on it went forward faster for the first three years than during the four or five years following', an eastern limb of three bays with Durham-style apses could have been completed by 1142 or thereby. (Figs. 1, 5.)

Fig. 1 End of Phase 1, *c.*1137-42.

It is interesting to recall the observations of the monk Gervase of Canterbury in his well-known and illuminating account of the rebuilding of that church after the great fire in 1174.[2] He relates how the first year was preparation, 'and in the following year . . . before the winter, he (William of Sens) erected four columns, that is, two on each side, and after the winter two more were placed, so that on each side were three in order, upon which and upon the exterior wall of the aisles he framed seemly arches and a vault . . . with these works the second year was occupied'. For St. Magnus that would give us vaulted aisles and the main choir arcade of three bays up to the level of the triforium, in two years, and in the third year the triforium and clearstory. Allow another year for the east end, the return of the aisle walls into the transepts, and a certain urgency in translating the relics from their temporary shrine in the other church, and we have a possible first dedication date of *c.* 1142. The transepts up to triforium level, three bays of the north wall of the nave up to the wall-head, plus half a window and a complete wall arcade of the fourth bay, with similar although not identical progress on the south side, and with columns to correspond, is the visible surviving extent of the first-period style. (Fig. 2.) It is characterised by exceedingly heavy window-heads with label-mouldings (Pl. IVd) and eight-sided cubical capitals for the principal piers.

Nothing of the original crossing remains, unless re-used in the new crossing which was boldly inserted about 1170, presumably after a collapse of the original crossing-tower. Although notably pointed, with deep mouldings and water-leaf capitals, the new work did not disdain the old, and the old arches adjacent to the new crossing were carefully re-fashioned. This evidence of medieval building methods, about which St. Magnus is uncommonly revealing, is there for the observant to see in all the arches adjacent to the crossing, for example in the first bay of the nave where incised chevron ornament partly represents the original arch which has been half-demolished and then rebuilt without it.

The polychrome treatment of the architectural elements of the earliest work, by a counterchange of red and white building stone (not just painted decoration) is worth a special mention, for it has never received due recognition, probably because some of it is not too easy to see, the choir having been, as Tudor remarked, at one time rendered hideous by pews, galleries, whitewashed, pinkwashed and yellow-ochred pillars.[3] It is a very remarkable scheme, especially so in a country where freestone is scarce, and it is thorough. The banded masonry of the east transept walls turns into the choir aisles and the very jambs of their windows. (Pl. IVa.) It is over a wide diapered string-course such as Dunfermline has, and this returns into the choir aisle also, as does the plain flagstone walling below it, which would be plastered. The arch-rings of the main and triforium arcades, and of the windows, exhibit all variations of red and white counterchange. (Pl. III.)

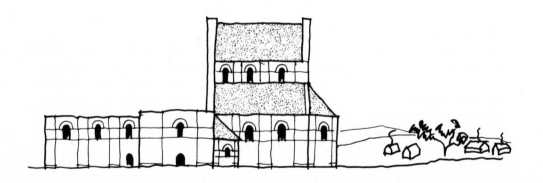

Fig. 2 End of the first-period style, *c.*1145.

The end of the romanesque building programme was a completed east limb with the transepts and three east bays of the nave up as high as the window-heads. (Figs. 2, 3.) The first piers next the crossing were completed and arched to buttress the crossing. The second were completed but not arched, the third were half-built and the fourth pair was started, all their bases having been laid, and the bench for the wall arcade, before building in height began. It is this sort of picture, therefore (Fig. 4), which we should have in our mind's eye when we think of St. Magnus Cathedral at the time of earl Ronald about 1150.

A fifteenth-century picture of the building of Vézelay shows work proceeding at just such different rates of progress, with high but uncompleted aisle walls and windows temporarily abandoned, all protected by straw upon the wall-heads, while work proceeds at the west front.[4] Another of about the same date shows a choir, furnished and obviously in use, with a temporary closing-screen fancifully depicted and work proceeding in the transepts and nave at a different rate, but lagging far behind the choir which was the important thing to complete, consecrate and forthwith put to use.[5]

It is singularly unfortunate that the east end was demolished in the early thirteenth century to make way for the additional choir, good though it is, for the surviving evidence suggests the influence of the cult of relics upon its plan and design. The eastmost bay of the romanesque choir, whose arches on north and south spring from massive rectangular piers, is uncommonly narrow, the arches noticeably small and underscaled. (Pl. IVc.) The sudden change in size suggests a passage across the choir between the apse and the reredos of the high altar. No better explanation suggests itself for this unusual deviation from the regular rhythm of the main arcade. The suggestion of a passage across the choir passing behind the altar and in front of the apse recalls the saga and the cult of relics. (Fig. 5.)

When Bishop William was struck by blindness while at his prayers in Christ Kirk a great fear fell upon him and he tearfully promised to take up (exhume) the holy relics of earl Magnus whether earl Paul liked it or not, and he summoned all the men of highest rank in the Orkneys and made it known to them that he was going to search the grave. It was opened, the coffin was raised and the bones were washed, the body evidently being disarticulated after twenty or twenty-one years in the ground. The bones were laid in a shrine and set over the altar, and the holy relics were kept there for some time. Then the farmer had his dream and the bishop his second change of heart and mind and expeditiously the relics were taken to Kirkwall and set over the altar of the church that was there, as we have seen. Now, *sette skrin ufir altari* is the phrase, and in the original Icelandic *skrin* is a loan-word from the Latin *scrinium* which at this date would have the meaning of portable shrine or reliquary. It is so used by Honorius of Autun in a near-contemporary record, *arca testamenti a sacerdotibus portabatur et scrinium vel feretrum cum reliquiis a protitoribus portatur.* Later in the Middle Ages the meaning was extended

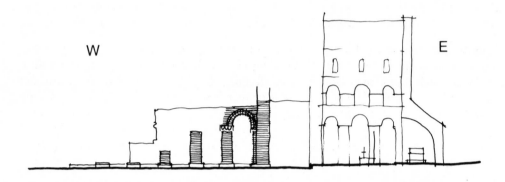

Fig. 3 Progress westwards after *c*.1142: north arcade of the nave.

to include the permanent architectural shrine which was a separate erection behind or to the east of the high altar.[6]

Many men and women from as far as Unst, the most northern of the Shetland Islands, now came to the shrine, and among them were two who despoiled it by stealing gold from it. The saga narrative is circumstantial, and we may conclude from it and the foregoing indications that the shrine was an enriched casket containing if not the whole body, then at least representative bones. This accords with the early twelfth-century practice of placing reliquaries in prominent places, frequently upon a beam over an altar, as Gervase of Canterbury describes in a vivid passage in his account of the great fire and rebuilding there, to which reference has already been made. 'And now the people ran to the ornaments of the church, and began to tear down the pallia and curtains, some that they might save, but some to steal them, the reliquary chests were thrown down from the high beam and broken, and their contents scattered; but the monks collected them and carefully preserved them from the fire'.

When the new cathedral was begun in Kirkwall, in the name of a saint to whom the founder felt a personal obligation, the shrine would inevitably be the most important thing about it and it would have been in accordance with the custom of the time to erect a permanent shrine of fitting splendour in the great eastern apse which St. Magnus Cathedral may be presumed to have had. There is good reason to believe that this is what was done.

Such an arrangement ingeniously adapted and prolonged the life of the traditional apse which had been the usual eastern termination since Early Christian times when it contained the benches of the clergy round its wall with the bishop's throne in the middle. With the development of the cult of relics and the consequent need to provide circulation for pilgrims within the church the apse ceased to be the synthronon and became the repository of the shrine. The east end of Durham, which was probably the model for Kirkwall, was sanctified by the shrine of St. Cuthbert in just this position, which was one of great convenience. At Kirkwall an ambulatory behind the altar screen would provide easy access to the apse by way of the side aisles of the choir and would ensure no distractions at the altar and choir stalls. This is good planning (Fig. 5) in reconciling very different requirements, and the cross passage in St. Magnus inferred from the smallness of the eastmost choir arches of the north and south sides can reasonably be explained as admitting to such an ambulatory. From the cult of relics there thus developed a division of the eastern limb of the greater churches. The arrangement is still preserved in Westminster Abbey, but few examples survive because the original romanesque apses have everywhere been demolished to make way for the inevitable later extension of the choir, which happened at Kirkwall too.

*   *   *   *   *

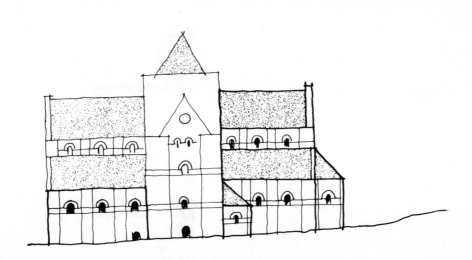

Fig. 4 The first completed church, *c.*1150.

The bones of St. Magnus, St. Ronald and Bishop William invest the church with a special distinction, even in this age. The remains of Bishop William who died *c*. 1168 were discovered in a tomb in the centre bay of the north arcade of the new choir, during Government repairs in 1848. They were accompanied by a leaden plate five inches long, crudely inscribed, with abbreviations, on one side H. REQUIESCIT:WILLIAMVS:SENEX FELICIS MEMORIE, and on the other P(RI)MVS EPIS(COPVS).[7] It is interesting to speculate that this might be a temporary identity label made during a general transference of distinguished remains from the old choir to the new in the thirteenth century.

In each of the massive rectangular piers at the east end of the early choir, which separated the aisle apses from the main apse, there is a cavity about nine feet above floor level. (Pl. IVb.) In each cavity was an oak coffin containing a skull and bones, disarticulated, of an incomplete male skeleton. The south pier contained the relics of St. Magnus, the north those of St. Ronald, who was slain in Caithness in 1158, buried in the cathedral, and canonised in 1192.

The cavity on the north side was discovered during the Government repair of 1848 and the bones were claimed to be those of St. Magnus, not without reason. But the third Marquess of Bute had his doubts and thought the skull a substitute. He referred to ancient acts of excessive piety, to the theft of the body of St. Mark from Alexandria, and of the skull of St. Andrew from St. Peter's. We ourselves can refer to the theft of the skull of the fourth-century Pope St. Silvester from a church in Rome in March 1969.[8]

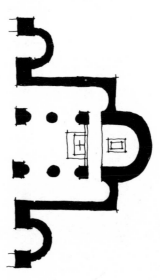

Fig. 5 Conjectural east end, 1137-*c*.1142, showing altar, cross-passage, and shrine in apse.

Baring-Gould records that relics of St. Magnus were taken at the Reformation to Aix-la-Chapelle and to the church of St. Vitus in Prague. Lord Bute communicated with Cardinal Manning, who replied with a letter from the Archbishop of Prague, which said that in 1673 the Dean of the Metropolitan church of Prague recorded that among the unadorned relics of his church were divers parts of St. Magnus the Martyr bequeathed by the Emperor Charles IV, a part of the shoulder blade brought from Aix-la-Chapelle in 1372, and a part of a leg; but, the Archbishop continues, although all the relics of the saints still remaining in St. Vitus have been most carefully examined no trace or part of those of St. Magnus was found. Yet the Marquess percipiently preferred St. Ronald for this north pier interment, and he did not know of the other pier burial which proved that he was right, for this was not discovered until 1919.

In 1925 the two collections of bones were examined by R. W. Reid, Professor of Anatomy in Aberdeen and one-time President of the Anatomical Society. He concluded that the remains conformed with the descriptions and histories of St. Magnus and St. Ronald in the *Orkneyinga Saga* and other relevant documents, and that those in the north pier were in all probability of St. Ronald; those in the south St. Magnus. Although three thirteenth-century wall burials in Christ Church Cathedral in Bergen can be quoted as parallels, namely those of King Sverre Sigurdsson in 1202 and the Maid of Norway in 1290 alongside her mother Queen Margaret, it is clear from contemporary accounts of the Kirkwall discoveries that the mural internments are not original, but crude insertions, probably made during the disturbances of the Reformation.[9]

The *Sturlunga Saga* says that in 1298 relics of St. Magnus were taken to Iceland and reverently placed in Skalholt Cathedral, and from the Faroes comes even more interesting evidence of widespread and continuing veneration. The uncompleted Magnus cathedral at Kirkjubøur, begun, but never completed, by Bishop Erlendur, who died in 1308, has eight exceptionally fine consecration crosses and on the outside of the east gable a carved panel of steatite or soap-stone, a Rood, depicting the Crucifixion in highly accomplished late Gothic style. A marginal inscription round the panel, in Latin, has been variously translated and one reading goes thus: 'This is the repository for the great Lord the holy Magnus' sainted relics Our Saviour's sacrifice . . . Virgin Mary . . . the sainted Magdalene . . .'. The slab was removed in 1906 and 1956. Behind it was a lead box. The box contained a linen packet wrapped in skin and cloth. In it were seven small linen parcels each stuck with a skin slip bearing inscriptions unfortunately illegible. In one was a splinter of wood and one or two bones, reckoned to be relics of St. Magnus and the Icelandic Saint Bishop Thorlacius (1178-1193) to both of whom the church is dedicated, the Faroes having no saint.[10]

Professor Reid's paper attracted the attention of a Mr. Brent in Torshavn who wrote to the minister of St. Magnus Cathedral in 1926, asking if the Kirkwall bones lacked a phalange, such as the Kirkjubøur packet contained.

As it so happens, they do. Had there been no phalange missing from the Kirkwall connection then either the Kirkjubøur relics were not genuine, or the remains in the south pier were not those of St. Magnus. The Kirkjubøur facts at least help to establish the authenticity of both.

The last historical reference to the relics in Kirkwall is for the winter of 1263. After its defeat at the battle of Largs, the remnants of the Norse fleet returned to Kirkwall and in the Bishop's Palace the great King Haakon died. Shortly before he died, thinking that a cure might be effected by the virtue of the relics of St. Magnus, he walked to the cathedral and round the shrine of St. Magnus the Earl. But his sickness steadily increased. For consolation he had Latin works read to him, but finding this too great a strain, books in the familiar Norse tongue were read instead, both night and day; first the lives of the saints, and then the sagas of the kings of Norway, one after the other. By 15 December he was too weak to speak; 'near midnight Sverri's Saga was finished, and just as midnight was past Almighty God called King Haakon from this world's life'. Until winter was over he was temporarily laid to rest in state before the shrine of the Saint in the adjacent cathedral, presumably in the new choir. On Ash Wednesday, 5 April 1264, his coffin was solemnly lifted and carried to his flagship in Scapa Flow and sailed back to Bergen for final burial in Christ Church there, a symbolic departure of the Norse power west-over-seas.

St. Magnus Cathedral was founded and endowed by Norsemen. Still as Earl's property it came into the possession of James III as Earl of Orkney, and by him as private property it was granted to the people of Kirkwall in 1486. Since then it has belonged to the Magistrates, Councillors and inhabitants of Kirkwall. Their right to ownership has been challenged from time to time by powerful forces. The various attempts which have been made to deprive the town of its most splendid possession are but repetitions of similar challenges to other Norse medieval private churches, especially in Iceland, where they have been likewise stoutly resisted.

The discoveries of 1848 occurred during a programme of clearance by the Government when the church had totally ceased to be a place of worship and for ten years (1844 to 1854) was an Ancient Monument. The Crown's claim to ownership was finally abandoned in 1851 and the £3,000 it had so recently spent on repair and renovation was gratefully acknowledged as a donation towards maintaining an object of public interest.

REFERENCES

1. All quotations in this paper are, unless otherwise stated, from *The Orkneyinga Saga*, ed. by A. B. Taylor (1938).

2. R. Willis, *The Architectural History of Canterbury Cathedral* (1845). The Latin text is given in *The Historical Works of Gervase of Canterbury*, ed. by William Stubbs (1879). There is an extensive excerpt in Elizabeth Holt, *Literary Sources of Art History* (1947), pp. 48–58.

3. J. R. Tudor, *The Orkneys and Shetland* (1883).

4. L. F. Salzman, *Building in England* (1952), Pl. 6b.

5. Miniature in *Givart de Roussillon*, National Library, Vienna. Reproduced in *The Flowering of the Middle Ages*, by Joan Evans (1966), Pl. 87, with notes.

6. For those two quotations and the interpretation I am wholly indebted to the generous scholarship of Dr. C. A. Ralegh Radford.

7. John Mooney, 'Notes on Discoveries in St. Magnus Cathedral, Kirkwall', in *Proc. Soc. Ant. Scot.*, Vol. 59 (1924–5), pp. 239–51.

See also Mooney, 'Discovery of relics in St. Magnus Cathedral', *Proc. Ork. Ant. Soc.*, Vol. 3 (1925), pp. 73–8. 'Further notes on Saints' relics and burials in St. Magnus Cathedral', *op. cit.*, Vol. 6 (1927–8). pp. 33–7. and 'Internments and excavations in St. Magnus Cathedral', *op. cit.*, Vol. 7 (1928–9), pp. 27–32. I am moved by those most valuable and original papers to pay tribute to the journal which published them, and to a great Orcadian scholar.

8. An unidentifiable Press cutting in the writer's possession states that the skull was broken out of its case (i.e., shrine or reliquary) on the altar of the church of San Silvestro in Capite, the parish church of the British Catholic community in Rome. It was handed back by the thief during a confession.

9. The oak coffin from the south pier is now on view in the Tankerness House Museum opposite the west front of the cathedral.

10. I am indebted to Mr. Sverri Dahl for this information. As well, he gives a short account of the church, with a photograph of the reliquary panel, *The Fifth Viking Congress* ed. Bjarni Niclasen, Tórshavn (1968), pp. 187–8.

Romanesque Bases, in and South-east of the Limestone Belt

by

S. E. RIGOLD

INTRODUCTION

BASE-MOULDINGS are seldom described with precision, yet those at ground-level are the easiest of details to examine and to draw from direct contact,[1] as well as the most closely tied to the beginning of any recorded building-campaign. Those characteristic of one campaign can usually be distinguished, but they may be altered without disturbing a large design sustained over several campaigns. They have that kind of independent serial variation that so commends pottery to archaeologists: they can be 'sectioned'; they are repetitive enough for easy classification; and they are stratigraphically 'sealed' by their superstructure.

Bases are here treated in isolation, by their own typology, without deference or prejudice to the chronological claims of other tests—of plan, composition or ornament, of liturgical convenience or technical feasibility. As far as possible, the terms used here imply a hypothesis of interpretation—how the masons may have 'read' mouldings, rather than a hypothesis of development —how he came to use them. As far as possible too, the only chronological evidence admitted here is 'historical' rather than 'archaeological'. In default of records it may be circumstantial, but the prime examples are from the greater and better documented religious and military monuments, many of them in the care of the Department of the Environment. Other examples have been introduced to give a wider distribution or simply because they come from well-known buildings which may have started snowballs of ill-founded stylistic argument.

Limits of the Enquiry

'Romanesque' here envisages a Roman or Byzantine precedent behind, often not far behind, any work, and the immanent possibility of 'correcter' classicism. This is more than an admission that Antique usages continued devolving until regenerated in a 'twelfth-century renaissance' by a fresh study of Roman models, particularly those in Christian Rome, and also of Vitruvius.[2] It recognises that 'revivals' could occur at any time and that masons might work at different intellectual levels in the same period, some copying classical forms naively, others conscientiously, others yet playing deliberate 'manneristic' variations upon them. The persistent model for bases was the

'Attic': it could be generalised enough to be maintained by craft-tradition, or, on occasion, made to conform with the prescribed proportions of Vitruvius,[3] whether or not other classical forms were also rationalised and interpreted in his terms. Lasteyrie noticed that 'Attic' of any complexion was less dominant in Normandy and Britanny than in the rest of France (to say nothing of the Empire) and plainly unclassical forms, sometimes claimed as 'Saxon', were correspondingly commoner.[4] After the Conquest they are actually more prevalent in the Caennais and Bessin than in England. Here the attention is rather to Roumois, Caux and Bray, closer to England as well as to central Christendom.

The area of England covered is also determined by accessibility, then and now: its bounds are geological and economic—to seaward the easy passage of Caen stone, to landward the Oolite belt. These two not dissimilar 'facies' provide the stone for a large proportion of the examples, and their distribution overlaps along the east coast to the Humber. The shelly limestone from Quarr, Isle of Wight, also moved coastwise eastward.[5] Ferruginous sandstones, such as 'Bargate' in the west Weald or 'Carstone' in west Norfolk, are much more restricted and Ragstone and such Greensand formations are rarely found. Clunch types are commoner and lend themselves to the deep mouldings of later Romanesque but not to preservation outdoors.

Within this limestone-bounded area there is a homogeneity of type which overrides, but does not suppress, local fashion. If the massive rolls of Tewkesbury and the muted ones of Norfolk typify local extremes, examples to the contrary can be found in the neighbourhood of each. The homogeneity extends beyond the Oolite into the Triassic sandstone and a few parallels are cited from this area,[6] but there are signs of a cultural rather than a geological inhibition before the hard rocks are reached. Whether or not St. John's Chester is as late, and therefore backward, as Clapham claimed,[7] the accepted dating of Penmon priory would imply that Anglesey lagged by two or three generations.[8] The North can certainly produce metropolitan detail,[9] but the mean standard of execution is coarser in a geologically diversified area.

There is no theoretical 'upper' limit of date to the enquiry: it is the nature of the material, not the Norman conquest, that leaves it little scope before the 1050s. A definition which avoids the teleological thinking implicit in the word 'transitional' allows the lower limit to pass 1200. In detail if not in structure, this last generation is as Romanesque and more truly Roman than anything before.

Limitations of the Evidence

Bases are seldom found 'roughed-out'[10] and were normally finished before laying, whereas uncompleted enrichments in higher situations show that these could be worked *in situ*.[11] The evidence is presented in the form of ortho-graphic elevations, based on sections taken from stones which do not appear to have been re-tooled. Comparison with genuine bases in the same building leaves little faith in any renewal.

As a rule, only integral bases of circular, or part-circular, plan are considered. Space does not allow the drawings to cover a full radius, but the general order of magnitude is given in the text. Only the top of the square plinth, which often expands at a chamfer or salient moulding, is shown, unstippled. The section is necessarily generalised for the earlier bases, which were cut by eye, without a template. Where much of the circuit is lost a protected section, often in the corner of a nook-shaft, must represent the whole.[12] Where one base is shown as typical of a concurrent set the others may vary in their proportions.

Whether as criteria of absolute date or of the relative staging of elements in a complex plan, bases are only valid for the part and the annual 'lift' in which they occur. There is no necessary connection between the bases and capitals even of one storey, nor between the shell of a building and its arcade. The value of bases at fundamental level, which is the same for a roofed building as for a ruin which stands only to a few courses, lies above all in their testimony to the laying-out of a plan. These reservations affect any assessment of Malmesbury abbey, for example, where a fair consistency *at base-level* between the nave and what remains of the eastern arm and between the wall-arcades and the great piers need not involve the sculptures, nor even the completion of the main arcade.[13] Such consistency reflects the confidence and the credit with which a great abbey or a great prelate might *plan* in totality. Thus, while Lanfranc completed Christ Church, Canterbury, in seven years from 1071,[14] John of Séez, who 'could not finish' Peterborough in seven years from 1118,[15] yet surely left his memorial in its lower courses, stopping only at the north-west part of the nave. This is in complete contrast with the guarded steps at Romsey, where the bases of almost every bay are different.

Execution

No prejudice about the development of tools should overrule the evidence of profiles. Workmanship is a function of the conditions of building, of the type of stone, of which each has its characteristic tooling, and of the value set upon a more or less precious material. The almost carpenterly delicacy of East Anglia persists in all phases, but becomes more noticeable the further from the source of stone. Nearer the Oolite quarries the treatment is bolder and more casual. It is not questioned that sharp arrisses are characteristic of the late Romanesque, but within the progress of one building there is no even or irreversible improvement—often there is deterioration. Abbot Scotland's bases at St. Augustines are remarkably smooth; less so those in the nave. In the choir of Norwich, though rugged for the district, they are neat; in the nave some are very slipshod, or even roughed-out. At Winchester those at triforium-level, some of which go with the tower rebuilt after 1107,[16] are awkward and ill-finished beside the fundamental bases. Explanations are not hard to find: a foreign master and raw journeyman, more attention to the monks' own choir or simply pressure to 'finish the job'. In a disputable history this kind of evidence is ambivalent. At Chichester, Ralph Luffa (1091–1123) is reported to have rebuilt, after a fire in 1114, the church he himself had built *a novo,*[17] whence it has been deduced that nothing remained of its predecessor, needed by the 1070s, and assumed that work progressed steadily westward, even after 1123. The bases in the choir are typologically later than those in the east nave, even perhaps than those in the west, and *better finished* than either. But finish contributes little to the thesis that only the choir was entirely renewed after 1114, while the five eastern bays of the nave may contain relics earlier than Ralph.

Documentation

Except where there are reliable summaries[18] only primary sources are cited. Clapham gives a 'lead' to many of these[19] but cites interpretive works on the same footing, without criticism, so that pyramids of argument have passed by default—arguments *ex silentio,* arguments from *Gefühl* and arguments based squarely on false premises. One instance involving all three will suffice:

Saxl, discussing the sculptures at Malmesbury, invoked Clapham's date of *c.* 1160 for the nave as preferable to Kingsley Porter's of *c.* 1140.[20] It does not help his case, for Clapham was simply citing a shaky pile of inference by Brakspear:[21] first, that the Saxon church was standing in 1143 because William of Malmesbury, in a work ended in 1125,[22] said that it lasted 'to his own day'; second, that the monks began rebuilding in delayed jubilation some years after they had been freed from their commendator, Roger of Salisbury, reaching the west end at leisure, by *c.* 1160—sheer supposition, started by a 'false scent'. William's apparent silence on the rebuilding of his own abbey has been taken as negative evidence, but the natural inference from the first citation is that the Saxon church had gone by 1125, while in the *Gesta Regum,* which *was* completed *c.* 1143, he grudgingly commends Roger's energy and perfection in building, *maxime in Salesbiria et Malmesbiria,* with no suggestion that this only concerns secular work.[23] William, though too proud to be specific, might equally be taken to imply that Roger had laid out the entire new abbey church. This is what the bases seem to say, but it is a hypothesis, not a premise.

Throughout the Romanesque period definite and acceptable sources are meagre. Even chronicles of individual houses may provide no more than a date of foundation or consecration. The bald chronicle of Thorney,[24] which completed a great church in some twenty years, under one abbot, yet delayed dedication for another twenty, is of unparalleled precision and also a warning against reading too much into dedication-dates. The more biographical chroniclers, such as Eadmer, add little despite their authentic emphasis on personal 'drive'. No record of expenditure survives outside the royal Pipe Rolls.

Although but a decade or two before the Winchester rolls open,[25] the *oeuvre* ascribed to Richard of Ilchester is inferred from one entry in the annals of Waverley.[26]

The most absolute credentials, dated building-inscriptions, are excessively rare in northern Europe. That which is one of the features combining to make St. Kyneburga's of Castor the most significant medium-sized Romanesque church in England has been a fulcrum of misunderstanding. To Clapham the building was 'definitely dated to the year 1124'[27] and a great deal followed on that. Nevertheless, the stone records dedication, not construction; it is in relief except for the end of the *millésime,* which is incised and may have been completed when the stone was re-set, *c.* 1200; and the year, as Ruprich-Robert saw, is surely 1114.[28] A neighbour and dependency of Peterborough, which was rebuilt from 1118, Castor is much closer in detail, including bases, to the nave of Thorney, finished in 1108.[29] The dedicatory-inscription of 1185 in the New Temple of London[30] is a firm point in the 'Attic revival' of the late twelfth century.

Working Generations

The interdependant records of Thorney, Castor and Peterborough are fundamental to the hypothesis that a new manner, a *style Henri 1er*, with its own fashion of bases, was emerging about 1115, to flourish for a full genera-tion until the 1140s, after which, for whatever causes—economic and political uncertainty (rather than 'anarchy' as such), or the Cistercian example—a chastened and eclectic spirit emerged. With this as its centre a rough scale of generations, allowing a deviation of perhaps half a working life, is used here, not as a substitute for individual dating, but as a convenient provisional grouping of works with some documentary credentials and no inconsistency of manner. The inclusion of any building should be falsified on documentary grounds alone. It may be of more than mnemonic use to associate the 'generations' with personalities:

GI, from the first Norman plantation under the Confessor to the late 1080s: with Lanfranc or with Scotland of St. Augustines;

GII, thence to *c.* 1115: with many Benedictine father-figures, or with Rannulf Flambard:

GIII, the high-point, from *c.* 1115 to the Cistercian climacteric of 1143–7: with Roger of Salisbury and the young Henry of Blois;

GIV, thence until the 1170s: an age of cross-currents (*c.* 1160 is an undes-criptive phrase): one manner may be associated with prior Wibert of Christ Church, Canterbury;

GV, the very distinctive and generally classical phase from *c.* 1175 until the Interdict: with Richard of Ilchester.

Previous Studies

The one substantial 'Essai sur les bases romanes', by F. Deshoulières,[31] treats only of France, with little interest in Normandy or regional variety as such. His large sample shows how tenacious the classical forms were, yet, from the English viewpoint, how little can be claimed as peculiarly northern, let alone Saxon. He comes straight to the question whether bases are valid criteria of date, but leaves it almost unanswered. This is as well for he is paralysed with the French malady of *siècles*. Even Ruprich-Robert[32] cannot escape the infection, but he takes bases seriously and separately, depicts them exquisitely and his great work remains indispensible for Norman parallels. No English work can touch these, despite a more pragmatic time-scale and the relative dullness of English capitals. To Bond, Romanesque is just an antecedent.[33] Clapham, in a page or two, with seventeen schematic and not very accurate profiles, only allows one non-Attic form more than a mention and neglects the whole range here called 'modified Attic'.[34] His general progression from shallow to deep cutting is fair enough, but not his 'two parallel developments', one upright, the other 'of great projection'. These extremes co-exist with intermediate forms, distending the same components horizontally to match the diameter of the shaft, occasionally observing the Vitruvian proportions in this plane only. With few honourable exceptions,[35] Clapham's generation recorded profiles less scrupulously than their Victorian predecessors.

The End and Utility of this Study

Hereinafter follows a classification, with some 350 specimens, of which 228 are illustrated. These do not form a corpus, but are chosen from a mass taken at random from each part of each major building and from a partly fortuitous choice of minor ones. They are thus a sample as well as a selection, and the classes they shape are empirical enough to stand even if the 'hypotheses of interpretation' should prove illusory. They are the product of a growing experience which came to recognise familiar forms, usually where expected, sometimes in surprising situations, but they are a beginning, not an end. An exhaustive corpus is impracticable, but the classification invites the collection of more data by the same tests and methods (not mechanical ones) and the amplification of the classes.

It is not claimed that bases provide a universal index of absolute date, that Tantalus's cup of archaeologists unable to think except in evolutionary terms. This study will serve its purpose if it raises questions and hypotheses to be tested by other means. If the crossing-bases at Wimborne resemble one, and only one, early, but not quite primary, stage at Winchester, does the smaller minster not have a nucleus from about the 1090s? Is Malmesbury a work of Bishop Roger? Or, to go outside the area, if the eastern arm of St. John's, Chester, has double hollows and the massively Romanesque nave has neo-attic bases, may there not be some eighty years between them? Plans and photographs neither answer nor ask these questions. That bases can ask them shows the need for further and finer recording of architectural details, whatever the context and at no more trouble than the interminable pot-sections. The matter is urgent, and it is not always considered part of an excavator's duty: certain bases, fast crumbling on exposure, might never have been drawn but for this paper.

A CLASSIFICATION

Definitions *(Fig. 1)*

Whenever possible a variant form will be related to and described in terms of the Attic. This calls for a more generalised anatomy than the orthodox one, of two rolls *(tori)*-t separated by vertical fillets (f) from a deep hollow

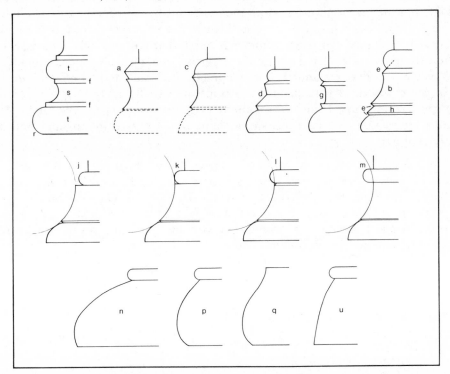

Fig. 1 Generalised Romanesque bases to illustrate terminology.

(trochilus, or *scotia,* i.e., darkness)-s. The three stages are here called an 'Attic sequence'. What serves for a torus is called a 'roll', even when angular (**a**) or no more than a quadrant (**c**). When a lower roll is constricted beneath to less than its full diameter (**r**) it is 'recurved'. When it is disproportionately heavy the base is 'weighted'. What represents the scotia is called the 'hollow', be it

concave, angled (d) or almost flat (g). One or both fillets may be lacking or feebly indicated, but when both are prominent they may look like the exposed edges of a band of definite thicknesses, applied to the hollow. A scotia thus seeming to stand proud is called a 'band' (b) and its fillets 'edges' (e). A radial or oblique edge or fillet is 'chamfered'. A roll is 'hooded' when part of it is masked by a short extra band, or 'hood' (h) emerging from under the main band. When the upper roll does not reach the projected arc of the hollow, it is 'recessed' (j); where it just reaches it, 'tangent' (k); where it overrides it, 'projected' (l). Where a projected roll intersects a band or hollow without exposing its edge, it 'occludes' it (m).

Other terms apply also to forms that cannot be construed as Attic, particularly those comprised of convex members only, which are classed as 'single', 'double' or 'multiple' according to the number of rolls. Where the lower roll or, in a 'single convex' base, the only roll, is, as Clapham says, 'of great projection' *in the horizontal plane only,* it, and by extension, the whole base, is 'expanded'. Such a roll or base is 'oblate' (n) when very expanded and little recurved; 'bulbous' (p) when somewhat expanded and strongly recurved, even when the curve is reversed at the top to give a cyma-profile (q); 'campaniform' (u) when neither expanded nor recurved, but tall and almost conical. A cylinder replacing a roll, in any position but usually at the top, is a 'collar'. A 'spur' means any form of ornament or *griffe* pointing to the angle of the plinth: these are typologically important, but are rare in England and here little explored.

To simplify location, 'west nave' means the western part of the nave, and such phrases likewise; any kind of door-surround is a 'portal'; and the abbreviations for the (historic) counties follow the *Oxford Dictionary of English Place Names,* with Cal. for Calvados, S.M. for Seine Maritime. Finally, 'Norman' is not used as a synonym for Romanesque but indicates a feature in, or closely matched in, Normandy itself.

Synopsis of Classification

A. Non-Attic forms found in archaic contexts:

      I. Reversed capitals.
     II. Truncated cones.
    III. Double hollows.
    IV. Double rolls.
     V. Multiple rolls.
    VI. Single convex forms.
   VII. Weighted double-convex forms.
  VIII. Projected hollows.

B. Attic forms in early and middle contexts:

      I. Complete sequences—

        1. Relatively orthodox.
        2. With reduced upper rolls.
        3. Assimilated to campaniform or bulbous.
        4. With rigid bands.
        5. With extended bands.

     II. Augmented and converted Attic.

    III. Modified Attic—

        1. Undifferentiated rolls.
        2. Secant rolls.
        3. Chamfered tops.
        4. Truncated bases.

C. Sculptural bases:

      I. Zoomorphic bases.
     II. Cylindrical bases.

D. Simplified bases:

      I. Hollow forms.
     II. Convex forms.

E. The Attic revival:

      I. Tentative forms.
     II. Mature forms—

        1. With both fillets vertical.
        2. With one or both fillets chamfered.
        3. Without a lower fillet.
        4. Without an upper fillet.
        5. With no fillets.

A. NON-ATTIC FORMS FOUND IN ARCHAIC CONTEXTS

A form is called 'archaic' if it is known from attested GI, or even pre-Conquest examples: a later or undocumented context containing such forms is 'archaic' by association. An 'archaic *mélange*' is a mixed assemblage containing such forms, whether it is attested early, as in Lanfranc's enlarged dorter-undercroft at Christ Church, Canterbury,[36] or only apparently so, as in the five eastern bays of Chichester have.

I. Reversed Capitals

Wide-chamfered squares, like the capitals in Repton crypt, Db[37], but serving as bases, as at Étampes, Essonne,[38] are hard to match in England. At Nately Scures, Ha,[39] or Eynsford church, K, door-quoins are chamfered steeply up to a roll below a nook-shaft, making 'square-campaniform' bases.

Upturned cushion-capitals are common in East Anglia under small shafts of portals, fonts, wall-arcades, etc., and occasionally support proper, moulded bases. A 'cushion' is a convex form, usually quadrilobe in plan, cut back to a square much larger than the shaft, from which it is separated by a roll. It tends to the campaniform on the portals of Haddiscoe, Nf (1),[40] Southoe, Hu, Great Wymondley, Ht, and the frater at Horsham St. Faith, Nf,[41] but commonly it is more expanded, as in other monastic contexts in Nf, some relatively late—the chapter-house at Horsham St. Faith, the slype at Thetford (abutting the transept completed by 1114),[42] the choir at Carrow, by Norwich (2) [43] and the west range at Binham.[44]

The form (3) in which the shaft directly penetrates a quadrilobe cut back to a square hardly more than its diameter, prominent at Cérisy-la-Forêt, Manche,[45] occurs much later on small, engaged shafts, as at Polstead, Sf, and Bibury, Gl.

II. Truncated Cones

This simple form, a chamfer or *glacis* at about 45deg., straight from shaft to plinth, or with a reservation above or below, but with no intervening roll, was used under the Conqueror in Basse Normandie, even on major columns of great churches, among them St. Nicholas[46] and both the abbeys at Caen.[47] No comparable Anglo-Norman church is known to have used it thus. On nook-shafts of portals it persisted in Calvados,[48] but rarely in England, as at Shalfleet, Wt.[49] English churches with conspicuous conical bases, though by no means all indisputably pre-Conquest, are insular or, at least un-Norman, including St. Martin, Wareham, Do,[50] Sompting, Sx (on the tower-arch),[51] Langford, Ox, a pretentious church on a royal manor,[52] with steep cones in two tiers (4).[53] The bases of the 'mid-wall shafts' of such 'late-Saxon' bell-towers, as St. Peter-at-Gowts, Lincoln,[54] or Marton, Li,[55] look conical but the comparable detail at Hadstock, Ess (5) includes bases broken into straight

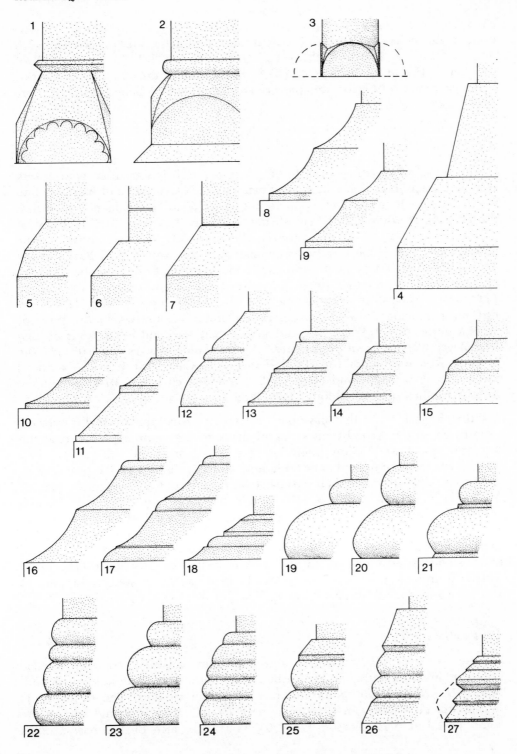

Fig. 2 Romanesque bases. Classes A I-IV. Scale 1:5

chamfers, in a *double talus* prefiguring form III.[56] In obscure positions, however, plain cones are very persistent and foundation dates provide such
'upper' limits as 1107 for the crypt at Old Sarum,[57] 1133 for the hall of
St. John's Hospital, Cirencester (6),[58] 1146 for the dorter-range of Carrow
(7)[59] and even 1177 for the passage-arcade of abbot Benedict's gatehouse
at Peterborough.[60]

III. Double Hollows

The double hollow, again without an upper roll, has been seen as a very
seal of the spiritual bond between England and Normandy and hardly found
beyond them. It marked the Confessor's apse (8) at Westminster,[9] as well as
the crossing at Mont St. Michel, whence came Scotland who used it just west
of the crossing (9) of St. Augustine's, the first truly spacious church of the
new dispensation.[62] One example remaining at the west end of Battle abbey
may mean that it was used throughout the church of this, the field-trophy
of conquest.[63] It is rather rough, like those on the tower-arch at Broughton,
Li,[64] whose claims to be pre-Conquest could find support from Hadstock.
But most documented early instances, including one or two in the transept
at Winchester (1079),[65] are fine and subtly shadowed and in contexts of high
patronage, like those in Normandy: the nave of Jumièges (by 1057);[66] the
crypt of Rouen cathedral (by 1063);[67] la Trinité, Caen;[68] St. Gervais, Falaise;[69]
the choir of Lessay;[70] and after 1082, the radial chapels (10) at Fécamp.[71]
In England the type was seldom copied later.

Other English bases that have been referred to this type are really hybrids,
assimilated to the Attic by inserting quadrant rolls at various places: if at the
top only, the lower hollow might be read as a 'converted' roll (cf. p. 114).
These, where documented, cluster about the beginning of GII but vary in
execution: at Canterbury they are coarse in the nave of St. Augustine's (11,12:
1087–91).[72] fine in the hall (13) and cloister (14) of the Christ Church
infirmary, which logically follows the dorter enlarged by 1089;[73] fine also on
the Caen-stone door of Colchester keep (15), which is consistent with a
primary date, before 1087, but may be an *early* alteration;[74] very fine in two
Quarr-stone variants on the façade of Winchester chapter-house (16, 17).[75]
Those in the choir of Bardney abbey, Li (18) can be classed as variants of
this form and, *pace* Brakspear, consistent with the refoundation of 1087.[76]

IV. Double Rolls

Bases of two rolls, expanded and somewhat weighted, come in archaic
contexts in Normandy, as at Authie, Cal,[77] and Ste. Marguerite-de-la-Mer,
S.M. (19), with simple spurs and raw acanthoid capitals. The form occurs
in the archaic *mélange* in Chichester nave (fourth from crossing) and on the
south portal at Brize Norton, Ox (20),[78] but most such English bases, unless

heavily weighted (A VII), seem to be late (cf. p. 129). The context at Sutton, Sx, where some have intervening fillets (21), and bold volute spurs, is difficult to match.[79]

V. Multiple Rolls

This unlearned form, comprising three or more evenly balanced rolls, suggests an archetype in turned timber. It occurs early in Calvados,[80] in an expanded version in the nave of Great Paxton, Hu,[81] and on the only surviving base of Remigius's Lincoln minster, begun c. 1072.[82] It is thus demonstrably 'archaic' and associated with, though rarer than, the next two classes. On the tower-arch at Netheravon, Wi, in a still 'Saxon' plan, fourfold rolls to the west (22) match big campaniform bases on the east.[83] At Stoughton, Sx, another 'Saxonising' church, the form is more expended on the medial bases of the chancel-arch than on the lateral (23).[84] A distinctive variant has the topmost roll, and sometimes others, obliquely flattened so that it resembles a 'band' with an 'edge'. This is seen in varying degrees among the coarse Oolite bases with three, four or five rolls, in the dorter-undercroft *mélange* at Canterbury (24, 25)[85] and on the massive Bargate-stone portal at Witley, Sy (26)[86] and on that at Elsenham, Ess (27),[87]—both with markedly archaic detail.

A second, widespread variant looks like a weighted double-convex form (class A VII) but with an hour-glass waist which is bound with a third roll, as on the portals of archaic two-celled churches at Smeeth, K (28)[88] and Egleton, Ru (where the chancel-arch has reversed capitals). At the comparable church of Stopham, Sx,[89] unbound hour-glass bases have *capitals* with multiple rolls; the forms are clearly related.

VI. Single Convex Forms

These may be oblate, bulbous or campaniform, and, like classes A V and A VIII, suggest timber prototypes. The ideal specimens are the great cheese-like bases to the corner-posts of the earliest stave-churches.[90] In stone this form and the related A VII belong with post-like members—nook-shafts and the relatively slender monolithic columns found especially in archaic crypts.

The oblate variety fits large supports in great churches: in the crypt of Bury St. Edmunds[91] its profile on the second pillar from the west (29) is a short arc, at the crossing it is near elliptical (30), as is that on the surviving pair (31) in Winchester choir, ready by 1093.[92] At Ickleton, Ca, a miniature 'great church' with monolithic columns, the form is half-elliptical at the west, less expanded on the paired crossing-shafts (32).[93] Bulbous versions may occur in smaller-scale but functionally similar positions, as at the crossing at Leonard Stanley, Gl (33), as late as the 1120s or '30s.[94] Less prominent situations include some unquestionably archaic, such as the windows in the top stage of the tower at Clapham, Bd, which has recently been shown to be of a piece with the 'Saxon' build.[95] On portals it may take the shape of a bulbous cyma,

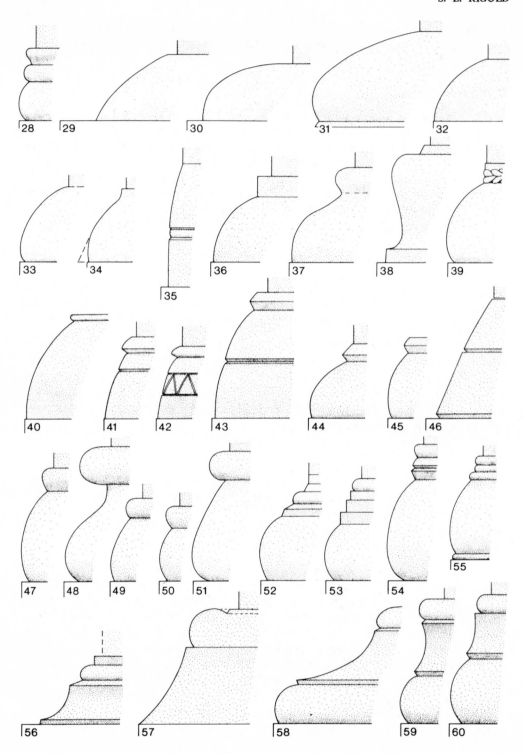

Fig. 3 Romanesque bases. Classes A V (variant) to A VIII and B I, 1 (Winchester). Scale 1:5.

as at North Ockendon, Ess (34), or Little Saxham, Sf, a dependency of Bury, or even be steep and campaniform, as at Poslingford, Sf (35).

The normal bulbous shape, however, exercises an almost modish influence in GI and GII: even Attic forms are assimilated to it. In Germany, despite the dominance of a purer classical tradition, simple or collared bulbous bases occur, as they do in the Clapham tower, side-by-side with Attic. Beneath the monolithic columns in the archaic round church at Druggelde, Westphalia, they have simple angular spurs just like those on such English examples as North Ockendon, Ess (34), or Milborne, Do, which is from GI if not earlier.[96]

VII. Weighted Double-convex Forms

This comprises all bulbous and campaniform bases having a proportionately small upper element, such as the collar (36) or the weakly defined upper roll (37) under the monolithic columns of Gundulf's part of Rochester crypt (soon after 1077).[97] Other archaic treatments include a reversed cyma carrying a collar (38) in Scotland's crypt at St. Augustine's,[98] and range from very bulbous with ornate collars (39), on the portal at Heckingham, Nf, to oblate with an attenuated upper roll (40) at North Elmham cathedral, Nf. In the last case the other face of the Oolite block was worked to an 'augmented' Attic base (130) for an inserted north door, so that it may derive from the suppressed west door or elsewhere in a build hardly later than the removal of the see, c. 1072.[99]

At Heckingham, too (41) and other early eastern churches, as Ilketshall St. Andrew[58] (42), a distinctive campaniform species occurs, with a sharp, carinate upper roll and a scoring round the bulge. The finest and largest, on the paired half-shafts at Isleham priory, Ca (43) might confirm the tradition that the Breton founder was an *ancestor* of Alan Fergant, i.e., probably Hoel (d. 1084).[100] An unscored and more oblate version (44) in North Elmham parish church could well be a relic of Herbert Losinga's abortive collegiate foundation there.[101] A very steep version on the portal of Reed, Ht, is associated with persisting long-and-short quoins.[102] On the similar but class A VI base at Poslingford (35) a bead replaces the scoring.

Contexts no less archaic further west produce comparable forms. At Pershore abbey, Wo, a re-set base (45) resembling that at Elmham (44) must surely antedate the standing church.[103] Scorings appear with a pronounced upper roll (still in Oolite) at Chepstow priory, Mon, founded in 1071,[104] and on a class A VI base in the north-east angle of Walter of Cérisy's transept at Evesham abbey, Wo, (46) begun soon after 1077.[105] But the plain and generalised bulbous form with a sturdy upper roll is more widely distributed and persists from the archaic *mélanges,* at Chichester (47 or with a cyma, 48), and in the Canterbury dorter-undercroft (49, the bulbous part facetted), to Folkworth, Hu (50), which is not conspicuously archaic, and even to the wall-arcade in the gatehouse at Evesham (51), considered part of abbot Reginald's precinct-wall (1122–49).[106]

In much the same early contexts are bulbous forms with more complex upper elements, as in St. Augustine's crypt (52) or the choir-aisles of Gloucester (53: soon after 1089).[107] They can sometimes be resolved into freakish Attic sequences: on the portal at Water Stratford, Bk (54) the band might be 'read' as folded in two.[108] At Duxford St. Peter, Ca, full of archaic detail, some bases add thin rolls above and below (55), others are scored or bear frets and beasts (not Scandinavian zoomorphs).

VIII. Projected Hollows

These comprise a large hollow and a recessed upper element of a roll and sometimes more. They are here classed, not as Attic sequences lacking a lower roll, but as oblate examples of class VII with the great roll 'converted' (see below) to a hollow. This finds them with their functional equivalents in classes A VI and A VII: at Bury St. Edmunds they occur in the apse of the crypt (56), soon after 1081;[109] at Gloucester the giant arcades have full upper rolls in the choir (57) and quadrants only in the nave—a normal progression.

B. ATTIC FORMS IN EARLY AND MIDDLE CONTEXTS

These are classified as 'Complete' where all three members of the sequence are present and distinct, 'Augmented' when extra members are added, 'Converted' when a hollow is substituted for a roll or *vice versa,* and 'modified' where the upper roll is deformed or suppressed. These are persistent differences: all may exist in the same phase of construction and all are affected by the same general tendencies, progressive or regional, which deviate from the true Attic in degree rather than in kind, and are reversed in the subsequent 'Attic revival'—diminution of the upper roll, less recurvature of the lower and narrowing of the 'edges'.

I. Complete Sequences

1. **Relatively orthodox**, i.e., well rounded, with broad edges or fillets and a suggestion of Vitruvian proportions at least in one direction. Their 'orthodoxy', though better than many provincial Roman works,[110] seldom rivals that of Jumièges or Rouen, to say nothing of the Rhineland. There is never much depth of scotia, with the result, well shown at the type-site of Winchester, particularly on expanded bases, that the upper roll is often forced back to a tangent or recessed position (58, 60). When projected it commonly occludes the hollow, as at Tewkesbury (61). These distortions may be regarded as normal and few English bases, even upright ones, are near Vitruvian even to the degree that the proportionate height of their members approaches 1:2:3 i.e., with the lower pair properly gauged, the topmost already diminished). Of those in the great churches of the Benedictine climacteric only the ground-bases of the Winchester transept (58, 59, 60) are demonstrably before c. 1090. The rest are contemporaneous with the spread of the less orthodox

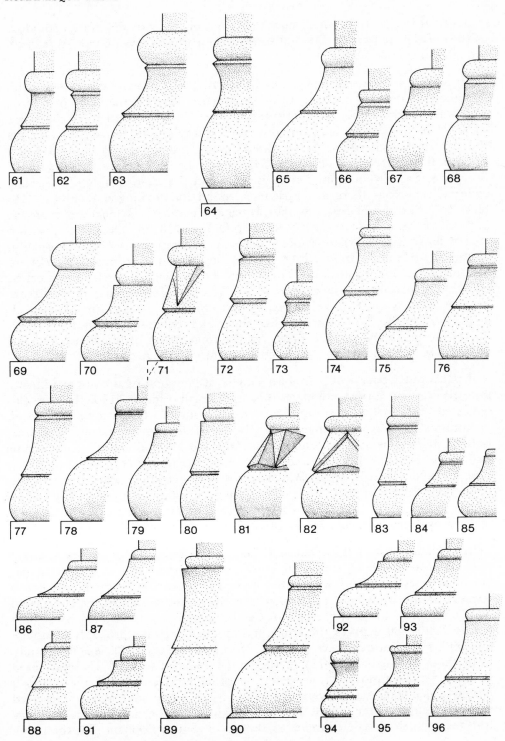

Fig. 4 Romanesque bases. Classes B I, 1-2. Scale 1:5.

'reduced' form (B I, 2) which may then be mingled with the more orthodox, as (65) in the transept at Ely and (66) in the eastern arm of Castle Acre, both probably from the 1090s.[112]

Sites with substantial upper rolls lie mainly, like Winchester, to westward. Benedictine contexts include: Tewkesbury (61, 62, 63), the most orthodox, with the fullest rolls, in an organised, even Vitruvian design, occupied in 1102;[113] Bath, contemporaneous but feebler in relief, at least on the crossing (64);[114] Gloucester, where the weighted bases in the slype (67)[115] and possibly those in the cloisterward nave-aisle (68) are primary; Romsey, on the crossing;[116] Boxgrove, Sx, settled from Lessay in 1105, in the chapter-house.[117] Among collegiate churches there is a varied set round the crossing at Wimborne, Do (e.g., 69), like the higher, not the primary, ones in the Winchester transept, but still pointing to c. 1100,[118] and a tufa base (70) in comparable position at Steyning, Sx, collegiate though held by Fécamp from 1085.[119] Finally, at the ever-relevant Castor, Nh,[120] the crossing-bases in particular (71, 72) are near-orthodox in proportions. These may be matched in archaic two-celled churches, especially those dependent on great establishments; the rolls are massive at Kensworth, Bd, (73) belonging to St. Pauls,[121] and on the chancel-arch at Lower Swell, Gl, they are like those of Tewkesbury, but more reduced on the portal. They are also heavy on the rough bases of the transept-arches at Bargham, Sx, ascribed to the eleventh century by the excavator.[122]

2. **Reduced Upper Rolls.** In East Anglia attenuation of the upper roll sets in early on all forms: compare those at North Elmham (40, 44), or the weighted Attic sequences on the 'mid-wall' shafts of a church so full of 'Saxonisms' at Great Dunham, Nf (74).[123] If the epicentre of 'reduction' is here, it has become widespread by GII and an equilibrium of moderate 'reduction' is established from about the date of Ernulf's crypt at Canterbury (75: c. 1098 onwards).[124] At Winchester it only becomes conspicuous on the upper west side of the transept (76), evidently rebuilt with the tower, after 1107. At Chichester it is confined to the choir (77), where the reconstruction of 1114 was seemingly almost complete.[125]

In order to define a fully 'reduced' roll, especially in eastern contexts, where they are found side-by-side with more orthodox ones, the discriminant has been taken as the point where the upper roll accounts for no more than a seventh of the total height. Thus, in the Ely transept 78 may be contrasted with 65 and, at the extreme east of Castle Acre, 79 with 66[126] both assigned to the 1090s. 80 typifies the choir and apse of Norwich, probably complete by 1096.[127] In Thorney nave (1098–1108) most bases (81, 82, 83) differ only from those at Castor (72, 73) in their fully reduced rolls.[128] These are used at Bury St. Edmunds on the eastern crossing-piers, antedating the claustral ranges which themselves were complete by 1119,[129] and also on inserted reinforcements in the crypt. In Norfolk they can be accepted as primary features of such archaic churches as Bawsey or South Lopham (84, the north portal).[130] Kent generally follows the Eastern fashion, but can be eclectic: the upper rolls are very slender on the recently excavated west crossing piers of St. Martin-le-Grand, Dover (85) a *collégiale* effectively *dissolved* in the 1130s,[131] even more so on the chancel-arch of Walmer Old church, with precisely Ernulfian detail: at St. James, Dover, with ornament recalling Castor and Thorney, rolls of both sizes occur.

All the foregoing point to GII. By GIII 'reduction' predominates everywhere and fuller rolls are conspicuous only on 'showpieces' in the resistant Cotswold area, such as Elkstone, Gl. This observation loses force from the fact that by GIII the complete Attic sequence was itself in eclipse, outnumbered in most mixed assemblages by 'modified' forms and retained chiefly in positions of functional emphasis, especially crossing-piers. Among smaller churches, Iffley, Ox (86) is typical in this respect, and at Rochester keep (soon after 1126) complete but 'reduced' sequences occur only on the great transverse arcade (87).[132] These later sequences can often be recognised by the small scale of the whole in relation to the shaft, by the feeble edges, by the light and generally recessed upper roll, with the lower seldom more than a quadrant—characteristics seen even on frontispieces, such as St. Botolph's, Colchester (88).[133] Among the exceptional cases where 'reduced' bases still display bold edges and massive lower rolls are the gate-tower of Bury St. Edmunds (89), confirmed by excavation to be no earlier than abbot Anselm's enclosure, after 1119;[134] and the crossing-piers of Reading abbey (90), after 1121, the last Benedictine church in the grand old manner.[135]

Two themes may further illustrate the diminution of the upper roll and enfeebling of the edges in circumstances which otherwise tend to conservatism. One is on tower-arches and crossings, where recurvature and depth of hollow tend to survive in a series of neat bases with recessed upper rolls. The earliest, with a pronounced edge (91), is on the massive, keep-like tower of Leeds parish church, K, which cannot be associated with a reported foundation in 1137.[136] Its successors are on Augustinian crossings, none very well documented: Christchurch (Twineham), Ha, probably from the time of Rannulf Flambard (d. 1128);[137] Dunstable, Bd, founded before 1125 (with firm edges but lower rolls not recurved);[138] Waltham, Ess (92), where the piers are integral with the suppressed apse, recently excavated;[139] and St. Bartholomew, London (93), after 1123 and probably after the chevet with modified bases (178).[140] The last two, in metropolitan buildings, with some royal patronage, are close to the great bases in Rochester keep (87) and consistent with the end of Henry I's reign.

The other is more difficult—the *Prunkstücke* where display extends over the whole church and full sequences are used profusely. There is a delusive tendency to think of them as late *because* they are ornate. A precious and eclectic expression of the idiom may indeed recur in G IV, for which the works of prior Wibert at Canterbury[141] are sometimes cited, and which seems

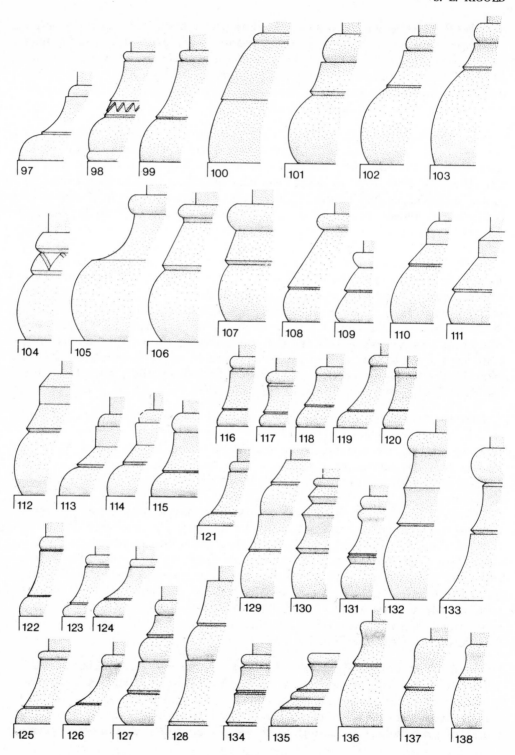

Fig. 5 Romanesque bases. Classes B I, 2 (elaborated) to B I, 5, B II and B III, 1 Scale 1:5.

also to appear, despite historical indications, at Patrixbourne, K (94).[142] Another possible instance is the so-called Infirmary chapel at Lewes priory (95), whose angle-shafts have very reduced and austerely refined bases.[143] This, however, may be a work of G III and in most cases the weight of parallels, not least in bases, points strongly that way. An instance is St. Peter's, Northampton, close to a castle in royal hands by 1130,[144] where the profiles, tangent or recessed (96, 97) again sometimes come close to Rochester (87). The elaborations, such as dagged 'hoods' (98) and 'worked plinths' (cf. p. 120) are those found in bishop Roger's buildings more often than in revivals of Wibert's age.

3. **Complete sequences assimilated to Campaniform or Bulbous.** These were early mutations with no future. At Pershore abbey, Wo,[145] they are close to the Thorney type east of the crossing (99) but in the nave exaggeratedly campaniform (100), as, in another form, at Evesham (46), but in strong contrast with Gloucester and Tewkesbury. In the bulbous kind the upper roll remains sturdy but the short, thick band is forced upwards by the excessively weighted lower roll. Dateable early instances include the simplest bases (101) at St. John's in the White Tower, after 1078,[146] and the apse-responds (102) at Gloucester, soon after 1089.[147] Undocumented contexts include the chancel-arches of St. Leonard, Wallingford, Brk (103),[148] showy, bourgeois but archaic, and the 'castle-church' of Essendine, Ru (104), merely clownish. Complete sequences, weighted and very expanded, but without edges, are used in the archaic crypt of St. Mary-le-Bow, London (105).[150]

4. **Rigid Bands.** This covers two more early mutations of the Attic, centering on Wessex and Sussex in the 1090s,[151] but used once or twice, at the same date, in the Ely transept. Again, a *locus classicus* is the Winchester triforium, which used both, well before 1107. In one mutation the band is straight, as in the previous sub-class (bulbous), but longer and more integral with the upper roll or collar: besides Winchester (106) it occurs on the third and fourth nave-piers at Chichester (107), about the crossing at Wimborne (108), the ambulatory at Romsey and the 'castle-church' of Great Canfield, Ess (109).[152] In the other the band is 'angled', or broken into oblique and upright strips, the upper roll recessed, reduced to a chamfer, or suppressed (these are 'modified' forms). Contexts are identical: the primary, east side at Winchester (110), the Wimborne crossing (111), the sixth Chichester pier (112), the Ely transept and, less weighted, in Christ Church crypt Canterbury (113), and a two-cell church at Selham, Sx (114), which can hardly be before *c.* 1090.[153]

5. **Extended Bands.** The distribution of this variety is markedly eastern. Where is occurs it is dominant: it is used throughout Castle Rising keep save for a few in the chapel. The lengthening band is already seen once or twice at Thorney (83), but what creates this sub-class is the reduction of the lower roll as well as the upper, so that the band occupies at least half the total height. At first the rolls are about equal but relatively heavy, as in the apse at Binham

priory (115), probably c. 1107,[154] the south door at Hales (116)[155] and the east crossing-arch of Castle Rising church (117),[156] all in Nf. The mature form is distinctive, uniform almost puritanical: the edges are slight, the band smooth, the rolls small and neat, the lower one sometimes a quadrant, but more often recurved and oblate, as at Mettingham, Sf (118). It characterises the crossing (119) and chapter-house (120) at Binham,[157] the entire nave of its twin at Wymondham (121), perhaps complete in the 1130s,[158] at Carrow the presbytery (122) that may have existed by 1146[159] and at Rising the west crossing of the church and almost the entire keep (123, 129) which was probably left unfinished in the late 1130s.[160] Where it occurs outside East Anglia the contexts again suggest the later 1130s or soon after, as in the frater of Dover priory (125)[161] and on both doors and the crossing (126) of East Meon church, Ha, probably from Henry of Blois's productive early years.[162]

II. Augmented and Converted Attic

'Augmentation' and 'conversion' are defined above (p. 114). Ernulf used both at Canterbury but the prime site for these rare and early phenomena is St. John's in the Tower,[163] with many permutations of increased (127) and converted (128) sequences. Among augmentations, a band may be added at the top, as on a pilaster in the transept at Norwich (129),[164] or the lower roll may be duplicated, as on a re-used base found at Weeting Castle, Nf.[165] But the most usual is an extra upper roll, as on the inserted lateral doors of North Elmham cathedral (130),[166] or the ornate chancel-arch of Petersfield, Ha (131).[167] There is a good classical precedent[168] for the kind seen at Gloucester (132), which doubles the hollow in an otherwise normal sequence. This, with the lower roll omitted, might account for the fairly common variety, noted by Clapham at Blyth priory, Nt, and seen at Tewkesbury (133) and the nave of Castle Acre (134), which has a heavy roll above two hollows. Alternatively, and since it is the exception among rows of normal sequences, it may be 'read' as a 'partial conversion', of the lower roll only.

Such liberties taken with the Attic sequence itself are distinct from the lighter, adventitious elaborations, particularly common in G III. The most persistent is the narrow extra band, or 'hood', often dagged or indented, which appears sporadically at Peterborough throughout the building begun in 1118,[169] but is often confined to 'showpieces', like St. Peter, Northampton, or façades. At Thetford it appears only on the west front: in a like position at Lewes priory,[170] in a late eclectic set, some quite neo-Attic, the hood has become the functional band of an odd augmented sequence (135).

The plinth may also bear elaborations, of which the most usual is a 'quirk' or reversed chamfer, cut into its uppermost 1.5cm. or so. It balances and responds to the 'hood', where present, but is also found with plain forms, as early as the Bath crossing (64) and in Normandy too, as at Neufmarché-en-Bray (158), rebuilt for a royal refoundation in 1128.[171] It is hard to find attested

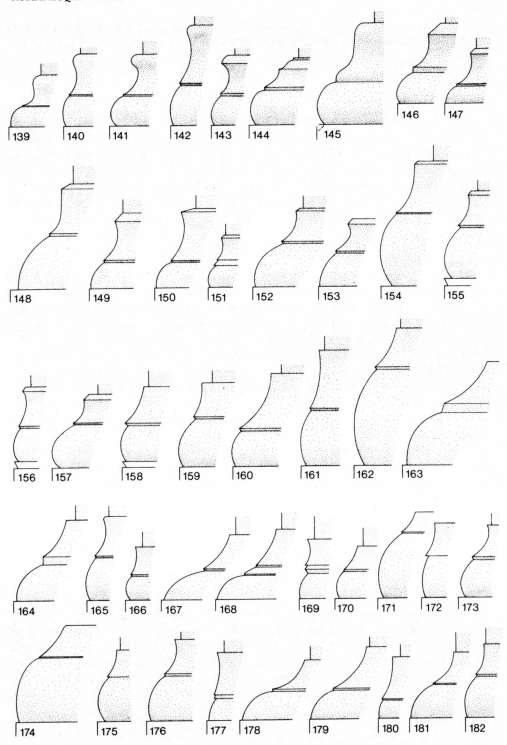

Fig. 6 Romanesque bases. Classes B III, 1-4. Scale 1:5.

examples later than GIII, which alone would support the attribution (cf. p. 101) of Malmesbury, where it runs through most of the church (155, 156) to bishop Roger of Salisbury (d. 1139).

III. Modified Attic

This, the most numerous class in England, can be divided into: (1) 'undifferentiated', where the upper roll makes a continous curve with the hollow; (2) 'secant', where the roll becomes an arc or cyma intersecting the hollow; (3) those where the roll is replaced by a chamfer of various breadth and inclination. (4) 'truncated' or 'decapitated', where the roll is totally absent. The last two are found at a date far too early for any gradual devolution from the norm to have taken place in England: an 'Ionic' model remains a possibility.

1. **Undifferentiated Rolls.** There are rough instances at Chichester, in the west nave (136) and elsewhere, but the usual kind, with a fine, often chamfered, lower edge is most typical of the age of bishop Roger. It is used at his castle of Sherborne, Do, on the columns of the upper hall (137) and the north-range wall-arcade (138),[172] and among mixed assemblages of the same general age: at Portchester, Ha, where the range of forms in the keep and the priory church, occupied in 1135,[173] is interlinked; on portals at Yaverland, Wt (139), Old Shoreham, Sx (140)[173] and Leonard Stanley, Gl (141),[175] the former two identical with Portchester in detail, the last comparable in plan and history; at St. Augustine's, Canterbury, only on the north-west (Ethelbert) tower, which is *not* numbered among the works of abbot Hugh (d. 1126), and may be ascribed to his immediate successor.[176] Such circumstantial inference would assign the portals of Wickham and Bishop's Sutton, Ha (142) to Henry of Blois, the latter acquired by him in 1136,[177] and the costly, varied but unfinished church of Iffley, Ox, to the wealthy burgess, Henry of Oxford, about the 1130s.[178]

2. **Secant Rolls.** These, again, are rare and occur in mixed assemblages. The short arc, or convex chamfer, is also at Portchester, on the crossing (143). The cyma is used in the transept at Christchurch, Ha (144), perhaps the work of Flambard,[179] and certainly antedating the truncated bases of the nave, which, in turn, must be presumed complete by *c.* 1150.

3. **Chamfered Tops.** These are found combined with rigid bands (B I, 4), as on the rough weighted bases (112), whatever their date, in the south-west nave and tower at Chichester, and at Wimborne (111). In the primary build at Thetford priory narrow and hesitant chamfers appear as a variant among 'truncated' bases (p. 125). Coarse ones are hard to distinguish from the 'undifferentiated' (B II, 1), especially when eroded or, perhaps, unfinished, as the great weighted bases in the crypt of St. Peter-in-the-East, Oxford (145).[180]

It may not be until G III that the chamfered top becomes a distinct alternative form, either dominant in its structure or mixed with others, as with secant rolls in the Christchurch transept, with 'undifferentiated', on the chancel-arch of Bishop's Sutton, with all sorts at Portchester (146, on the west front), Yaverland (147, on the chancel-arch), and St. John, Devizes, Wi, probably an early work of bishop Roger,[181] on the inward faces of the crossing. Most noticeably, it is one of the three forms in close combination at the keep of Norwich (148), which is unfortunately not closely documented,[182] the others being 'reduced' Attic and 'truncated'.

In the east it is dominant in the nave of Ely (149), probably laid out by 1115,[183] and her dependent parish-church of Lakenheath, Sf (150); so also at the grange of St. Augustine's at Minster in Thanet,[184] the keep of Hedingham, Ess,[185] which resembles Rochester, and at Polstead, Sf, with some hooded forms (151). In Wessex and the Cotswolds it is perhaps even commoner. The treatment in the nave of Wimborne resembles that in the chapter-house at Gloucester (152), each structurally later than their crossing (69, 108) and slype (67) respectively. At Bishop's Waltham palace, Ha, it was used by Henry of Blois in the chapel-crypt (153), matching work at Wolvesey of the 1130s.[186] At Malmesbury it runs throughout the church, the nave (154), crossing (155), transept wall-arcades (156) and what remains of the choir (157) and argues once more for unity at base-level and for the claims of Roger.

4. **Truncated Bases.** This form, comprising lower roll and hollow only, is found occasionally in England from an early stage. In Normandy it appears in the *chevet* at Fécamp, soon after 1082, but remains rare—the instance at Neufmarché-en-Bray (158) may be an atypical anglicism. Yet its spread in England within the range of G III is almost explosive. It becomes the commonest form of all, and, in its turn, the most utterly exterminated. Though 'actuarially' a shade later than the other modified Attic forms, like them it is not found in documented contexts after *c.* 1160.

In the early cases the single edge is often chamfered and the roll often well recurved, as in the Canterbury dorter *mélange* (159), the Wimborne crossing (160), the west portal of Ickleton, Ca (161), and, beside full sequences treated in the same bulbous fashion, at Bury, Hu (162), an archaic church, near and dependent on Ramsey abbey, whose style it doubtless reflects. A few in the eastern arm at Romsey, Ha, include that beneath the capital signed 'Robertus'. Among these early cases are expanded, unrecurved and generally wide-edged bases in the transept at Evesham (163), the west nave at Ickleton,[187] the east nave of St. Leonard's priory, Stamford, Li, established by 1087,[188] and, not earlier than Henry I, the west tower of Goring priory, Ox (164).[189]

The last-named are bold enough, on the other hand, there is a hesitance, an admixture of feebly rounded (165) or chamfered tops, in the earliest case where the truncated form is dominant in a large structure, the choir and crossing of Thetford priory, begun late in 1107.[190] In the chapter-house the bases are either distinctly chamfered (166) or distinctly not. The nave of Old St. Paul's seems to have used the form after 1108[191] and at Peterborough, as rebuilt from 1116,[192] it is universal (167), allowing for hooded rolls and minor variations (168, 169). From that point until just after mid-century it is the most expected form, the latest attested situations being parts of Wibert's work, at Christ Church, Canterbury,[193] and the infirmary chapel, St. Catherine's, at Westminster (170), ascribed to abbot Laurence, soon after 1159.[194]

The earlier examples show much local variation. In Rutland, at Preston and Braunston, they are expanded, with a short hollow and heavy roll; at Ancaster, Li, which has strange ornaments, the band is extended in eastern fashion and the roll a short quadrant. The same is true of those from bishop Roger's works, arguably among his earlier ones:[195] Old Sarum cathedral (171, 172); St. John's Devizes (173), again by the crossing; the east respond of the nave arcade of Sherborne abbey (174), where they are weighted and slightly rounded as in the crypt of St. Peter's, Oxford (145).[196]

In the raised choir of the last-named (175) the mature, delicate and well balanced form is used, as it is in some, but not all, of the much-cited 'mixed assemblages', which all point to the climacteric of G III, around 1130: it is absent from Portchester, confined to the tower-arch at St. Peter's, Northampton, but conspicuous at Iffley and at Norwich keep (176). At Avening, Gl, it is general except on the portal, which has chamfered tops, both forms closely matching those in Gloucester chapter-house, where they are also used in combination.

Of documented buildings from the 1120s to the 1140s where it is the dominant or only form, Rochester keep, which has it everywhere except on the great arcade (87) and sometimes hooded (177), was begun in 1126;[198] the grand *chevet* of St. Bartholomew's, London (178) cannot be long after the foundation of 1123[199] and is close in detail to the naves of Waltham, Ess (179)[200] and Christchurch, Ha;[201] the chancel of Stow, Li, is ascribed to bishop Alexander, between 1123 and 1148;[202] the nave of Bourne, Li (180)[203] and the Cistercian transept-chapels of Bordesley, Wa (181),[204] are both in foundations of 1138, and the latter at least soon after that. All parts of Lilleshall, Sa (182) that were necessary for the occupation, c. 1146, use the form;[205] so, generally, does the refectory of Dover priory, needed for the Benedictine 'take-over', c. 1136.[206] The nave of her dependency at St. Margaret's, K, somehow privileged during the reorganisation of the 1130s, has bases (183) matched among those in Rochester keep. The same can be said of some primary bases (184, 185) in St. John's hospital, Huntingdon, whose founder, earl David, cannot be other than the king of Scots, who resigned the earldom in 1136.[206]

In the same great generation must surely come Stewkley, Bk,[207] ornamented with discretion, which uses only the truncated form (186), as do the

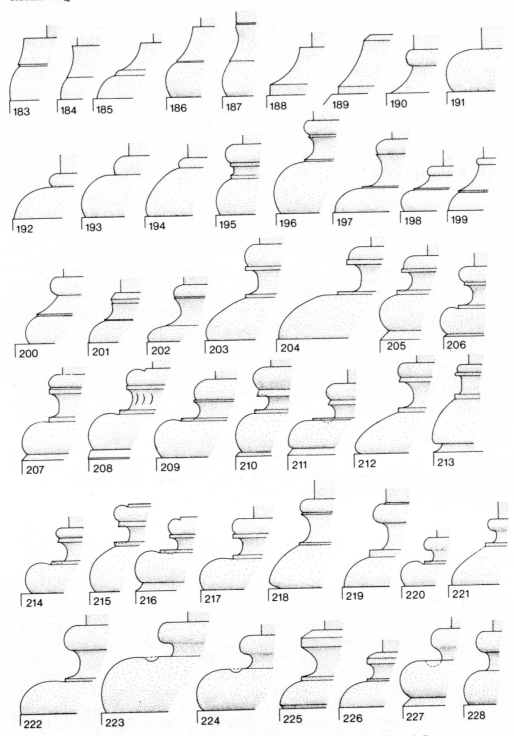

Fig. 7 Romanesque bases. Classes B III, 4 (end), D and E. Scale 1:5.

unexpectedly delicate bases of Tickencote, Ru, which, by contrast, is down-
right vulgar, yet seems to be another work of the Scots earls, David, or his son
Henry (deprived 1141).[208] The same form in secular contexts would suggest
no later an origin for two English stone houses: 'King John's House',
Southampton (187) and the 'Priest's House', Malling, K.[209]

C. SCULPTURAL BASES

Carving, other than mouldings, can almost be ignored as a factor in English
bases, whereas it plays a large part in Deshoulière's survey. A brief fashion
for enrichment in G II and early in G III seldom tries anything more difficult
than dags and cables. In this context the ascription to Ernulf (1114–24) of the
exceptionally delicate ornament, with scalloped hoods and pearls, in the east
claustral range of Rochester becomes acceptable.

I. Zoomorphic Bases

These exotic devices, sometimes supporting moulded bases, are found as
near as the Limousin but hardly known in England. The Prior's door at Ely
had human and animal supporters, now very eroded.[210] The ultimate is a
squashed little lion on the south door at Iffley. The animals at Duxford
(p. 114) are superficial decoration.

II. Cylindrical Bases

Carved drums, foliated or just moulded, are also crude and few. The best
known carry the nook-shafts beneath the inelegant tympanum at Dinton,
Bk.[211]

D. SIMPLIFIED BASES

The changed and chastened temper of English Romanesque after the middle
of the twelfth century is nowhere more sensible than on bases. The truncated
form is already prognostic of this mood, but at the same time as the hint of
nostalgia for the riches of G III, noticed in Wibert's works, and before the fresh
infusion of *disciplina romana* in the 'Attic revival' a home-bred group of bases
appeared which took the 'modified Attic' idiom to its ultimate conclusion in
cultivated simplicity.

I. Hollow Forms

A type-site for these is Denny, Ca, a cell of Ely, laid out on some scale from
c. 1159 and abandoned within ten years to the Templars.[212] The primary bases
in the crossing (188) and nave, matched in Ely parish church, consist of a
single hollow with a fillet or reservation below. A large version was used on
the crossing of Crowland abbey, Li, some time after a fire in 1146,[213] and
the form appears with a deep chamfered top (189) in the chancel at Hemel
Hempstead, Ht. where the nave, not obviously much later, has neo-Attic bases.[214]

A hollow chamfer with an upper roll may first appear at this time, but that in the vault under Canterbury guildhall (190)[215] carries a multiscalloped capital responded to waterleaves which belong with the neo-Attic idiom. There is even a revival of plain truncated cones (class A II), in conspicuous positions, as the arcade at Everton, Bd, matched by an ultimate neo-Attic one (form E II, 4).

II. Convex Forms

A more usual 'simplified' form is the revived double roll (class A IV), rather depressed but sometimes recurved. Even the single roll appears, as in the nave (191) of Blackmore priory, Ess, founded 1152–62.[216] Both forms carry multi-scalloped or waterleaf capitals and clearly endure until late in the century. They fit well with the Cistercian ethos, as in the transept and slype of Stoneleigh, Wa (192), where the church was begun in 1155,[217] but they are also common in parish churches, as at North Leigh, Ox (193). On the west door of Denny abbey which belongs to the phase after c. 1169, when waterleaf first shows there,[218] they are remarkably weighted (194), a reversion to type A VII.

E. THE ATTIC REVIVAL

Neo-Attic bases are readily distinguished from earlier complete sequences by a true concavity in the hollow which, when expanded, soon becomes 'water-holding', and by a return to recurvature on the lower roll, by extending the arc or, more often, and less classically, by a compound curve of two arcs or by a minor arc intersecting the major from below. The lower fillet recovers its classical, vertical position; on 'water-holding' bases it may be turned through a right angle, but yet expose a vertical edge. This elastic, 'mannerist' treatment assumes an easy familiarity with the orthodox form which it hardly ever appears unaltered in England or northern France. The twelfth-century 'renaissances' differ from others by this sort of irreverence. A new set of 'modifications' breaks out almost at once, and in England 'neo-Attic' must comprehend bases that have lost one or other, or both, of their fillets and revel in distortion. Again, the arrangement is typological and the chronology contingent.

I. Tentative Forms

The first appearance of a neo-Attic profile, with both fillets clear and vertical (195) is in the *mélange* at Portchester, chancel and keep. It is an oddity even by Norman standards. In Normandy a correcter Attic can be felt in such bases as those of Fécamp after a fire in 1162 (196), which refine the older idiom but keep the light fillets. Though more curvaceous, they recall the rather timid antiquarianism seen in some works of prior Wibert's age (p. 119) and evidently widespread about the 1160s. The lower edge is attenuated, the upper roll, still small and neat, may intersect the hollow of a quadrant or less, seldom a proper scotia. One of the few relatively bold examples is at

Dunstable (197), second pier from the west. More typical are the chancel-arch of Oxhill, Wa (198), the door to the prior's lodging at Castle Acre (199)[219] and, on a larger scale, reponds in the infirmary at Bury St. Edmunds (200) and in the aisled hall at Warnford, Ha.[220] At Orford, Sf, those on the wall-arcade of the chapel in the keep (201), with an angled upper roll, are from the later 1160s[221] and those in the east nave of the church (202), probably of like date.[222]

II. Mature Forms

1. **With both fillets vertical.** This is the quintessential neo-Attic form, however the rolls and the generally deep hollow are distended. It was complete in central France, as at Sens, by mid-century, but that does not make it usual in Normandy much earlier than in England, nor does it make it 'Gothic'. It appears instead of forms like Fécamp (196) in the choir of Gournay, S.M. (203), probably after a fire in 1172 and with completely Romanesque, finely drilled detail. Christ Church, Canterbury, in 1174 may not have been the first English work of high patronage to use it,[224] but from about that time there was no self-respecting alternative in either country. It is used in St. Frides-wide's, Oxford (204, 205) which was complete and ready for a re-enshrinement by 1181,[225] and its characterises those buildings which, with varying probability, may be counted among those for which the Waverley annalist praised the cosmopolitan Richard of Ilchester, bishop of Winchester, 1173-88.[226] The precise kind of neo-Attic is not clear from the engravings of his Magdalen hospital at Winchester,[227] but both fillets are vertical on the stair-turret at Bishop's Waltham palace (206)[228] and on the east processional door (207) and the cloister-bases of St. Mary Overie, Southwark.[229] A rare enrichment, a row of nicks in the hollow, known earlier from Chartres, appears on the Southwark cloister-bases and also at Norwich, at the cathedral infirmary, built by bishop John of Oxford not before 1175,[232] and at the stone hall called the 'Music House' (208), where they would fit best in the career of its tenant Jurnet just before 1177.[231]

Broad, paired, vertical fillets hardly had time to become acclimatised in England and buildings with them, as the choir of New Shoreham, Sx, look exceptionally French. In the thoroughly English Peterborough they are confined to three piers in the north arcade (209) which precede the completion of the nave by abbot Benedict (1177-94),[223] and the fillets are still rather narrow. They are little wider on the very similar primary bases of Leiston abbey, Sf, founded 1183.[232]

2. **With one or both fillets chamfered.** Where the edge is broad this is a clear reassertion of a radial fillet (usually the upper one only), as at the screen-door of Farnham Castle (210),[234] Graffham, Sx (211), the New Temple, London, dedicated 1185,[235] the nearby tower of St. Bride's,[236] and the south transept at Bardney.[237] This 'impurity' affects England and Normandy alike, with vertical and radial constantly intermingled and with every grade of arc in the

hollow. The narthex at Trie-Château, S.M.(212) which is like the Bardney transept, may be contrasted with a domestic window from the same town (213).[238] In Dover keep, ready by 1186,[239] the upper chapel (214) has both fillets radial, as does the crossing of Lesnes abbey K (215: not long after 1178)[231] and the west nave at Binham; the lower chapel at Dover (216) has both vertical, or rectilinear, as does the nave of Framlingham, Sf. (217).

Narrow fillets, chamfered or not, may be quite persistent, but where both are found, the wider is the later, at Dunstable, where it is confined to the west front. St. Cross, Winchester, has the narrower form on all its untouched bases (218) supporting the tradition that it may be the ultimate work of Henry of Blois, laid out by 1171,[240] rather than another of Ilchester's.

3. **Without a lower fillet.** This early variant is found beside those with upright fillets in the choir at Gournay and the crossing of St. Frideswide's, Oxford. It simply avoids the problem of adapting fillets to water-holding hollows.

4. **Without an upper fillet.** The will to simplify asserts itself so soon that at Peterborough the transition from double but narrow fillets (209) to this form (219) is direct and evidently made in the 1180s, for work complete by 1194. Here it has the regular form, with the upper roll bold and round, which marks the final phase of many English Romanesque churches, such as the west fronts of St. Leonard's, Stamford (220)[241] or Boxgrove,[242] and plentiful isolated features, few precisely dated, such as the portal of Little Snoring, Nf (221). Among secular examples, the hall of Oakham castle, Ru (222) was almost certainly built for Walkelin de Ferrers (d. 1201), perhaps to receive the king, whose release he had negotiated in 1193-4.[243] On the large bases in the west nave of St. Leonard's, Stamford (223), and in Moyses Hall, Bury St. Edmunds (224),[244] the remaining fillet is reduced to a channel, foreshadowing the next variety. In a variant found at Bibury (225) and Ampney Crucis, Gl, and at Compton, Sy (226), under the eastern stage with its Romanesque timber balustrade, the upper roll is squared and remarkably heavy.

5. **With no fillets.** This is the end of the second cycle of simplification. It is used on the arcade at Everton, Bd, and beside another two-storey sanctuary at Darenth, K (227). The last has bases very like those in the guest-house at Dover priory of which a depressed version is on the tower-arch of St. Margaret-at-Cliffe, K, and an upright one on the south-west tower of St. Margaret's, King's Lynn (228). These works, if free and plastic, with such ornaments as 'trumpet-scallops', are purely Romanesque, not 'Early English'. It is arguable that this idiom may have lasted, besides others (the Dover guest-house also has form D II), until the Interdict.

REFERENCES

Abbreviated References. The following denote works cited many times; those marked * are taken, unless specifically excepted, as valid bodies or digests of records (but not of opinions); those marked † as bodies of examples only:

†*AN* V. Ruprich-Robert, *L'architecture normande aux XIe et XII^{e}s. en Normandie et en Angleterre* (1884-9).

An. Mon. *Annales Monastici*, ed. H. R. Luard (R.S., 36, 1865).

†*ASA* H. M. and J. Taylor, *Anglo-Saxon Architecture* (1965).

CAF *Congrès archéologique de France* (sub anno).

ERA A. W. Clapham, *English Architecture after the Conquest* (1934).

GP William of Malmesbury, *Gesta Pontificum*, ed. N. E. S. A. Hamilton (R.S., 52, 1870).

*HKW H. M. Colvin, R. A. Brown, A. J. Taylor, *The History of the King's Works* (1963).

**Mon.* W. Dugdale, *Monasticon Anglicanum*, ed. J. Caley, etc. (1817-30).

*MRH D. Knowles, R. N. Hadcock, *Medieval Religious Houses, England and Wales*, 3rd edn. (1971).

†*NCB* D. F. Renn, *Norman Castles in Britain* (1968).

†*RC* *Inventories* of the Royal Commission on Historical (in Wales, on Ancient) Monuments, under counties.

R.S. Rolls Series.

VCH *Victoria History of the Counties of England*, under counties.

1. As all those shown here have been drawn, except Great Dunham (sketched from ground). For Bardney, Lesnes and Westminster the sources are given in the notes. The writer is indebted to his colleagues for the following, whether reproduced or not:—to A. J. Fleming for Stanton, Bucks., and Wickham, Hants.: to R. Gem for Battle and Sherborne abbeys; to D. Sherlock for Orford church; to P. White for Sherborne castle. All the rest were drawn to full scale by the writer on site, freehand, without a 'comb'.

2. For interest in Vitruvius, especially in Ottonian Germany, cf. W. Oakshott, *Classical Inspiration in Medieval Art* (1959), pp. 69-70.

3. Vitruvius, *De Architectura*, III, v, 1.

4. R. de Lasteyrie, *L'architecture réligieuse en France à l'époque romane* (1912), p. 633.

5. For mouldings as far east as Old Shoreham, Sussex; for running ashlar as far as Canterbury keep: cf. C. F. Hockey, *Quarr Abbey and its Lands* (1970), pp. 2, 59, 118.

6. e.g., Bordesley, Lilleshall, Stoneleigh.

7. *ERA*, pp. 120, 123.

8. *RC, Anglesey* (1937), pp. 119-21.

9. Discussed with E. Gee: the archaic forms (multiple rolls at Richmond keep; Attic at Lastingham) and the neo-Attic forms are much as in the south.

10. Possible exceptions cited include the nave of Norwich cathedral and the chancel of Stewkley, Bk.

11. e.g., on the E. face of the gate-tower at Bury St. Edmunds, and the tower of Iffley, Ox.

12. e.g., at Colchester keep.

13. Relevant to the discussion on Malmesbury, p. 106.

14. *GP*, 69; Eadmer, *Historia Novorum*, ed. M. Rule (R.S. 81, 1884), p. 13; Gervase, *Opera*, ed. W. Stubbs (R.S. 73, 1879-80), ii, p. 368.

15. *Hist. Coenobii Burgensis*, in *Scriptores varii*, ed. J. Sparke (1723), p. 71, tr. W. T. Mallows, *The Peterborough Chronicle of Hugh Candidus* (1949).

16. *An. Mon.*, ii, p. 43.

17. *GP*, p. 206.

18. i.e., the asterisked items in the abbreviated references above.

19. *ERA*, *passim*, usually in footnotes.

20. F. Saxl, *English Sculptures of the 12th Century* (1964), p. 58.

21. *Archaeologia*, lxiv (1912-3), 339-436, exp. p. 401.

22. *GP*, p. 361.

23. *Gesta Regum Anglorum*, ed. T. D. Hardy (1840), ii, p. 637.

24. *Mon.*, ii, p. 611, cf. *VCH, Cambs.*, ii, pp. 211-3.

25. In 1208.

26. *An. Mon.*, ii, pp. 245-6.

27. *ERA*, p. 105.

28. Photograph in C. E. Keyser, *List of Norman Tympana and Lintels* (1927), Fig. 7. The stone has been closely examined. The part with the incised lettering is not a repair from the time of the re-setting, but the semi-circle may have been cut from the bottom at that date. If so, the C^o in relief is an attempt to complete it like the rest, then given up. More probably it was left unfinished at 'MC . . .', and the date completed *c.* 1200. One serif covers the double stroke, which is normal epigraphy, especially *c.* 1200, another the single, and there is room for a second 'X' if it had been needed. The implication is that the stone was pre-cut after 1100, but not before 1110 (?), and completed to read 1114.

29. See note 24.

30. cf. R. W. Billings, *Archit. Illustration and Account of the Temple Church* (1838), p. 28 (before it was re-cut).

31. *Bull. Monumental*, lxxv (1911), pp. 77-101.

32. *AN.*, *passim*; few examples have been personally verified.

33. F. Bond, *Gothic Archit. in England* (1906), p. 694; *English Church Archit.* (1913), ii, pp. esp. 549-51.

34. *ERA*, p. 119-21.

35. P. M. Johnston is especially useful for Sussex examples.

36. Completed in his lifetime: Eadmer, as in note 14.

37. *ASA*, ii, p. 512, Pl. 558.

38. For discussion of the Carolingian origins of reversed capitals, A. Choisy, *Hist. de l'architecture*, ii, p. 170.

39. R. and J. A. Brandon, *Analysis of Gothic Architecture* (1847), Pl. 1.

40. *ASA*, i, pp. 270-1—an archaic. round-towered church.

41. Founded 1105, according to a late and lost source: *VCH, Norfolk*, ii, p. 346.

42. According to a late but probably trustworthy source: *An. Mon.*, iii, p. 342.

43. Whither the convent moved in 1146-7 (*VCH, Norfolk*, ii, pp. 351-2), but cf. *J. Brit. Arch. Ass.*, xxxviii (1882), pp. 167-7, for possible indications of a pre-existing hospital, from which this part might derive.

44. Foundation as dependency of St. Albans, whether or not there was an earlier cell, shortly before 1107 (from the attestations of *Mon.*, iii, p. 345, No. 1): the W. range is considerably later.

45. *AN*, Pl. LXXIII: *CAF*, clxxii (1908), pp. 545-87, for full context.

46. *CAF*, *ut supra*, p. 52.

47. *Ibid.*, pp. 1, 21: *AN*, Pl. LXXV.

48. e.g., Anisy, Hérouville, Tilly-sur-Seules: *AN*, Pls. C, CXVI, 4, CXIV.

49. For the archaic-looking typanum, Keyser, *op. cit*, in n. 28, Fig. 86.

50. *ASA*, ii, 636, Fig. 324.

51. *ASA*, ii, 562, Fig. 274.

52. *ASA*, i, 371, Fig. 168.

53. cf. the steep cones in St. Germain, Auxerre (*Bull. Monument.*, lxxv [1911], p. 85).

54. *ASA*, i, 395, Fig. 179.

55. *ASA*, i, 413, Fig. 191.

56. *ASA*, ii, 272-5: recently disentangled by W. Rodwell's excavations.

57. See R. A. Stalley in *J. Brit. Arch. Ass.*, 3rd ser., xxxiv (1971), pp. 62–83, for an assessment of Roger's patronage, and esp. p. 71, for indications that his work at the cathedral began as late as *c*. 1125.

58. *VCH, Glos.*, ii, p. 122; a late foundation of Henry I, but the context might be the appropriation by Cirencester Abbey in 1155.

59. Certainly conventual; see note 43.

60. *Op. cit.*, in note 15, p. 97. Cleaning in 1976 shows these to have been renewed.

61. *RC, London, i, Westminster Abbey* (1924), Fig. on p. 22.

62. Gocelin,*Translatio S. Augustini*, II, ii, in Migne, *Patrologia Latina*, clv, col. 15. For Mont St. Michel, cf. *AN*, Pl. xlviii, 79.

63. Complete by 1087: *Chronicon de Bello*, ed. J. S. Brewer (1846), pp. 26, 37. The surviving detail was noticed by R. Gem.

64. *ASA*, i, pp. 115–7. The form also occurs at Kirkdale, Y (*ibid.*, i, p. 360, Fig. 160), which is pre-Conquest if the inscription is integral.

65. *An. Mon., ii, p.32.*

66. R. Martin du Gard, *L'abbaye de Jumièges* (1909); details not very clear, but cf. Fig. 11, and *AN*, p. 120.

67. Mixed with Attic forms: *Bull. Monumental*, xcv (1936), pp. 181–201.

68. See note 47: *AN*, i, 120, Pl. xlvi, cites 'conique' *and* 'double talus' at the abbaye aux Dames only.

69. *AN*, i, p. 214, Fig. 272; *CAF*, clxxii (1908), pp. 373.

70. *CAF, ut supra*, p. 244.

71. *AN*, i, 185, Fig. 218 (misdated: it was probably built by abbot William de Ros).

72. See note 62.

73. See note 36: though not strictly documented, it is possible that the infirmary too was a late work of Lanfranc.

74. *HKW*, i, p. 31; the archaeological argument for a widening of the door is not entirely convincing. Is it prompted by an assumption that the door must be 12th century?

75. Not documented. Is it an independent royal work of the Conqueror?

76. *Arch. J.*, lxxix (1922), p. 17, Fig. 2–3;

77. *AN*, Pl. CXXIII, A.

78. For the simple, chequered tympanum, Keyser, *op. cit.*, in n. 28, Fig. 33.

79. It was granted to Lewes priory before 1130: *Sussex Arch. Coll.*, lxviii (1927), but the spurs suggest No. 200, below.

80. As at Bully and Biéville: *AN*, Pls. CI, XL, B.

81. *ASA*, ii, p. 486, Fig. 237.

82. *Mon.*, vi, 1270. This detail, internal, at the west end, was noted by P. Kidson in his recent survey.

83. *ASA*, i, p. 457, Fig. 219.

84. *ASA*, ii, p. 582, Fig. 288.

85. v. note 36.

86. On a rich manor, the only holding of the honour of L'Aigle in Surrey: *VCH, Surrey*, iii, p. 61.

87. *RC, Essex*, i, Pl. opp. p. 83.

88. A chapelry on the great archiepiscopal fee of Aldington.

89. *ASA*, ii, pp. 578–80.

90. e.g., Holtalen, Trøndelag (A. Bugge, *Norwegian Stave-churches* [1953], Pl. 31); for a grooved campaniform base (as at Isleham, *v.i.*) cf. Hoprekstad (*ibid.*, Pl. 20).

91. Chronology discussed, with plan during excavation, by R. Gilyard-Beer in *Proc. Suffolk Inst. of Archaeol.*, xxxi (1970), pp. 256–62.

92. *An. Mon.*, ii, p. 37.

93. Insufficient reason to ascribe the church to the priory there, as in *Proc. Cambr. Antiq. Soc.*, xi (1907), p. 181, and *Arch. J.*, cxxiv (1967), pp. 228–9.

94. A presumably Augustinian foundation, hardly older than 1121, existed when, and

for some eight years after, it was granted to Gloucester, *c.* 1138: *Hist. et Cartul. S. Pet. Glouc.*, ed. W. Hart (R.S. 93, 1863), i, pp. 113, 224.

95. *ASA*, i, p. 158, citing the long-assumed view that they are separate builds. The unity was noticed by T. P. Smith and verified by myself. Associated bases are weighted Attic.

96. *ASA*, i, pp. 424-8, Fig. 201. The beast-ornaments are probably post-conquest.

97. *GP*, pp. 136-7. It would be circular to argue from bases alone against the contention (cf. *Arch. J.*, lxxxi [1930], pp. 188-212) that the west crypt is not primary; with most modern students, I accept the more obvious hypothesis.

98. See note 62.

99. *Med. Arch.*, vi-vii (1962-3), pp. 67-108, esp. 74-8 (Fig. 35, 4 only shows the secondary working; the primary was uncovered on the suggestion of R. Gem).

100. A twin-cell, with Linton, of St. Jacut-de-la-Mer; cf. *Arch. J.*, cxxiv (1967), pp. 253-4 and, for the thin documentation, *VCH, Cambs.*, ii, p. 314.

101. cf. *The first Register of Norwich Cathedral Priory*, Nf. Record Soc., xi (1930), ed. H. W. Saunders, pp. 32-3, 36-7, 52-3.

102. *ASA*, ii, pp. 509-10; *VCH, Herts.*, ii, pp. 252-3.

103. Presumably that which a late but apparently internal source, *Leland's Collectanea*, ed. T. Hearne (1774), i, p. 242 mentions as rebuilt 'by 1020, where the order of annals suggests emendation to 1120.

104. cf. *J. Brit. Arch. Ass.*, 3rd ser., xxxv (1929), pp. 102-211.

105. *Chronic. de Evesham*, ed. W. Macray (R.S. 29, 1863), pp. 55, 97; the tower presupposes a transept.

106. *Ibid.*, p. 98; his accession may be as late as 1130.

107. The primary build, begun 1089, was dedicated in 1100 (*Hist. et Cartul. S. Petr. Glouc.*, as in n. 94, pp. 11-12; fires in 1102 and 1122, *ibid.*, 12, 14; *An. Mon.*, i, p. 43) imply neither complete renewal of any part, nor that the church was incomplete in 1100.

108. Undocumented but arguably not long after 1100; for the tympanum, in the 'Winchester' manner, cf. T. D. Kendrick, *Late Saxon and Viking Art* (1948), p. 143.

109. See note 91.

110. Such as those of the cross-hall of the York fortress, one now re-erected outside the Minster,

111. *Anglia Sacra*, ed. G. Wharton (1691), p. 294 (an internal chronicle ending 1277).

112. *Ibid.*, i, p. 613; *Liber Eliensis*, ed. D. J. Stewart (1848), p. 253; the Ely transept was certainly complete by 1106. Castle Acre priory was moved to the present site soon after 1087-9; *Mon.*, v, pp. 46-8.

113. *An. Mon.*, i, pp. 44-5; P. Kidson has recently pleaded the Vitruvian intention. It is the most classical of early Anglo-Norman buildings an any reckoning;

114. *Ang. Sacra.*, as in n. 111, i, p. 560; *GP.*, p. 196. For other remains, cf. *J. Brit. Arch. Asso.*, xlvi (189), pp. 85-94.

115. *v.s.*, note 107. The slype is integral with the choir.

116. *VCH, Hants.*, ii, pp. 126 ff; no building-reference for this period.

117. Now rather patched, cf. *VCH, Sussex*, ii, p. 56.

118. *VCH, Dorset*, ii, p. 109, n. 22. The evidence that bishops Hugh (d. 1085) and Maurice (d. 1107) of London held the minster is tenuous but plausible on historical analogy: the bases may indicate their work.

119. Granted by the Confessor; *VCH, Sussex*, ii, pp. 121-2.

120. See p. 103.

121. *Arch. J.*, lxx (1912), pp. 69-82, with generally good drawings but the door-bases are inaccurate, showing them as double rolls, when in fact they are sturdy, recurved Attic with chamfered edges.

122. *Sussex Arch. Coll.*, xcix (1961), pp. 38-65, Pl. V, a, b (but no drawn profiles).

123. *ASA*, i, pp. 217-221.

124. *GP*, p. 138: Eadmer, as in note 14.

125. For untouched but fire-damaged early work on the concealed side of the choir-triforium, see *Sussex Arch. Coll.*, cxi (1973), pp. 20–25.

126. *v.s.*, n. 112.

127. *Chron. Barthol. Cotton Mon. Norvic.*, ed. Luard (R.S. 16, 1859), p. 4. The completion of the apse with its *synthronon* was requisite for the long-planned removal.

128. See pp. 105, 118.

129. *Mon.*, iii, p. 162.

130. *ASA*, i, pp. 400–1.

131. When most of the endowments were transferred to the new priory. The occasion for the splendid rebuilding of the old minster is uncertain: much of the eastern arm remained until *c.* 1880 and is recorded in plan but not in detail (*Arch. Cant.*, iv (1861), pp. 1–16, Pl. V; xx (1893), pp. 295–304, Pl. opp. pp. 120, 121); the crossing and unfinished nave have been recently excavated by B. J. Philp.

132. *HKW*, i, p. 39.

133. The first minster in England to adopt the Augustinian rule in the 1090s, sending out colonies in the 1100s and building on a large scale, quickly, in rendered brick: it would hardly be slow in completion.

134. *Mon.*, iii, p. 162; apparently named as *turris S. Iacobi.*

135. *An. Mon.*, ii, p. 218.

136. 'Chronologia Augustinensis' in T. Elmham, *Hist. Mon. S. Augustini Cant.*, ed. G. Chadwick (R.S. 8, 1858), p. 33; this must surely refer to the priory which held the older church, now being excavated by P. J. Tester and the Kent. Arch. Soc. On preliminary examination bases in the transept-apse and chapter-house are consistent with this assumption.

137. He built some part but the church was *iam surgens* under his successor and unfinished even at the Augustinian foundation, *c.* 1150 (*Mon.*, vi, p. 303).

138. The internal chronicle, *An. Mon.*, iii, pp. 14–15, says only *temp.* Henry I, but cf. *MRH*, p. 156, for evidence that it existed by 1125.

139. East end suppressed for incorporation into the great double-armed church of the royal Augustinian refoundation in 1177 (cf. J. C. Dickinson, *Origin of the Austin Canons* [1950], pp. 135-41). The building is otherwise unrecorded, but cf. the plan in *HKW*, i. p. 89.

140. Dickinson, as in note 139, pp. 121, 135. It seems most probable that the priory was not an enlarged hospital but that the two were side-by-side and nearly simultaneous, but it is not certain that the ambitious *chevet* was planned from the beginning.

141. The water-tower, perhaps the treasury, and like adjuncts of the cathedral (cf. *Arch. Cant.*, vii [1868], pp. 4, 74). Some of the detail appears to be re-used.

142. Contains at least two Romanesque phases (cf. *Arch. J.*, cxxvi (1969), pp. 214-5), but the dominant ornament seems too early for the 1190s, the earliest possible date for the small alien priory, assuming it used the church.

143. i.e., the free-standing chapel, recently excavated, east of the great church that appears to imitate Cluny, for whatever purpose. It is perhaps exotic in detail too. Discussed with W. E. Godfrey.

144. cf. *VCH, Northants*, iii, pp. 34, 56, *HKW*, ii, p. 750. Though not mentioned before 1200, the church was in dispute between the Clunaic priory, founded by 1100 by Simon of Senlis, lord of the castle, and the King, who obtained the castle before 1130 and held it until his death, when Simon II regained it.

145. See note 103.

146. *HKW*; i, pp. 29–31.

147. See note 107.

148. Passed to St. Frideswide of Oxford when the Honour of Robert d'Oilly was stripped and possibly due to his patronage. Descriptions in *J. Brit. Arch. Ass.*, xlvii (1891), pp. 132–4 (where the Association is asked to settle *once for all* whether it is Norman or Saxon!).

149. *VCH, Rutland*, ii, pp. 230, 275; castle held of the bishop of Lincoln.

150. No real documentation, but a strong tradition, e.g., in Stowe, assigned this privileged church to the Conqueror; see *Med. Arch.*, iv (1960), p. 143.

151. For documentation of the principal contexts see notes to their more generalised bases.

152. A classic motte-and-bailey (*NCB.*, p. 128) on a Vere tenure (Round and Fox in *Trans. Essex Arch. Soc.*, new ser., xvi (1923), p. 138).

153. *ASA.*, ii, pp. 536-9.

154. See Note 44.

155. *ASA*, i, pp. 278-9.

156. There are apparently three builds—east and west of the axial tower, and the W. front.

157. cf. notes 44 and 148. They would appear to mark a campaign following fairly soon after that probably to be assigned to *c.* 1107.

158. Attestations (*Mon.*, iii, p. 330; *MRH*, p. 81) put the foundation-charter precisely in 1107 (again, cf. n. 44). The nave may have been completed in the 1130s.

159. See note 43.

160. The top storey suggest a completion rather than just a reconstruction. The dating is circumstantial but accords with Albini's marriage to the queen dowager. cf. *NCB.*, p. 43.

161. Rival convents disputed (and added to?) the same buildings between 1131 and 1139, when the colonisation from Christ Church was complete: Gervase, *Opera*, (as note 14, i, pp. 96-9, ii, p. 287-9.

162. Again, circumstantial; the bishop held the church and 6 hides of the parish; *VCH, Hants,* iii, pp. 65, 75.

163. See note 146.

164. See note 127: this part too should antedate the removal;

165. Detached from a window-jamb, but hardly deriving from the standing castle.

166. See note 99.

167. The ambitious east end of an ill-documented chapelry: archaic in detail, but perhaps a forerunner of the Portchester-Yaverland manner.

168. The double scotia is a well-known classical usage. Palladio, in the Redentore of Venice, no doubt citing a Roman precedent, combines it with a single-scotia base on a higher stylobate so that the roll of this runs level with the lower scotia of the other, implying equivalence if not actual conversion.

169. See note 15.

170. Part of one west tower survives, undocumented. I owe the details to W. E. Godfrey.

171. Ordericus Vitalis, *Hist. Eccl.*, ed. A. le Prevost (1838, ff.), xii, ch. 46; J. M. Besse, *Abbayes et Prieures de l'anc. France*, vii (1914), p. 86, is inadequate.

172. Presumably complete at his fall: *Gesta Stephani*, ed. R. Howlett (in R.S. 82, 1886), iii, pp. 49, 53. See also *op. cit.* in note 57, pp. 65-8.

173. *VCH, Hants.*, iii, p. 159.

174. A possession of St. Florent, Saumur, under the exalted Braose patronage; plan in *Arch. J.*, cxvi (1959), p. 245.

175. See note 94.

176. *William Thorne's Chronicle*, tr. A. M. Davis (1934), pp. 63, 67.

177. Bishop Henry obtained the manor by exchange in 1136: *VCH, Hants.*, iii, p. 42.

178. *VCH, Oxon.*, v, p. 191. At the relevant time it was a chapelry of Cowley, *ibid.*, p. 201. It looks like a private effort. Contrast *RC, City of Oxford* (1939), p. 151.

179. *MRH*, p. 154, a fair summary of an ill-documented issue.

180. cf. *Arch. J.*, lxviii (1911), p. 203.

181. *op. cit.* in note 57, pp. 81-3, for a suggestion that St. John's is after Roger. But it is parcel of his new borough, it not a unitary building, and, in part, looks *earlier* than his greater works.

182. H. of Huntingdon, *Hist. Anglorum*, ed. T. Arnold (R.S. 74, 1879), pp. 244, 159; implying it was probably complete by 1122, certainly by 1136.

183. cf. *GP*, p. 324, and *VCH, Cambs.*, iv, p. 50, but no absolute dating.

184. *Arch. J.*, lxxxvi (1929), pp. 213–223, Fig. 1.

185. A Vere tenure, but otherwise undocumented.

186. Both Waltham and Wolvesey were begun in 1135 or soon after: *An. Mon.*, ii, p. 51. Waltham was dismantled *c.* 1155 except the chapel, which has the peculiar 'ribbon' flintwork of the earliest work at Wolvesey.

187. See note 93.

188. A cell of Durham, quite large but afterwards run down.

189. *VCH, Oxon.*, ii, 103–4.

190. i.e., before the death of Roger Bigod, to be occupied in 1114 (see note 42); the chapter-house may be after 1114.

191. So it seems from Hollar's sensitive engraving.

192. See note 15.

193. See note 141;

194. W. R. Lethaby, *Westminster Abbey re-examined* (1925), p. 28, citing evidence that it was complete by 1163.

195. See Note 57.

196. See note 180.

197. A dependancy of Minchinhampton, so ultimately of the 'Dames' of Caen. *Tr. Bristol and Glos. Arch. Soc.*, xliii (1921), pp. 180–90.

198. See note 132.

199. See note 140.

200. Apparently of one build with the crossing and suppressed apse: see note 138, and esp. plan in *HKW*, i, p. 89.

201. Apparently structurally after the crossing: see note 137.

202. cf. *op. cit.* in note 57, p. 67; I have found no confirmation of the essentially likely tradition that Alexander built at Stow.

203. An Arroasian abbey: *VCH, Lincs.*, ii, p. 177.

204. *VCH, Worcs.*, ii, p. 151.

205. The convent was moved from elsewhere: *VCH, Salop.*, ii, pp. 70–71.

206. Later the Grammar school; it contains a second Romanesque phase; *VCH, Hunts.*, p. 397 (note 1).

207. *VCH, Bucks.*, iii, p. 426. Robert of Gloucester and Reginald of Dunstanville both had an interest in the parish under Henry I. The church is *not* to be explained by its subsequent gift to Kenilworth priory.

208. *VCH, Rutland*, ii, pp. 275 ff.; part of the Honour of Huntingdon.

209. M. E. Wood, *The English Medieval House* (1965), pp. 11–15 (Southampton, which she indeed dates early), and p. 346 (Malling, briefest notice).

210. G. Zarnecki, *Early Sculpture of Ely Cathedral* (1958), pp. 23 ff., Pls. 79, 80.

211. *RC, Bucks.*, i, pp. 123–4.

212. *Liber Eliensis*, as in note 112, pp. 387 ff.

213. *VCH, Lincs.*, ii, 107.

214. A new town on the manor of Berkhampstead, in existence by 1167–8; *VCH, Herts.*, ii, p. 217.

215. *Arch. Cant.*, lxxxiii (1968), pp. 2–11, Figs. 1, 3.

216. *MRH*, p. 148, pp. 11, 39, 42 (concerning the *same* building).

217. *MRH*, p. 216.

218. *VCH, Cambs.*, ii, p. 259. Recent examination has shown that the nave was completed on a plan shorter than that laid out under Ely; cf. note 212.

219. The similar bases in the Thetford prior's lodging have been shown to be re-set.

220. M. E. Wood, *op. cit.* in note 209, pp. 11, 36–40 (the same building): circumstances suggest soon after 1180, rather than as *Arch. J.*, cxxiii (1966), p. 190.

221. *HKW*, ii, 769–70. The biggest expense was in 1165–7.

222. All part of royal encouragement of the borough: cf. *Arch. J.*, cviii (1952), pp. 148–50.

223. L. Regnier, *Gournay-en-Bray et Saint Germer* (Caen, 1903), pp. 32–5: the extensive

fire was caused by an attack on Henry II, but it is admitted that the rebuilding is not explicitly connected with it.

224. Recent excavation has shown that the new work in the choir of St. Augustine's, after a fire in 1168, was almost as advanced: details not yet worked out. *Op. cit.* in note 176, p. 94.

225. *VCH, Oxon.*, pp. 97-8.

226. See note 16.

227. *Vetusta Monumenta*, iii (1796), pp. 1-12, Pls. I, II, III.

228. The rebuilding, after Henry of Blois, was complete enough in 1194 for a royal council to be held there: R. of Hoveden, *Chronica*, ed. W. Stubbs (R.S. 51, 1868-71), iii, p. 250.

229. *Arch. J.*, lxxi (1914), pp. 155 ff. for the bases from the cloister, which was destroyed by fire in 1212; one processional door remains.

230. *Op. cit.* in note 101, pp. 82-83, with a suggestion that it is *after* 1183.

231. V. D. Lipman, *The Jews of Medieval Norwich* (1967), pp. 27-32, 96-99. M. E. Wood, *op. cit.* in note 209, pp. 5-6, 19-20. A slightly later date is possible.

232. cf. note 15.

233. Re-set on the present site in 1380; *MRH*, p. 190.

234. Presumably another work of Richard of Ilchester.

235. See note 30.

236. W. F. Grimes, *The Exploration of Roman and Medieval London* (1960), pp. 182-97, and Pl. 84-6, which shows a form that might be still 'tentative'. An exact profile is needed.

237. *Arch. J.*, as in note 76, pp. 21, 23, Figs. 3, 4.

238. The window is in the Victoria and Albert Museum.

239. A. W. Clapham, *Lesnes Abbey* (1915), esp. Pls. ix, xi, xii.

240. Only a fragment, in the sacristy, remains of Henry's first building, *c.* 1137. The rest is a complete and extensive rebuilding, ready for a doubling of the hospitality in 1185 (*MRH*, p. 404), but Henry was always honoured as the sole founder.

241. See note 188.

242. See note 117.

243. *VCH, Rutland*, ii, pp. 8-11.

244. M. E. Wood, *op. cit.* in note 209, pp. 5-6, 19, 32.

Usk Castle and its Affinities

by

J. K. KNIGHT

USK CASTLE[1] overlooks the present town of Usk and the site of the Roman *Burrium* which lie below it in the floodplain of the River Usk (Pl. V). *Burrium*[2] occupied a strategic keypoint where the Usk valley, a major route into the interior of Wales, is joined by an overland route from the English midlands, both being followed by Roman roads. After Hastings, William fitz Osbern was given the task of subduing this area, which had given the English so much trouble in the reign of the Confessor. He overran most of Gwent between the Wye and the Usk and sometime before his death in 1071 divided the tithes of his lands *'inter Waiam et Oscham'* between the abbeys of Lyre and Cormeilles, south-west of Rouen.[3] William died in 1071 and his son, Roger, forfeited his lands in 1075. At the time of the Domesday Survey, Thurstin fitz Rolf held extensive estates between the Usk and the Wye and beyond the Usk,[4] which must correspond broadly both with Fitz Osbern's lands between the two rivers and with the later lordship of Usk. The two keys to the control of this area are Raglan, at its centre, and Usk, on its southern boundary, and the latter was probably already occupied, if not fortified, at this date.

Thurstin apparently died without issue, for about 1115 the lordship of Striguil, including Usk, was granted by the king to Walter de Clare, and in 1138 the first documentary reference to Usk castle occurs.[5] In 1173 money was spent provisioning 'the Castle of Usk, which the men of Earl Richard [de Clare] hold against the Welsh',[6] and in the following year the Welsh, under Hywel ap Iorwerth, lord of Caerleon, seized it. Richard de Clare died in 1176. Hywel was still alive, allied to the king and with his seizure of Usk apparently regularised, in 1183,[7] but shortly afterwards the castle was betrayed to the Normans and Hywel mortally wounded in the assault.[8] In 1185, Usk was in royal hands, the king spending £10 3s. on repairs to the castle and to the houses in it, the garrison then comprising ten sergeants, ten archers, four watchmen and a flying squad of fifteen 'mobile' sergeants.[9] These entries, restored to Usk in 1947 by Arnold Taylor after having been attached to Chepstow by J. H. Round[10] contain a hint that the twelfth-century keep at Usk (Pl. VIa) may date from *post* 1185, for they refer to the *'turris et castellum'* of Chepstow, but only to the *'castellum'* of Usk. Historically the possible dates for the keep are before Hywel's seizure of 1174 (and Gilbert's death in 1176) or after 1189, when the de Clare heiress married William Marshall. If the latter dating is correct, the keep provides a surprising contrast to such innovating works usually attributed to 1190s as the Longtown (Herefordshire) keep or William Marshall's additions to Chepstow, if these are correctly dated, but the wording may reflect only the relative importance of the two castles and, the keep may date to the time of the de Clares, before 1174.

The Earthwork Castle and the Norman Keep *(Figs. 1–3)*

Before the building of this keep, the castle consisted of a sub-rectangular scarped and ditched enclosure forming a flat plateau 300 ft. by 250 ft., though subsequent erosion on the north-western side has given it a more irregular shape. Most of this plateau is now occupied by the Inner Ward of the later stone castle. On all sides save one the ground drops steeply away, but on the north, where Castle Hill continues as a ridge of high ground, the castle is protected by an outwork covering its northern front. Opposite this, on the south, is a rectangular outer ward in the area of the present house and gardens, which lie below the Inner Ward at the foot of a short but steep scarp. This outer ward was walled in stone in the fourteenth century, but may already have existed, in the form of an earthwork, in the early days of the castle. The same plan recurs in other early castles of the area, notably at White Castle. As at White Castle, the Usk barbican was left outside the later stone defences, since the line of access, originally across the barbican, had been altered when the stone castle was built.

The keep still stands to its full height at the western corner of the Inner Ward. It is trapezoid in plan and much altered by successive rebuildings, though there is no doubt that the irregular plan is original. Its interior has been remodelled more than once: it was heightened by some 8 ft. in the fourteenth century and its north wall was entirely rebuilt in the fifteenth, but in its original form it consisted of a three-storey tower 31 ft. by 33 ft. square in average dimensions, and some 31 ft. high. Its date, as we have seen, probably lies before 1174.

Its lowest storey is an unlit basement with no original external access. Entry to the upper floors would have been by way of a stair from the inner ward, though the original first floor door, at the south end of the west wall, has been destroyed by a later enlargement. No original features survive at first floor level, but on the floor above two blocked round-headed double-splay windows remain in the south wall, and there is a third, also blocked, in the centre of the east wall. They have unchamfered ashlar rear arches and those in the south wall have recessed window surrounds in a yellow (Triassic) sandstone, which contrasts with the red Devonian sandstone dressings of all other periods. A door at first floor level in the western end of the south wall is a renewal of the early thirteenth century, when the projecting latrine block to which it leads was added against the keep, but it may originally have served the stair to the upper floor of the keep and perhaps also an earlier latrine.

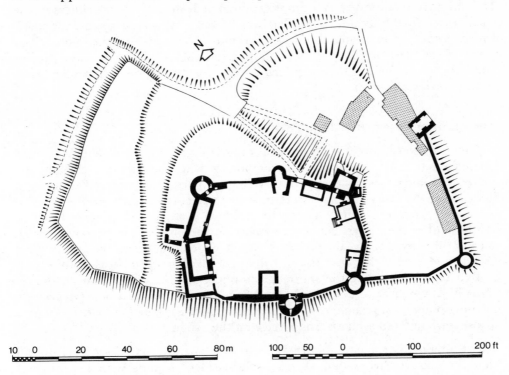

Fig. 1 Usk Castle. General plan.

The keep projects from the line of the later curtain over the scarp down to the inner ward. Outside the curtain, its base is buttressed by a massive sloping plinth of large squared blocks, cut through on the east by the approach to an inserted ground floor door to the keep. This plinth is probably a later addition. Medieval alterations to the keep are dealt with below, in their chronological contexts.

The Castle of William Marshall the Elder (Fig. 2)

The next phase of the castle's building history transformed it from an earthwork with a stone tower into a major castle. The inner ward was enclosed with a curtain wall of sandstone rubble, running in straight lengths to enclose an area which, though strictly speaking octagonal, is perhaps better regarded as a rectangle, its corners set towards the cardinal points[11] and its sides angled outwards into shallow echelons, multiplying its four faces into eight. At each of the four corners was a tower, the western one being the twelfth-century rectangular keep, the others round. At the south-western angle is a higher and more massive round tower, known in the thirteenth century as 'the round tower of the castle'[12] and today as the Garrison Tower. The entrance to the ward is a simple pointed arch through the thickness of the curtain, set directly opposite the Garrison Tower, close to the north-west angle, which carries a fourteenth-century half-round tower covering the approach at close range. The north-west and south-west angles of the curtain project unprotected to the field, though the former has an added rectangular tower of the fourteenth century.

The Garrison Tower *(Pl. VIb and Fig. 4)*

The Garrison Tower, of four storeys, with an added corbelled out and battlemented top is otherwise contemporary with the adjacent curtain, the angled quoining linking the two surviving in part. It is entered at ground floor level by way of an inserted late thirteenth-century doorway with bull-nosed (quarter round) jambs, from which a short wall passage leads to the foot of a spiral stair set in the angle between tower and curtain, though because of alterations in the ground level since medieval times, the ground now rises to the level of the first floor of the tower within a few yards of this door, so that seen from inside the ward, the tower appears one floor shorter than it actually is. Opposite the inserted entrance, a second, similar door, gives access to the ground floor chamber. This inner door is set in an earlier, wider, opening whose unchamfered ashlar jambs survive on the inside.

The original entrance is above the inserted one, at first floor level, its sill eight feet above the ground. A tall round-headed opening with two rings of small squarish voussoirs, it would originally have been reached by way of an external wooden stair, probably a vertical two-storey porch, as at Tretower, for a lateral stair would have obstructed one or other of the two openings (a firing slit and a loop lighting the stairs) which flanked it. Both lower floors of the tower are lit by sets of three loops, with round-headed unchamfered rear arches, which emerge as long firing slits with serifed bases. Similar slits occur on the two towers at Chepstow attributed to William Marshall the Elder. One of the first floor set is angled to open inside the curtain, covering the approach to the tower. Another of the same set has an altered splay, its inner part narrowing inwards, with substantial jambs of standstone blocks.

The spiral stair continues to the second floor landing, which is lit by a loop similar to those below, but shorter, set directly above the entrance door. From this landing, two passages run along the inner face of the tower, to the wall walk of the curtain wall, through two late thirteenth-century rectangular doors with chamfered surrounds, but there was probably no original direct access between tower and curtain. The western passage curves round in the thickness of the wall to a garderobe chamber which discharges on the outside of the tower through a projecting garderobe chute of ashlar, also added in the late thirteenth century. From close inside the eastern door to the wall-walk, a curving wall-stair with lintelled roof rises to the top floor and to the roof. On the second floor, as on the first, one of the windows has been altered, but here the opening is enlarged to a broad lancet and the remodelled splay, which, like that below, narrows inwards on the interior, has been given a low two-centred rear arch.

The levels of the first and second floors are marked externally by chamfered offsets of ashlar, that of the third floor by a ring of beam holes, for a projecting wooden hourd or gallery, like that which still survives at Laval (Mayenne).[13]

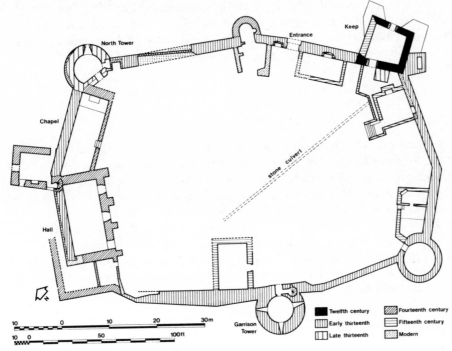

Fig. 2 Usk Castle. Plan of inner ward.

Similar rings of beam holes survive at Pembroke, Caldicot and several French round keeps,[14] and at Pembroke there are also vertical beam holes, encased in stonework, marking the rear face of the hourd.[15] Usually there is little evidence whether tower and hourd were roofed together or were structurally independent, though at Pembroke the stone vault which roofs the keep is surrounded by a rainwater drain, suggesting that here the hourd was roofed separately. A single firing slit, blocked internally by an added fireplace, remains at this level. Its fellows were perhaps enlarged to produce the inserted windows of this upper floor. On the inner face of the tower, immediately above the entrance door and the slit above it, is a rectangular blocked door, the lower part of one of its ashlar jambs remaining, presumably giving access to the hourd. Built into its blocking is a window with pointed trefoiled head. There is a second patch at the head of the stairs, also with a window built into it, but this is of irregular shape and shows no sign of replacing an earlier opening.

The upper floor was remodelled in the late thirteenth century. The external door was blocked, the tower heightened by three courses of yellow sandstone and a corbelled out and battlemented top. A hooded fireplace with joggled lintel and three windows with trefoiled heads were added, one window in the filling of the blocked door opening. The stair head landing also received a window, but this has a simple pointed head and is on a slightly different sill level, so that is probably not exactly contemporary. The added windows, fireplace and bull-nosed jambs, find parallels in the work carried out for Gilbert de Clare, at Caerphilly *post* 1271, and there is documentary evidence that in 1289 work was in progress on the alteration of the windows of the Garrison Tower.

The Entrance and Mural Towers

The gateway to the inner ward (Pl. VIIa), a simple archway through the curtain, is surprisingly simple for the entrance to a major castle, but can be paralleled at Chepstow, where the entry to William Marshall's castle was by way of a very similar arch, covered at short range by a mural tower, just as the (later) north-west tower at Usk covers the entrance at a range of 20 ft. The Usk gateway has a pointed and chamfered outer arch with one tongue and bar stop (which can be paralleled, e.g., in King John's work at Corfe) and with a portcullis slot behind. The rear part of the passage is slightly wider than the outer and the rear arch chamfered but unstopped. There is little trace of the chamber above the gate.

Of the three early thirteenth-century corner towers, little remains. The north tower was totally rebuilt by Gilbert de Clare shortly before 1289, and the east tower was replaced in the fourteenth century by the service end of the hall block. Of the southern tower, only rear door and foundations remain.

Seen from the foot of the scarp the Garrison Tower is impressive, with a battering base and a series of ashlar chamfered offsets punctuating its considerable height. There are the blocked remains of two or more firing slits in the curtain between the Garrison Tower and the south tower, suggesting a regular series which would have supplemented the series of long serif-based slits in the tower. The defences of the new castle must have been complete by 1233, when they withstood siege by Henry III, during the latter's quarrel with Richard Marshall. Richard made terms with the king, including a *pro forma* surrender of the castle as a sop to the royal dignity, but when Henry was slow in returning the 'borrowed' castle, Richard re-took it.

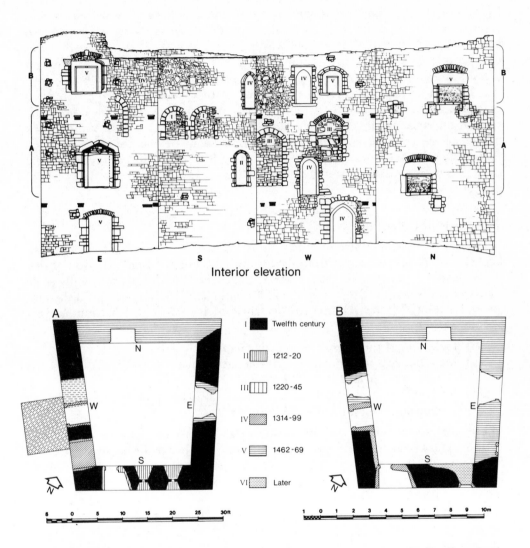

Interior elevation

Fig. 3 Usk Castle. Plans and internal elevations of twelfth-century Keep. A: first floor level,
B: upper floor.

The First Remodelling of the Norman Keep *(Fig. 3)*

During the time of the younger Marshalls (1219–1245), the interior of the
Norman keep was remodelled as a two-storey chamber block, the two upper
floors being thrown into one. This work is later than the remodelled door to
the latrine block which was added against the keep when the curtain was
built and its own door was blocked when the keep was again remodelled in

the early fourteenth century. The original entrance to the keep was replaced by one over 10 ft. high in the same position and a large and broad window was inserted beside it. Both have unchamfered ashlar surrounds with two-centred heads, though that of the window was later renewed. The style and character of the openings recalls the rectangular tower built by one of the younger Marshalls at the south-west corner of the upper ward at Chepstow[16] and both the Usk and Chepstow blocks consist of a lofty room with large windows over a high basement. Both were obviously intended to provide accommodation of importance, and Perks has suggested that the Chepstow chamber block might be the *camera comitisse*—the retiring room of the countess—referred to in 1271–2. A domestic use by the lord or his family (in preference to the spartan accommodation provided by the Garrison tower at this date) seems probable at Usk.

The Castle of Gilbert de Clare

In 1245, Anselm Marshall, the last of William's five sons, died and Usk became the head of a separate lordship under Richard de Clare, the son of one of William's daughters. Richard was succeeded in 1262 by his son, Gilbert de Clare 1st. A Minister's Account of 1289 relating to Usk has been published by Arnold Taylor.[17] Items relating to the fabric of the castle may be summarised as follows:

   (i) lock bought for door of the castle chapel.
  (ii) lock bought for the door of 'the new tower where the Lord Earl's treasure is placed for safe keeping'.
(iii) 'for altering the windows of the Round Tower of the castle, let to contract to John Mayel by writ, 7 s.'.

These correspond neatly to the main works of this period now to be seen in the extant remains: the north angle-tower which can be identified as the 'new tower', alterations to the access and windows of the Garrison Tower (the 'Round Tower' of the castle); and the insertion of a new chamber on its upper floor. The chapel mentioned cannot be the present chapel, which is later, and the key must have been for its now vanished predecessor.

The North Tower

The D-shaped North Tower is of late thirteenth-century date and is probably the 'new tower' built shortly before 1289, in which Gilbert de Clare's treasure was stored. There are two ground floor doorways. One, obviously recent, cuts through its outer face, largely destroying a cruciform firing slit. The other, with renewed stop chamfered jambs, leads from the inner ward. In the south-east corner of the tower, a latrine chamber is contrived in the angle between tower and curtain and is lit by a slit covering the approach to the entrance. Above the slit, at first floor level, is a squinch arch recalling contemporary work at Caerphilly.

At first floor level, cruciform firing slits cover the north-east curtain, but the surviving slits are all in the eastern half of the tower, and others must have been lost in an extensive refacing of the western half which has left its mark in a prominent series of external putlog holes. The first floor, reached from the ward by a stone stair, was a well appointed chamber. Its entrance has bull-nosed jambs like those in the Garrison Tower[18] and is one of a trio of openings set in the flat rear wall at this level. That in the centre is a fireplace resting on three corbels and with a head of three joggled blocks, the centre corbel being a re-used impost with dog-tooth decoration. On the opposite side, the door is matched by a now much ruined window recess. The symmetry is increased by a pair of attached shafts set in the inner sides of window and door, emphasising the tripartite division of the wallspace. Of the upper (second) floor, very little survives, but the brothers Buck in 1732 (Pl. V) show the North Tower standing to its full height, with a corbelled out top like that on the Garrison Tower. Two openings are shown in the upper floor, one a cruciform slit covering the west curtain.

The work of Gilbert de Clare at Usk forms part of an enormous programme of castle building which he was carrying out in these years, but emphasis was shifting away from lesser castles like Usk to the major strategic fortresses like Caerphilly or the abortive Llangybi.[19] The alterations to the Garrison Tower were domestic rather than military and the other major work, the North Tower is referred to as the tower where the Lord Earl's treasure (i.e., revenue?) is stored for safe keeping. With such an expensive programme of building on hand, the collection of revenue would loom large in the affairs of Usk lordship and its castle in those years.

The Fourteenth Century—Elizabeth de Burgh and the Earls of March

Gilbert de Clare II, was killed at Bannockburn in 1314, Usk passing to his sister, Elizabeth de Burgh. In 1322–6, it was in the hands of the younger Despenser, but was recovered by Elizabeth on the accession of Edward III, when she proved that she and her child had been held in prison by Despenser at the time of the 'voluntary' exchange. Along the north-west side of the inner ward are a range of domestic buildings which can probably be attributed to Elizabeth de Burgh. They comprise a two-storeyed buttressed hall-block with a square tower on its northern angle, outside the curtain wall, forming a chamber block and a single-storey chapel at the east end of the hall. The household accounts for the Christmas celebrations of 1327 at Usk castle, have survived[20] and the quantities of food consumed make it clear that Elizabeth was in residence with a large household. The details of the chamber block in the square tower are of early fourteenth-century character, and in the 1930s excavation of the chapel produced a sculptured corbel—the head of a long-haired male. My colleague Mr. S. E. Rigold comments[21] that this wears the long 'bobbed' hair with curvilinear curls of the early fourteenth century, rather than the long but straight hair represented by sculptural convention from the mid-fourteenth century onwards. He would date it to *c.* 1325, plus or minus twenty years. It represents a young dandified noble (who wears a fillet) who could be the younger Despenser. It is possible that the range was built by Despenser in 1322–6, though one doubts whether his portrait would have been allowed to remain after Elizabeth had recovered her property. Despenser seems to have been involved in local feuds during his stay at the castle, for in 1322 one of two rival priors of Goldcliff Priory was abducted and carried off to Usk castle, but was freed after paying a ransom.[22] The whole episode was repeated in 1442 with a subsequent prior.

The hall, of three bays, is entered at ground floor level through a door at its lower end with renewed stop chamfered jambs. There are much ruined window openings between the buttresses. At first floor level, the door to the screens passage is set above the entry to the ground floor. There is a large fifteenth-century fireplace in the north wall. The service range lay west of the hall in the area of the western angle tower. It has gone, but its outline is preserved by a masonry revetment wall enclosing it and apparently continuing eastward as a terrace or platform along the north side of the hall. The western gable of this hall block is a prominent feature of the castle ruins as seen from below on the west and appears in Bucks' print.

The chamber block on the north angle of the hall lies outside the curtain. It has a fireplace on each floor and windows with hollow moulded jambs. A spiral stair in the south-west angle gives access between floors and both of the inner angles of the tower contains a postern-like door giving access to the berm outside the curtain. On the west this is in part formed into a terrace by the revetment wall of the service block. The chapel, east of the hall, was excavated in the 1930s. Little detail remains. A similar arrangement occurs in Warkworth Castle, Northumberland,[23] in a range which assumed its present form in the early fourteenth century and is also known at Boulogne.[24]

The Outer Ward

Elizabeth de Burgh died in 1360 and her great granddaughter, Philippa, married Edmund Mortimer, Earl of March. The Earls of March held the lordship from 1368 to 1399, and the outer ward, with its great gatehouse (Pl. VIIb), and the north-west angle tower of the inner ward, can be attributed to them. The gatehouse, an imposing stucture, still inhabited, consists of a vaulted gate passage below, with a single large room over the gate. From the gatehouse, the curtain of the outer ward runs westward to a circular corner tower of two storeys and a basement, both upper floors lit by narrow rectangular slits with recessed rectangular panels in the jambs of the rear arches. The tower is entered through two tall superimposed round-headed doors, the lower with ball-shaped stops. The interior was fitted out at a later date as a Columbarium. From this tower, the curtain of the outer ward returns to the southern angle tower of the inner war, with a small postern gate just before it reaches it.

The north-west angle tower of the inner ward has recessed panels in what remains of its rear entrance door, like those in the windows of the Columbarium tower. Little remains of it, but on the inside, on the side facing the gate, is a semi-circular recess, perhaps for a stair to the upper floor.

The Fourteenth-Century Remodelling of the Keep

With the building of the new Hall early in the fourteenth century, the accommodation inserted by the younger Marshalls in the Norman keep was no longer required. The level of the first floor was lowered and the upper floor was heightened by some 8 ft. in order to accommodate an upper floor, the addition being particularly evident on the west exterior face. New doors to each of the three superimposed rooms were provided on the west, a solid square masonry foundation providing the base for a vertical timber stair to the two upper floors. There are two small rectangular window openings with chamfered surrounds on the upper floor, blocked by the fifteenth-century alterations, but otherwise little detail survives.

These rooms were no doubt intended for members of the household. There is not enough evidence to date them closely, and they could belong to the time of Elizabeth de Burgh or to that of the Earls of March.

The Fifteenth and Sixteenth Centuries

Edmund, the infant fifth Earl of March, on hereditary principles heir to the throne, was kept a prisoner throughout the reign of Henry IV. In 1405, Usk Castle, 'in some measure repaired for defence',[25] probably in response to one of a series of writs issued by the king on 8 September 1403, ordering the owners or constables of twenty-two Welsh castles to look to their furnishing and guard 'with men, victuals, armour, artillery and all other things' in view of the 'Glyndwr revolt'[26] was attacked by a Welsh force led by Gruffyd, son of Owain Glyndwr, which suffered a disastrous defeat, after which three hundred prisoners were massacred near the Castle.[27] When Edmund died, his lands passed to his sister, whose son ascended the throne as Edward IV in 1460. In 1431, William ap Thomas, a new man who had married the heiress of Raglan, was created steward of the lordship. He was to rise high in the service of the house of York and was to be progenitor of the house of Herbert. In a dispute over the election of a prior of Goldcliff in 1441, one candidate was seized at the Priory by a band of eighty armed men belonging to ap Thomas and taken to Usk Castle, where he was kept, chained, Sir William threatening to force him to resign 'even if he were on the high altar of the Priory'.[28]

The north-west wall of the keep was rebuilt at this time from the ground up, presumably after structural failure. The work is characterised by a prominent series of external putlog holes and an identical series occur in the rebuilt western half of the north tower. This rebuilding (of a distinctly non-military character) implies repair after a period of neglect, and its character, taken with the alteration of the upper floors of the keep into a pair of well-appointed chambers, is in keeping with the use of the castle by the Herberts, acting as royal stewards, and by their retainers. The new work in the keep included two large fireplaces in the rebuilt north wall and a large rectangular window, mullioned and transomed, overlooking the outer ward at first floor level, with moulded drip stone and two centred moulded rear arch with small pyramidal stops. The upper floor has two simple rectangular openings. Work of this period elsewhere in the inner ward includes lodgings set against the inner faces of the curtains of the inner ward, several with fireplaces like those in the keep, and a large fireplace in the first floor of the hall.

This work (particularly the large window in the keep) is similar to work at Raglan attributed to Sir William ap Thomas's son, William Herbert, who succeeded his father in 1445, was created Earl of Pembroke in 1468, and executed after the Yorkist defeat at Edgecote in 1469. Under William Herbert Raglan was removed from the Lordship of Usk and elevated into a separate lordship (1465). He was a man of great wealth, with wide interests in commerce and property and a fearsome reputation for the ruthless pursuit of his own interests. In 1457 he was outlawed for robbery, murder and causing grievous bodily harm to the king's subjects. According to his kinsman, Sir Thomas Herbert of Tintern, writing in the seventeenth century, 'so soon as he [Sir William Herbert] was made a Baron' (in 1462) he 'was at great charge in repairing several Castles within his jurisdiction and hereditary seignories of his own'.[29] This statement that he repaired not only his own castles ('hereditary seignories of his own'), but also others of which he was the Constable, is particularly relevant to Usk, which fell within the latter category.

In 1511, Henry VIII reunited the lordship by purchase, but it is doubtful whether the castle, save for the outer gatehouse, the residence of the steward, was occupied after the execution of William Herbert in 1469. When Leland visited 'cairuske' in 1536-9 he noted that 'The castle there hath bene great, stronge and fair', but spoke of it in the past tense.[30] In 1550, the castle was granted to Sir William Herbert, whose family had continued to serve as royal stewards, but when Thomas Churchyard saw it in 1587 it had been long in ruins.[31]

The Date of Usk Castle

Usk seems to belong to the period when the new models of fortification of the early thirteenth century were still novel on the March and their lessons not yet fully learnt. The wall passage in the ground floor of the Garrison Tower (repeated at Longtown) was a potential weakness which a later builder would probably have avoided and two angles of the Norman keep, as well as two of the angles of the curtain wall, were left projecting to the field unprotected. These weaknesses may have been theoretical rather than practical, but a hand more practised in the new modes of fortification would probably have avoided them. The clearest indication, however, of Usk's 'first generation' status is the entrance, a simple archway through the curtain, without flanking towers or projecting members and like the gateway of William Marshall the Elder at Chepstow. In 1938, O'Neil contrasted Usk with the more advanced work of Hubert de Burgh, *post* 1219, at Skenfrith and Grosmont and went on to attribute Usk to William Marshal the Elder, who died in that year.[32] The Skenfrith round keep is a maturer version of its type than the Garrison Tower, and the gatehouse is a stronger and more elaborate version of the Usk/ Chepstow 'simple arch' type, with the entrance arch raised to first floor level.[33] It is now possible to add to O'Neil's thesis with evidence from the newly excavated Montgomery, where work began in the autumn of 1223, probably under the advice of Hubert de Burgh.[34] This has a large, twin-towered gatehouse.

Although integrated with the curtain wall, the Garrison Tower has many of the features of the circular keeps of the southern Marches. This is not so much of a paradox as might at first seem, since in France circular keeps are, at this date, usually integrated with the line of the *enceinte*, as at Dourdan, Coucy or Gisors, or of the town defences, as at Villenueve-sur-Yonne or Aigues Mortes. Renn has argued for a date of 1185–95 for the Longtown keep,[35] whilst William Marshall's work at Chepstow, with its rounded mural towers, is usually dated to soon after his marriage to the *pucelle d'Estriguil*[36] in 1189, but if these are really so early, they exercised surprisingly little influence on the castle building of the following generation. Curtain walls with projecting round towers were used by John, but his larger towers were normally conservative multangular structures, like Odiham (1207–12) which harks back to Chilham and Tickhill in the 1170s, in marked contrast to Philip Augustus's circular keeps at e.g., Rouen (1207) or Villeneuve-sur-Yonne (1205–11).[37] Recent work by Mr. Richard Hartley at Longtown has shown that the Romanesque voussoirs which form a major prop of its late twelfth-century dating are re-used pieces, demanding a date after, not before 1200,[38] whilst the Grosmont hall of 1201–4 is a conservative structure of late twelfth-century type.[39] Usk would thus seem to date to between the conservative phase of *c.* 1200–10 and the new style castles built after 1220. Can the career of its builder help us to define its date more closely?

From 1207 to 1212, William Marshall was in Ireland and his relations with the king were bad. At one stage, his castles were in the king's hands as a pledge for his good behaviour and it is most improbable that he would have begun a major new castle in these years, particularly after John had seized the castles of another absentee marcher lord, Hubert de Burgh, in 1205. By 1212, however, the political wheel had come full circle, and William was back from Ireland, fighting for John against Llywelyn ap Iorwerth and from then onwards he was foremost among John's advisers. In 1214, he was granted Haverford-west, Carmarthen, Cardigan, and Gower, and was left in charge of England during John's absence in Poitou. Llywelyn Fawr was also at the height of his power in these years and actively allied with the baronial opposition against

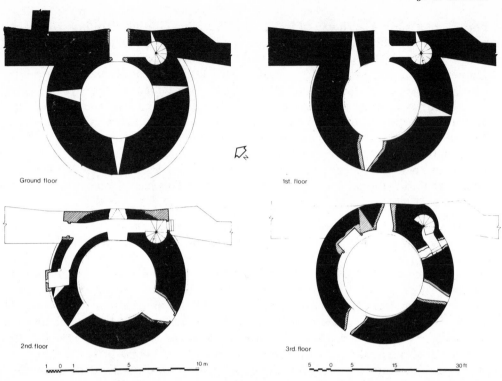

Ground floor

1st. floor

2nd. floor

3rd. floor

Fig. 4 Usk Castle. Plans of Garrison Tower.

the king, whilst Reginald de Braose, the rival of the Marshall–de Burgh alliance on the March had in 1215 recovered by force the extensive territories in northern Gwent, Brycheiniog, and the central March forfeited by his father. De Braose was in alliance with Llywelyn and was the northern neighbour of the Marshalls on the March. As the holder of extensive lands in west Wales and as a major prop of the English royal power, William represented one of the biggest barriers to Llywelyn's plans. In such circumstances, and in a worsening political climate, a prudent man would look to his castles, and William was well placed, both financially and politically, to plan major new works. The years 1212 to 1219 thus provide an excellent historical context for the building of Usk.

William Marshall died in 1219. In December of the previous year, the king's court had restored Grosmont, Skenfrith, and White Castle to Hubert, leaving him free to build. In 1220, Ralph de Blundeville, Earl of Chester, returned from the crusades and probably began the building of Beeston, Chartley, and Bolingbroke.[40] In 1223 Henry III began on (New) Montgomery. Between them, these castles have several twin-towered gatehouses and two developed round keeps. They are technically in advance of Usk and, taken together, show a more fluent use of the new modes of fortification. They may perhaps be taken as providing us with a *terminus ante quem* for the latter.

REFERENCES

1. For previous accounts of the castle see A. J. Taylor, 'Usk Castle and the Pipe Roll of 1185', *Archaeologia Cambrensis* (1947), pp. 249-55, and B. H. St. J. O'Neil, *Usk Castle* (privately printed, 1938).

2. C. W. Manning, Burrium, *Roman Frontier Studies 1969*, ed. Birley, Dobson and Jarrett (Cardiff 1947), pp. 61-69. Grid Ref. S.O. 377011, O.S. 1 in. map sheet 171.

3. Dugdale, *Monasticon* (ed. Caley, 1830), Vol. VI, p. 1076.

4. *Domesday Book* (ed. Farley, 1783), Vol. I, 1856.

5. Ordericus Vitalis, *Historia Ecclesiastica*, ed. A. le Prevost (Paris, 1838-55), V, 110. See also J. E. Lloyd, *A History of Wales* (London, 1912), Vol. II, p. 478.

6. *Publications of the Pipe Roll Society*, Vol. XXI, p. 22.

7. *Publications of the Pipe Roll Society*, Vol. XXXIII, p. 59-60 (though Novus Burgus, where Hywel was stationed with his sergeants, is surely Newport (Mon.), not Newton Nottage (Glam.). See also Lloyd, *History of Wales*, pp. 545-6 and 572.

8. Giraldus Cambrensis, *Itinerarium Kambriae*, Bk. I, V.

9. *Publications of the Pipe Roll Society*, Vol. XXIV, p. 10.

10. Round, *Publications of the Pipe Roll Society*, Vol. XXXIV, p. xxvii. Taylor, *Arch. Camb.*, 1947, pp. 249-253.

11. This is a feature which recurs in a number of the geometrically planned castles of the thirteenth century, e.g., Dourdan (Seine-et-Oise), Skenfrith (Mon.), Kidwelly (Carms.), Rhuddlan (Flint.). On geometrically planned castles of the early thirteenth century see O. Heliot, 'La genèse des châteaux de plan quadrangulairs', in *Bulletin de la Société Nationale des Antiquaires de France* (1965), pp. 238-52.

12. Taylor, *Arch. Camb.*, 1947, p. 255.

13. C. Enlart, *Manuel D'Archéologie Française II*, II (Paris, 2nd ed., 1932), Fig. 256. P. Heliot, in *Bulletin archéologique du comité des travaus historiques et scientifiques*, 1969, Fig. 38, p. 185.

14. At Loches (Indre-et-Loire) and Loudun (Vienne), P. Heliot, 'L'évolution du donjon dans le nord-ouest de la France et en Angleterre aux XIIe siècle' (*op. cit.* in n. 13), pp. 184-6. There is also documentary evidence for hourds among the castles of Philip Augustus.

15. I am grateful to my colleague Mr. Bengt Petersen for showing me his measured drawings of the Pembroke timberwork. See also D. F. Renn, 'The Donjon at Pembroke Castle', *Transactions of the Ancient Monuments Society*, new series XV (1967-8), pp. 35ff.

16. J. C. Perks, Department of the Environment Official Guide, *Chepstow Castle*, pp. 24-5.

17. A. J. Taylor, *Arch. Camb.*, 1947, pp. 254-5, citing P.R.O. S.C.6 926/30.

18. These are characteristic locally of work of the late thirteenth century. They occur, for example, at Caerphilly in work which Mr. C. N. Johns dates to c. 1284-7 (Official Guide, forthcoming); at Chepstow Castle in the cellarage of Roger Bigod III's range of domestic buildings, begun in 1278, in the newly excavated guest house at Tintern Abbey, probably contemporary with Roger Bigod III, in work at Goodrich Castle in progress from c. 1280 and in a number of less well dated buildings in southern Monmouthshire and east Glamorgan. I am very grateful to Mr. Johns for fruitful discussion of this point.

19. C. King and C. Perks, *Arch. Camb.*, 1956, pp. 96-132. Work involving masonry was in progress at Llangybi in 1286, but the position is confused by the presence of an earlier adjacent castle.

20. P.R.O. Exchequer Accounts Bundle 91, No. 14. I am very grateful to Mr. Isca Bowen for drawing my attention to this document and for sending me a photocopy of a transcription by Lady Jenkinson.

21. *in litt.*, 1 Feb. 1973.

22. D. H. Williams, 'Goldcliff Priory', *Monmouthshire Antiquary*, Vol. III, pt. I (1970-1), p. 44.

23. C. H. Hunter-Blair and H. L. Honeyman, Official Guide, *Warkworth Castle*, pp. 13-18.

24. P. Heliot, 'Le Château de Boulogne-sur-Mer et les Château Gothiques De Plan Polygonaux', *Révue archaéologique*, 6th ser., 27 (1947), pp. 41-59.

25. *Chronicon Adae de Usk* (ed. Thompson, 2nd ed., London, 1904), p. 103, ('aliqualiter ad defensionem reparato').

26. *Calendar of Close Rolls*, Henry IV, ii, III. I am very grateful to my colleague, Mr. David Morgan Evans, for this reference.

27. On the exact siting of this battle see J. E. Lloyd, *Arch.Camb.*, 1933, pp. 347-8.

28. D. H. Williams, 'Goldcliff Priory', *Monmouthshire Antiquary*, Vol. III, pt. I (1970-1), p. 47.

29. A. J. Taylor, Official Guide, *Raglan Castle*, 10. See also *Dictionary of Welsh Biography* (London, 1959), pp. 354-5;

30. Lucy Toulmin Smith, *Leland's Itinerary in Wales* (London, 1906), p. 44.

31. Thomas Churchyard, *The Worthines of Wales* (1587), ed. of 1776, p. 19.

32. *Op. cit.* in n. 2.

33. O. E. Craster, 'Skenfrith Castle: When Was It Built?' *Arch. Camb.*, (1967), pp. 133-47. More recent excavations, by the present writer, have included the area of the gate.

34. J. D. K. Lloyd and J. K. Knight, Official Guide, *Montgomery Castle* (H.M.S.O., 1973). The definitive report on the excavations is forthcoming (in *Archaeologia Cambrensis*).

35. D. F. Renn, 'The Round Keeps of the Brecon Region', *Arch. Camb.* (1961), pp. 133-4, 141.

36. The phrase is that of the verse biography *Histoire de Guillaume le Marechal* (ed. P. Meyer, Paris, 1891-1901). Striguil is of course another name for Chepstow.

37. On Villeneuve-sur-Yonne see J. Vallery-Radot, 'Le donjon de Philippe-Auguste à Villeneuve-sur-Yonne, *Château Gaillard II, Colloque de Büderich* (Köln, 1967), pp. 106-112. The keep is firmly dated by its surviving devis or building specification. See also J. Vallery-Radot, 'Quelques donjons de Philippe Auguste', *Bulletin de la Société Nationale des antiquaries de France*, CXIX (1964), pp. 155-160.

38. I am very grateful to Mr. Hartley for allowing me to quote the results of his current work.

39. Suggested dating is based on the grant of the Three Castles to Hubert in July 1201 and his departure for France by the spring of 1204. A pre-Hubert date is precluded by the documentation of the previous (royal) phrase and by very early thirteenth-century detail which still survived in the 1930s (C. A. R. Radford, Official Guide). Mr. Peter Simpson points out to me that the hall has marked similarities to that at Christchurch (Hants.) which Hubert acquired by marriage in 1200.

40. M. W. Thompson, 'The Origins of Bolingbroke Castle, Lincolnshire', *Medieval Archaeology* X (1966), pp. 152-8.

ACKNOWLEDGEMENTS

I am very happy to express my thanks to the present *seigneur* of Usk, Mr. R. H. J. Humphries and his lady for their constant encouragement and interest during my many visits to their home, for the loan of ladders and for much fruitful discussion of the castle. The plans of the castle and the survey on which they are based are largely the work of my colleague, Mr. Peter Humphries, without whose help this paper could hardly have been written.

The Wakefield Tower, Tower of London

by

P. E. CURNOW

INTRODUCTION

IT IS NOW well over a hundred years since G. T. Clark wrote his account of the Tower of London. It appeared first as a monograph and then slightly amended in his *Medieval Military Architecture.*[1] It remains as an unrivalled description of the Tower, although the works of John Bayley[2] and Britton and Brayley[3] were worthy predecessors. Clark was writing during the period when the Tower was being cleared of its eighteenth-century military buildings and was undergoing 're-medievalisation' at the hands of Salvin. As a result Clark's work is even more valuable than just a description of existing remains, for as many features of the Tower have been revealed since his time, so during the time of restoration did many original details disappear, and these latter were often noted by him. Nowhere in the Tower is this more true than in Clark's final detailed account of the Wakefield Tower; an account which took note of two successive restorations of the tower since it was first written, and which explains, for example, the evidence left on the ground floor by supports to the earlier timber ceiling joists. Above all, however, the careful description of that ceiling which he made before the brick vault was inserted in connection with the installations of the Crown Jewels in the Wakefield Tower, facilitated the decision to remove that same vault in 1970 after the regalia were removed to their new home in 1967. The demolition of the reinforced concrete floor and the brick and cast-iron vault which bore the cage containing the Crown Jewels was thus achieved in the knowledge that the original form of the first floor timber work was fully known, and had only been removed after 1867. After recording the original floor construction and noting its destruction, Clark commends the proposal to rebuild the bridge linking the Wakefield and St. Thomas's Towers, but comments 'to vault the ground floor would be a mistake, the lower floor covering was always timber, and of a curious pattern. It should be replaced'. It is gratifying to be able to rectify the mistakes of the past and it is even more pleasing to feel that the reinstatement of the original floor design can in some way be regarded as an act of piety to one of the greatest writers on military architecture. It is only to be regretted that our knowledge of the Palace which formed the background historically and architecturally to the Wakefield Tower on the north-east is (apart from the copious documentary evidence) virtually limited to a very few early illustrations, and that no detailed plans of the Wakefield Tower or the eighteenth-century buildings which stood against it on the east can so far be traced.

HISTORY

The Wakefield Tower (Pl. VIIId) stands midway along the inner south curtain of the Tower of London and also formed the south-west angle tower of the

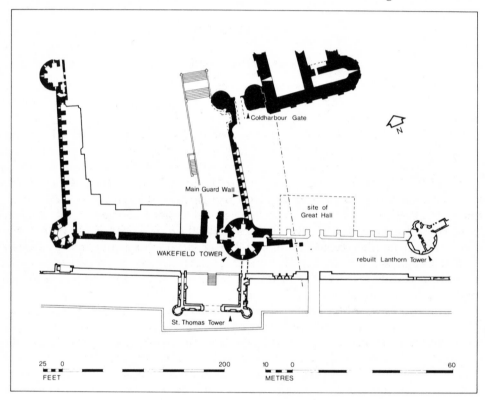

Fig. 1 The environs of the Wakefield Tower.

innermost or Palace Ward of the castle. Its importance derives both from this and the fact that it was built to command the principal water gate as well as the palace postern gate. Its proximity to the almost contemporary Great Hall of the palace is indicated by one of its four names[4]—the Hall Tower. It dates from the early years of the reign of Henry III (commenced in 1221),[5] a period of great activity in the development of circular towers and donjons, although earlier writers have suggested that the upper and lower storeys were of widely different dates.

The external aspect of the tower was substantially altered by Edward I, who, in the late thirteenth century, built the outer south curtain, pushing the river back and infilling the space between the two curtains to within two or three feet of its present level. This had the effect of truncating the Wakefield Tower by concealing its plinth and thus rendering it far less imposing. At the same time a bridge linking the upper storey with the new gate (St. Thomas' Tower) was constructed.

In the fourteenth century part of the tower became a repository for documents, a use which was subsequently extended and continued up to the nineteenth century and which gave rise to it also being known as the Record Tower. In 1737 a building known as the Old Treasury House was constructed on the site of an older building of that name, which in turn had replaced the curtain wall immediately to the east of the Wakefield Tower (Pl. VIIIa). This was linked with the Wakefield Tower and also used as part of the Record Office being so inscribed on the lintel of the door below a tablet bearing the arms of Queen Elizabeth I which had been re-set there.

The Wakefield Tower suffered two mid-nineteenth century restorations, the most extensive being undertaken in 1867-9 for the reception of the Crown Jewels, after which the tower and a new staircase building to the north were opened to the public. In 1886 the Old Treasury House was demolished (Pl. VIIIb) and the present curtain wall constructed between the Wakefield and Salt Towers.

To the north of the Wakefield Tower there stood until 1940 a block known as the Main Guard, the last of a succession of buildings on this site which incorporated the remains of the western wall of the Palace Ward and ran from the Wakefield Tower to the twin-towered Coldharbour Gate, the principal entrance to that ward. Demolition of the Main Guard building enabled the thirteenth-century wall to be exposed and consolidated.

The Wakefield Tower itself was not cleared of later accretions both externally and internally, until after the removal of the Crown Jewels in 1967 and the consequent demolition of the nineteenth-century staircase and ticket office in 1970-71 (Pl. VIIIc). After cleaning, the repaired tower was opened again in 1973—to be seen, for the first time in some three hundred years, free of unworthy appendages.

SUMMARY OF EXCAVATIONS 1957-73

Whilst the general date and significance of the Wakefield Tower have never been in serious doubt, its original design, its archaeological context within the south curtain and the part it played in the innermost or palace ward—and indeed in the palace itself—were uncertain. The recent clearance and investigation of the Tower itself (1970-3) was only the most important of a series of investigations aimed at resolving some of these uncertainties.

In 1957-8 an area east of the Wakefield Tower, and south of the nineteenth-century curtain, was excavated, revealing a hitherto unknown postern through the early thirteenth-century curtain which had been razed, prior to the building of the early eighteenth-century Old Treasury House (Pl. IX a,b). This was followed in 1958 by an excavation in Water Lane against the south-west jamb of the Bloody Tower gateway, and extended westward, to reveal the footings of the twelfth-century curtain (Pl. IXc), and northwards within the west side of the gate passage to reveal the original road surface and the base of the original jambs[6] (Pl. IXd). The results of this work were embodied in the *History of the King's Works* which forms the essential basis for all subsequent research on the Tower of London.

As noted above, further work had to await the removal of the Crown Jewels to their new home in 1967. Only after this was done and the nineteenth-century vault removed could the tower be examined, especially the ground floor now freed from its forest of iron supports and central piers (Pl. X, a, b, c). Excavation was undertaken both within to restore the original ground floor level, and outside against the north face. The latter revealed a great depth of finely faced ashlar indicating that it was designed to be exposed (Pl. XIa).

The repair work to the tower and the small guard-room to the west, to allow access by the public, included re-opening the original doorways on both floors of the tower. This was followed by further excavations in 1974–5 which were directed to the area fronting the wall of the Main Guard running northward from the Wakefield Tower to the site of the Coldharbour Gatehouse. This wall was presumed to follow the line of the west ditch of the eleventh-century bailey, and the first archaeological evidence for it was found by B. K. Davison in 1964 at a point north-west of the White Tower.

The relation between this early ditch and the main guard wall were, and at the time of writing, still are, being examined as also the relationship between the ditch and a hitherto unknown Roman building. These findings will be the subject of a separate report.

The main results of these excavations, together with the known and observable details of the Wakefield Tower and adjacent buildings, are now briefly described in the context of the general development of the Tower.

THE DEFENCES WEST OF THE WAKEFIELD TOWER

The architectural growth of the Tower of London from its inception by William I has been authoritatively set forth in the *History of the King's Works*.[8] Immediately after the publication of that work, however, excavation, necessitated by the building of the new underground Jewel House north-west of the White Tower, produced evidence that led to a substantial modification to the hitherto accepted line of the north and north-east defences of *c.* 1200 AD.[9]

The plan prior to the major remodelling of the defences by Henry III and Edward I, which occupied much of the thirteenth century, showed the east curtain still following the Roman wall.[10] The north and west defences, then only recently formed (c. 1190), ran from the Roman wall at a point just north of the north-east angle of the White Tower westward to the site later occupied by the Beauchamp Tower and from thence southwards to the Bell Tower, on the line of the present (thirteenth century) curtain. Apart from the Wardrobe Tower, which has a claim to be the earliest mural tower, the Bell Tower, and its contemporary south curtain, are all that remain of the pre-Henry III *enceinte*.

The exact position and nature of the junction between this early curtain and the work executed under Henry III and associated with the Wakefield Tower were examined in 1958. In 1928, the purbeck plinth, with seven offsets, common to both the early curtain and the Bell Tower, had first been exposed next to that tower, and some 7 ft. below the present roadway; the 1958 excavation showed that this distinctive plinth extended intact as far as the western jamb of the gateway now known as the Bloody Tower gate. At this point it gradually steps downward and dies beneath a triple offset Reigate ashlar plinth, which was grafted onto it beneath the gateway—which of course became the principal water gate, the whole of the south curtain being washed by the river until Edward I pushed the river back and built St. Thomas's Tower and an outer south curtain. The manner of the junction of these two plinths suggests that the earlier work on the south curtain was left incomplete— perhaps at the death of King John, and at a point where it approached the ditch which almost certainly must have formed part of the western defences of the eleventh- and early twelfth-century castle. The position of the new work, and the fact that behind it the ground rises on either side, strongly suggests that at its centre the Wakefield Tower was set over, or partially within, this pre-existing ditch. Indeed it is quite possible that the gap in the southern defences left by this ditch had not hitherto been filled.

The Bloody Tower gateway is part of this build, although its proportions have been somewhat altered by a later rise in the level of the roadway. The contemporary road surface was revealed some 2 ft. down, together with the cill, the bar-stops of the two straight chamfered orders of the pointed segmental outer arch and the base of the portcullis groove.[11] As first built, this, the principal water gate, was perhaps of rather modest strength; only the later provisions of a lengthened gate passage with vault and a super-imposed tower turned it into a gatehouse proper. Thus, on its west side, the gate-passage extended only to the thickness of the curtain and a small return nib. It was defended by a portcullis—the present one a sixteenth-century replacement—and a gate behind the inner arch.

On the east side, a small guard room (Fig. 2), which is of one build with the gateway and the Wakefield Tower, commanded the gate passage. Approximately 10 ft. square internally, it lies half within the circumference of the Wakefield Tower, but there appears to have been no communication

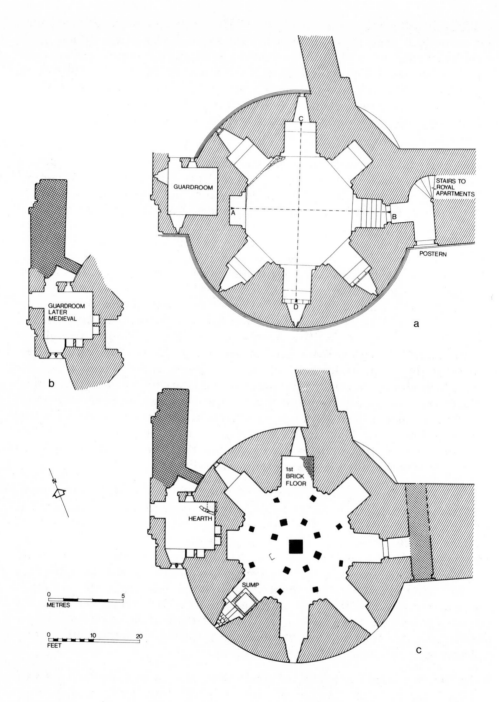

Fig. 2 Wakefield Tower: ground floor plans. a: Early thirteenth century as excavated (slightly restored), b: alterations to Bloody Tower and Guardroom, c: timber supports and other post-medieval alterations.

between them, the present doorway having been forced through recently. The flattened barrel vault is original, but the room has been much altered. Originally it must have been entered from the rear (north), where remains of the doorway and a small window survive, the former becoming blocked by the latter rearward extension of the gate passage (Fig. 2 b). The presence of the small rectangular window goes to confirm that the openings in the south and west wall were at first only loops. That in the south wall has clearly been enlarged into a two-light cusped window probably in the fourteenth century, whilst the present modern doorway opening westwards into the gate passage is in fact obscured when the gate is open. If, as suggested, there was a loop in this position, it would have been placed to command the gate passage when the gates were shut, but it may have been turned into a doorway, despite its inconvenience, as early as the fourteenth century when the rear door was blocked off. The series of cupboards, at one time four in number,[12] in the south and east walls were not original features but may have been of late medieval or sixteenth-century date, possibly associated with the insertion of a fireplace in the north-east angle of the room. The hearth (Fig. 2 c) was discovered during the removal of the later floors, its flue cut into the vault, and was taken up close to one of the reveals of the upper floor of the Wakefield Tower and perhaps from thence into the thirteenth-century flue of the Wakefield Tower—but nineteenth-century restoration has erased all evidence of its upper course.

As noted above, there was no access to the Wakefield Tower from the west, and the small guard room, although integral with it, was used solely to control the water gate. There may have been a small portcullis chamber approximately on a level with the high ground of Tower Green, and either reached directly from it, or by a flight of steps to the north-west of the gateway.

The upper chamber, if it existed,[13] was replaced by the Bloody or Garden Tower and above only the front wall with its portcullis slot and housing survive.

THE DEFENCES EAST OF THE WAKEFIELD TOWER

As has been seen the Wakefield Tower could not be entered directly from the outer bailey but could only be approached either via the Coldharbour Gate, the principal entrance to the innermost ward situated against the west side of the White Tower, or directly by water, by means of a postern in the south curtain immediately adjoining the Wakefield Tower on the east.

The curtain which stood up to 5 ft. above plinth level extended for some 35 ft. to the east at which point it abutted a short north-south wall of buttress-like appearance (Pl. XIb). That the curtain was contemporary with the tower was indicated by the careful bonding of the ashlar faces which were found in almost pristine state; in addition, the uppermost of the three offsets of the tower plinth was carried along the curtain wall with the angle being formed of a single stone. Further evidence is provided by the banker marks of the stonemasons; the same masons can be seen to have left their marks on the ashlars of the curtain and both the external and internal faces of the tower (Fig. 7). The remarkably good state of the Reigate ashlar—a soft stone of poor weathering qualities—is responsible for the preservation of both the scratched bankers marks and the mainly vertically combed tooling, and indicates that it could only have been exposed to the weather for a short period, thus providing visual evidence supporting the historical evidence for the late thirteenth-century date of the burial of the lower part of the wall and tower.

The depth of the plinth decreased from west to east as the foreshore rose. Two drains through the wall discharged by means of rectangular openings below plinth level. Their substantial size indicates that they may have been connected with the kitchens which lay north of the Wakefield Tower and also the well which was discovered between the site of the great hall of the palace and the Wakefield Tower at a point just north of the postern.

The postern itself, sited only 18 in. from the tower is just over 4 ft. wide within. Between the two chamfered orders with bar-stops, the cill is pierced with small weep-holes, no doubt to allow any water which penetrated into the passage to run back out. The combination of raised cill and steps at the end of the passage strongly suggests that the passage would have been duckboarded; Royalty disembarking here would not expect to get their feet wet. The passage was closed only by a gate, the drawbar-hole for which survives. Being a water-gate the plinth runs continuously beneath, but there is no evidence at or below cill level for fixings for landing stage—or a drawbridge. However, timbers found in front of the postern indicate the likelihood of the former; indeed the relative shallowness of the water at this point—the cill of the postern stands only some 3 ft. above the gravel of the short—would make a stage imperative except at high tide. The upper part of the gateway is missing, but the surviving details of the jambs may be paralleled on the Bloody Tower gateway, and the shape of the missing arch may be inferred from another postern visible in Henry III's east curtain between the Salt and Broad Arrow Towers, i.e., flattened, pointed-segmental.

As noted above, the curtain associated with the building of the Wakefield Tower butted against a pre-existing structure; in fact two similar and parallel buttress-like features were uncovered 8 ft. apart. Unlike the neighbouring curtain they were built of rubble with Reigate dressings and a single chamfered offset plinth of shallow projection. Each was deeply founded, the foundation extending southwards; it is quite possible that they had been dressed back to their present face. That they were earlier than the curtain is proved by the latter oversailing timber revetting associated with the projections. Drains from the palace complex have been mentioned above, however, what may be called the great drain from the White Tower was carried between these twin features in a stone conduit large enough to walk up, although the nineteenth-century curtain wall has blocked if off. Before the foreshore was pushed to the south by Edward I this drain must have discharged between these flank walls. It seems improbable, nevertheless, that these features originally acted solely as part of an outlet for a drain—even a large one—and while lack of evidence precludes any firm conclusions, the width of the opening and the depth and southward projection of the foundations of these flank walls suggests arrangements associated with some earlier, i.e., twelfth-century water-gate or postern. It is almost inconceivable that the original inner bailey should not have access from the river.

ST. THOMAS'S TOWER AREA

The extension of the fortifications of the Tower of London during the reign of Edward I modified the whole of the pre-existing south front by the construction of a new outer curtain provided with a vast new water-gate—St. Thomas's Tower. The infilling of the area between the new outer curtain and the earlier curtain necessitated the extension of the drains so that they would again discharge into the river beyond the new alignment. Those already noted adjacent to the postern were carried in roughly-built chalk conduits which were angled to join the extended great drain, so that only a single outlet was required through the new curtain. The infilling also raised the new ground level above the cill of the postern and a flight of steps had to be built leading down to it. A new cill was added and the level within the passage was raised to eliminate two steps at the farther end (Pl. IXa). At the Bloody Tower the evidence has been somewhat disturbed, but the condition of the stop-chamfers and jambs suggest that here the level was only marginally raised at this time. The raising of the external levels will also be seen to have a bearing on the contemporary change of level within the tower.

THE WAKEFIELD TOWER

The discovery and clearance of the postern passage disclosed the original entrance to the ground floor of the Wakefield Tower (Fig. 2 a), and also revealed the base of a spacious new stair, 10 ft. in diameter, which led upwards to state apartments, one of which would have been the upper room of the Tower. Although Clark shows the entrance to the ground floor of the Tower as occupying the eastern recess, the postern[14] passage had by the nineteenth century long been filled in, and the surviving internal part of the doorway lay below both internal and external floor levels. This did, however, demonstrate the fact that the ground floor of the tower was always entered at this point by successive doorways on the same site. It was only during the restorations of the 1880s that a loop was formed in the original

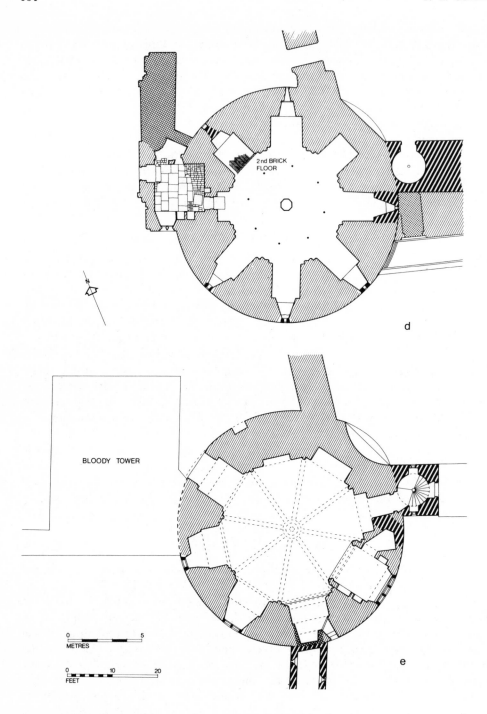

2nd BRICK
FLOOR

d

BLOODY   TOWER

0   5
METRES

0   10   20
FEET

e

Fig. 3 Wakefield Tower: d: ground floor 1867-1970, e: first floor as existing.

opening (Fig. 3) and a new way in forced through from the small guard room on the opposite (west) side. The rebuildings and blockings associated with this new loop totally obscured the surviving parts of the original entrance which had to be cut and drilled out.

The internal entrance arrangements and indeed the ground floor as a whole could not be examined until its original floor level was established and this could not be done until the 1867 vault and its massive supports were removed (Pl. X). The clearance of the brick floor revealed the emplacements for the timber props noted by G. T. Clark,[15] which were inserted to support the original ceiling. These props were required to support the weight of the records stored above as well as to counteract the decay of the ceiling beams also noted by Clark. Two successive brick floors were encountered over the whole area; the upper floor pre-dated the jewel cage supports and respected the double ring of timber props (Fig, 2 c) which, in some cases, still rested on pad stones. These latter may have been inserted when the upper brick floor was made, but it is clear that timber supports initially stood on the lower brick floor. The date of the brick floors is uncertain, although pottery evidence, notably from the south-east loop, suggests a late sixteenth-century date for the lower floor. The upper brick floor could easily date from the refurbishing of the tower in 1728.[16]

The original floor was only reached at a depth of 8 ft. 6 in. below the upper brick floor, of this at least the lower 5 ft. 6in. represented an infill of late thirteenth-century date. (Fig. 9 and Pottery Report). The clearance of the infill almost doubled the height of the chamber to over 19 ft., giving it a scale and grandeur hitherto unsuspected (Fig. 4, Pl. XIc). The buried ashlar like that found externally proved to be in perfect condition and exactly comparable in detail and masons' banker marks. The round-headed recesses in each of the sides of the octagon which because of their shape have misled many earlier historians into pronouncing the lower part to be of Norman date, were found to have bar-stops to each of their straight chamfered orders. In any event, the homogeneity of the ashlar work throughout, combined with its quality and fine joints, leave no doubt as to its early thirteenth-century date, and here, as nowhere else in the Tower of London, it shows the excellence of the masonry of the Royal Works at this time. The floor of the chamber was of ragstone rubble, but it is possible that a finished floor level may be represented by the upstand which follows the line of the internal face of the wall. Irregularity of line below the top of this step may be connected with the setting out and would hardly be expected to be visible in the finished job. When described by Clark and in the Commission volume[17] the recesses in the ground floor chamber were, of course more than half buried. It is now possible to describe the features not hitherto visible.

On entering the eastern recess (Fig. 2 a) already referred to, a rebated doorway, of which the lower part ot the jambs remains, is set half way within the wall thickness. A broad flight of steps then leads down to the interior; it should be noted that the internal floor level is appreciably below the external plinth on the south (river) side. On the south side the three recesses terminated in loops of which the lower parts survived, the upper parts previously visible, having been completely reformed (Pl. XIc). It was necessary for a guard to mount a tall step which brought the cill of the loop to breast height. From this point they were splayed downward to command the water or foreshore almost immediately beneath the tower. In height they could hardly have been less than 6 ft. , but their most pronounced feature was their narrowness—1½ in. Such loops with their step set 6 ft. back from the aperture and plunging splay would almost require an act of *legerdemain* to aim or shoot through, unless the archer was something of an acrobat to get right into the sloping embrasure.[18] Since only the lower part of the loops survive there is no evidence of cross-slits. However, near the base there are cut-out recesses as if to receive a short cross-timber, perhaps for fixing some sort of shutter, or perhaps a

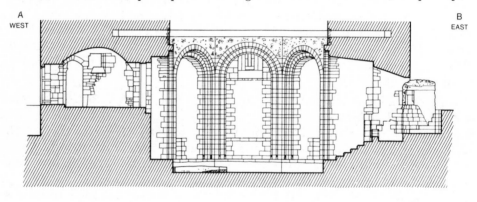

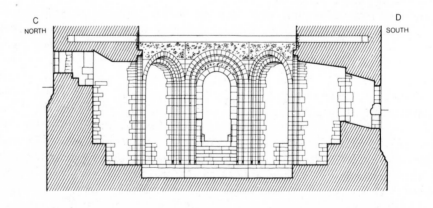

Fig. 4 Sections across the ground floor of the Wakefield Tower.

platform. Whatever the question of the utility of such loops for an archer, they were certainly efficient in commanding a good visual range and give some degree of light. But most of the light to the lower chamber was derived from small rectangular windows high up in the north-west and north recesses (Fig. 4), their heads being raised higher than the level of the main soffit of the of the recess. Their cills are at precisely the same height (3 ft.) above the triple offset plinth on the north as the cills of the loops on the south. However, the plinth on the north is set 8 ft. higher for reasons discussed on page 171 (below). The remaining recesses are blank as they back on contemporary buildings, that on the west the main gate guardroom and that on the north-east the great hall complex.

The ceiling of this lower chamber spanned a maximum 25 ft., and as the plan shows (Fig. 5) its design was of some interest, but had it not been for Clark who drew it before its destruction in 1867-9 the evidence for its beam slots would have been insufficient for an accurate reconstruction. Indeed it would

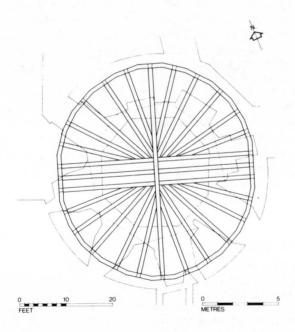

0 10 20
FEET

0 5
METRES

Fig. 5 Wakefield Tower: plan of first floor joists and ring-beam.

have been questionable to remove the nineteenth-century vault were it not that Clark's plan matched perfectly the beam slot evidence which was uncovered first. Few towers in England retain floors and those that do have in most cases been extensively restored. The confirmation of the design of this one is therefore all the more important as it shows not a simple spanning as might be expected but a radiating system of some complexity. At least part of the reason for this was found during investigation, for the joists extended almost to the outer face of the wall where they were dovetailed (Fig. 6) into a sectional ring-beam set just within the facing ashlars of the tower. Timber lacing was not an infrequent feature of 'romanesque' building practice[19] but is not commonly attested to later.[20] Its function in this case may have been two-fold, to bind the drum of the tower together in the same fashion as a modern ring-beam, and by anchoring the joists to provide a rigid web for the floor, reinforcing the cantilever effect of the former which are embedded within the wall for some 9 ft. of their length. (Fig. 6.) It seems unlikely that the central post recorded by Clark and replaced in the reconstruction was an essential part of the original design, although it is needed now because the ring-beam has virtually disappeared and the joists themselves could not be replaced to their full length without rebuilding the Wakefield Tower. The ashlar facing of the lower part of the tower extends above the ring-beam and indeed above the bottom of the reveals of the upper floor, and it is difficult to see how the timber work could be regarded as other than an internal feature of the first phase of construction, i.e., c. 1225.

It has been argued that the change from ashlar to rubble facework represents the external evidence for a substantial rebuilding of the upper storey by Edward I, at the time when it was linked to his new water gate, St. Thomas's Tower.[21] The documentary evidence is imprecise, perhaps referring to the works necessitated by the actual linking of the two towers which seems a more likely explanation. Virtually no evidence at parapet level survived the nineteenth-century restorations, and in default of such evidence the nature of the wall head in both the early and late thirteenth century must remain uncertain. Clark, however, mentions a line of blocked up arches[22] which could signify a loop-holed parapet or a covered wall-walk, and with the eye of faith it is just possible to see what may be traces of blocked loops at the height of the vault. A work of this nature would conform to the ideas of concentric defence carried out for Edward I elsewhere, with the inner defence commanding the outer.

Internally there are no primary features in the first floor chamber which unequivocally indicate a fundamental change of design. On the contrary, there is one feature which in the writer's opinion is clearly secondary and strongly suggests that the extent of the alterations carried out by Edward I was limited to the modification of the south recess to receive the bridge from St. Thomas's Tower. Thus the reveals of the recess can be seen from the plan to be unnecessarily awkwardly placed in relation to the bridge (Fig. 3 e);

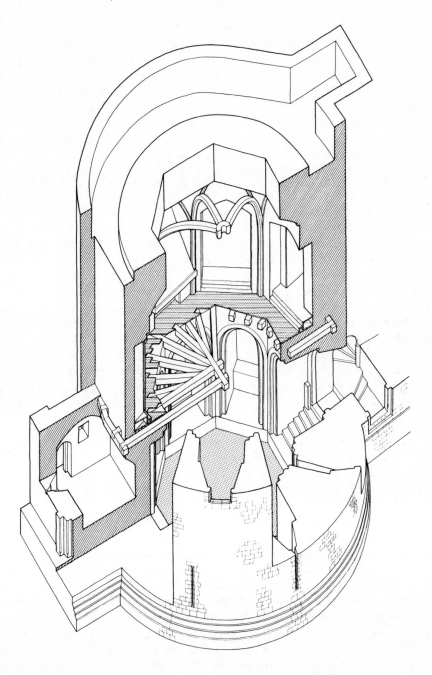

Fig. 6 Axonometric view. Details — e.g., loops and fireplace hood restored.

more important, the canted window has a two-centred head with a hollow chamfer which can be paralleled exactly in the turrets of St. Thomas's Tower. Further, the stone of the head differs from the otherwise ubiquitous Reigate, the reveals are ashlar as opposed to rubble in the remainder, and do not course with the ashlars of the jamb. Finally, the rubble fill between the window head and the top of the recess is totally dissimilar from the neighbouring rubble work. Thus there can be little doubt that the doorway and window are an insertion and it follows that the upper floor was already in existence prior to the construction of Edward's new water gate.

Taken cumulatively, a number of other features in the tower also tend, in the writer's opinion, to confirm this view. In the context of the Tower of London, Edwardian vaults normally spring from some form of bell capital; here, although the actual vault is nineteenth-century, there is no suggestion of a capital to the continuous wall shafts. The ashlar work and the form of the drop arches to the recesses would fit quite well with a Henrician date and the double chamfered orders of the ground floor recesses which, now that they are fully exposed, are comparable both in scale and detail to those of the upper chambers. Perhaps more significant is the fact, also noted by Clark, that the missing hood to the fireplace was supported on wooden brackets and is likely therefore to have been of plaster; the fireplaces of the latter part of the reign of Henry III and of the Edwardian period within the Tower of London are without exception of stone. An echo of the round-headed arches of the ground floor may also be observed in the two sedilia in the oratory (one subsequently cut through for a doorway probably in the eighteenth century) which bear the traces of bar-stops to their chamfers.

The planning of the upper floor is of some ingenuity, its octagon is twisted from that of the lower chamber so that four rather than three recesses on the south had windows. The chamber is entered through the internally rebated doorway set within a high and narrow arched passage through the wall and opening to the east recess. The south-east recess is occupied by the oratory containing an aumbry, piscina and opposed sedilia. It is differentiated by projecting spurs of masonry corbelled out above on each side which assisted in separating the oratory from the body of the chamber. This separation was enforced by the provision of a timber screen in 1238[23] and it may not be entirely fortuitous that stones had been pieced in at some time in a position compatible with the cutting in of a bearer—possibly, in view of its height—the rood beam of a screen. The south recess, as already noted, receives the bridge from St. Thomas's Tower—originally it, no doubt, had a window similar to that which must have existed in the south-west recess. Unfortunately all traces of the medieval windows were removed partly when Georgian sashes were inserted and partly in the nineteenth century when these were replaced by the present unsatisfactory medieval pastiches. The next recess has a half window to avoid the junction with the south curtain. The north-west recess, originally a window,[24] was made into the entrance to the Jewel House and the doorway has been retained. Next comes the fireplace with a nineteenth-century head; the outline of the original hood is now visible after the removal of the cement rendering, as are the holes for the timber supports. Between the fireplace and the original entrance, which also led to the rest of the Palace, is a blank recess facing the largest windows. Considering that this palatial room with its private oratory could be little less than one of Henry III's inner *cameras,* it would not be improbable for a chair of estate to occupy this blank recess.

It is customary for a private oratory to be attached to an inner chamber as instanced by the provision of such a one in the state suit above Edward's water gate. That he would have provided one in a rebuilt upper chamber of the Wakefield Tower which had ceased to be an inner chamber and would needs be traversed by the occupants of St. Thomas's Tower is possible, but inherently improbable.

The original form of the vault remains a problem. Clark surmised that it was never completed as there was no evidence for it remaining before the 1867 work, but it is surely inconceivable that a royal *camera* of such a fastidious monarch as Henry III would not have been carried to completion. Since a completed stone vault—rare in English as opposed to continental towers—might have left at least some indication for such an acute observer as Clark it is surely possible that the English weakness for wooden vaults obtained in this instance? It is the more to be regretted that the topmost part of this tower is almost devoid of medieval masonry for there must have been some form of access to the wall head from the neighbouring curtain walls. Although extensively restored and shorn of a number of its original features, including window seats, the upper room must be regarded as one of the noblest tower chambers we possess, and is the only surviving room of the Palace proper within the Tower of London. (Pl. XI D.)

THE DEFENCES NORTH OF THE WAKEFIELD TOWER

There remains to be considered the north side of the tower and its junction with the Main Guard Wall (called after successive buildings which housed the Guard, the last a substantial building removed after 1940); the latter already mentioned in relation to the line of the eleventh-century defences. The excavation of the full depth of the north face, barely complete at the time of writing, has exposed fine ashlar rising 13 ft. 9 in. from a foundation offset (Pl. XIa) to the top of the plinth which is here 8 ft. higher than on the south (Fig. 4c-d). The most obvious reason for this—and probably the correct one—is that the finished ground level on the north would be that much higher due to the observable upward slope from the riverside, and indeed visually the ground level here would relate to this plinth level whether the ground actually abutted the tower as was the case finally, or whether there was an intervening ditch round the north-west quadrant of the tower, as was the case initially.

Located and excavated in 1975, the ditch proved to be from 12 to 15 ft. in width and falls into two parts: a steep-sided open ditch approximately 9 ft. deep levelling off to a sloping ledge and then falling sharply again to form the construction trench for the tower (Pl. XIa). Below the footing offset the foundations were trench built; above, the ashlar was all face built, but it is clear that the bottom courses were covered almost immediately, there can be little doubt, nevertheless, that when built the bulk of the ashlar was intended to be seen.

BANKER MARKS	OCCURRENCE				TOTAL
	TOWER			CURTAIN WL.	
	NTH. FACE	STH. FACE	INT. GD. FLR.	POSTERN	
☆	7	1	10		18
✕	11	1	1	3	16
Ƶ	7			2	9
→	4	1		2	7
⌐	3		2		5
<	2			2	4
⋈	3				3
⊢	2	1			3
▽	2	1			3
⋈	2		1		3
A	2		1		3
W	2				2
Ö	2				2
△				2	2
Ã	1				1
⩗	1				1
⟨		1			1
⋊			1		1
⟨⟨			1		1
⟨				1	1

Fig. 7 Table of masons' marks.

Almost simultaneously with the building of the tower the Main Guard Wall was commenced. But although its footings are some 2 ft. above those of the tower it is immaculately bonded to it for a height of 10 ft. 6 in., the bonding quoins bearing identical masons marks. Up to this height and extending northwards as far as the side of the ditch the wall itself, although of rubble, is carefully face built and smoothly rendered. Above this, however, the wall sets back slightly and the quoins although bonding with the tower are roughly constructed and the wall itself is much less carefully built until an ashlar face is reached. This compares with the wall footings north of the ditch where it has been demonstrated archaeologically that the early ditch in which they were set had already been infilled and that they were thus trench built.

The finished ground level is marked by courses of ashlar which run from the Wakefield Tower towards the Coldharbour Gate stepping up to follow the slope. The upper part of the wall is well bonded but it seems quite clear that two major phases involving a slight change of plan are represented here, even if they are only separated by a short period. Thus the lower part of the tower must be contemporary with the open quadrant ditch; itself of unfinished appearance, and with the faced wall which formed its eastern termination— this being the only part of the no doubt intended Main Guard Wall to be executed in the first phase.

Subsequently it appears to have been decided that the ditch should be filled and the Main Guard proceeded with as a replacement of an earlier defence which must have existed at this time.

A historical context for these two phases may be put forward which not only fits the sequence of tower and Main Guard Wall but also suggests the date for the possibly significant change from Ashlar to rubble at the mid-height of the Wakefield Tower.

CONCLUSIONS

That the first major task of the new reign at the Tower of London should be the completion of the south curtain between the work of John, west of the Bloody Tower and the Roman wall, involving the commencement of the Wakefield Tower (and its linking curtains east and west) together with the building of the Lanthorn tower (at the south end of the Roman wall) is indicated by the documents, and dated c. 1220-5. It is clear that the Wakefield Tower was far from complete in 1226[25] and the authors of the *History of the King's Works* state that 'little appears to have been done to the fortifications between 1230 and 1238'. A great deal, however, was being done to the palace at this time (c. 1230-34), for example, the reconstruction of the Great Hall and provision of kitchens which relate to the Wakefield Tower and (perhaps) the Main Guard Wall respectively. Following the major building work external rendering (c. 1234) and internal fitting and decoration (c. 1238-40) followed. Included in these operations is the upper chamber of the Wakefield Tower which as we have seen is very much a part of the palace complex.

If two phases are indicated by the change from ashlar to rubble[26] in the Wakefield Tower and it has been shown above that they must fall within a single reign, the building history north of the tower is only explicable on the basis of two phases. It is therefore suggested that the first phase ordered by the regents, with defence the prime motive, saw the Wakefield tower raised in ashlar to a defensible height and made more defensible on the north by the provision of a ditch in 1220-5. The second phase followed shortly after, possibly as much as ten years, probably less, and was linked with the reconstruction of the palace which must have necessitated the provision of a new enclosing wall and gatehouse to the innermost ward, i.e., the Main Guard and Cold Harbour Gate. If the view put forward above be accepted, the Wakefield Tower with its attendant curtain walls and the rebuilding of the Great Hall complex can be seen to fall into the two successive decades 1220–1240, the former to a single plan and integrated closely with the latter which no doubt fell more directly under the personal eye of the king, who had become of age.

It is difficult nowadays to appreciate the impression which the Wakefield Tower must have made before it was masked by the massive changes wrought by Edward I only fifty years after it was built. Quite probably whitewashed (the Hall and Great Chambers were so treated in 1234), it would have dominated the whole river front of the castle, the magnitude and importance both defensive and domestic can appropriately be regarded as being in the tradition of those massive cylindrical 'Great Towers' which were being attached to the enceinte of polygonal or quadrilateral castles at this time. By far the largest tower in the castle—excepting of course the White Tower—and containing one of the lord's principal chambers—in this case the King's—it fulfils two of the fundamental conditions of a Great Tower of the type made fashionable by Philippe Auguste in France only a decade or so earlier. Falaise, Gisors and, perhaps, especially comparable in view of its position, the Tour du Coudray at Chinon may be quoted. In England, in the 1220s another Blundeville, Ranulph Earl of Chester was building castles one of which, Chartley, had a great round tower on the curtain. Other late examples may be met with in England and also in Scotland where Bothwell, Dirleton, and Kildrummy are all so provided.

The later medieval use of the tower to store state records, appositely illustrated by the finding of a papal bulla of Innocent IV during the recent excavations (Fig. 8), heralded the long-continuing erosion of its military and domestic role: an erosion which also affected the fabric and which was only reversed in the last few years.

Fig. 8 Papal Bull of Innocent IV from fill of the Wakefield Tower.
Scale 1:1.

REFERENCES

1. G. T. Clark, *Medieval Military Architecture* (1884), Vol. 2, pp. 220–26

2. J. Bayley, *The History and Antiquities of the Tower of London* (1825).

3. Britton and Brayley, *Memoirs of the Tower of London* (1832).

4. For a short period at the time of its building it was known as the Blundeville Tower after the contemporary constable of the Tower of London.

5. H. M. Colvin (ed.), *The History of the King's Works* (1963), Vol. 2, pp. 710–4, 719, and references. Referred to hereafter as *King's Works*.

6. *King's Works*, p. 711 and Pl. 46 B.

7. B. K. Davison, 'Three Eleventh Century Earthworks in England', in *Château Gailliard* II (1967).

8. See also *Royal Commission on Hist. Mons.: (East)*, 1930.

9. Davison, *op. cit.*

10. Davison, *op. cit.*, showing development plans of the Tower of London.

11. See note 6 above.

12. A drawing by T. Wykeham Archer shows the room before the door into the Wakfield Tower was cut. B.M.

13. Could the upper part of this guard room be the crenellated chamber being built in front of the Blundeville (i.e., Wakefield) Tower? See *King's Works*, p. 714, and Pipe Roll, 19 Henry III, rot. 11.

14. Clark, *op. cit.*, p. 221.

15. Clark, *op. cit.*, p. 222.

16. This date is cut on one of the ashlars on the south-west side of the tower.

17. See note 8.

18. The general development of both the form and function of loops has not always received the attention that it deserves. The refinement of masonry detail and the rapid development of mural towers characteristic of the later twelfth century and early thirteenth century resulted in a wide variety of loops—differing in length, splay and cross-slit; the last a recent feature. The elongation and narrowing of the loop which seems to have taken place at this time—thanks partly to the high quality ashlar work—culminated in such remarkable loops as those to be found in the Tour de Constance at Aigues Mortes much later in the thirteenth century. Less extreme forms, however, set in the deep reveals of mural towers abound in the Welsh border castles of the earlier part of the thirteenth century, e.g., White, Skenfrith, and Grosmont, and the inner east curtain of Chepstow; the latter *c.* 1200, at Corfe the North Upper Gate tower of *c.* 1245 has loops of exceptional length and narrowness; *c.* 10 ft. by 1½ in. The south-east tower being cleared and consolidated has loops 7 ft. 6 in. in length and of equal narrowness (1½ in.). Such a width begs the question as to how practical these are to shoot through. It would be essential for the archer to be close to the actual aperture—possibly in many cases with a short bow, but often impractical for the cross-bow (the normal castle defence weapon) due to the acute splay within the embrasure. Loops obviously designed for the cross-bow may be seen in many of the Edwardian castles of the late thirteenth century. Exceptionally, D. F. Renn discusses loops and their defensive potential, see 'The Avranches Traverse at Dover Castle' (the comparison with the Bell Tower and south curtain at the Tower of London is also instructive here), in *Arch. Cant.*, LXXIV (1969), pp. 79-92. 'An Angevin gatehouse at Skipton Castle' (Yorks. W.R.) in *Chateau Gailliard*, VII (1975), pp. 174–82; 'Defending Framlingham Castle', *Proc. Suffolk Inst. of Arch. for 1973*, Vol. XXXIII, part 1 (1974), pp. 58–67.

19. Examples are to be found at Walmer Court: the Old Manor House, Ludgershall Castle, Lewes Castle. I have to thank Mr. S. E. Rigold for drawing my attention to the two latter examples.

20. Bronllys Tower, Brecon, is an example in a round keep roughly contemporary with the Wakefield Tower.

21. *King's Works*, pp. 719-20, and quoting Pipe Roll 9, Edward I, rot. 2.

22. Clark, *op. cit.*, p. 223.

23. *King's Works*, p. 714. The Chapel was also painted at this time. Clark observes (*op. cit.*, p. 225) that there were traces of wall painting found during the 1867 restoration and that the windows were narrow with drop arches.

24. Bayley, *op. cit.*, p. 262 illustrates a window in this position.

25.*King's Works*, p. 711.

26. The problem posed by the change from ashlar to rubble cannot be answered with certainty but it is worth noting that the lower part of the Bell Tower and of the south curtain up to the Bloody Tower are built in a similar manner and it is by no means certain that all the upper part of the latter is of later date especially that part immediately adjoining the Bell Tower. The base of St. Thomas's Tower is likewise of ashlar—especially cramped and waterproofed. It may not be coincidence that this ashlar work is not found in the other towers of Henry III enceinte and seems to be limited to the walls washed by the river itself with its tidal scour.

APPENDIX

WAKEFIELD TOWER POTTERY

by

STEPHEN MOORHOUSE AND JAMES THORN

INTRODUCTION

THE POTTERY associated with the Wakefield Tower is principally of four main groups. Of these two were found by the cill and in the passage of the Postern (Fig. 2 a), the others in the make-up of the ground floor (Fig. 9) and in the south-west loop of the tower (Fig. 2 c). These have been dealt with as separate sequences in the text.

According to the documentation of the tower, the deposition of the associated material (Figs. 10–12) should not be dated earlier than the completion of the lower part of the tower *c.* 1230, and not later than the reign of Edward I (1272–1307) when the outer curtain was built causing the in-filling of the earlier ditch and raising of the floor levels within the tower.

———————

List of Layers shown on Section Drawings (Fig. 9)

1	Herringbone brick floor.	7	Black ash.
2	Rubble, soil and ash.	8	Light brown gravel.
3	Brick built drain.	9a	Yellow gravel.
4	Brick floor and mortar.	9b	Brown clay.
5a	Soil and ash make-up for brick floor.	10	Clean green Chilmark chippings.
		11	Yellow gravel.
5b	Brown soil.	12a	Brown clay and earth mixture.
5c	Black ash.	12b	Yellow gravel.
5d	Light grey ash.	12c	Black ash mixed with soil.
6a	Chilmark chippings mixed with earth. In section A-B there are also thin layers of chalk chippings, and black ash.	12d	Dark silty earth.
		13	Green Chilmark chippings.
		14a	Earth fill of central pillar pit.
		14b	Lime-mortar cement.
6b	Large chips of green Chilmark.	14c	Stone-built central pillar.
6c	Undisturbed green Chilmark chippings.	14d	Concrete support for jewel cage structure.
6d	Stony earth mixture.	14e	Stiff brown clay.
6e	Yellow gravel.		

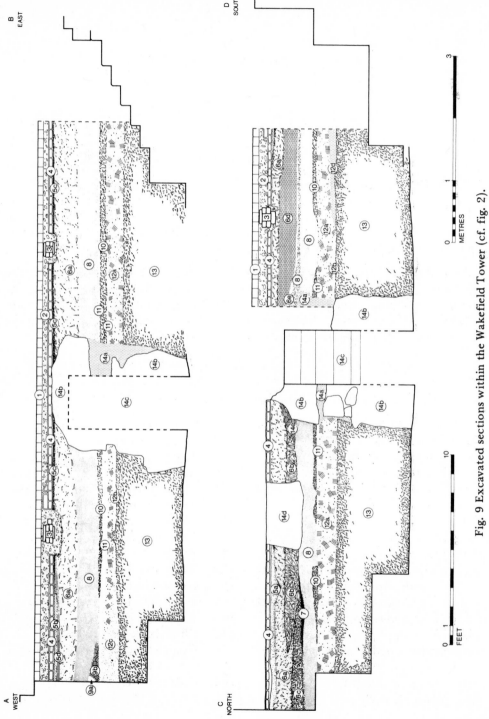

Fig. 9 Excavated sections within the Wakefield Tower (cf. fig. 2).

MATERIALS FROM IN-FILL OF DITCH OUTSIDE POSTERN *(Fig. 10)*

This group came from beneath the level of the lower cill 70 cm. down. It consisted mostly of cooking pots of shell-tempered ware, Nos. 2–4, and a body fragment of a decorated jug, No. 1. Above this were a few Roman sherds in disturbed levels which contained some medieval fragments such as Nos. 3, 5–6; Some of the material from the ditch definitely has a late thirteenth-century origin.

Lower Level

Red Ware

1.—Jug. Very hard, fine, sandy, grey fabric with bright orange outer margin and surface, covered externally in a bright, shiny, clear, deep orange glaze. The decoration appears to be linear strips of white clay with a round pellet of red clay at the intersections. A similar sherd was found at the Custom House, London, in Group C. 2 (No. 222).[1]

Shelly Ware

2.—Cooking pot. Similar fabric to No. 3 below, but with a sand content making the fabric harsher; externally the surface has been smoothed, internally it is rough and uneven. The rim shows a set of finger impressions on edge. Cf. a similar sherd at the Custom House, London, in Group C.2 (No. 366).

3.—Cooking pot. Hard fired, very smooth fabric with dull buff surfaces.

4.—Cooking pot. Hard, fine, sandy fabric, light purple core with red-purple margins. The sherd appears to have been heavily burnt and has been deposited in building mortar or lime.

Upper Levels

White Slipped Red Ware

5.—Jug. Very hard, fine sandy grey fabric covered with dull white slip, external vertical rouletted strip decoration covered with glossy mottled apple-green glaze. The rim form is similar to a complete jug found at Mark Lane,[2] London, and also the fabric is similar to No. 30.

6.—Body sherd. Very hard, fine, sandy, light blue-grey fabric with a bright purple-red outer margin and surface; decoration in a white clay, covered externally in a patchy clear glaze leaving the decoration a light yellow ochre.

GROUP FROM FLOOR OF PASSAGE *(Fig. 10, Pl. IXb)*

A group of pottery was found in the raised floor level sealed below the solid in-fill of the passage. It consisted of a decorated jug, No. 9, which is a similar type of white slipped ware jug to those found in the Tower (Nos. 16, 29, 30,

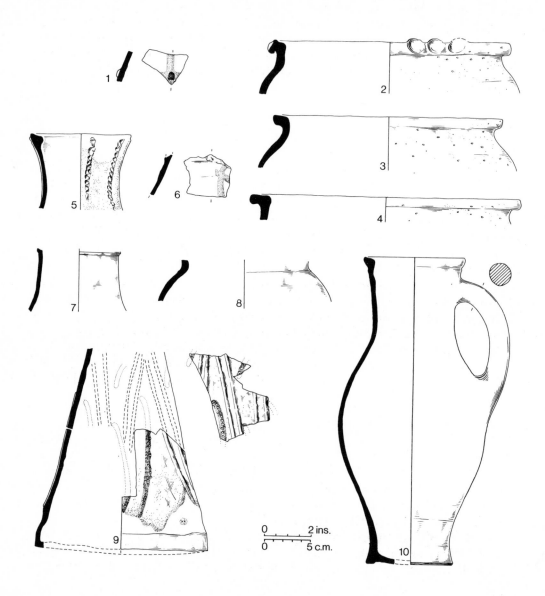

Fig. 10 Coarse pottery associated with postern. Scale 1:4.

etc.), while No. 7 is a fairly unusual developed jug from the Surrey kilns; the coarse cooking pot, No. 8, is known among the earlier Surrey types. A date around the middle of the fourteenth century is therefore likely for this group.

White Ware

7.—Neck sherd. Thin, completely oxidised light buff fabric with external shiny, patchy, khaki-green glaze with lighter mottling in places. Identical in fabric to sherds found at Winchester Palace, Southwark.[3]

8.—Cooking pot. Hard, granular, gritty, dull buff fabric, externally blackened.

White Slipped Red Ware

9.—Jug. Hard fine sandy fabric reduced to a blue-grey core, the inner surfaces varying from grey to dull salmon-red. External decoration consists of near vertical applied strips of body coloured clay, possibly in an acute chevron form, with intermediate red coloured strips, with diamond notch-rouletting on top. Externally covered in a white slip and a mottled, apple-green glaze, both the slip and glaze coming to within 3 cm. of the base.

10.—Jug, with rod handle and recessed footring. Smooth, sandy, friable, dull pinky-red fabric. Covered with patchy, dull-green glaze and dull-cream underslip.

Many fragments (not illustrated) belonging to baluster jugs with rod handles, similar to No. 17, were also found.

Red Ware

Body sherd (not illustrated) of fine, pale-red fabric similar to an example found at the Custom House, London, in Group A.3 (No. 14).

GROUP FROM INNER FILLING OF WAKEFIELD TOWER *(Figs. 11 and 12, Pl. XIc)*

This is the largest group found in five separate layers below the brick floor make-up of layer 5a–d which contained a sixteenth-century handled bowl, No. 32. A wide range of jug forms are represented in this group.

The white slipped jugs, Nos. 17, 23 and 29, are similar to types found in west Kent, but have a wide distribution around London, and their production centre is uncertain. A more characteristic and distinct type of jug is represented by Nos. 19 to 21. These are presumably manufactured somewhere in the London area and traded through the London markets. Their characteristics include hard bodies, rich dark-red glazes and a variety of decorative motifs in a white slip or clay. Their style of decoration and general vessel form resembles jugs found at Rouen,[4] and it is evident that the jugs found in the

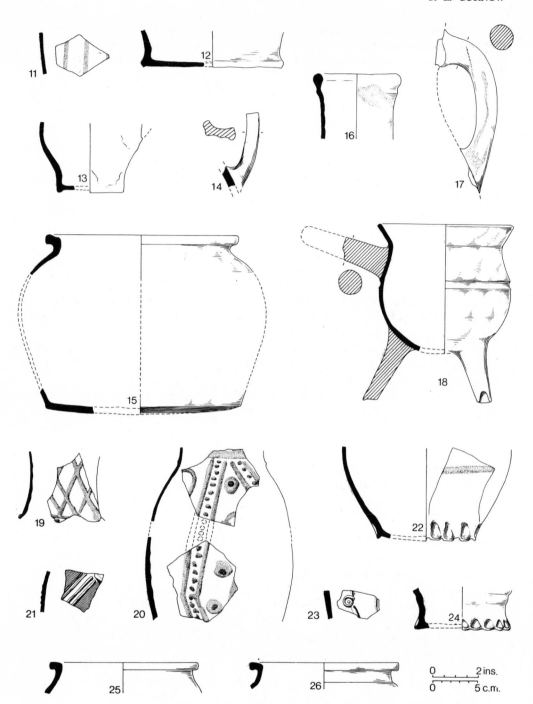

Fig. 11 Coarse pottery from basement in-fill. Scale 1:4

London area were copying these products.[5] The two jugs, Nos. 11 and 12 are similar to products from the Oxfordshire area[6] but the strap handle is likely to indicate a north Midland kiln source.[7]

It is evident that a large number of kiln centres surrounded London in the medieval period and not only supplied the city and surrounding area with pottery, but used its markets and ports for trading.[8]

There were two examples of reduced grey wares—Nos. 15 and 28. These are basically of a sandy, lumpy, totally-reduced fabric, a product of the Hertfordshire area,[9] which has a wide distribution to the north and north-west of London. A number of groups containing these wares are now known and range in date throughout the thirteenth century.[10] The thumbed handle on No. 28 is a feature of jugs in the general area to the north of London, dating to the later thirteenth and early fourteenth century.[11]

Layer 12 a—d

Red Ware

11.—Body sherd in similar fabric to No. 12 with external, neatly-applied, vertical strips of red clay covered overall externally in a shiny, dull, olive-green glaze. A similar sherd was found at the Custom House in Group C.2 (No. 220).

12.—Jug. Very fine-grained, sandy, bright-red fabric with external bright, browny-orange glaze with dull lime-green mottling, which extends under the base.

13.—Body sherd in identical but slightly darker fabric to No. 22, but totally oxidised throughout. A plain recessed footring. The handle base shows the extension of a shallow groove which presumably went down the length of the handle. The inside of the jug is crudely made, while externally it is well finished off and smooth.

14.—Handle base. Hard, sandy fabric with small, white inclusions, bright, salmon-red surfaces and margins with grey core. Deep, shiny, olive-green glaze down the centre with patches underneath.

Grey Ware

15.—Cooking pot. Hard, fine, sandy reduced light-grey fabric; soot-blackened exterior.

Red Ware

Roof furniture? One large sherd (not illustrated), coarse sandy fabric with dull pink surfaces, a blue-grey core and external lumpy, glossy, dull, orange-brown glaze.

Layer 11

White Slipped Red Ware

16.—Jug. Fine smooth fabric with dull, brick-red margins contrasting with a blue-grey core. External dull, creamy slip and streaky patches of dull to light green glaze.

17.—Complete rod handle and part of base (not illustrated). Similar fabric to No. 29 with all-over white slip, patchy in places, and sporadically covered in a light apple-green glaze with darker mottling. These sherds would seem to be part of a London Classic Baluster Jug, a good example of which is the Lesnes Abbey jug.[12]

Red Ware

18.—Tripod pipkin. Hard, fine, sandy fabric with smooth, dull, pale-red surfaces and a grey core. Covered externally by a dull, olive-green glaze, to which mortar adheres. The vessel has copied a contemporary metal form, seen in manuscript illustrations from the thirteenth and fourteenth centuries.[13]

Layer 8

Red Ware

19.—Jug. Very thin, fine, hard, sandy fabric totally oxidised to a dull salmon-red. External decoration of white clay lattice-work under a rich, uniform, light ox-blood glaze.

20.—Jug. Similar fabric to No. 19, but with a reduced, light-grey core. External decoration in a white clay under an all-over, rich, uniform ox-blood glaze.

21.—Body sherd in a thin, fine, sandy fabric with red surfaces, darker internally, with a dark grey core. Chevron decoration of parallel white strips, apparently unglazed on this sherd.

22.—Lower part of globular jug in a smooth, fine, sandy fabric with dull, salmon-red surfaces and a well-defined grey core throughout. Pronounced thumbings on the base forming a foot stand. Horizontal band of white slip, covered with a watery, dull-orange glaze.

White Slipped Red Ware

23.—Body sherd. Very hard, sandy, grey, reduced fabric, dull red outer surface with applied strip under a dense green glaze, over which mortar adheres.

24.—Jug. Hard, sandy, bright, brick-red fabric with a light blue-grey core. Rough coarse-grained, internal sandy surface. Small, shallow finger impressions above the base angle, over which is a white slip, covered by spots of orange and light green glaze.

25 and 26.—Cooking pots in similar fabric to No. 1; light grey fabric, darker surfaces.

Saintonge Ware

Two sherds (not illustrated), in a fine, smooth, off-white fabric with external, bright, mottled, apple-green glaze, from the shoulders of monochrome green glaze jugs characteristic of those from the Saintonge area of south-western France.

Layer 7 *(Fig. 12)*

Red Ware

27.—Jug. Fine, sandy, friable fabric with dull, pinky-brown surfaces and a light-grey core. There are two applied, leaf-shaped ears at the top of rod handle reminiscent of French contemporary examples from the Normandy area.

Grey Ware

28.—Jug. Hard, fine, sandy, totally reduced, light-grey fabric with small white inclusions and dull red ochre margins. The rod handle has alternate side thumbings down the back with a stab mark in the centre of each. An interesting feature of this jug is the separately applied base.

Layer 6

White Slipped Red Ware

29.—Jug. Fine, sandy, smooth fabric with dull salmon surfaces and a dark grey core. Covered externally in a white slip with external, rich, apple-green glaze over applied dot and strip decoration of white clay.

30.—Jug. Hard, fine, sandy totally reduced grey fabric covered all over in a thick, creamy slip with an external mottled, apple-green glaze thickening towards the rim, suggesting an inverted firing position in the kiln.

31.—Jug. Fine, sandy, reduced grey fabric with extremely smooth, dull, salmon-red outer surface. There is a dull creamy slip on the upper half of the sherd with the suggestions of the termination of a rouletted strip (too faint to show in the drawing). Wide spaced thumbing around the slightly recessed footring.

Layer 5 a—d

32.—Handled bowl in a fine, smooth, light-buff, sandy fabric with extremely smooth surfaces. Covered internally in a bright, glossy, light apple-green glaze with darker mottling. The fabric and glaze suggest a date around the middle of the sixteenth century although the general form is known earlier in Surrey white ware.

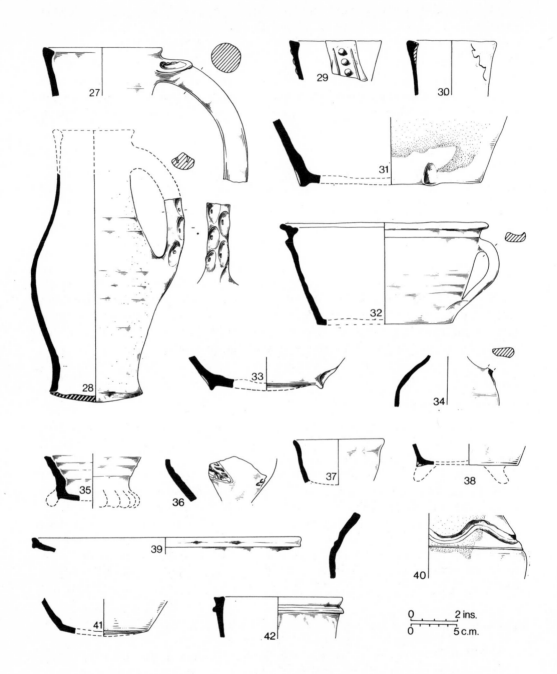

Fig. 12 Coarse pottery from basement in-fill and south-west loop. Scale 1:4

Layer 2

33.—Jug. Very hard, fine, sandy fabric with dull brown surfaces and a light-grey core. The fragment shows the remains of a pulled foot similar to those found on typical Dutch vessels later in the Middle Ages.

GROUP FROM FILLING OF SOUTH-WEST LOOP

This group is a completely isolated group found within the Wakefield Tower sealed by a probable late Tudor brick floor. Although small and undated by documentary evidence it is important as it contains vessels that would, out of context, suggest dates at either end of the sixteenth century.

Typological evidence suggests that the Raeren stoneware (Nos. 34–35) belongs to the earlier or first half of the sixteenth century, while the Surrey white wares (Nos. 36–38) belong to the latter part. However, the moulding on the Cologne piece (No. 36) supports a later date in the sixteenth-century,[14] and the Raeren mugs, although most commonly found in the early sixteenth century, are known to continue throughout the century into the early seventeenth.[15] Recent evidence suggests, moreover, that the emergence of the post-medieval Surrey white wares occurred much earlier in the sixteenth century than was previously thought. Bearing these somewhat conflicting factors in mind, a date for the group around the middle of the sixteenth century (if not slightly earlier) seems reasonable.

Raeren Stoneware

34.—Jug. Fine, light-grey stoneware with internal, light-matt, purple surface and external all-over rich glossy, mottled, light grey and light brown glaze.

35.—Jug. Fine light grey stoneware with external glossy glaze similar to No. 36, but darker; unglazed internally.

Cologne Stoneware

36.—Jug. Fine light-grey stoneware, moulded leaf decoration covered by a uniform, internal, light watery purple-brown glaze and an external, dark, glossy uniform glaze.

Surrey White Wares

37.—Shallow bowl. Smooth creamy off-white fabric, with a bright creamy yellow internal glaze.

38.—Pipkin. Smooth, fine, sandy fabric with internal bright yellow glaze and mottled apple-green speckling beneath the base.

Red Wares

39.—Plate. Sandy dull brick-red friable fabric with smooth surfaces, blackened internally.

40.—Jug. Hard, fine, smooth sandy fabric with dull-pink surfaces and a blue-grey core. Externally, bright olive-green to orange glaze, more watery and patchy below the girth groove.

41.—Jug in identical, slightly redder, fabric to No. 39 above, with a splash of similar glaze on the external base angle.

42.—Jug. Fine sandy bright brick-red fabric with grey inner surface covered all over externally in a glossy dull metallic brown glaze.

REFERENCES

1. *Trans. London and Middx.*, 25 (1974), pp. 180-183 and 26 (1975), pp. 118-151.

2. B. Rackham, *Medieval Pottery* (1948), p. 28, Pl. 37.

3. Information from Dr. Francis Celoria.

4. *Arch. Journ.*, CXXII (1965), pp. 74-85.

5. *London Museum Medieval Catalogue* (H.M.S.O., reprinted 1967), Pl. LXIII, No. 1.

6. For the form of vessel of similar date see *Oxoniensia* IV (1939), p. 106, Fig. 25.

7. The general fabric of this handle together with its section and 'splash' glazing technique suggest a northern-Midland source, although the white inclusions are not found in similar products from the Nottingham kilns.

8. *Trans. English Ceramic Circle*, 2 (1945), pp. 234-6.

9. *Med. Arch.*, V (1961), pp. 267-70.

10. An earlier thirteenth-century group from Sopwell Nunnery, Herts., a group from the middle of the century from Berkhampstead Castle, *Herts. Archaeology*, 2 (1970), pp. 69-71; various stratified groups from The More, *Arch. Journ.*, CXVI (1959), p. 163, Figs. 8-9, and a late thirteenth-fourteenth century group from Chequer Street, St. Albans, *Herts. Archaeology*, 3 (1972), pp. 121-2, Fig. 1:5.

11. *Herts. Archaeology*, 1 (1968), pp. 124-127, with a distribution map on p. 125.

12. *Antiquaries J.*, XLI (1961), pp. 1-12, Figs. 1 and 5.

13. *Op. cit.*, note 6, Pl. LV, and Fig. 68, No. 4.

14. Jugs from the various Cologne factories have recently been discussed by J. G. Hurst, 'A Sixteenth-Century Cologne Jug from the Carmelite Friary, Newcastle-upon-Tyne', *Archaeologia Aeliana*, 4th ser., XLVIII (1970).

15. Originally discussed in J. G. Hurst 'Flemish Stoneware Jugs', in *Winchester Excavations 1949-1960* (Winchester, 1964), pp. 142-3. Evidence for their continuity is given in *Wilts. Arch. Mag.*, LXII (1967), p. 74, and *Post-Med. Arch.*, 4 (1970), p. 76, n. 161.

De Ireby's Tower in Carlisle Castle

by

R. GILYARD-BEER

SQUARE, SQUAT AND FUNCTIONAL, the outer gatehouse of Carlisle Castle looks out across ditch and glacis towards the city today as it has done for six centuries past. It is not an attractive structure and, if it has commanded a measure of regard from historians, this has been because it belongs to the small and select company of medieval buildings for which original documents exist.[1]

From about 1383 until 1962 it was in constant use and no opportunity for a comprehensive examination of it occurred, although the fact that it had been placed on Schedule B of buildings in military occupation following the 1911 agreement between the War Department and H.M. Office of Works ensured its survival. On 15 February 1962 the last garrison was withdrawn from the castle and its buildings were transferred to the Ministry of Works for preservation as an ancient monument. The gatehouse, latterly in use as a guard room and as a meeting place of the Old Comrades' Association of the Border Regiment, became vacant and it was at last possible to consolidate its fabric and to explore its historical potential.

This article is based on the results of that work, undertaken at intervals over a period of some eight years, working back slowly and painfully through the cream and olive paint of service occupation, through hard and unsympathetic proprietary plasterwork, through brick partitions and casings, to stonework itself changed and counterchanged by centuries of alteration and renewal until few external openings in the building could be claimed to bear more than an accidental relationship to their medieval predecessors. At the end of it all, the gatehouse is still as unlovely as ever, but it is now vastly more informative and it displays its information for all to see. Moreover, it is now possible to see how far it corresponds to the terms of its fourteenth-century documents.

The gatehouse takes it name from a William de Ireby who in 1212 was a tenant-in-chief of King John as his ancestors had been since the time of Henry I.[2] Although the names of castle towers have a notorious habit of changing with the years, it is possible that it was built as a successor of a William de Ireby's tower, damaged when the castle was taken in 1216 by Alexander II, King of Scots, and notable as late as the middle of the thirteenth century for the fact that it was fractured from top to bottom and had not been repaired.[3]

On 13 April 1378 an indenture[4] (Pl. XII) was made between the new King Richard II and John Lewyn,[5] mason, for the building of a gate and a tower on the side of the castle towards the city. This new gatehouse was to be 55 ft. long and 32 ft. wide, and was to stand 34 ft. high to the base of its battlements. The gate passage, 11 ft. wide, was to be covered by a barbican with double battlements, projecting 10 ft. in front of the gate and entered by an arch springing from a flanking tower containing a kitchen. In this kitchen tower south of the barbican there was to be a vaulted cellar 28 ft. long and 18 ft. wide, with a fireplace and a privy, and on the north side of the gate there was to be a 14 ft. square prison and a chamber of the same dimensions with fireplace and privy. The gate passage was to be vaulted and to be flanked by two buttresses 5 ft. square at ground level, as high as the main building, and battlemented. The kitchen tower towards the castle ditch was to be 32 ft. long and 20 ft. wide externally and was to contain two vaulted chambers with fireplaces and privies. Above the gate there was to be a hall 30 ft. long and 20 ft. wide, with a timber screen wall. The kitchen was to have two stone fireplaces, and there was to be a chamber behind the hall dais with fireplace and privy. All walls were to be 6 ft. thick from ground level up to the vaulting and 5 ft. thick above that, and the partition walls within the building were to be of reasonable thickness. The king was to provide a quarry for the stone, and timber for scaffolding and centering, whilst Lewyn was to work the quarry and to provide lime, sand and transport. The contract price was 500 marks.

For some years it has been realised that the building described in this indenture is the existing gatehouse to the outer ward of the castle (Fig. 1). There are inconsistencies both in the description and in some of the measurements given but, allowing for an occasional lack of precision in the wording of the indenture, there can be little doubt about the identification.

The building is two storeys high with external walls of red sandstone ashlar that weathers indifferently and has been subjected to much renewal in times gone by. On plan it resembles a capital letter L with its long arm roughly on the axis of the south curtain of the outer ward. This long arm is traversed by the gate passage immediately above the short arm of the L which projects in advance of the curtain. A barbican occupies the re-entrant angle formed by the two arms.

There are several irregularities in the plan. The main ones are that the gatehouse masks a change in the direction of the curtain, and that the top end of the long arm is set at an angle to the rest of the building and probably incorporates part of an earlier building on a different alignment.

The gatehouse is not truly orientated and for the sake of simplicity its outer face towards the castle ditch is described in this article as the south face, and its face towards the outer ward as the north face. But in the indenture of 1378 these were regarded, excusably enough, as the east and west faces respectively. For simplicity again, the long arm of the L is here referred to as the hall range, and the short arm as the kitchen tower, although strictly speaking the latter is not a structurally independent tower

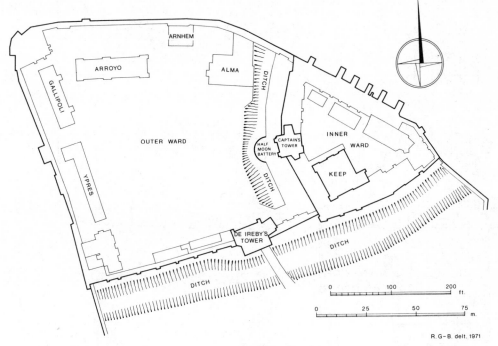

Fig. 1 Carlisle Castle, plan.

but is simply a projection from the hall range. For the sake of brevity the following account concentrates on the medieval features of the gatehouse, particularly those discovered during the work of 1962-70; the details of its plan and of the later alterations made to it can best be studied in the figures.

Description (*Fig. 2*)

The south front of the gatehouse is formed by the barbican flanked on the west by the kitchen tower and on the east by the curtain of the outer ward which here overlaps the hall range (Pl. XIIIb).

The front of the barbican itself (A on Fig. 2) is flush with the south face of the kitchen tower, but is only one storey high against the tower's two storeys. Its entrance archway, of two orders chamfered on both sides and dying into the flanking walls, was never intended to be provided with gates, and the fact that it is set within a rectangular recess in the wall face suggests that the present stone bridge over the ditch may have been preceded by a

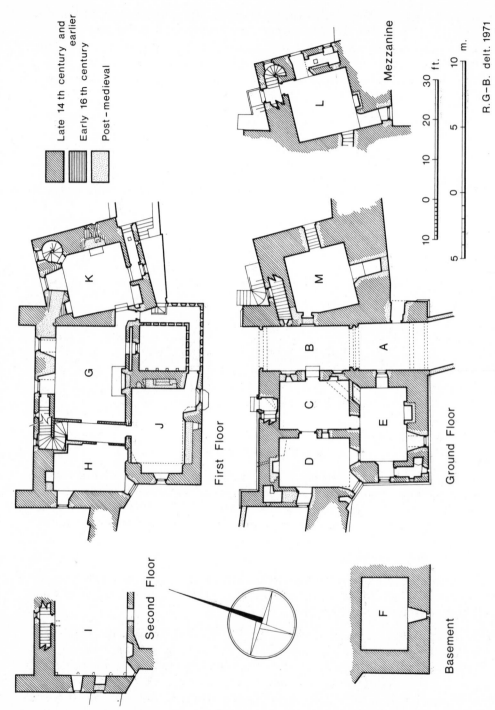

Late 14 th century and earlier

Early 16 th century

Post - medieval

Mezzanine

Second Floor

First Floor

Ground Floor

Basement

Fig. 2 De Ireby's Tower, plan in 1962.

R.G–B. delt. 1971

turning bridge capable of closing the arch when raised. Above the recess there is a rectangular panel with a moulded frame, bearing a coat-of-arms now too heavily eroded to be identifiable.

The wall walk of the barbican has battlements on both its inner and outer faces which in their present form have feather-edged eighteenth-century musket loops. Within the barbican and on the same level as its wall walk there are four corbels on the east face of the kitchen tower, suggesting that the barbican passage was once capable of being decked over at this level, although the rebuilding of the parapets has destroyed any evidence for the corbels on the wing wall that would have been necessary for this.

A misleading doorway through the eastern wing wall is probably of seventeenth-century date; although described as a sally-port on eighteenth-century plans,[6] it is rabetted for a door closing against the barbican passage, and it once led to a post-medieval building, destroyed before the eighteenth century, on the berm of the ditch outside the curtain.

The barbican abuts on the south face of the hall range which is here pierced by the gate passage (B). The massive iron crooks behind both jambs of the arches at either end of the passage and the pockets reserved in its barrel vault show that it was designed for two sets of double-leaved doors closing against the barbican and against the outer ward. The southern arch still has a fine plank door in two leaves with a small wicket, and is framed externally by a higher arch of two orders covering the grooves for a portcullis which could be lowered in front of the door. The iron-shod portcullis survives, long since fixed in its raised position.

Access to the rooms west of the gate passage is now through a post-medieval doorway forced through the wall between two blocked fourteenth-century doorways. It leads first into a barrel-vaulted room (C) that was originally reached through the northern blocked doorway in the passage. A straight flight of steps rises within the thickness of the north wall of this room to the first floor. In the fourteenth century a doorway in the north wall of the room led to these steps, but in the nineteenth century this was blocked and replaced by a doorway from the steps to the outer ward. The blocking and the paving of the landing at the foot of the stairs have now been removed to reveal the mutilated eastern jamb of the original doorway and the three winders by which the stairs turned southwards into the room.[7]

In the west wall of room C a fourteenth-century doorway leads to another room (D) of similar dimensions, also barrel-vaulted. Beneath the north-eastern corner of the vault a pair of massive corbels carries oversailing chamfered courses of masonry to support the stairs from room C where they turn out of the thickness of the north wall into the room above. The fourteenth-century fireplace of room D was found behind a series of superimposed surrounds in the north wall of the room; at the back of its hearth a narrow channel leads through the wall to a small loop in its outer face, presumably a device to make the fire draw. The west wall has a window set in a mutilated fourteenth-century embrasure. Walled over within the northern reveal of this embrasure there was found a doorway to a blocked wall passage leading north and then turning east to serve a privy; this passage has now been reopened. The only other original features in room D are a loop in the south-west angle, widened almost out of recognition, and a small squint alongside the doorway, also later remodelled.

A forced doorway now leads from room C to another room (E) which occupies the ground floor of the kitchen tower. It has a barrel-vault, is much the same size and has the same features as room D. Its fourteenth-century fireplace has been discovered in the south wall, and alongside this is the embrasure of a loop later widened to form a window. In the southern reveal of a second embrasure in the west wall a doorway leads to a wall passage and to a privy contrived within the south-west angle of the building. In the east wall a casement window probably occupies the embrasure of a loop commanding the interior of the barbican. As originally built, room E was not accessible from room C; it was reached through the southern of the two blocked fourteenth-century doorways in the gate passage B, from which a diagonal passage led south-westwards cutting off the angle of room C. The upper part of the wall of this passage survives within room C supported on a stop-chamfered beam inserted on brick packers, and a small part of the slab roof of the passage with its continuous chamfered corbel courses has been revealed by removing the lining and back of a cupboard in the north wall of room E.[8]

When the walls of room E were cleaned down they showed clear signs that its original floor had been at a higher level than the modern boarded one. The hearth of the fourteenth-century fireplace was 2 ft. 6 in. above the level of its successors, and the jambs of the embrasures of the south and west windows and of the doorway to the privy had been cut down by an equal amount. The boarded floor rested on made ground, and excavation revealed the main walls of the room going down 10 ft. 8 in. into the ground to form a cellar (F). This had a clay floor, and the only feature in its walls was an embrasure high on the south side with a sill sloping steeply upwards to a small loop set above the head of the embrasure and obviously intended as a ventilation shaft rather than a source of light. The cellar had had a barrel-vault, the haunches of which remain although the crown was destroyed to give room for lowering the floor of room E. Cellar F had been deliberately filled with earth, clay and rubble containing no dateable material. There were no stairs down to it and access must have been through a trap in the missing crown of the vault.

The first-floor rooms of both hall range and kitchen tower are reached by the stairs in the north wall of room C. These stairs, although slightly altered, are basically of the fourteenth century. The room into which they emerge now occupies the whole of the first floor above B, C and D, and measures 41 ft. 6 in. by 18 ft. 10 in. It had been divided by modern brick partitions into two rooms separated by a passage opposite the stair well, and although these partitions have now been removed the room is best considered in two parts, the part (G) east of the stairs and the part (H) west of them.

The north wall of room G had been much altered. It now has two nineteenth-century sash windows set in embrasures. Only the west jamb of the west embrasure belongs to the fourteenth century, the whole wall east of this and up to the heads of the embrasures having been rebuilt with re-used masonry.[9] In this west reveal of the west embrasure an original doorway leads to a flight of steps rising westwards in the thickness of the wall. The east embrasure also had a fourteenth-century predecessor, but in a different position, for exploration of the straight joint between the north and east walls of the room has shown that the face of the east wall was originally carried through to form the eastern side of a recess or embrasure in the north wall where the jamb of a fourteenth-century doorway leading eastwards into the thickness of the wall remains.

The south wall of room G has also been extensively patched, but towards its east end there was a fourteenth-century loop overlooking the barbican. The lintel of this loop survives in the head of a larger and later window inserted here which cuts through the portcullis slot within which the mutilated remains of the portcullis can be seen. Just to the west of this window a large quadrant corbel set high on the wall may have been one of a pair to support the portcullis mechanism. The only other fourteenth-century feature in the south wall is the fireplace, robbed of its dressings and uncovered from beneath a series of army stoves and fireplaces. The wall around it is much patched, but by unexpected good fortune still retains three stones cut to a skew that gives the rake of the great tapering hood above the fire.

Room H has a small fourteenth-century fireplace at the west end of its north wall and just enough original stonework in the embrasures of its two windows to show that they belong to that date although both were later widened. The south wall has two doorways side by side, the west one of the fourteenth century and the east one an early sixteenth-century insertion.

Rooms G and H are now open to the roof, but there was once another room (I) above H, reached by the stairs rising in the north wall of room G. About halfway up this flight a landing and doorway open into room I, which has a fireplace in its south wall, and two windows in its west wall with a doorway to the wall walk of the south curtain between them. All these were probably fourteenth-century features, although the doorway to the curtain was later blocked, both windows were widened, and another doorway was forced through the south wall near the fireplace.

The evidence for the vanished floor of room I can be seen on its north and west walls. Below the west jamb of the doorway from the stairs there is a large hole capable of housing the end of a massive beam, the upper surface of which would have been 7 ft. 3 in. above the floor of room H; the hole for the other end of the beam was destroyed when the later doorways were inserted in the south wall of rooms H and I. At the north end of the west wall there is a large quadrant corbel, and examination of the masonry along the rest of that wall shows where four more corbels of similar size, fairly regularly spaced at the same height, have been dressed back flush with the wall face. The upper beds of all these corbels are 7 ft. 4 in. above the floor of room H, so that the soffits of joists supported on them would rest on the upper surface of the great beam beneath the doorway to the stairs. These joists were probably cantilevered out to the east beyond the beam to enable the floor to cover the doorway, and the east wall of this suspended room must have been framed of timber.

The doorways in the south wall of room H lead to room J on the first floor of the kitchen tower. The removal of an army stove and blocking walls has uncovered two large fourteenth-century fireplaces occupying most of the south and east walls of the room. The one in the south wall has kept its fine chamfered segmental head of 10 ft. 6 in. span, and some 3 ft. above hearth level a blocked loop is set in the back of its flue.[10] The other fireplace has a span of some 8 ft., but has lost its dressings; there is a recess for a cupboard alongside it. The west wall of the room is wholly taken up with a recess that has a segmental head matching that of the southern fireplace; within it is the embrasure for an original loop, cut down by two courses when it was later widened into a window. In the fourteenth century there was probably a sink below the loop, for the spout of a drain can be seen in the external face of the wall at this point.

The south-east corner of room J has been greatly altered by the insertion of a doorway to the wall walk of the barbican with a sash window alongside it. Enough evidence remains to show that in the fourteenth century there was no access to the barbican here, and that the window replaces an embrasure which led to a half-octagonal turret projecting from the wall on a corbelled base which still survives outside. The function of this turret would be to provide enfilade fire across the face of the barbican.

Returning to room G, a modern opening in its east wall leads to room K which is about 16 ft. square and which, with the two rooms beneath it east of the gate passage, is set at an angle to the rest of the gatehouse. This irregularity of alignment and the character of the masonry in parts of the walls suggest that this end of the building is an older structure incorporated in the fourteenth-century gatehouse and remodelled out of recognition in the process. The greater part of the south-west angle of room K was rebuilt when the doorway from room G was made and when another doorway was forced through the wall to give access to the wall walk of the barbican, but the east jamb of a fireplace remains near this point and alongside it the embrasure of an original loop later replaced by a window. From the east reveal of this embrasure a doorway leads to a passage in the thickness of the south wall and eventually through another doorway forced through the end of that wall to give access to the east curtain. Originally this passage was a privy, the drain of which has been found under the floor, and its side walls show rough masonry where the solid end of the passage was cut through to form the doorway.

The removal of a fireplace against the east wall of room K brought to light the mutilated remains of its brick predecessor of early sixteenth-century date. It has lost its surround, but above it are parts of a moulded and plastered panel that formed its overmantel, and the back of the flue contains a small brick cupboard and a sloping channel leading to a ventilation loop in the outer wall. The insertion of this fireplace blocked an earlier window, remains of which can be seen both internally and externally.

The north wall of room K has also suffered much alteration. Originally there was a plain rectangular opening like a doorway without jambs near the west end of the wall, and an embrasure alongside it. When the brick fireplace was inserted in the east wall the embrasure was widened to the east and provided with a segmental brick head, a passage was forced through its west reveal, and the earlier rectangular opening was blocked in brick. Later, the whole of this passage was filled up with rubble. Enough rubble has now been removed to show that the sixteenth-century passage replaced a fourteenth-century one which had been entered through the rectangular opening, led northwards for some 4 ft., and then turned westwards to the doorway already mentioned in the thickness of the wall at the north-east angle of room G. Access from G to K in the fourteenth century was therefore not in its present position at the south-east angle of G, but through the wall at the north-east angle.

In the north-east corner of room K a doorway leads to a newel staircase which goes up to the parapet. Today it also goes down to room L beneath room K, but this was not the fourteenth-century arrangement. A quarter-turn down from K the east wall of the stair well has a window inserted in a blocked doorway. Immediately below this the sides of the stair well and the rough and improvised newel stones show that the stairs have here been cut through the wall to link with the passage outside room L. The steps between room K and the blocked doorway were renewed to a more gentle rake than they possessed originally, thereby covering a landing which once existed behind the doorway. In the fourteenth century, therefore, there was no direct access from K to L; the stairs from K ended at a landing behind the doorway, from which there would perhaps be an external flight of wooden steps down to the outer ward.

Room L lies below room K and is of much the same dimensions. Its north wall contains a passage with a flight of stone steps descending steeply westwards to the level of the gate passage. From the landing at the head of these stairs an original doorway leads into the north-east corner of L, the east wall of which has a recess into which the door swung. This wall also has an embrasure, much altered and with a doorway forced through its south reveal into a small passage within the wall thickness. The passage was originally reached by a doorway with a very heavy quadrant-shouldered head towards the south end of the east wall, and it served a privy, the drain of which has been found under the floor. In the south wall a small late fireplace is contained within the surround of its fourteenth-century predecessor, and beside it in the south-west angle of the room there is a window, parts of the embrasure of which are original.

At the foot of the stairs in the north wall a doorway, later blocked, led into the gate passage. The south wall of the staircase alongside this doorway shows the straight joint of one jamb of a blocked opening, and the length of the joint shows that this was a rabetted trap or hatch rather than a doorway. This trap led into room M which lies below room L and is of the same size. Access to M is now by a forced opening through its east wall with a steep flight of steps down from the level of the outer ward. In the south wall there is an early recess later extended through the wall to communicate with the seventeenth-century building that stood on the berm of the ditch and that has now gone. The whole of the north-west angle of the room was rebuilt when the trap from the stairs was blocked and replaced by a doorway in the west wall leading to the gate passage. Room M has no windows and no fireplace.

The Gatehouse and the Indenture Compared *(Fig. 3)*

From the description just given it will be apparent that some parts of the gatehouse can be identified in the terms of the indenture of 1378, that some parts cannot, and that there are both major and minor discrepancies.

Although the battlements have all been renewed, the height of the sills of their embrasures above the level of the outer ward correspond well with the 34 ft. of the indenture. The southern or outer face of the building is slightly higher because it projects on to the lip of the ditch.

The wall thicknesses specified tally well with those of the fabric. The outer walls vary in thickness from 5 ft. 9 in. to 6 ft., compared with the 6 ft. of the indenture, and from 4 ft. 6 in. to 6 ft. on the upper storey as compared with the 5 ft. of the indenture. The two buttresses on the north face can be regarded as roughly 5 ft. square if the plinth is included, and this again conforms to the specification.

It is more difficult to reconcile the overall measurements of 55 ft. by 32 ft. given by the indenture. The full length of the gatehouse is really 77 ft. and more, and its width including the kitchen tower is 43 ft. 6 in. A length of 55 ft. cannot be achieved even by subtracting the part of the hall range that lies east of the gate passage, which might reasonably be done because it appears to be part of an older tower rather than a piece of new building in the fourteenth century. However, by including the buttresses and excluding the kitchen tower the width of the building can be reduced to 31 ft.

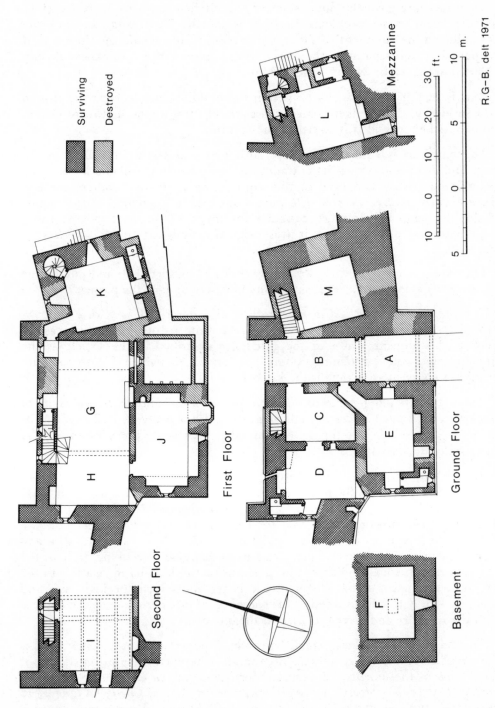

Surviving

Destroyed

Mezzanine

L

Second Floor

I

First Floor

K

G

H

J

Basement

F

Ground Floor

M

B

A

C

D

E

10   0   10   20   30 ft.

5   0   5   10 m.

R.G.-B. delt 1971

Fig. 3 De Ireby's Tower, reconstructed plan in fourteenth-century.

The indenture gives the dimensions of the kitchen tower as 32 ft. by 20 ft. and this again causes problems. Its front is actually 28 ft. 6 in., and in order to produce a measurement of 20 ft. it is necessary to include the thickness of the partition wall separating the tower from the hall range, a thickness already included in the 31 ft. width of the hall range.

But the major discrepancies lie within the building, and to clear the ground for considering them it is best to list first of all those rooms and features that can be satisfactorily identified from the indenture.

The barbican is easily identifiable, although it is 16 ft. instead of 10 ft. long. The manner in which its entrance dies into the wing wall and the kitchen tower is admirably conveyed in the words *et se tournera a trauers par une vousure entre lentree vers la dite porte tanq' sur une meindre Tour,* whilst its double parapets, although designed for musketry in their present form, perpetuate the memory that it was originally designed to be *doublement embataillez.*

The gate passage is 11 ft. wide and vaulted, all as specified, and one of the two *botraces* is indeed *sur les iowes* of the northern arch of the passage.

The *meindre Tour q' serra une Cusyne,* also described as *la dite Tour q' serra la Cusyne cestassauoir deuers la fossee* despite its differences in measurement is the projecting arm of the gatehouse described in this article as the kitchen tower and containing rooms J, E and F, of which J with its *deux chemynez couenables de pere* is the kitchen itself.

Room G extending *paramont la dite porte* is the *sale de trente pedz en longure et vynt pedz en laeure,* although its width is really 18 ft. 10 in. and its length to the socket for the great beam that represents the position of the *mur parclos de maerisme* is 27 ft. 6 in.

To the east (north in the indenture) of the gate passage room M, although roughly 15 ft. square, is the *prison q' contendra quatorze pedz squarr'* correctly described as being *a lautre part de la dite porte deuers le North.* The qualification *outre celle prisone* shows that the *Chambre ouesq' chemyne et priue de quatorze pedz squarr'* is to be looked for on this side of the gate also, and room L with its fireplace and privy and its measurements echoing those of the prison is the obvious candidate. The position of the kitchen in relation to the hall shows which is the low end of the latter and which the high end, and enables room K to be identified as the *chambre estante deriere le dees* complete with the fireplace and privy specified in the indenture.

The *deux mesons voutees* could be rooms C and D were it not that C lacks the fireplace and privy specified. But the most detailed description of any of the rooms in the indenture is reserved for the cellar: *en la meindre Tour a la port de lentree vers le suth un celer contenant vynt et oyt pedz en longure et dys et oyt pedz en laeure voutez ouesque un chemyne et un priue.* Room E corresponds to the position described and has the vaulting, fireplace and privy, but is only half the size. Nor is it a true cellar, and its claim has been further damaged by the recent discovery of the true cellar F beneath it, but a cellar that again is half the size specified and that lacks both fireplace and privy.

This lack of correspondence between the ground floor and basement rooms west of the gate passage serves as an introduction to the major discrepancy between the indenture and the fabric. The indenture is concerned with the building of a gatehouse that was to contain eight rooms of various kinds besides a barbican and a gate passage. As built, the gatehouse contained eleven rooms in addition to barbican and gate passage, and some of its dimensions were notably in excess of those specified. The inescapable conclusion is that the indenture as we know it was not faithfully executed, and that there were substantial variations of contract during building.

The king twice appointed commissioners to survey the work on the gate-house. On the first occasion in 1383[11] the commission was for Carlisle Castle alone and the commissioners were to report on the quality of the work. But in 1387[12] a second commission covered both Roxburgh and Carlisle Castles and the commissioners were to inform themselves and to certify how much the works exceeded the agreements made between the king and Lewyn, and how much would still be needed to complete the works in excess of those agreements. This excess could well refer to Roxburgh where the works were long drawn out and where Lewyn claimed that he had suffered losses and depredations;[13] but it could equally well refer to Carlisle where it would suggest that there had been some departure from the contract.[14]

The information provided by the documents and the fabric can there-fore be treated as complementary rather than contradictory if the easy assumption is abandoned that because a contract exists it must necessarily have been executed, and if it is remembered not only that documents may throw light on a building but also that a building may throw light on its documents.

Taking documents and fabric together, it can be seen that the indenture and the subsequent accounts and surveys provide a firm series of dates that cannot be won from a mutilated fabric singularly devoid of stylistically dateable features. They throw light on the supply of materials for the work, the manner in which it is to be carried out, and its cost. But they give at best an imperfect picture of the structure, of its defensive arrangements and of the accommodation it contained. We learn that it was to be an embattled tower pierced by a gate passage, covered by a barbican and flanked by a projecting wing, and that within it there was to be accommodation corresponding to that of a fairly substantial medieval house and including a small prison. They specify the fireplaces and privies needed for various rooms, but they tell practically nothing of the relationship and communications between these rooms and therefore of how the building actually worked as a house. It is only by turning to the fabric that these bare bones can be clothed with the flesh of actuality and that we can appreciate in some detail how the gatehouse was intended to be used both as a military and as a domestic building.

The Gatehouse as a Military Building *(Fig. 3)*

The shape of the gatehouse is unusual. It does not conform to the twin-towered type that appeared at Dover Castle before the end of the twelfth century and became dominant in the thirteenth, or to the simple tower with central gate passage that had been in use since the late eleventh century. Its L-shape is a compromise between these two types, providing a flanking tower on one side only of the gate. A gate flanked by a single mural tower appears at Robin Hood's Tower in Richmond Castle before the end of the eleventh century, but there the gate is a simple opening through the curtain and is not enclosed within a building. Lewyn's idea had been more closely anticipated in the gatehouse of Goodrich Castle about three-quarters of a century before the date of the Carlisle indenture and, more significantly, was again to be used by him in a form modified to suit the needs of a quadrangular castle in work at Bolton Castle that was the subject of a contract drawn up between him and Sir Richard le Scrope and dated only five months after the Carlisle indenture.[15]

The barbican occupies the re-entrant angle of the L, and the lack of gates at its entrance perhaps dictated the use of the interesting double battlements that protect both sides of its wall walk; indeed it has the appearance of having been designed to 'welcome little fishes in, with gently smiling jaws' so that, once inside, a plunging fire could be directed on an attacker from all four sides.

The other interesting feature of the barbican is that, as originally built, there was no means of access from its wall walk to the gatehouse; both the doorways that now provide this access are relatively modern insertions. In this it differs from such fourteenth-century barbicans as those at Tynemouth, Alnwick and Warwick. Nor is there access to the wall walk from stairs within the barbican itself, as at Prudhoe. Instead of this, advantage is taken of the change of direction in the curtain at this point to allow the east curtain to overlap the front of the gatehouse as far as the barbican, thereby creating a terrace along which the wall walk of the barbican could be manned from the curtain. In short, the defence of the barbican reads with the defence of the curtain and not with the defence of the gatehouse, and a successful assault on barbican and curtain would not involve the fall of the gatehouse which stood above them and would still be capable of independent resistance.

This independence is underlined by the provision of gates closing against the outer world at both ends of the gate passage and by the manner in which the gatehouse itself interrupts circulation along the curtain. The doorways now leading from the outer ward to the stairs in room C, and from room L to the east curtain are both modern insertions. In the fourteenth century the interior of the gatehouse could only be reached from within the gate passage, from the outer ward by wooden stairs to the newel staircase leading to room K, and possibly from the wall walk of the west curtain to room I, these last two being concessions to the domestic functions of the building.

The Gatehouse as a Domestic Building *(Fig. 4)*

The ability of the gatehouse to be militarily independent of the rest of the castle is matched by its self-contained and independent character as a house. Its most striking feature, apparent in the fabric but not in the documents, is that it contains three sharply defined sets of accommodation, differing in elaboration and purpose, and that although the gate passage acts as a common entrance to all three sets, from that point onwards considerable ingenuity has been exercised to keep each set independent of its neighbours. These arrangements are best expressed in the planning diagram (Fig. 4) from which it can be seen that there were two small apartments, each of two rooms, and a large suite of seven rooms.

The entrance to the first set of two rooms was through the doorway on the west side of the gate passage just within the gates. This led to room E on the ground floor by means of the angled passage, a devious but effective way of ensuring that this room in a tower projecting in front of the gates could only be reached from behind the protection of those same gates. Room E is a living room with fireplace and privy, and with a loop commanding the barbican and the outside of the gates. Its position suggests a porter's room or guardroom controlling the entrance. Beneath it, room F conspicuously lacks any domestic comforts, and has no fireplace, no privy, no direct light, and no paved floor. The only commodities it can offer are air and water, the former from an inaccessible vent and the latter from constant seepage that makes its walls run with damp and keeps its clay floor a perpetual puddle. Accessible only through a trap beneath the feet of the guard it was clearly designed for security.[16] The damp makes it unsuitable for storage and it is likely that it was a prison associated with the guard, but not the prison mentioned in the indenture, for which a likelier candidate exists elsewhere.

The prison of the indenture forms part of the second set of two rooms and lies on the opposite side of the gate passage. Here a doorway led to a flight of stairs rising steeply to a landing from which another doorway leads to room L, which is a living room equipped with fireplace and privy. Near the foot of the stairs a trap provided the only access to room M. Like F, M lacks all domestic comforts, and its relationship to L mirrors the relationship of F to E. There can be no reasonable doubt that M is the prison of the indenture and that L housed the person or persons whose duties included the custody of this second prison.

The third, and by far the largest, set of rooms was entered from the second original doorway on the west side of the gate passage. This led first to room C which has no fireplace or privy. Through a doorway to the west C communicates with D which is a living room with fireplace and privy and has a squint through which its occupant could keep C under observation. In the north wall of C was the doorway to the stairs leading up to G on the upper floor.

G was the hall, with its low end to the west and its high end to the east where the dais would be. It had a hooded fireplace in its south wall and two windows in its north wall, and through the sides of the embrasures of these windows there was access to chambers beyond both the low and the high ends. The high-end chamber is K, with fireplace, privy and its own stairs down to the outer ward. The low-end chamber I lay above the great beam hole that marks the west end of the hall. Chamber I had a fireplace but no privy, the occupant probably using a privy on the wall walk, for the stairs to the chamber carry on up to the leads of the gatehouse, and the adit of a drain, otherwise unexplained, appears at ground level near the south-west corner of the building.

H with its low headroom was for service and, in view of its fireplace, may have provided accommodation for a servant as well. It lies between the hall and room J which was the kitchen.

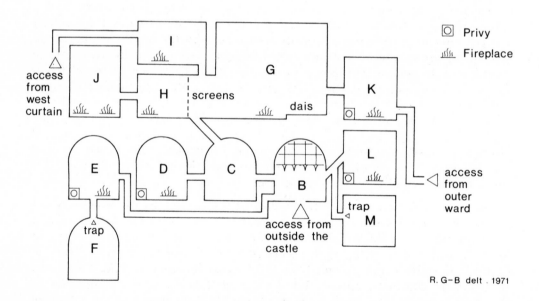

Fig. 4 De Ireby's Tower, planning diagram.

This suite of seven rooms therefore represents a complete medieval house, suitable for the household of a man of substance. The visitor to it, having passed the guard at the gates, was admitted from the enclosed gate passage B to a lobby C which was itself controlled by the occupant of D, perhaps best thought of as a steward who supervised admission to the rooms above. From the lobby the visitor went upstairs to the low end of the hall G which was served by the kitchen J through a service room H. Beyond the hall dais was the chamber of the master of the household, K, and above the service room the less elaborate chamber I could accommodate guests or other members of the household.

Independent of this house and of one another, the guard chamber E with its attendant prison F, and a second prison M, with a gaoler's chamber L above it suggests the incarceration of prisoners derived from two different types of jurisdiction exercised by the master of the household.

The Reason for Building the Gatehouse

It remains to consider why the gatehouse of the outer ward was rebuilt between 1378 and 1383 and why in its final form it departed from the details of the indenture, and here one can leave the rigours of fact for the comforts of hypothesis.

If the present gatehouse was the successor of its namesake which received so unfavourable a report in the survey of 1257, then it is not surprising that it needed complete rebuilding in 1378[17] and that advantage should have been taken of this to incorporate in the new structure the more sophisticated living accommodation required by late fourteenth-century standards. From early times a hall and state apartments for the use of the king on his visits to the castle had existed in the inner ward, and the new gatehouse was now to provide a smaller but complete lodging for another household, in a position where it could control access to the castle, and to a design that made it capable of acting in isolation both as a strong point and as a house. The most likely household to occupy such a building would be that of the constable as guardian of the castle on behalf of the king. It was not uncommon to use the principal gatehouse of a castle as a lodging for its constable. The gatehouse known as the Constable's Tower was built at Dover Castle between 1220 and 1227 to serve this purpose;[18] the gatehouse to the inner ward of Scarborough Castle was also known as the Constable's Tower in 1361;[19] and the great residential gatehouse built early in the fourteenth century at Kidwelly Castle and reconstructed between 1399 and 1422 was known as the 'constablery' later in the fifteenth century.[20]

If the constable can be accepted as the occupant of the gatehouse at Carlisle, then an explanation can be suggested for the failure of the fabric to correspond exactly with the indenture of 1378, and for the need for the survey of 1387. From the end of the twelfth century the maintenance and custody of Carlisle

Castle were generally entrusted to the Sheriff of Cumberland, and from the fourteenth century it was customary for the sheriff also to be one of the four or five wardens appointed by the king to keep the March. For instance, in 1378, the year of the indenture, the sheriff, William Stapleton, undertook to reside in the castle and to maintain it with his household, and he was succeeded in this duty from 1380 to 1381 by Matthew Redman, one of the wardens of the western March. But in 1381 there was a change of policy, and the keeping of the March by a group of wardens, rarely ranking higher than knights, was supplanted by an arrangement whereby a more considerable lord was appointed principal warden of the western March and keeper of the castle.[21]

One may guess that more than coincidence lies behind these curiously apt dates; that the gatehouse of the 1378 indenture was commissioned to provide enough accommodation for the household of a constable with the rank of knight; that in 1381 it was realised that this accommodation would not be appropriate to the more exalted rank and larger household of the newly-appointed principal warden; and that in consequence the size of the gatehouse and the number of rooms within it were increased, although much of the basic plan of 1378 was still retained. The dual nature of the warden's responsibilities to the March and to the castle may perhaps be the reason for providing two prisons deep in the earth beneath his new house.

One may even point a finger at the man whose demands perhaps upset the indenture of 1378. The first principal warden of the western March, who entered into office in 1381 when John Lewyn was in the early stages of work on the gatehouse, was that same Richard le Scrope, Lord of Bolton, for whom Lewyn contracted to build part of Bolton Castle only five months after he had contracted to build the gatehouse for the king. Here, then, is a man whose own castle shows that he had decided ideas about the scale of accommodation appropriate to his dignity and that he was not afraid to change his mind during the course of a building campaign, and a man who already had a working relationship with the master mason in charge of the works at Carlisle.

If these suggestions be accepted, then there need be little wonder that the gatehouse does not conform to the indenture, and still less wonder that by 1387 the king wished to know just how much his new warden's requirements had cost him in the building of de Ireby's Tower in Carlisle Castle.

REFERENCES

1. The essential documents are listed in H. M. Colvin, ed., *History of the King's Works* (1963), Vol. 2, p. 599.

2. *Book of Fees 1198–1242*, Vol. 1, pp. 199, 266.

3. *Royal Letters, Henry III*, Vol. 2, pp. 124–5.

4. P.R.O., E.101/483/31; printed in L. F. Salzman, *Building in England* (1952), pp. 456–7.

5. Lewyn was the most prominent master mason in the north of England during the latter part of the fourteenth century; for his career see J. H. Harvey, *English Mediaeval Architects* (1954), pp. 166–9.

6. e.g., Department of the Environment, Ancient Monuments Plan Room, Works 31/1040.

7. The old internal access to the stairs is shown on eighteenth-century plans, Works 31/1040 and 31/1046. The external doorway is not yet present on an engraving of c. 1835.

8. The sequence of post-medieval alterations to rooms C and E can be recovered with the aid of early plans (Works 31/1046). By the eighteenth century room C had been partitioned into two smaller rooms, the northern one reached by the original doorway of C and the southern one by the new doorway forced through the wall of the gate passage. After the middle of that century the partition was removed, the northern doorway was blocked, and the new doorway kept as the entrance to the whole of C. The original doorway to E was also blocked, the diagonal passage demolished and the space it occupied thrown into C, and another new doorway was forced through the south wall of C to give access to E.

9. The rebuilding took place before the middle of the eighteenth century (Works 31/1055). It is marked by a change in the alignment of the wall face.

10. For inglenook windows of this kind see E. Viollet-le-Duc, *Dictionnaire raisonné de l'architecture française* (1875), Vol. 2, pp. 419–20; Vol. 3, p. 200.

11. *Cal. Patent Rolls, Ric. II, 1381–5*, p. 353.

12. *Ibid.*, 1385–9, p. 367.

13. For Lewyn's work at Roxburgh see *History of the King's Works*, Vol. 2, pp. 819–20.

14. Although the accounts in the Public Record Office enable the general progress of the work to be followed, they are not specific enough to identify alterations to Lewyn's indenture of 1378. His final account for nine years' work at Roxburgh and Carlisle between 1378 and 1386 (E. 364/21/rot. G) summarises the terms of the indenture and contains a reference to the works at both castles having been increased by order of the Council, but the only additional building material charged for Carlisle is 66s. 8d. worth of stone from the quarry of Sir Robert Prenyng. Scaffolding is mentioned in the sheriff's accounts for 1379, and lead for the new tower that was then boarded (E. 364/13/rot. B). In 1380–1 timber is provided for the tower and a wooden 'peel' is built outside the gates (E. 101/39/11), probably the successor of one built in 1307–8 (*History of the King's Works*, Vol. 2, p. 598). In 1381–2 the new gatehouse receives the woodwork, ironwork and leadwork for its fittings, the work being carried out *de avisamento et ordinatione Ricardi lescrop quem rex ordinavit custodem ejusdem castri* (E. 364/18/rot. B dorso) and the double doors for the gate passage are made (E. 101/554/24). In 1384–5 the bridge before the gatehouse is being built and the windlass, pulley and axletree, probably for the portcullis, are being installed (E. 101/554/25).

15. Printed in Salzman, *op. cit.*, pp. 454–6 from *Ars Quatuor Coronatorum*, Vol. 10, p. 70. The pattern of events at Bolton seems to have repeated that at Carlisle, in that the actual building differs substantially from the terms of the agreement, pointing to variations of contract that have not survived in documentary form.

16. Compare the trap door access to the cell below the floor of the porter's room beside the stairs to the great hall of Bolton Castle; to the cell below the floor of the guardroom in the great tower of Warkworth Castle; to the basement of the Prison Tower of Conway Castle, etc.

17. The great gate is mentioned as being ruinous in 1315 and 1335, but this may equally have been one of the two gatehouses to the inner ward (*History of the King's Works*, Vol. 2, p. 598).

18. *Ibid.*, pp. 634-5.

19. *Ibid.*, p. 832.

20. *Ibid.*, p. 686.

21. For the custody of the castle see J. L. Kirby, 'The keeping of Carlisle castle before 1381', *Trans. Cumberland and Westmorland Antiquarian and Arch. Soc.*, N.S., Vol. 54, pp. 131-9. For the wardens of the March see R. L. Storey, 'The Wardens of the Marches of England towards Scotland 1377-1498', *English Historical Review*, Vol. 72, pp. 593-615.

Three Stages in the Construction of the Hall at Kenilworth Castle, Warwickshire

by

M. W. THOMPSON

THE GREAT CASTLE at Kenilworth, a few miles west of Coventry, has perhaps achieved its widest fame through Sir Walter Scott's novel of that name, but it is a splendid monument in its own right. The main castle is concentric, an outer curtain wall of the thirteenth century enclosing an inner core of twelfth-century origin. The east side of this inner ward between the twelfth-century keep on the north and the tall block erected by the Earl of Leicester in c. 1570 on the south is missing. The whole of the group of buildings running round the west side of the court between these two structures is a single functional unit: hall in the middle, services to the north, and chambers of various kinds running south to the chapel that impinges on Leicester's building (Fig. 1). The arrangement is very similar to that revealed by the writer at Conisbrough,[1] and indeed was probably normal in a castle bailey in the decades before and after 1200.

The curious fact at Kenilworth is that as a result of massive reconstruction all the buildings appear to be late fourteenth century in date, as can be seen on the plan dated by the late P. K. Baillie Reynolds (Fig. 1). So thorough has been the remodelling that even the curtain wall can be regarded as original twelfth century only at the north and south ends. The design looks two hundred years older than the detail; there must be a great deal of masonry earlier than late fourteenth century concealed in the core and foundations of the walls. It is with the problem of the early development of the key building, the hall, that this paper is concerned, but before entering into this it will be wisest to describe the extant remains.

The ruin leaves no doubt that when completed in the 1390s the hall was intended to be a buiding of rare splendour on which no expense had been spared. It was two-storeyed, measuring 89 ft. by 46 ft. and divided into six bays, the vault of its undercroft supported on a double row of columns, the stumps of which survive (Pl. XVb). There is an oriel window in the south-east corner and doorways at the north-east corner at both floor levels (Pl. XIVb). The upper doorway, sheltered by a porch, was reached by a long flight of steps

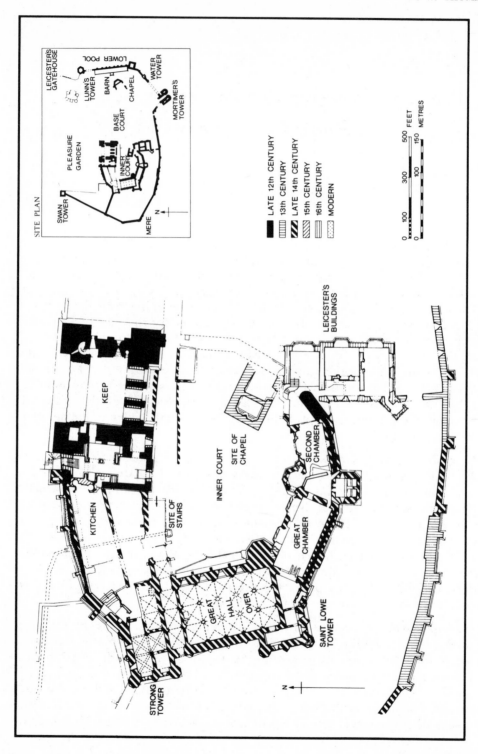

Fig. 1 Inner bailey of Kenilworth Castle.

at right angles to the building that have now vanished. There is a cross range of two-bays' width at the north end projecting westwards as the Strong Tower (Pl. XIVa). The Saint Lowe Tower at the south end is symmetrical only externally, for half of it is occupied by the southernmost bay of the hall, so that it does not constitute a true cross range. This curious anomaly evidently implies that the late fourteenth-century builders found themselves constrained by the form of earlier structures, particularly the hall. The evidence for the roof trusses consists of deep slots roughly 4 ft. long by 1 ft. wide, set 2 ft. below the wall top (Pl. XVa). At the lower end of the slot there is a deeper cavity apparently for a stone or wooden corbel, while the upper part may have received the brace for the sole piece of a hammer beam. This is perhaps the most reasonable although not the only possible interpretation of how these slots were intended to be used.

It is unlikely that we shall learn more about the earlier stages of the hall from the visible masonry, and even more improbable that this will be dismantled to examine what is hidden within it. Excavation may have an interesting tale to tell, particularly on whether a ground-floor aisled hall preceded the present first-floor hall: arcades would be on a different alignment to the evenly-spaced arcades of the later undercroft columns. The purpose of this paper is to discuss the one relevant document, a contract of 1347 for a new roof for the hall, which survives among the Duchy of Lancaster records at the Public Record Office. A transcription has already been published by the late Dr. Salzman,[2] but hitherto only in a footnote in the Victoria County History has there been any hint of its interest for the study of the hall.[3] A transcription carefully checked against the original and with the lines numbered for reference concludes this paper as an appendix.

The contract survives in two copies in one of the Duchy of Lancaster miscellaneous volumes (DL 42/11, 52v–53r, 61v–62r) bearing the marginal heading 'Lendenture Mestre Richard de ffelsted'. The two parties entered into the contract at the Savoy house of the Earl of Lancaster on 16 October 1347 (26), and as such a document would be worthless after completion of work and final settlement it is fair to assume that it was copied out at the time. Henry, Earl of Lancaster (c. 1299–1361, created Duke 1351), on whose behalf the work was to be carried out, had in that year succeeded to his father's earldoms, so that we can perhaps regard the contract as arising from his alterations and improvements. The earl was then in France and his agents in this agreement were John Gynewell, Bishop of Lincoln, Sir Peter de la Mare, Seneschal of Lands, and Sir Peter de Wotton, Receiver-General of the household. John Gynewell, the retiring steward of lands, had been consecrated bishop of Lincoln in the previous month (27 September), but in October was apparently still giving guidance to his successor.[4] The carpenter contractor, Richard of ffelsted (Felstead in Essex), citizen of London, is known only from another contract of 1342 between himself and William Marberer for whom he built a timber-frame tavern in Paternoster Row.[5]

Master Richard (4-15) was to make a roof (*somet*) measuring 89 ft. along the plate (*assise*) and 46 ft. in breadth for the hall (*sale*) at Kenilworth, together with its window shutters (*fenestres*), doors (*huys*) and three screens (*espeeres*). He was to make a low roof for the panrty and buttery at the end of the hall and another roof for the kitchen beyond the buttery and pantry. Master Richard will be responsible for the carpenters and sawyers, and the carpentry and sawing that will be necessary when the masons have finished. The earl will find all wood and arrange for carriage. Master Richard will carry out the work well, as it is arranged and planned, and will find scaffolds, cords, hoists and equipment for which the earl will supply the wood. As soon as the masonry is ready Master Richard will be ready to carry out the specified tasks without anything being found at fault (23-4).

During the execution of the task Master Richard was to be furnished by the earl with gentleman's robe of livery (23). He was to be paid (16-21) a total of 250 marks in the following instalments: £40 on St. Martin's day (11 November 1347), £20 at the Purification of Our Lady (2 February 1348), £30 at Easter (20 April), £30 at the Nativity of St. John the Baptist (24 June), £20 at the Decollation of St. John the Baptist (29 August 1348) and the remaining £26 13s. 4d. when the task was complete. Evidently it was envisaged that the work was to start almost immediately and be finished in about twelve months. Covering the roof with slates may have been a subsequent operation since it is not mentioned and required the services of a slater or tiler.

Three questions are at once prompted by this document. First, was the work ever carried out? A sealed contract must be regarded as a solemn and binding agreement, each party no doubt having its own copy of the original. More conclusive is the indication in the contract that the masons were already at work, indeed almost finished, on what was presumably a roofless shell that would be unusable until Master Richard had covered it. Having regard to this there can be little doubt that the work was carried out.

Second, as the dimensions of the hall in the contract are identical with the surviving ruin does it record the construction of the latter? It might be possible to misdate a building on architectural grounds by forty years in the twelfth or fifteenth centuries, but hardly between these particular dates; the lavishly decorated ruin is a Perpendicular building; one erected in 1347 would be Decorated. The answer must be no, and it follows that two phases of constuction for the hall, 1348 and *c.* 1390 must be assumed.

The third and most difficult question is whether the work in 1347-48 represents a remodelling of an old hall or the construction of a new one. Had it been a new structure one might have expected a complete contract for the whole operation; the document itself suggests a reconstruction. There was to be no new roof for structures at the upper end of the hall, which is not easily reconcilable with a hall erected on a new site. These considerations taken with the older lay-out implied by the disposition of the buildings at Kenilworth have inclined the writer to the view that the work was a remodelling of an earlier hall. As Master Richard had to make doors, window shutters and screens a very drastic reconstruction was envisaged. This would imply three phases (at least) for the hall: an inferred pre-1347 stage, a drastic remodelling in 1347–49 and another drastic remodelling in c. 1390.

The span of 46 ft. at Kenilworth is too great for it to have been roofed without sub-division into aisles before the fourteenth century. The width would have been normal for a late twelfth- or thirteenth-century aisled hall, and indeed could be regarded as standard in the late twelfth century.[6] During the course of the fourteenth century various experiments in abolishing tie beams and bracing the principal rafters to the inner face of the wall led finally to the ingenious device of the hammer beam which permitted uninterrupted spans of over 60 ft. The great triumph of the new roofing technique was at Westminster Hall, where the eleventh-century arcades were swept away at the end of the fourteenth century and replaced by a combination of hammer and arched brace that spanned little short of 70 ft. One result of this greater skill in roofing was that halls with undercrofts, hitherto very constricted by the limit of roof span, could now be built as wide as aisled ones, or an undercroft could be inserted into a former aisled hall. These matters are common knowledge, but what bearing do they have on the alterations at Kenilworth?

It is tempting to suggest that at Kenilworth the first hall was a normal aisled building, that the arcades were removed in 1347–48, and that a further drastic remodelling took place in c. 1390 when the undercroft was inserted and the structure made two-storeyed. The decoration on the springing of the under-croft vault leaves no doubt that it belongs to the last remodelling. Unfortunately the second phase cannot be demonstrated from the contract, since there is no conclusive evidence in it that indicates whether the finished building was to be aisled or aisleless. The three screens (espeeres) that Master Richard had to make suggest an interior free of arcades, but an aisled building would require screens of some kind. Another suggestive point is the need to bring a London carpenter to the Midlands, as if a special skill was required that could not be met locally. The aisle walls would have to be raised and strengthened and new windows inserted, which could explain the work that the masons had to complete before the carpenter arrived from London. If, as has been suggested, this was an alteration to an existing building, why should the entire roof need replacement—a very unusual event except in the case of fire—unless the object was to alter its form?

It is not certain whether the existing slots at each truss were intended for hammer beams, although it is probable that they were. Did they support trusses of c. 1390 or those retained from 1347? Could a span of 46 ft. have been achieved without hammer beams and if not were they available as early as 1347? The comparison that at once springs to mind is the splendid roof of the

1340s over the hall at Penshurst Place, Kent, which spans 39 ft. without the assistance of hammers. Most students would hesitate to concede that hammer beams were in use as early as 1347.[7]

If it will not be allowed that 46 ft. could have been spanned in 1347 with the consequence that the arcades in the hall remained until the last decades of the fourteenth century, then the results might be even more interesting. In that case John of Gaunt would have swept away arcades and inserted the undercroft in one operation, a change more spectacular than that at Westminster Hall! On the whole the present writer finds it more credible that the two changes were made at different times.

There the matter must be left: the slender evidence renders further discussion unprofitable. Through the contract of 1347 one can dimly see the shapes of two earlier buildings before the present magnificent hall of John of Gaunt covered over what went before; it is to be hoped that other evidence will gradually sharpen these shapes and make the sequence of alteration more intelligible.

APPENDIX

This transcription is based on the copy of the contract which runs over from folio 52v to 53r in DL 42/11. Except for slight spelling variations this is the same as the copy on 61v–62r in this volume. It is written in French and consists of 26 lines varying from 17 to 21 cm. in length. There are a few minor differences between this transcription and that published by the late Dr. Salzman.

Marginal Heading: *Lendentures Mestre Richard de ffelsted.*

1   Ceste endenture faite parentre le tresreuerent piere Johan par la grace de dieu Euesque de Nicole,[8] Mons.' Piers/de la Mare Seneschal des terres le noble homme Mons.' Henri Counte de Lancastre et Sire Piers de Wotton Receivour/ General le dit Counte dune part et Mestre Richard de ffelstede citeseyn et carpenter de Loundres dautr. part/tesmoigne qe le dit mestre Richard ferra une

5   somet a une sale de Kenilworth de la longur de iiij ix/pees de assise et en leoure xlvj pees ensemblement oue toutes les fenestres et huys apartenantz a la/dite saele et oue tres espeeres en la sale susdite. Item, il ferra au boute de la dite sale une bas somet pur panetr. et butr. Item, il ferra une sumet pur une cusine a boute de la dite sale par/dehors la panetr. et botrie. Et pur la dit oueraigne faire le dit Mestre Richard trouera carpentiers/et sarrers a toute manere de carpentrie et sarure, qapendra a la dite oueraigne del hure qil le/ merisme soit mys en la place ou les ditez mesons serront faites. Et lauantdit

10   Counte de Lancaster trouera/tote manere de merisme at cariage tanqe en la dite place ou le dit oueraigne serra leuee. Et le dit/Meistre Richard ferra le dit oueraigne bien at couenablement com il est ordeigne et deuise. Et auxint/acorde est entre les dites parties qe le dit/Mestre Richard pur le oueraigne a sez custages demeigne trouera skaffoldes, cordes, ginnes[9] et toutes autres instrumentz qe apartenent pur lauantdit oueraigne faire et louer. Mais Mons.' de Lancastr.'

15   /susdit trouera merisme pur les dites skaffoldes, ginnes et pur toutes les autres Instrumentz. Et pur loueraigne susdit auera/le dit Mestre Richard deux centz et sinkaunte marcz desterlings. De lez quex ccl marc. desterlings le dit Mestre Richard serra/paie en la feste de Seint Martin en yuern lan du regne le Roi Edward tiers puis le conquest vintisme primer/de xl liurees desterlings, en la feste en la Purification Nostre Dame adonqes proschein auenir xx li. dester'., en la feste du/Pask adonkes prochein auenir xxx li. desterlings, en la feste de la

20   Nativite de Seint Johan le Bapt.' adonkes prochein/ensuant xxx li., et en la feste de la Decollacion Seint Johan le Bapt.' adonkes prochein suant xx li. Et ceo qe remandra/aderere adonqes de les ccl marcz le dit Mestre Richard serra pleinement paie com le dit oueraigne soit tout parfait./Et auera le dit

Mestre Richard de dit Counte robe de liuere de gentils hommes par tout le temps qe le dit mestre/Rochard esterra en le dit oueraigne faire. Et si tout come la masonrie de piere isoit prest le dit Mestre Richard/y serra prest de sa partie aperformer lez dites besoignes issint qe nulle defaute ne serra en lui

25 troue. En temoignaunce/de quele chose les auantditz Euesqe, Sire Piers et Piers et le dit Mestre Richard a cestes endentures entrechauge/-ablement ount mys lur seals. Escript en le manoir de Sauuoye pres de Loundres le xvje iour Octobr'. lan susdit.

REFERENCES

1. *Med. Arch.*, XIII (1969), pp. 215–16.

2. L. F. Salzman, *Building in England down to 1540* (London, 1952), pp. 436–37.

3. *VCH, Warwickshire*, VI, p. 135, note 57a. This volume was edited by Dr. Salzman.

4. For further details on the earl's chief household officers see Sir R. Somerville, *A History of the Duchy of Lancaster, 1256–1603*, pp. 358–59.

5. Salzman, *op. cit.*, pp. 432–34.

6. All the aisled halls from the second half of the twelfth-century listed by Mrs. Kaines Thomas are of this width to within a few feet: Margaret Wood, *The English Medieval House* (London, 1964), p. 45.

7. I have been in correspondence on this matter with Professor Barley and Dr. Alcock, the authors of a recent paper on roofs of this period (*Ant. J.*, lii [1972], pp. 132–68) who both doubt whether the arcades could have been removed at this date.

8. Lincoln.

9. Hoists.

Langerwehe Stoneware
of the Fourteenth and Fifteenth Centuries

by

J. G. HURST

Introduction

LANGERWEHE LIES between Aachen and Raeren, and Cologne and Frechen on the northern border of the Eifel, in the Duchy of Jülich. It was well situated for a kiln site, with clay suitable for making stoneware, fuel nearby, and on a

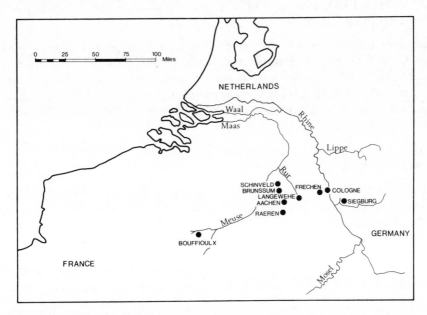

Fig. 1 Map showing position of Langerwehe and other stoneware producing centres

trade route down the Rur to Jülich and the Maas and thence to the Netherlands and Britain (Fig. 1). It was also on the Imperial east-west route from Frankfurt to Aachen. This enabled it to become one of the major centres of stoneware production in the fourteenth and fifteenth centuries.

Langerwehe ware has been much neglected by scholars and there has been no major study nor has it figured in the general works on stoneware.[1] This is partly because it never developed in the sixteenth century into a fine decorated phase as did the Siegburg, Cologne, Raeren, and Frechen kilns. Solon describes Langerwehe as a factory emulating the style in vogue at Raeren at a later period and refers to two late jugs and Tilman Wolf who was a master potter in 1661.[2] He goes on to say that 'nothing more being known of the place, or of the master, we shall make no further reference to it'. This is typical of the attitude of early writers who were only interested in the art–historical vessels and not in the coarser utilitarian wares of Langerwehe or other pottery centres. Von Bock[3] has only a brief mention saying that 'Pottery of high artistic quality appears hardly at all to have been made there, but rather the simple undecorated domestic ware indispensable in every medieval household . . . As the household wares were very ordinary in appearance Langerwehe pottery was never sought by collectors and is not represented in collections abroad or museums'. This is the crux of the matter and why nothing of note has been written on Langerwehe ware by art historians, but this makes it doubly interesting for archaeologists. Only four short articles have appeared on the subject, one in 1937, two in 1959 on the occasion of the museum opening[4] and the fourth (a guide to the museum) in 1971.[5]

While the outside world has largely ignored Langerwehe there has been intense local interest centred on the work of the local schoolmaster, Josef Schwartz (1892-1964), who systematically collected pottery from houses in the town and building sites. A museum was started in 1925 and found a permanent home in 1959 in an old farm provided by the town. This provides a useful display of Langerwehe ware and other local material.

Historical Evidence

It is likely that pottery was made at Langerwehe from an early date, but the first firm evidence is a series of wasters of Pingsdorf-type ware found near St. Martin's Church in a context of the last quarter of the twelfth century.[6] In the thirteenth century Siegburg-type near-stoneware was produced[7] but the first documentary evidence comes in 1324 with a reference to '*om Uhles*' ('around the potteries'). This must be about the time of the first production of true stoneware, which is the main subject of this paper.

There is little further documentary evidence until the sixteenth century, but from then on, and particularly in the seventeenth and eighteenth centuries, more is known about the industry. In the sixteenth century the potters' emblem of three jugs was placed alongside the lions of the Jülich family in the arms of Langerwehe. In the seventeenth century the pottery trade played an important role as a source of revenue to the ruling Dukes of Jülich. In the ordinances of 1624 it was laid down who might sell so many pots and what payments should be made subsequently to the duke. The number of firings each potter was allowed was fixed, depending on the number of persons in the family. Even more stringent rules were set out in the Guild ordinance of 1706. Everyone was aware how often he was allowed to fire a kiln. The period of firing, from April to November, had to be observed under the threat of penalty. Only those who were townspeople of Langerwehe were allowed to become potters and a six-year apprenticeship was prescribed. If a potter suffered misfortune and his products were destroyed in the course of firing, his colleagues in the Guild helped him, or he was permitted an additional firing. These strict rules of the Guild were adopted in order to safeguard the market, to meet competition from outside and above all to maintain the quality of the wares. From 1823 various agreements were made based on the 1706 rules till in 1870 the potters organised themselves into a strictly organised potters' union, with the object of competing more effectively with the industrial products which were newly coming on to the market. By the early twentieth century, however, industrial products almost entirely ousted the Langerwehe wares.

Late Pottery Types

From the sixteenth century there was no development of decorated wares such as was made at other stoneware centres. Langerwehe specialised in large storage jugs and jars with medallions bearing either the potter's mark or the arms of the customer. Some of these had Bellarmine masks[8] while others had the English royal arms[9] with the date of 1594.[10] These were often dipped in a slip twice, from above and below, and care was taken to leave an area in the middle which was not covered with the slip resulting in characteristic light bands.[11] Large sauerkraut pickling jars, called *Kappeskrug*, were a feature of the nineteenth century[12] and were traded widely, especially in the last quarter of the century, to the Netherlands, but not to England where there is little evidence of any Langerwehe imports later than the middle of the sixteenth century. These jars had large indented footrings, reminiscent of the medieval frilled bases, designed to allow passage of air on the damp floors of cellars. Other late products include roofing tiles, water pipes, chimney pots, and floor tiles.

Pottery is still made in Langerwehe by the Kuckertz-Renner family at the *Uhlhaus* (Pottery) in the Dorfstrasse. Types include globular or oval forms in a grey stoneware with blue-painted decoration. Others in a dark-grey stoneware have scratched decoration or the so-called *red-Knibis* ornamental style.[13] The tradition is also being kept alive by the manufacture of pottery in a workshop across the courtyard from the museum.

British Finds

Langerwehe stoneware has been known from British sites for the last ten years since an examination of the material enabled the three basic fabrics of Siegburg (light grey), Raeren (dark grey with brown and grey glaze) and

Langerwehe (dark grey with purple or brown wash) to be distinguished. In 1968[14] it was possible to list thirty-four sites in England where Siegburg was found, one hundred and three Raeren and twenty-two Langerwehe. All these numbers may now be greatly increased, and it is unusual to have a site of the fifteenth century, especially in the eastern half of England, without at least one Langerwehe sherd. Now that it is possible, as described below, to assign other sherds, previously thought to be Raeren, to Langerwehe, the find spots can be increased still further. In the 1960s it was assumed that Langerwehe ware began in the fifteenth century and extended into the sixteenth century, as did the classic Raeren drinking mugs.[15] Then finds both from the Netherlands and Britain made it clear that Langerwehe wares were in fact produced as far back as the beginning of the fourteenth century and as early as the Siegburg stonewares.

The most important groups of Langerwehe wares comes from Southampton where it is first found in early fourteenth-century contexts before the French raid of 1338;[16] from Stonar, Kent, in fourteenth-century contexts (mainly the second half);[17] from the London Custom House, datable to the mid to late fourteenth century; [18] from Edinburgh which has produced the largest group of any site, comprising 313 sherds from at least 131 vessels, datable to the late fourteenth and early fifteenth century;[19] from Newcastle Black Gate, datable to the early to mid-fifteenth century;[20] and from Sandal Castle, Yorkshire, of similar date but extending into the sixteenth century.[21]

The number of sites where a full Langerwehe series is still present in the first half of the sixteenth century is disturbing for, in the Netherlands, it seems to be replaced by Raeren c. 1500. There is no doubt that on most sites in Britain, too, this is also the case, but there is a substantial quantity of Langerwehe, for example at Mount Grace in Dissolution contexts.[22] It is reasonably easy to distinguish the classic forms of Langerwehe and Raeren, but many sherds could be either, which is an added hazard to identification since the Edinburgh series shows most clearly how like the classic Raeren fabric and glaze many Langerwehe sherds are. The same applies to other sites and so unfortunately lessens the dating value of, especially, the fifteenth-century types.

As so much of this British material is fragmentary (of the Edinburgh material 266 were body sherds, and only fifteen bases and twenty-six rims, from 131 different vessels) there is a need for a type series of complete shapes. This is best provided by a series of examples from the Kreissparkasse kiln site in Langerwehe and other finds from Langerwehe and the Netherlands preserved in the Van Beuningen collection[23] to which all the illustrations refer.[24] Many of the British examples have come from rescue excavations financed by the Department of the Environment in recent years and this paper is offered as a contribution to the understanding of the mass of imported pottery recovered from such excavations.

Langerwehe Fabric and Forms

Langerwehe was in the van of developments and started to make true stoneware in the early fourteenth century as soon as Siegburg[25] or Brunssum/Schinveld.[26] It copied traits from both these centres but had a distinctive method of production and decoration of its own which makes its main types readily recognisable. The Brunssum/Schinveld industry stopped because of political difficulties in the middle of the fourteenth century, almost as soon as stoneware started. Langerwehe continued through the fourteenth and fifteenth centuries and, together with Siegburg, provided the main exports of domestic stonewares to the Netherlands and Britain. All the examples have not yet been collected but there is little doubt that in Britain it largely outnumbers Siegburg imports.

Langerwehe stoneware is easily distinguished from Siegburg by its dark grey colour, while Siegburg is always light, and by the addition of an iron wash, which in unglazed examples gives a characteristic purple matt finish quite unlike any other stoneware. Unfortunately glazed examples have a patchy brown and grey colour very similar to Raeren which also has a dark grey fabric, so that many sherds from the two sites are indistinguishable. This means that in most cases only the unglazed or partly glazed examples have been identified as Langerwehe and that many so-called Raeren sherds, especially from fourteenth- and fifteenth-century levels, have not been correctly identified. Although the Langerwehe pots are well made and as good as many Siegburg examples, their methods of firing do not seem to have been as efficient, especially in the control of air in the kiln, although it is not clear whether this is deliberate or accidental. Langerwehe vessels not only have a varied surface colouring, but many examples are underfired and not fused, so that they have a buff or reddish hard earthenware fabric. The large numbers of vessels so underfired suggests that this could have been intentional. There may well have been deliberate deception here since many jugs which looked like stoneware externally were not fused and would therefore be porous and not so efficient as the Siegburg examples. Alternatively, it is possible that they were deliberately less well made, and for this reason cheaper and more readily available for the general market.

The two most popular types of Langerwehe ware were jugs of three main sizes and two-handled cups of distinctive shape. Other vessels included cooking pots, costrels, horns and a wide range of other cups and beakers, but these are less common and were rarely exported. In addition to stoneware the Langerwehe potters made a range of off-white and buff earthenware with mottled green and yellow glazes.[27] In this material the two most usual forms were pilgrim horns, mainly made for the Aachen market, pipkins and small jugs with and without spouts. These are a continuation of the Andenne tradition[28] and similar types were made at Cologne. Some thought should be given to the influence of these wares as well as the imported French wares on Tudor-Green,[29] especially now the earliest examples of Tudor-Green are being dated back to the beginning of the fifteenth century.

The typical Langerwehe jug has an upright rim with an external bevel, sometimes with rectangular-notch rouletting on it. Very typical are two rows of rectangular notch rouletting on the shoulder. This rim and the simple rouletting is confined to Langerwehe except that, as the fifteenth century progresses, Raeren pots are increasingly found in similar forms and with the same decoration. The origins of Raeren pottery are not known and it is not clear to what extent it developed parallel with or was copied from Langerwehe, but pottery of Pingsdorf type was being made in the Raeren area in the twelfth century. The products of the mid-fifteenth-century kiln at Raeren Neudorf[30] however were identical to the later Langerwehe products. This obscures the nature and timing of the change from Langerwehe to Raeren imports which occurred in Britain in the last quarter of the fifteenth century.

Collared rims with complex rouletting were copied from Brunssum/ Schinveld[31] in the fourteenth century as were the cordonned rims of Siegburg.[32] The latter can be identified readily because of the light fabric, and because Siegburg jugs are not usually rouletted, but there is a difficult problem in distinguishing between late Brunssum/Schinveld and early Langerwehe wares since both have a dark fabric.

Jug Size

The jugs vary in height from 7–19 in. but fall into three distinct groups as shown in Table 1. There is a definite gap between the large and the medium sizes, but there is less difference between the medium and the small examples. The large and medium jugs are mainly ovoid or pear-shaped with no clear divisions, but there is a gradation in maximum body diameter which enable some sherds to be assigned to their jug type. The same applies to bases, but the rims have a smaller variation from only 3–4 in. so without a shoulder it is not so easy to state the jug size of smaller rim sherds. The small jugs have a wider variation in shape as they range from globular to the tall-necked Jacoba ovoid jugs. Unfortunately as so much of the British material is fragmentary it is almost impossible to assign jug sherds to their sizes as has been shown by the difficulties in working on the Edinburgh material. Nevertheless, it is important to draw attention to these three basic sizes which presumably reflect differences of function from the point of view of storage, decanting and drinking.

Table 1

	Height	Rim Diameter	Body Diameter	Base Diameter
	in.	in.	in.	in.
Large	18–19	4	12–14	8–9
Medium	12–15	3–3½	8–10	6–7
Small	7–10	3	5–6	2–4

Surface Treatment

The wide variation in the surface treatment, and therefore the appearance of the sherds, has been a major hindrance in the identification of Langerwehe sherds, especially those from undated contexts. The Edinburgh group of 313 sherds, all datable from the start of Raeren imports in the late fifteenth century, provides for the first time an opportunity to classify the various surface colours. Miss P. Clarke has divided them into groups, according to the more readily recognised internal surface appearance, and then classified within these groups according to the degree of colouration the external surface showed. The glazes ranging from glossy grey to deep purple black indicate the use of a thick iron slip.[33]

Jug Types

Langerwehe jugs may be divided into four main types based on rim forms with sub-divisions for different shapes and sizes.

I. —Jugs with collared rims

These are the earliest type datable to the fourteenth century. The shape is copied from the late period IV and V at Brunssum/Schinveld. The Brunssum/Schinveld trait of complex rouletting is also used.

II. —Jugs with cordoned rims

This is a Siegburg type which is found over a long period in the thirteenth and fourteenth centuries but seems to die out in the fifteenth century. These are therefore also likely to be early and contemporary with type I. They often have the Langerwehe rouletting which is not found on the Siegburg prototypes.

III. —Jugs with bevelled rims

This is the classic Langerwehe type. It is already found in the earliest examples of the fourteenth century but seems to run on right through to include some examples as late as the sixteenth century. It is not therefore useful as a dating criterion but is a fairly safe guide to a jug being Langerwehe if the fabric is dark with an iron slip.

IV. —Jugs with simple upright rims

Many of these are similar to the basic Siegburg types of the fourteenth and fifteenth centuries but are often simple forms so may not necessarily be copies but part of the fourteenth- and fifteenth-century pottery tradition of that time. They are likely to have been made in parallel with type III as they would have had a different use. While types I–III were likely to have been used for the storage or decanting of liquids with their complex rims, it is likely that many of the simple-rimmed type IV jugs were in fact drinking-jugs as we know from pictorial evidence the later Raeren examples were.[34] The change from complex to simple rims, together with the vast number of stoneware cups and beakers of all shapes and sizes, was all part of the revolution in drinking habits in the fourteenth and fifteenth centuries[35] made possible by the production of non-porous containers when stoneware became available. This revolution was only transferred to glazed earthenware containers in Britain in the later fifteenth and sixteenth centuries with the production of Tudor-Green and Cistercian ware cups.[36]

Langerwehe Type Descriptions

All the vessels illustrated come from the Van Beuningen Collection at Langbroek, Netherlands, the reference number is given when there is one together with the catalogue reference (Cat.).[37] where appropriate.

Jugs

I.—Jugs with collared rims

Fig. 2, No. 1. From Langerwehe, casual find, Van Beuningen, unnumbered. Rim sherd from jug similar to No. 2, below, grey stoneware, matt glossy iron wash outside and unevenly inside to just below collar, tall collared rim with complex chevron roulette at bottom, plain rounded rim, neck closely rilled.

Fig. 2, No. 2. From Langerwehe, Kreissparkasse, Van Beuningen, F1524. Small ovoid jug, brown-buff stoneware with almost overall iron wash giving a matt brown finish and then patches of grey and mottled brown where glazed, fine rilling on body but not below or on neck, no division till alternate oblique rouletted cordon at junction with cylindrical neck, deep collar with alternate oblique rouletting at bottom, plain rounded rim, grooved strap, frilled base, unglazed inside iron wash only going down to about bottom of collar.

Fig. 2, No. 3. From a pit in Boschstraat, Zaltbommel, Netherlands, Van Beuningen, F297 (found with No. 4). Small ovoid jug, grey stoneware with fairly thin overall grey glaze with only a few mottled brown patches, body rilled at centre but not below or above double cordon with rectangular notch rouletting. Another double cordon at junction, with cylindrical neck square notch rouletted, neck rilled, deep cordon with long rectangular notch rouletting at bottom, plain rounded rim, wide grooved-strap, frilled base. Unglazed inside, except just over rim.

Fig. 2, No. 4. From the same pit, Van Beuningen, F456. Medium jug, grey stoneware with overall matt iron wash except in a few patches where the dark-grey body is exposed or there are patches of grey and brown salt glaze, pear-shaped body with heavier rilling on upper half, two cordons on shoulder with alternate oblique rouletting, then bare shoulder before rilled vertical neck with collar and complex-rouletting, plain-grooved strap and frilled footring, bare dark grey stacking ring on base, unglazed inside with buff inner surface and iron wash down inside neck.

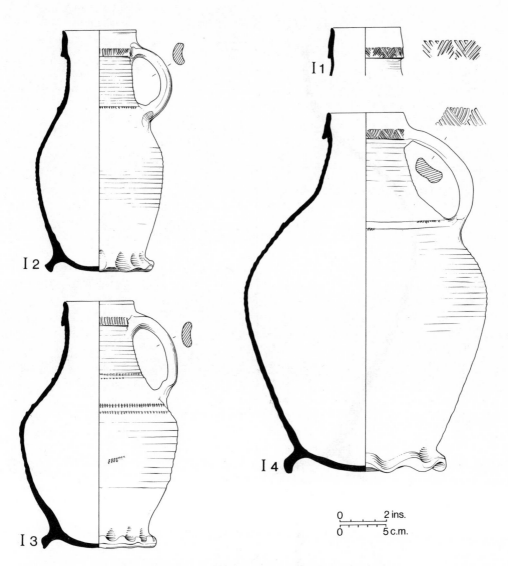

Fig. 2 Langerwehe: type I jugs with collared rim. Scale 1:4.

A sherd from *Boudewijn* has a double cordon with alternate oblique roulet-ting, datable before 1372.[38] There is a very similar jug, a waster with same decoration gap on shoulder, Van Beuningen F1536, from Kreissparkasse. Illustrated in Cat. No. 92.

Collared rim jugs with complex roulette are well dated to the middle of the fourteenth century. This is one of the last forms found at Brunssum/Schinveld, while there are two jugs, one purple and the other already brown and grey glazed, from *Nieuwedoorn Castle,* Netherlands, datable before 1370.[39]

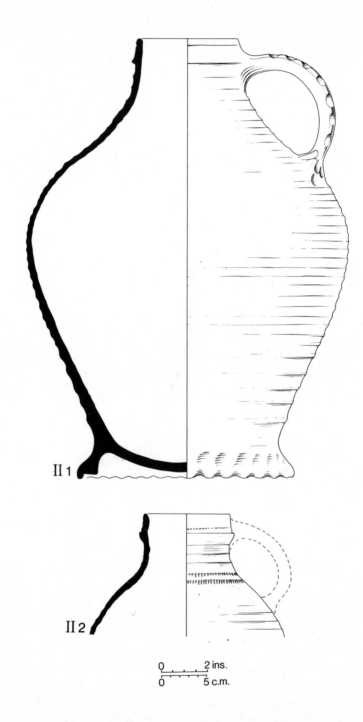

II 1

II 2

0 ___ 2 ins.

0 ___ 5 c.m.

Fig. 3 Langerwehe: type II jugs with cordoned rim. Scale 1:4.

II. – Jugs with cordoned rims

Fig. 3, No. 1. Unprovenanced in the Van Beuningen collection, unnumbered. Large jug dark-grey stoneware with overall mottled-brown salt glaze with a few grey patches, pear-shaped body heavily rilled and no rouletted bands or cordons, upright single rim with cordon below making a flush collar, lightly thumbed grooved strap with four thumbings at base, large frilled footring, unglazed inside with iron wash down inside neck.

Fig. 3, No. 2. From Langerwehe, casual find, Van Beuningen, unnumbered. Medium jug, dark-grey stoneware with buff inner margins and surface, outside overall mottled-brown saltglaze with bare patches of red-brown, globular shoulder rilled with usual two bands of rectangular-notch roulette under rilled vertical neck, cordon forming a flush collar with a band of square-notch roulette below plain rounded upright rim, unglazed inside with iron wash extending below cordon. There is a similar jug from *Southampton*,[40] No. 1126, from High Street C, pit 258 datable to the first half of the fourteenth century.

III. – Jugs with bevelled rims

Fig. 4, No. 1. Unprovenanced, Van Beuningen, unnumbered. Large jug, grey stoneware with matt iron wash glaze with some patches of grey and brown, tall pear-shaped with wide even rilling, two bands rough rectangular-notch roulette or shoulder and under bevelled upright rim, rounded and not angular like earlier examples, wide thumbed strap, large roughly thumbed footring, handle set out from rim unlike earlier examples where they are set below the bevel, unglazed inside with slashes and drips of iron wash over part. There is a similar jug from *Edinburgh* (No. 9) also with a thumbed handle.

Fig. 4, No. 2. From Langerwehe, Kreissparkasse, Van Beuningen, unnumbered. Medium jug, shoulder and part of neck with handle, light grey stoneware, overall mottled-brown salt glaze with thin wash inside, two bands rectangular-notch roulette on small cordons on neck above junction of plain grooved strap, upright neck with bevelled rim and rectangular-notch roulette, handle set just below unlike later examples which are flush.

This is the classic and most common type found on many sites usually datable to the late fourteenth and early fifteenth century. Netherlands finds include:

Aardenburg, complete ovoid medium jug (12 in. high) with plain bevel and double rouletted bands on shoulder. Datable to the late fourteenth and early fifteenth century.[41] *Spangen,* Fig. 6, No. 6, complete jug dated to the early 15th century but Dr. J. G. Renaud now thinks it is more likely to be late fourteenth century.[42] *Ter Does,* complete pear-shaped medium jug (14 in. high), rouletted bevel and two rouletted shoulder bands, *c.* 1420;[43] *Valckensteyn,* complete ovoid medium jug (12 in. high), rouletted bevel and two rouletted shoulder bands, last quarter of the fourteenth century.[44]

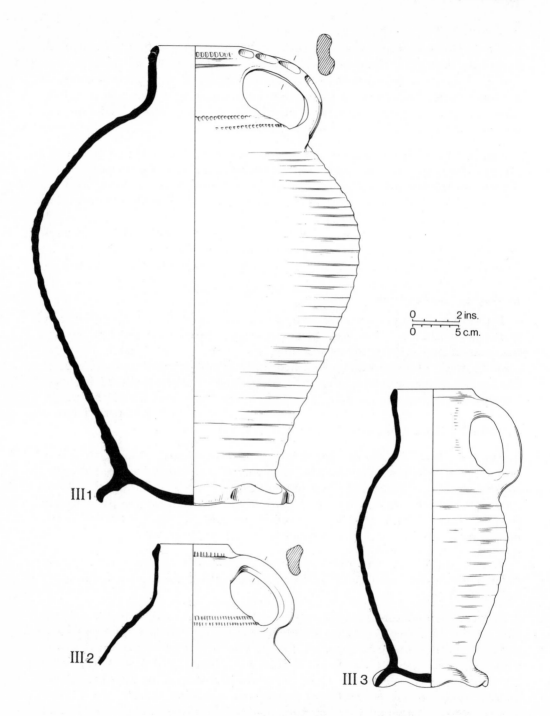

Fig. 4 Langerwehe: type III jugs with bevelled rim. Scale 1:4.

English finds include an ovoid sherd from a medium jug from *Boston*, No. 52,[45] which is likely to come from one of these jugs, as is No. 47, with two rouletted bands on the shoulder, as the type IV jugs are not usually rouletted; and *Edinburgh* (No. 8) together with about ten rouletted body sherds. These are datable to the mid- and early-mid-fifteenth century. But there are early fourteenth century examples from *Southampton* (Nos. 1124, 1126) and later ones (Nos. 1144 and 1145).

Fig. 4, No. 3, from Langerwehe, Kreissparkasse, Van Beuningen, unnumbered. Narrow medium jug of a form more usually associated with type IV jugs, pale yellow underfired stoneware with orange surfaces, brown slip on upper part of jug and inside the rim. Body heavily grooved but not rouletted. Other examples from the Netherlands include:

Medemblik, Van Beuningen, F2827, Cat. 93, casual, undated find. *Spangen,* dated to the late fourteenth or early fifteenth century.[46] English examples may include the *Colchester,* medium jug, No. 32[47] which was mis-identified as Siegburg, but the grey stoneware with the purple finish now clearly identifies it as Langerwehe, datable to the first half of the fifteenth century. There are about ten rims from *Edinburgh.* There is an example from *Vianen Castle,* Netherlands, datable before 1372[48] though in this find, as on most early sites, Siegburg predominates. It is not until the fifteenth century that Langerwehe imports overtake Siegburg. In England there has never been the same quantity of Siegburg, and at *Edinburgh* in the early fifteenth century there are forty-one sherds from twenty-six Siegburg vessels as opposed to 313 Langerwehe sherds from 131 vessels.

IV.—Jugs with simple upright rims

Fig. 5, No. 1. Unprovenanced, Van Beuningen, F218. Globular small jug, typical grey stoneware with patchy iron wash mainly one side only giving a quadruple effect of plain grey, matt iron-brown and on the other side, where salt has had effect, the usual patchy grey and brown mottled as pre-sixteenth-century, globular biconic body, heavily rilled below and lightly rilled above in typical fashion, cordon at junction of neck which is cylindrical and heavily rilled with another small cordon just under handle, grooved strap, simple rounded rim, frilled base, unglazed inside, iron wash unevenly about half way down neck.

The shoulder of a jug from *Stonar,* No. 21, with its angular profile, is very similar.

Fig. 5, No. 2, from Langerwehe, Kreissparkasse, Van Beuningen, F1389, Cat. 71. Small jug, grey stoneware with overall light-brown iron wash and patches of salt glaze with brown and grey patches, unglazed inside with iron wash going down inside the neck, ovoid heavily rilled body with cylindrical neck also heavily rilled with simple rounded rim distorted as a waster, small strap handle and frilled base.

Jug No. 36 from *Sandal* is very similar.

Fig. 5, No. 3. From Raeren, Neudorf kiln 1972, Van Beuningen, F2890. Small jug, grey stoneware, when fired normally typical grey and brown patches though more mottled than sixteenth-century, ovoid body, frilled base, short cylindrical neck with loop strap handle, early to mid-fifteenth-century, the typical pre-Raeren type.

From a round single-flue kiln, unlike the rectangular sixteenth-century examples, excavated with large numbers of wasters. There is a wide range of colour due to differential firing. The clay is off-white with red-buff surfaces if underfired. It becomes dark red-brown when fired almost to a stoneware then, when it becomes Raeren dark grey, it has a matt purple surface if an iron

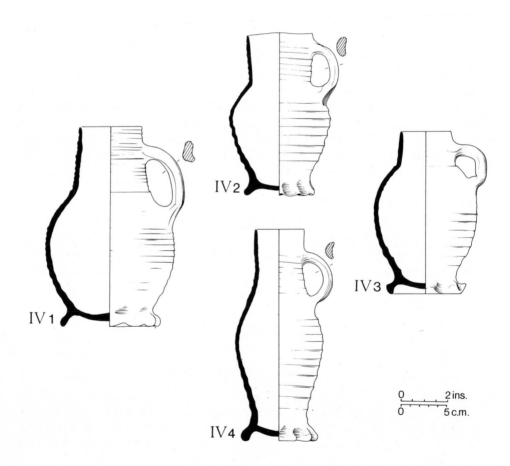

Fig. 5. Langerwehe: type IV jugs with simple upright rim. Scale 1:4.

wash is added (i.e., very like Langerwehe). If it is salt glazed the surface becomes typical Raeren grey and brown but with a somewhat mottled effect. If it is overfired the surface becomes dark purply brown.

This kiln is datable to about 1460 and demonstrates the similarity of Langerwehe and Raeren jugs in the two middle quarters of the fifteenth century before the typical late fifteenth- and early sixteenth-century Raeren type develops which swamps all other stoneware imports to Britain. *Sandal*, No. 39, may be closely compared with this type. There are two coin-dated jugs of this general type in the Langerwehe museum. One is a find from Langerwehe dated 1438[49] which shows the typical wide range of colour and the other from *Wickrath*, Kreiss Grevenbroich, dated 1423.

Fig. 5, No. 4, from Langerwehe, Kreissparkasse, Van Beuningen, F1500, Cat. No. 72. Tall narrow Jacoba-type jug, grey stoneware with overall brown and dark-brown iron wash worn off in places to expose grey body, patches of salt glaze with grey and brown. Ovoid rilled body with more heavily rilled narrow neck with simple rounded rim, small strap handle and frilled base. Unglazed inside with iron wash going down inside neck.

This type was also made at Raeren, Neudorf, *cf.* Van Beuningen, F2896. The *Hangleton* jug,[50] is of this type, in which context it was first suggested this type came from Langerwehe; datable to the first half of the fifteenth century. There are several heavily-rilled necks of this type of the same date at *Edinburgh* (Nos. 11–14).

Other Shapes

I.—Globular costrels

Fig. 6, No. 1, from Cologne, Kölner Stadlader, Van Beuningen, F1186. Globular costrel, dark-grey stoneware only partially glazed with patchy brown and grey Raeren-type glaze, back rounded, side rilled, front rilled with nipple, short neck with two thin strap handles.

II.—Barrel costrels

Fig. 6, No. 2. Unprovenanced, Van Beuningen, F722. Barrel costrel, dark grey stoneware with matt iron-wash partly flaked off, small patch green-brown glaze, rilled with central cordon where jointed to vertical neck with everted rim and two suspension handles.

These costrels have not been found at actual kiln sites at Langerwehe but from an examination of the large quantities of wasters from the many kiln sites at Raeren it does not seem to have been made there. A Langerwehe source is therefore more likely. Both types were also made at Siegburg.[51] The above examples were traded to the Rhine and the Netherlands, but are very rare in Britain. The only costrel so far identified here is a fragment from the Black

Gate Ditch, Newcastle,[52] in an early fifteenth-century context. It is likely though that more examples will be located if sherd collections are examined for them.

Standing costrels of Siegburg types 44–48 are found in the Netherlands, but have not so far been fully identified from British medieval sites. These were also made in the Kreissparkasse kiln.

III. – Cups

Fig. 6, No. 3, from Langerwehe, Kreissparkasse, Van Beuningen, F1462, Cat. No. 63 and Pl. Grey stoneware with overall salt glaze mainly grey with a few mottled-brown patches, matt iron wash inside, biconic cup with typical central groove and two loop handles, plain simple rim sloping in, frilled base, top deformed as waster.

The best example in Britain is the complete cup from *Southampton,* No. 1143, from High Street C, pit 213, datable to the first half of the fourteenth century but nearer 1350. In the Netherlands there is a slightly later example from the second half of the fourteenth century from *Aardenburg,*[53] and one datable before 1370 from *Nieuwedoorn Castle*[54] with a grey glaze. Other English examples come from *Stonar,* No. 30, from a fourteenth-century context, and much later from *Sandal* (No. 28).

Examples have also been found at Brunssum/Schinveld in the last period, but there are in fact very few examples and no wasters, so it is not fully certain they were made there.[55] Although the main type is fourteenth century, and most late fifteenth-century examples do have a taller different form, there are cups of the classic form clearly associated with sixteenth-century sites.[56] A further complication is the suggestion that they were also made at Bouffioulx[57] though these are the taller developed type. So like so many 'closely dated' foreign imports this type in fact has a wide date range and cannot be used to date a layer to the fourteenth century.

In addition to this form there is a wide range of other cups and beakers[58] Many similar to the Siegburg types.[59] None of these have so far been recognised in Britain and may not have been imported. It is not clear why only this one type comes in.

IV. – Horns

Fig. 6, No. 4, from Utrecht, Nutspaarbank in Dom Straat, Van Beuningen, F99, Cat. No. 50. Fine, off-white, fluted horn with two suspension loops, pale-yellow glaze round the outside of the top only, with light iron and copper flecking, scalloped knife-trimmed pattern on the rim. This earthenware example was drawn as a complete example; they were also made in stoneware. These were called *Aachen-* or *Pilgerhorner,* and were blown by Aachen pilgrims during their processions, every seven years, and at the coronations of the Holy Roman emperors.

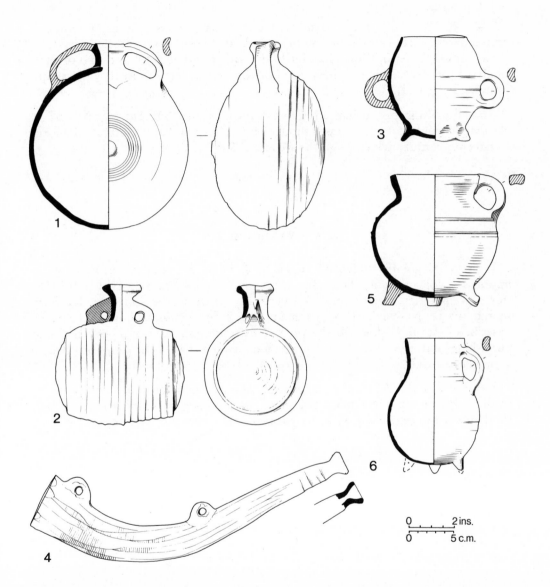

Fig. 6 Langerwehe: 1-2: costrels, 3: cups, 4: horns, 5: pipkins and 6: tripod jugs. Scale 1:4.

V.—Pipkins

Fig. 6, No. 5, from Langerwehe, Kreissparkasse, Van Beuningen, F1477. Globular pipkin with one strap handle and slightly thickened slightly everted rim, pale-yellow underfired stoneware with brown and purple iron slip on the outside and inside the rim.

VI. — Tripod Jugs

Fig. 6, No. 6. From Langerwehe, Kreissparkasse, Van Beuningen, unnumbered. Grey stoneware with overall iron wash outside and inside of neck trailing down in dips, globular body with rounded base and two or three small tripod feet, slight cordon at junction with vertical neck with simple rounded rim, small loop strap handle.

This type was not usually imported into Britain but *Sandal,* No. 31, is almost certainly of this type though it is from a later context than the fourteenth century which might be expected for this type.

ACKNOWLEDGEMENTS

I am very greatly indebted to H. J. E. Van Beuningen for making his important collection available for study and for his assistance in publishing this type material. For the past ten years my work on the collection has been shared by D. N. Neal, who has made the drawings while I have classified, described, and photographed the pots. This represents part of a programme of publishing pottery from the Netherlands which has a bearing on British imported wares.[60]

I must also thank all the excavators and museum curators who have so readily shown me their material, often in advance of publication, so that their forms can be linked with my proposed Langerwehe type series.

REFERENCES

1. O. Von Falke, *Das Rheinische Steinzeug* (Berlin, 1908), and K. Koetschau, *Rheinische Steinzeug* (Munich, 1924).

2. M. L. Solon, *The Ancient Art Stoneware of the Low Countries and Germany* (London, 1892), Vol. I, p. 43.

3. Gisela Reineking-Von Bock, *Steinzeug*, Katalog des Kunstgewerbemuseums, Cologne, Vol. 4 (1971), pp. 39–40.

4. L. J. Schwarz, Die Bedeutung des Langerweher Töpfergewerbes in der Verdangheit' (1937); H. Samlowitz, 'Das Töpfereimuseum Langerwehe', *Keramos*, Vol. 6 (1959), pp. 33–5, and J. G. Renaud, 'Een nieuw museum voor ceramiek te Langerwehe', *Meded. Vrienden v.d. Nederlands Ceramiek*, No. 17 (1959), pp. 34–5.

5. Ohm, Schmitt and Brockneier, 'Die Langerweher Keramik', *RWE-Verbund Werkszeitschrift*, Vol. 76 (Oct., 1971), 7 pp.

6. *Ibid.*, Pls. 1–2.

7. *Ibid.*, Pls. 3–5.

8. *Ibid.*, Pl. 15.

9. Ohm *et al.*, *op. cit.*, in note 5, Pl. 14.

10. A. Thwaite, 'The Chronology of the Bellarmine Jug', *Connoisseur*, Vol. 182 (1973), pp. 255–62.

11. *Ibid.*, Pl. 16, and Von Bock, *op. cit.*, in note 3, No. 336.

12. *Volkskunst in Rheinland*, Führer und Schriften des Rheinischen Freilichtmuseums in Kommern, Vol. 4 (1968), pp. 109–10. Nos. 345–9.

13. Ohm *et. al.*, *op. cit.*, in note 5, Pl. 17.;

14. J. G. Hurst, G. C. Dunning, and K. J. Barton, 'List of Saxon and Medieval Imports into Britain' (stencilled list, 1968).

15. J. G. Hurst, 'Stoneware Jugs' in B. Cunliffe, ed., *Winchester Excavations 1949–1960*, Vol. 1 (1964), pp. 142–3.

16. C. Platt and R. Coleman-Smith, eds., *Excavations in Southampton, 1953–1969* (Leicester, 1975), Vol. 1, pp. 153–6.

17. N. Macpherson-Grant, report forthcoming in *Med. Archaeol.*

18. J. C. Thorn in T. Tatton-Brown, 'Excavations at the Custom House Site, City of London, 1973', *Trans. London and Middlx. Archaeol. Soc.*, Vol. 25 (1974), pp. 180–3, and *ibid.*, Vol. 26, pp. 150–1.

19. P. Clarke in J. Schofield, report forthcoming in *Proc. Soc. Antiqs. Scot.*

20. Information Miss B. Harbottle.

21. S. Moorhouse, 'The Medieval Pottery from Sandal Castle, Yorkshire', Undergraduate Thesis, University College, Cardiff (1974).

22. Jean Le Patourel in L. Keen, report forthcoming.

23. Verzameling H. J. E. van Beuningen, *Verdraaid Goed Gedraaid* (Rotterdam, 1973).

24. See also J. G. Hurst, 'North Holland Slip', *Rotterdam Papers*, Vol. 2 (1975), pp. 47–65; J. G. Hurst, 'Sixteenth- and seventeenth-century imported pottery from the Saintonge', in V. I. Evison *et al.*, eds., *Medieval Pottery from Excavations* (London, 1974), 221–225, and J. G. Hurst, 'Spanish pottery from Sluis', forthcoming.

25. B. Beckmann, 'The main types of the first four production periods of Siegburg pottery', in V. I. Evison, *op. cit.* in note 24, pp. 183–220.

26. A. Bruijn, 'Die mittelalterliche keramische Industrie in Südlimburg', *Ber. v.d. Rijksdienst v.h. Oudheidkundig Bodemonderzoek*, Vol. 12–13 (1962–3), pp. 356–459.

27. Ohm *et al.*, *op cit.* in note 5, Pl. 9.

28. R. Borremans and R. Warginaire, *La Céramique D'Andenne* (Rotterdam, 1966).

29. J. G. Hurst, 'Tudor-Green Ware' in B. Cunliffe, *op. cit.* in note 15, pp. 140–2.

30. Excavated by Dr. O. Mayer in 1972.

31. Bruijn, *op. cit.* in note 26, Figs. 72 and 75.

32. Beckmann, *op. cit.* in note 25, pp. 213, types 74 and 75.

33. Miss P. Clarke report forthcoming as note 19. Hereafter referred to as Edinburgh in the text.

34. F. Grossman, *Pieter Breugel* (London, 1973), Pls. 131–2, 'The Peasant Wedding'.

35. A. Bruijn, 'Drie eeuwen drinkgerei', *Meded. Vrienden v.d. Nederlands Ceramiek*, No. 22 (1964).

36. P. C. D. Brears, *The English Country Pottery* (Newton Abbot, 1971), pp. 20 and 24.

37. Van Beuningen, *op. cit.* in note 23.

38. J. G. N. Renaud, 'Een Middleleeuwse Hoeve in de Polder Boudewijn Hartsland', *Ber. v.d. Rijksdienst v.h. Oudheidkundig Bodemonderzoek*, Vol. 6 (1955), p. 147, Fig. 7, No. 7.

39. Information Dr. J. G. N. Renaud.

40. Platt, *op. cit.* in note 16. Hereafter referred to as Southampton in the text.

41. J. A. Trimpe Burger, 'Ceramiek uit de bloeitijd van Aardenburg', *Ber. v.d. Rijksdienst v.h. Oudheidjundig Bodemonderzoek*, Vol. 12–13 (1962–3), p. 544, Fig. 68, No. D26.

42. J. G. N. Renaud, 'Vondsten van Spangen', *Rotterdams Jaarboekje* (1953), p. 121, Fig. 6, No. 6.

43. J. G. N. Renaud, 'Ter Does', *Leids Jaarboekje* (1954), p. 84, Fig. 16, No. 3.

44. C. Hoek, 'Kastelan binnen de hoge heerlijkheid Putten', *Ber. v.d. Rijksdienst v.h. Oudheidkundig Bodemonderzoek*, Vol. 12–13 (1962–3), p. 485, Fig. 20.

45. S. Moorhouse, 'Finds from the Excavations in the Refectory at the Dominican Friary Boston', *Lincs. History and Archaeol.*, Vol. 1, No. 7 (1972), Fig. 4.

46. Renaud, *op. cit.* in note 42, Fig. 6, No. 10.

47. B. P. Blake, J. G. Hurst, and L. H. Gand, 'Medieval and Later Pottery from Stockwell Street, Colchester', *Trans. Essex Archaeol. Soc.*, Vol. 1 (1961), pp. 43–7.

48. Information H. L. Janssen.

49. Ohm., *op. cit.* in note 5, Pl. 7.

50. J. G. Hurst, 'Flemish Stoneware Jug', in E. W. Holden, 'Excavations at the Deserted Medieval Village of Hangleton, Part I', *Sussex Archaeol. Coll.*, Vol. 101 (1963), p. 138, Fig. 27, No. 245.

51. Beckmann, *op. cit.* in note 25, p. 210, types 54–5.

52. Information Miss B. Harbottle.

53. Trimpe Burger, *op. cit.* in note 41, p. 543, Fig. 65, No. D23.

54. Information Dr. J. G. N. Renaud.

55. Bruijn, *op. cit.* in note 26, pp. 440–1, 82–3.

56. For example from Wisbech, Cambs., information S. Moorhouse.

57. A. Matthys, 'Les Grès Communs de Bouffioulx et Cot Châtelet', *Repertoirs Archaeol.*, Vol. 6 (1971), Fig. 7, No. 34.

58. Van Beuningen, *op. cit.*, in note 23, pp. 12–14, Nos. 56–69.

59. Beckmann, *op. cit.* in note 25, types 110–160.

Craignethan Castle, Lanarkshire:
an Experiment in Artillery Fortification

by

IAIN MACIVOR

INTRODUCTION

CRAIGNETHAN CASTLE (N.G.R. NS816464) was given by Lord Home of the Hirsel, then Earl of Home, into the guardianship of the Ministry of Works in 1949. Conservation of the fabric began soon afterwards. The excavation of overgrown debris leading to the final definition of the castle has been protracted and the definition is still not quite complete; but all the critical parts of the defences are now fully revealed.

The site is a spur formed by the deeply eroded beds of the Water of Nethan and the Craignethan Burn (Fig. 1). To north, south, and east the ground falls away steeply, in places precipitously, to ravines. To the west, at the base of the spur, the ground rises abruptly to overlook the site.

The structures of the castle are laid out on an almost symmetrical elongated plan on the spur (Plates XVI, XVII; Fig. 2). A large squat towerhouse stands within an inner close or courtyard surrounded by a rectangular barmkin or enceinte. The three fronts of the rectangle overlooking the ravines are flanked by rectilinear towers of different sizes. The west front consists of a straight massive masonry rampart, rising vertically from a deep ditch cut right across the spur, defended by a caponier and a loopholed traverse. West of the ditch is an outer close with small towers at its western angles. A house dated by an inscription to 1665 stands with lesser buildings in the south-west angle of the outer courtyard.

The high ground to the west is 270 ft. distant from the west rampart. The high ground on the opposite sides of the ravines is to the east about 400 ft., to the north about 525 ft., distant from the nearest buildings.

HISTORICAL BACKGROUND

The lands of Draffan, on which Craignethan stands, are first recorded in the reign of David I as a gift to Kelso Abbey. The abbey seems to have retained the superiority until the Reformation. It has been stated[1] that the lands were held by James, first Lord Hamilton (d. 1479), but there is no documentary

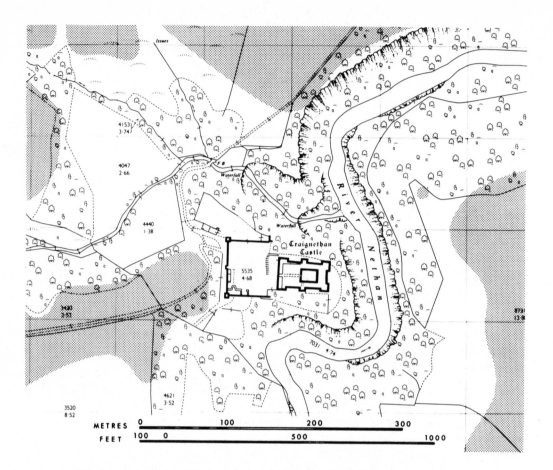

Fig. 1 Ground above 400 ft., the level which commands the site, is tinted.
(Crown copyright.)

evidence which establishes the first connection of the Hamiltons with
Craignethan more precisely than that it began at some time before 1532.

In a charter of 1532[2] Kelso Abbey, as superior, feus to Sir James Hamilton
of Finnart, the castle and fortalice of Nauthane and adjacent land. The charter
confirms an existing state of affairs, for in it Sir James is described as being
in possession of the subjects; and the castle is described as being then in course
of building by Sir. James.[3] The charter, and another later in the same year,
make the first mention of Craignethan Castle.

Sir James was a favoured natural son of James, second Lord Hamilton,
who had been created first Earl of Arran in 1503. The Bastard of Arran helped
eagerly in the Hamilton feuds, and on his father's death in 1529 was appointed

sole executor of the Earl's will and tutor to the infant second Earl of Arran. Sir James' influential position in one of the most powerful Scottish families was thus reinforced, and his standing was further raised by the friendship of King James V. The latter bestowed Crown offices on Sir James, which gave him the exercise of patronage at Royal buildings, including Linlithgow Palace and perhaps Blackness Castle.[4] It is clear that after 1529 Sir James had resources well beyond those that might have been expected from his titular station.

Sir James's prosperous career ended abruptly in 1540 when he was executed on a charge of treason, and his lands forfeited. The charter evidence quoted is only evidence that Sir James was involved at some stage of the building. His involvement is also attested by fragments of a pair of armorial plaques bearing the arms granted him in 1530/1,[5] both re-used in recent structures. At the end of Sir James's tenure Craignethan had become a place of some military consequence: in 1541 guns were taken from it[6] and in 1545 its gunner attended the siege of Lochmaben Castle, Dumfriesshire.[7]

On the death of James V in 1542 the second Earl of Arran became Regent of Scotland. Soon afterwards Sir James Hamilton's forfeiture was recalled in favour of his son, but Craignethan was acquired by Arran himself, in discharge of claims alleged against Sir James.[8] The castle was now closely involved with the varied fortunes of one raised to the highest rank in his country, who reached his zenith of prosperity in 1549 when he was created Duke of Châtel-herault in France. Contemporaries regarded him as a man of weak character and inconstant purpose; nevertheless, with Scotland divided by strong opposing pressures from France and England, by increasingly disruptive forces of religious conflict, as well as the traditional feuds of the great families, the Duke continued as Regent for twelve years. He was replaced in office by Mary of Lorraine, James V's widow: the Queen Dowager had opposed the Duke in the past, and continued to come into political conflict with him until her death and the return to Scotland of Mary Stuart to begin her personal reign as Queen of Scots.

The Duke was proclaimed a traitor, and in 1566 banished to France for opposition to the marriage between Mary and Henry Darnley; and Craignethan and Cadzow Castle, near Hamilton, his other principal strength in Lanarkshire, were occupied on behalf of the Queen. He was in Scotland again at the time of Mary's enforced abdication in 1567, when the Earl of Moray was proclaimed Regent for the year-old King James VI. The Duke and the family at once manoeuvred against the new Regent by supporting Mary. They colluded in her escape from Lochleven, entertained her at Hamilton, and tried to convoy her to safety to Dumbarton Castle. The Queen's small army with the youngest son of the Duke, Lord Claud Hamilton, was intercepted on the way and defeated by Regent Moray at Langside on 13 May 1568; Mary fled to England, the Duke withdrew to the island of Arran. Cadzow was given up to Moray, who then went to Craignethan to demand and receive its surrender.

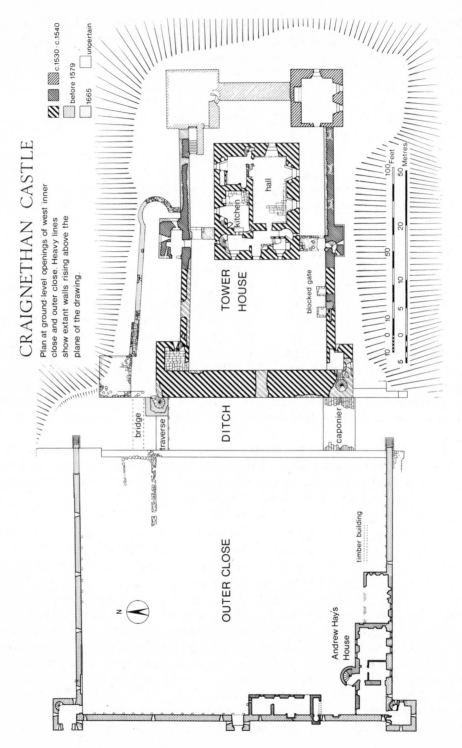

CRAIGNETHAN CASTLE

Plan at ground-level openings of west inner close and outer close. Heavy lines show extant walls rising above the plane of the drawing.

c.1530 - c.1540

before 1579

1665

uncertain

TOWER HOUSE

kitchen

hall

blocked gate

DITCH

bridge

traverse

caponier

OUTER CLOSE

N

Andrew Hay's House

timber building

100 Feet

50 Metres

Fig. 2

The opposition soon rallied after this serious reverse. The Hamiltons recaptured both castles late in 1568, the Regent's garrison at Craignethan capitulating to the threat of a cannon taken from the royal arsenal.[9] In January 1570 the family had the Regent shot at Linlithgow, but the opposing faction stayed in power, and to consolidate it called in English help under Sir William Drury, Governor of Berwick. Minor pieces ('shott') were brought into Craignethan, but Drury dismissed the place in a report—'a strong house of the Duke's, but situate in a hole, so that it is commanded on every part, and has no ordnance'.[10] He did not, however, attempt to take it.

The Earl of Lennox, father of the unfortunate Darnley, had been appointed Regent to succeed Moray; on 23 July 1570 the Hamiltons foregathered with Lord Claud at Craignethan and eighty horsemen with fifty hackbutters from the Craignethan garrison set off thence to ambush the new Regent on the road between Edinburgh and Stirling.[11] Lennox escaped by changing his travelling plans, on 7 August moved his forces and artillery from Stirling on an abortive attempt to clear the Hamiltons out of their 'den' at Craignethan,[12] but withdrew from Clydesdale with the family still undeterred, raiding supporters of the regime and holding one of them, Lord Sempill, imprisoned at Craignethan. Lord Claud made another foray with twenty hackbutters on 11 October.[13]

The cause to which the Hamilton adhered was, however, gradually declining. In April 1571 the Regent's men seized Dumbarton Castle by surprise, captured John Hamilton, Archbishop of St. Andrews (another of the Duke's illegitimate half-brothers), and hanged him at Stirling. In that town soon afterwards another *coup* was attempted and again failed, for although the Regent Lennox was killed, Mary's supporters were dispersed, and the next Regent, the Earl of Mar, was once more chosen from the opposite side. Regent Mar's death in 1572 came naturally; his successor was the most implacable of the Protestant Lords, the Earl of Morton.

An uneasy pacification, signed by the Hamiltons, was made between the factions in February 1573. Two months later Edinburgh Castle was taken by English troops and guns for the Regent, further adjusting the realities of power in his favour. Early in 1575 the Duke of Châtelherault died, and his insane eldest son succeeded as third Earl of Arran, living at Craignethan with the widowed Duchess, while his brother, Lord John Hamiton, with Lord Claud, took charge of affairs. Their hold on the family possessions and castles in Clydesdale was left unchallenged until 1579.

In May 1579 proclamations were issued against the Hamiltons for past alleged crimes, and levies were raised to besiege Cadzow and Craignethan castles. Protracted sieges were anticipated, but after brief operations Craignethan was abandoned during the night, and Cadzow surrendered. An order was issued for the fortifications of Craignethan to be slighted:

The King and Council, 'considdering the oft rebellioun and defectioun schawin and maid be the keiparis of the castell and fortilice of Draffen, als weill to his Majesteis predicessouris, of worthie memorie, as to his Hienes self in his awin tyme', ordain 'that James Hammiltoun of Libertoun sall, betuix the date heirof and the Feist of Michaelmes nixt to cum, caus dimolische and cast doun to the ground the inner barmkin of the said hous, and the tour upoun the south nuke of the samin, as alsau the tour upoun the north nuke at the entres, and the fowse thairof fillit; and that na thing remane within the clois about the rute of the tour bot the dur thairof, to oppin plainelie in the clois; as alsua na thing to remane bot the garding dike on the west hand without flankis, and that the bigging upoun the eist side of the tour, and the clois dykis on the south and north side, remane without flankis'.[14]

While nothing had been done by June 1580 the present state of the castle shows that most of the demolitions were eventually carried out.

The 1579 demolition order establishes a firm end-date for all the buildings and fortifications (including by inference the defences in the ditch ordered to be filled in), save for the 1665 house and the structures reasonably associated with it.

The towerhouse in the slighted castle was inhabited until Andrew Hay bought Craignethan from Anne, Duchess of Hamilton, and built a house in the outer close in 1665. Hay's house has been almost continuously occupied until the present day, while the rest of the castle gradually fell into ruin. In about 1730 Craignethan was bought by the Duke of Douglas, from whom it descends to Lord Home. In 1799 it was visited by Sir Walter Scott. Craignethan is an uncertain model for the Tillietudlem Castle of Scott's *Old Mortality,* but the association has attached prestige to the castle from Scott's romantic invention. The fabric was consolidated by the twelfth Earl of Home in the late nineteenth/early twentieth century.

The first antiquarian reference to Craignethan, in the eighteenth century, attributed the castle to Sir James Hamilton of Finnart.[15] MacGibbon and Ross attributed the inner barmkin to Sir James without qualification, and accepted that the outer close also appeared to have been built by him; but observed that the keep seemed to belong to the latter part of the fifteenth century.[16]

In 1956 Dr. W. Douglas Simpson read a short paper discussing architectural affinities of the building and attributed the towerhouse and both closes to Sir James. The paper was published in 1963 with a note of the excavation and clearance then in progress.[17]

DESCRIPTION

The rectangular tower (Plate XVIII a, Figs. 2, 3) measures externally 52 ft. 6 in. north and south by 69 ft. 6 in. east and west. Its west elevation is 34 ft. 10 in. high from the courtyard to the string above the corbelling.[17] Because of the eastward fall in ground level the basement was originally exposed on the east elevation, giving there a height of 48 ft. 8 in. Above the ground floor the west wall is massive, varying from 10 ft. 7 in. to 17 ft. 6 in.

The only openings towards the west are the central round-headed door symmetrically flanked by small windows, and a similar upper window offset to the south. There is a decayed armorial device above the door.[18] The other three sides are more generously fenestrated. There are no gunloops.

The ornate west parapet (Plate XVIII b) rises from a double staggered row of corbels with angle rounds, and a median round. The parapet has had enriched water spouts, and spirelets rising from the rounds. Heraldic beasts probably stood on the roof ridge.[19]

The plan is compact and ingenious: above a basement, a lofty hall to south rises through two storeys to north; overall there is an upper storey. In cubic capacity the Craignethan towerhouse is among the largest of Scottish rectangular towers, rivalled only by Newark Castle, Selkirkshire, Spynie Palace, Moray, and Threave Castle, Kirkcudbrightshire. It is only called a towerhouse for lack of a better word: comparative analysis of towerhouses in any of the works on Scottish historic architecture shows how unusual it is alike in proportions and planning.

The basement has four vaulted rooms arranged chequer-wise, the south-east room containing a well, and a fifth to south-west beside an awkward stair from ground floor to basement. Narrow openings light only the south-west stair and the two eastern rooms. The north-west room has a tortuous cramped stair up to the ground floor kitchen. The ground floor has a transverse north-south passage on its west side, articulated in two parts with vaults of different spans. The entrance leads into this passage; from it open the hall, a stair at each end down to the basement and up to the higher floors and the parapet, and a serving-hatch to the kitchen. The latter has been altered (with other parts of the passage) during the twelfth Earl's repairs, and may replace a door.

The barrel-vaulted hall is 30 ft. 9 in. by 19 ft. 9 in./20 ft. 6 in., and 24 ft. 4 in. high. It has three large windows with stone seats, the latter being continued as benching along all the walls save the west. These windows make a marked domestic contrast to the under-fenestrated west elevation. The hall fireplace was near the north-east angle, adjoining a door to a private suite of two superimposed rooms, both with garderobes, the upper one vaulted at the same level as the hall.

The kitchen is now entered only from the stair up from the basement. The entresol room above the kitchen, unlike the rest of the towerhouse at this level, is unvaulted. It is entered from the north-west stair.

At the west end of the hall is a narrow gallery at the same level as the entresol, entered from the stairwell at the south end of the ground floor passage. The well is roughly constructed and surprisingly spacious for its limited function since, although it reaches the top storey, there is no indication that its steps ever rose above the hall gallery. At entresol level the west wall of the towerhouse, supported on the vaults of the passage below, is 16 ft. 6 in./17 ft. 6 in. thick.

CRAIGNETHAN CASTLE

Tower-House and East Range

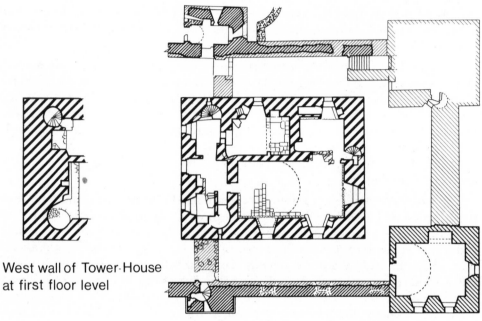

West wall of Tower-House
at first floor level

Plan at principal floor level of Tower-House

N

Heavy lines show extant
walls rising above the
plane of the drawing

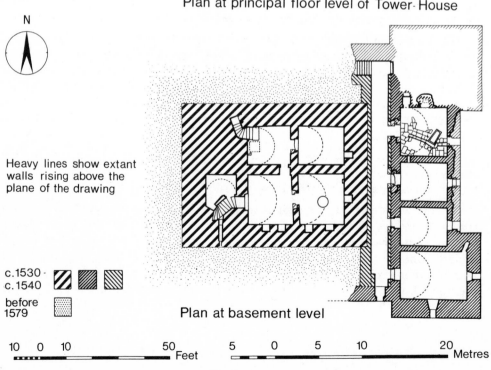

c.1530 -
c.1540

before
1579

Plan at basement level

10   0   10   50 Feet   5   0   5   10   20 Metres

Fig. 3

The upper floor is completely ruinous. Heavy concrete weather-tabling, part of the twelfth Earl's repairs, has preserved the plan of four rooms, all reached from the north-west stair. The west wall at the level of the upper floor and wallhead is 10 ft. 7 in. thick.

The platform behind the west parapet is 7 ft. 9 in. wide, conventionally saddled and sloped towards the parapet spouts for drainage, with two stepped longitudinal rows of flags. The generous scale suggests that this parapet of the towerhouse at least was armed, either with hand-manipulated or wheel-carriage mounted pieces.

The many awkwardnesses throughout the west part of the towerhouse suggest modification during building, but any change has defied analysis. The massive west wall suggests protection from artillery bombardment on its most vulnerable side.

As the weakness of the towerhouse west wall at ground floor level demands the protection of a rampart beyond it if the wall thickness above is to make sense, the barmkin must have been in course of building or at least contemplated when the towerhouse was built. Since the cross walls linking the towerhouse with the north and south walls of the barmkin are integral with the barmkin walls, while they are butt-jointed against the towerhouse walls, the lower part at least of the towerhouse must have been completed when the barmkin was constructed to north and south of it.

The area about the towerhouse, paved with stone setts, extends to the west 65 ft. by 83 ft., narrows to about 15 ft. to north and south; and is reduced to a 7 ft. 6 in. wide alley (subsequently further narrowed and vaulted over: see p. 254) between the towerhouse and the east range.

The barmkin around the towerhouse is a unit of design, though its construction, apparently from west to east, may have been protracted and detail changed. The special nature and tactical importance of the west rampart and ditch (Figs. 4, 5) suggest that they, with the caponier, the towers at each end of the west rampart, and the lengths of curtain beyond them up to a point beyond the blocked south gate, were begun first.

The west rampart is drawn in a straight line. It survives to an average height of 3 ft. 11 in. above the close: the demolition ordered in 1579 has here been thoroughly executed. At this height it is a solid wall on average 16 ft. 4 in. thick, with two adjacent stairwells entered from the south-west tower. One stair leads down to the caponier:[20] the other, almost completely destroyed, has presumably led up to the wallhead of the rampart.

The west rampart above the level of the close is supported by a cellular vaulted construction immediately below. Ten segmental vaults, 7 ft. by 6 ft. spring from cross-walls on average 2 ft. 3 in. thick. Vaults and cross-walls are contained between the 5 ft 4 in. scarp and the slightly narrower rear wall.

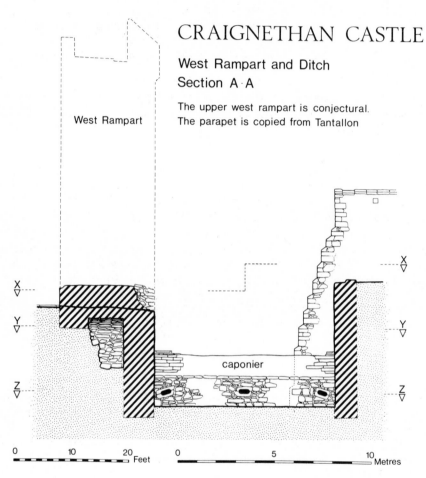

CRAIGNETHAN CASTLE

West Rampart and Ditch
Section A·A

The upper west rampart is conjectural.
The parapet is copied from Tantallon

West Rampart

caponier

0   10   20 Feet   0   5   10 Metres

Fig. 4

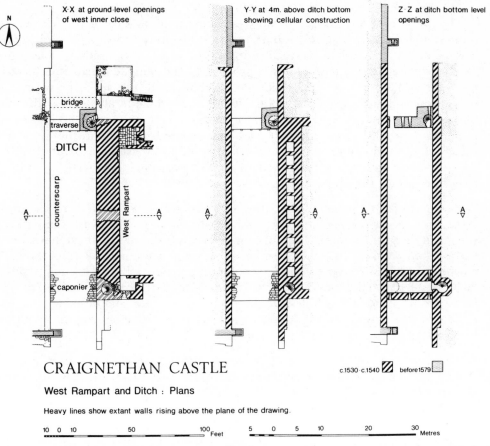

X·X at ground-level openings of west inner close

Y·Y at 4m. above ditch bottom showing cellular construction

Z·Z at ditch bottom level openings

N

bridge

traverse

DITCH

counterscarp

West Rampart

A

caponier

CRAIGNETHAN CASTLE

c.1530·c.1540   before 1579

West Rampart and Ditch : Plans

Heavy lines show extant walls rising above the plane of the drawing.

10 0 10   50   100 Feet   5 0 5   10   20   30 Metres

Fig. 5

The foundation of the rear wall is just below close level, so that at the springing level of the vaults the plan-form of the west rampart is a scarp with internal buttresses or counterforts about 6 ft. long. The counterforts decrease in projection towards the ditch bottom and terminate altogether 7 ft. above the ditch bottom where there is only the scarp on the 1 ft. 11 in. deep foundation.

The curious design is presumably a constructional expedient. The scarp face of the ditch as dug left a battered face of sandy subsoil. The scarp wall was founded and raised vertically from the foot of the subsoil face, the counterforts added to it as building progressed and lengthened to abut against the subsoil face as the latter receded. Concurrently the space between the scarp wall and the subsoil face was filled with rammed clay so that the top of the scarp, the counterforts and the rammed clay were kept to the same level. At courtyard level the inner wall was founded just behind the lip of the subsoil face. The rammed clay was then moulded to serve as centering for the transverse vaults which formed, with the scarp and rear walls, a unified structure to take the upper rampart.

Because of the instability of the subsoil face as excavated at an angle averaging 16 deg. from the vertical, construction of the west rampart to sufficient height to reach the springing level of the vaults must have been carried out rapidly to avoid collapse under weathering. The method of construction is suspiciously like jerry building, with the continuing danger during and after the building of the upper rampart that the weight of the latter would cause the whole structure to slip forward and collapse into the ditch. Bombardment of the upper rampart might have shown the work to be less durable than it superficially appeared.

The character of the demolished upper rampart is conjectural.[21] Dressed stones from the ditch excavation showed that it rose to a parapet with corbels similar to those *in situ* elsewhere on the barmkin, and that it had been furnished with gunloops. The loops may have alternated with embrasures on the parapet as at Carberry Tower, Midlothian,[22] they may have opened from casemated recesses above close level, or—perhaps most likely—they may have pierced the whole rampart thickness as in the south curtain of Blackness Castle, West Lothian.

The height of the west rampart is unlikely to have been more than 37 ft. 9 in. from close level to wallhead, and may well have been less.[23] At such a height the wallhead armament would still be below the rising ground 270 ft. distant. The wallhead armament could not, without a much greater and improbable height, effectively command the rising ground.

There were more than fifty gunloops throughout the castle, and the survivors are all of the same type: throats flush with the internal wall face or inset very slightly in cupped recesses, a single outward horizontal splay, the vertical splay varied and sometimes negligible, horizontal-axis round-ended external openings. Surviving throats are round or square, almost all 7 in. across, with 8½ in. below the south-east tower parapet only. None has any provision for a wooden bar on which to rest a gun, or to receive the swivel pin of a gun.

There are no intact examples of the largest kind of loop, with throat 1 ft.– 1 ft. 6 in. across, which were most probably designed for carriage-mounted artillery. All the surviving throats of 7 in to 8½ in. are suitable only for hand-manipulated guns.[24] The west parapet of the towerhouse suggests by analogy that the wallhead of the west rampart may have accommodated either hand-manipulated or wheel-carriage mounted pieces.

At each end of the west rampart a rectangular tower, of integral build with the rampart, is attached to its inner face. These towers, which probably rose only to the height of the rampart, will be described with the south and north fronts of the barmkin. The line of the west rampart scarp is extended beyond the north-west and south-west towers by revetting walls for 29 ft. to north, 33 ft. to south, of integral build with the rampart. Part abutting on the north revetting wall, part on the west rampart, is the stair tower (butt-jointed in a manner clearly secondary) of the traverse in the ditch. The bridge approach crossed the north revetting wall immediately beyond the traverse. A structure, probably secondary, so badly preserved as to be indefinable on plan, was sited at the northernmost end of the revetting wall.

The ditch beyond the west rampart is 31 ft. wide within the vertical walls of scarp and counterscarp; its bottom 16 ft. below the inner close. The ditch bottom is cut level right across the spur on which the castle stands and its ends open on the ravines to north and south.

The stair in the thickness of the west rampart descends to the level of the bottom of the ditch to give access to the caponier (Plate XIX a, Fig. 6). The stair has a loop immediately above the ridge of the caponier roof. Although the caponier is butt-jointed to the scarp and counterscarp, the intimate relationship of the caponier stair to the west rampart implies convincingly that the caponier was planned when the west rampart was constructed.

The caponier at the south end of the ditch extends across its full breadth. It is a barrel-vaulted gallery, externally 20 ft. wide, with walls of different thicknesses: the north wall 7 ft. 8 in., the south wall only 4 ft. 9 in. The flagged low-pitched roof is solid above the vault. Each of the caponier's walls is pierced by three loops to scour the ditch. The north outer loops are externally angled, giving this elevation of the caponier an odd slant-eyed appearance. The caponier gallery, 7 ft. 7 in. wide, rises 8 ft. 3 in. to the crown of its vault. It has no light or ventilation apart from the stair and the small square inner openings of its loops.

In the north part of the ditch, in a position corresponding to the caponier at the south, a thick-walled stair turret butt-jointed to the scarp face leads

CRAIGNETHAN CASTLE : Caponier

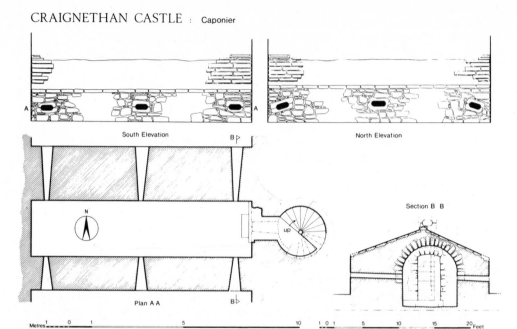

Fig. 6

down to the ditch bottom. The north face of the turret has a loop. From the west side of the stair turret a wall 7 ft. 8 in. thick traverses the ditch, and is butt-jointed against the counterscarp. The traverse has two loops and its west end is pierced by a door leading to the north end of the ditch. Remains of mortar against the turret show that the traverse had a cope gently sloping from south to north. At a height of 10 ft. 4 in. above the ditch bottom on the south face of the traverse are corbels to hold a roof structure. The corbels suggest a massive timber roof to protect the defenders and the traverse from above, giving what would be in effect a variant of the caponier design, open to the rear and so better ventilated.

The upper courses of the counterscarp had fallen when consolidation began. It was much simpler than the scarp; merely a vertical wall averaging 4 ft. thick at the top (the thickness of its lower part has not been investigated) without counterforts. It has been later extended 40 ft. 9 in. to the north.

The bridge, below the general level of the counterscarp, was approached by a broad roadway of setts. Nothing is known of the bridge save its location. It was presumably all of timber: perhaps a fixed span on either side of a central movable span with an upper counterpoise beam.

The south and north fronts of the barmkin had each the same basic plan, three towers jointed by two lengths of curtain. In detail and in state of preservation, however, the two fronts are very different.

The south front is much the best preserved part of the barmkin. Save for the south-west tower (ruined as an inevitable result of the demolition of the west rampart), it has not been slighted. The west length of curtain and the mid-tower still survive in part to wallhead level; the south-east tower survives intact save for its parapet. After the demolition of the west rampart, the slighting seems to have proceeded on the north front and then stopped, leaving the south front and the outer close intact.

At the west end of the south front is the rectangular tower built with the west rampart, its south and east walls varying slightly from the 5 ft. 6 in. general thickness of the south curtain; these together with a very thin north wall enclose an unvaulted chamber, 9 ft. by 10 ft. 4 in. In its east wall the tower has a fireplace, and, immediately beside it, a loop flanking the adjacent curtain. The tower probably had three floors; the fireplace suggests that the rooms were means as living quarters.

The curtain between south-west and mid-towers is well preserved with some corbels surviving at 28 ft. above ground level. It contains a blocked gate with two bar holes and, within the curtain, foundations 7 ft. apart for a short transe. The most likely explanation of the gate is that the first stage of building took in with the west rampart and ditch the north and south fronts as far as the mid-towers, and at this stage a south gate was designed as a principal access. When the next part of the barmkin was built, a change of plan produced the existing entry through the mid-tower of the south curtain, and the south gate was blocked.

The mid-tower contains an eccentrically-placed stair with two loops through its west flank and face. There is no loop in its east flank: the deficiencies of the flanking defence of the barmkin are noted below. Some corbels of the parapet of the mid-tower survive 4 ft. 2 in. above the corbels of the adjacent curtain to the west. The much reduced cross wall linking the towerhouse with the south barmkin extends from the mid-tower, 9 ft. 2 in. wide, with double gates opening inward to a small chamber from which the mid-tower stair is entered.

The east length of the curtain of the south front contains the postern already mentioned, opening within to the alley between towerhouse and east range, and the remains of three high-level openings through the curtain. The only one of these with any surviving detail has bar-holes but no checks for shutters or glazing, suggesting that the openings were to improve the lighting of the towerhouse hall. These openings, with the low-level windows of the east front, show that around the spur security was readily sacrificed to domestic convenience.

The south-east tower is part of the overall plan of the east front, which was laid out symmetrically with two projecting blocks 31 ft. 6 in. north and south by 34 ft. east and west joined by a range 44 ft. 6 in. north and south by 26 ft. 6 in. east and west. The original scheme was that the central range should rise above a vaulted basement possibly to the same level as the terminal blocks. The design was changed when the vaulted basement was completed. The projecting blocks were carried up as towers, the basements of the central range topped with a sloping weatherproofed surface, which was continued right to the east wall of the towerhouse over a vaulted pend newly built between the east range and the towerhouse. Access to all the east range basements was by the pend from a flight of steps leading down to its north end. Access to the east and west towers was from the new surface above the basements. The curtain between the towers was massively raised with a thickness of 11 ft.—a much greater thickness than at basement level.

The barrel vault of the south-east tower has a heavy stone-slabbed pitched roof of secondary but undatable construction, the ridge being at the same level as the corbel table. Accessible from the roof are the five loops which open to the exterior just below the corbel table. Their soles slope steeply downwards in the 3 ft. 8 in. thick walls in an unconvincing attempt to command the steep slope down to the Nethan Water. The south-east tower has no loops at ground level.

The north-east tower was demolished to its basement after 1580 and at the time of writing the debris has not been cleared. It had a small loop in its south flank.

The north barmkin has a mid-tower larger—24 ft. by 14 ft. 2 in.—than the corresponding tower to the south. The mid-tower contains the main entrance to the inner close, by an inward opening door leading into the vaulted interior of the tower and thence to the close at a point adjacent to the north link wall. The tower has a loop on each of its faces.

The north-west tower is also larger than the corresponding tower to the south, with the same elements though differently arranged, and with a garde-robe chute from one of its lost upper rooms. Outside the mid and north-west towers, paving leads to the bridge over the ditch. The paving was bounded to the north by a slight 2 ft. 9 in. outer wall which ends with the fragmentary structure already mentioned in describing the scarp north extension. This outer wall, obstructing the east gunloop of the mid-tower, is presumably an addition.

The arrangement of loops to flank the barmkin is haphazard and incomplete. Five flanks have ground-level loops and one has a loop skied at 12 ft. above ground level, and three have no loops at all. The west flank of the north-east tower is so far destroyed that it cannot be seen whether it had a loop. Two of the flanking loops are badly laid out so that they do not command the adjacent curtain.

The towers of the barmkin which survive to a sufficient level all have loops in their faces towards the field. These are at different heights: in the mid-north tower at ground level, in the mid-south tower at 8 ft., in the kitchen tower just below the parapet. The oddity of the kitchen tower loops, in attempting ineffectively to command a steep slope, has already been noticed. Though lower, the other face loops have the same defect.

The counterscarp was extended 40 ft. 9 in. to the north as a preliminary to the construction of an outer close west of the ditch, externally 192 ft. east and west by 156 ft. north and south, with crenellated walls to north, west and south, and towers about 18 ft. 3 in. square at the north-west and south-west angles. A low wall to the east above the counterscarp seems to have been raised to stop people from falling into the ditch and not as part of the defences.

The curtain and towers of the outer courtyard (Plate XIX b) reproduce several features of the works east of the ditch, though the curtains are much slighter and lower, averaging 3 ft. 9 in. thick and 12 ft./13 ft. 6 in. to the parapet walk. Curtains and towers are pierced with low-set loops. There has been a continuous corbelling round all three inner wall faces of the courtyard, as for a plate to take a roof round the three sides. Excavation in 1971 showed the foundation-trench of a timber range on the south side, and the existence of a narrower stone range along part of the north half of the west curtain. No range was ever built against the north curtain.

The twenty-two loops of the outer courtyard, unlike those of the inner enceinte, are regularly and systematically placed. Each flank has a loop, which is well-sited and completely answers its purpose. Because of the small size and shallow projection of the towers, the west front is as completely flanked as in a bastioned system.

For some reason not apparent, a round-headed opening has been slapped through the west face of the north-west tower. The opening is flanked by loops. It is not clear whether the alteration was made before or after 1579.

The north and south curtains of the outer courtyard are carried down to the ditch bottom by stepped buttresses. At ditch bottom level these buttresses are pierced by small loops. Both command a minimal field of fire because the edge of the spur drops away sharply just in front.

In the south-west angle of the courtyard is a roofed rectangular two-storey-plus-attic house with central projecting round stair and entrance turret on its north elevation, dated 1665 on the door lintel. To the rear the house incorporates the south-west tower of the courtyard. A low single-storey range, including a kitchen, lies adjacent to the house on the west curtain. A two-storey-plus-attic south wing, attached to the partly rebuilt south curtain, is now much ruined.

DISCUSSION

In the building of Craignethan three major elements may be distinguished: the towerhouse with the enceinte round it including the west rampart, ditch and caponier; the outer courtyard; Andrew Hay's house and its adjoining ancillary buildings. There are, besides, minor modifications and additions; the change of entrance gate position; the alteration of the original plan of the east range of the enceinte; the addition of the traverse in the ditch; the addition of the wall and ruined structure (not all of the same period of building) beyond the mid and west towers of the north enceinte.

The date of Hay's house is known, the association of the neighbouring buildings with it reasonable: so the place in the sequence of these structures need not be further discussed.

Although no evidence conclusively dates the main programme (towerhouse, barmkin, ditch and caponier) the charter evidence of building in 1532 may be straightforwardly taken to mean that this programme was then under way. The pair of Sir James Hamilton of Finnart armorial plaques may come from any part of the castle except the known seventeenth-century works. There is no way to determine whether or not the programme, including the modification of the original plan of the east range, was begun before or completed before or after Sir James's time: a bracket of about 1530 to about 1540 may have to be extended each way.

There is no way to determine whether the outer courtyard and the wall and ruined structure beyond the north enceinte were begun by Sir James, or by the second Earl of Arran after 1540. The traverse, implying a drastic reappraisal of the ditch defences because the caponier had been judged insufficient, may be the latest of the pre-1579 works.

The main programme included the principal residential unit, the towerhouse, with further accommodation—reduced by the modification of the east range layout—scattered round the close, and the main fortifications. It is tempting to think of the west front as an ingenious application of the lessons apparently offered by the siege of Tantallon Castle in 1528, using as a basis a free adaptation of Tantallon's medieval plan.[25] At Tantallon prolonged bombardment by James V's artillery left the castle unscathed. This and other episodes seemingly demonstrated that good defences in the medieval style were by no means obsolete. On the exposed west front, defence towards the field was totally separated from defence of the flanks by the provision of the simple and massive rampart, with the caponier extending from its base. The caponier and the base of the west rampart were shielded from battering fire by the counterscarp.

It is impossible to conjecture the original armament of Craignethan with any confidence. It may become possible with systematic study of surviving weapons and documents relating to the artillery used in the contemporary defence of Scottish places. The wallhead armament of several major places of strength included wheel-carriage mounted pieces ('mountit upoun thair stokis quheillis and aixtree' or 'with hir furnist stok and quhelis') ranging from cannon properly so-called, through culverins to double falcons.[26] It may also include small-bore hand-manipulated pieces, usually breech-loading, with or without stocks, maybe sometimes swivelled. A conventional crenellated parapet could also readily take a hackbut, rested with its hook in front of the crenel.

The largest of Scottish gunloops with throats between 1 ft.–1 ft. 6 in. in diameter, in works such as the blockhouse at Dunbar Castle,[4] Blackness Castle, and the curtain north of David's Tower at Edinburgh Castle probably accommodated wheel-carriage mounted pieces, though I have found no certain documentary confirmation. Most gunloops, however, including the middle size found at Craignethan, accommodated the same variety of hand-manipulated pieces as the parapet: breech-loaders with chambers, named variously, and rather inscrutably, double or single (i.e., large or small) *cutthrottis, heidsteikis* and *slangis*; muzzle loaders, including the lesser falcons and the hackbut-sized lesser culverin.[27] Because of its hook, a hackbut would be awkward to work in a gunloop; yet it might seem odd if the hackbuts certainly used by the Craignethan garrison in forays (p. 243 above) could not also serve for defence.

Hand-manipulated guns of various types must have been quantitatively the principal armament of Craignethan. The parapet of the west rampart and the west parapet of the towerhouse may have accommodated wheel-carriage mounted pieces of modest size, perhaps no larger than double falcons.[6] There is no suggestion that heavy guns (cannon, culverins, sakers) could have been defensively emplaced.

In two important respects the work has no analogies in the surviving body of evidence for its Scottish contemporaries: the system of 'perpendicular fortification' with field defence and flank defence sharply distinguished; and the protection given by the counterscarp to the low-level flank defence and the scarp base.

The first known designs using roofed caponiers in permanent fortification for ditch defence and for communication between the works were made by Francesco di Giorgio Martini towards the end of the sixteenth century. The roofed caponier for ditch defence was elaborated by Albrecht Dürer,[28] but with the development of bastioned systems it fell into disfavour, save to overcome the problems of an intractable site,[29] until revived in principle by Montalembert and in practice by the new fortification of the nineteenth century.[30] Unroofed caponiers for communication were still used in classic bastioned fortification, but although the same name was used this is really a different type. The immediate parentage of the Craignethan caponier is obscure. In spite of shortcomings of detail (lack of ventilation, limited field of fire) it is the most remarkable element of the monument.

In planning Craignethan the high ground west of the site must have been taken into account. We do not know whether the west rampart was designed to withstand 'great artillery' or lesser pieces; but it was obviously assumed that its sheer massiveness could withstand a battery established on the commanding west eminence 270 ft. distant, and that a breaching battery must be brought closer to the rampart to be really effective. At such a range the armament of the rampart was reckoned to be a sufficient deterrent, while the caponier gave separate defence against close assault.

On the three other fronts no especially strong defence was judged necessary against bombardment, so there the design reverted to traditional forms, which had no comprehensive low-level flank defence. The extra thickness of the later work on the east front, however, suggests that the high ground 400 ft. distant was beginning to seem uncomfortably near.

The proposed function of the outer courtyard in the domestic economy of the castle is obscure. In 1579 the open space of the courtyard was a garden[31] and this may have been its proposed use from the beginning. The corbels around the inner wall faces show that lean-to buildings were intended round all three sides. Excavation has demonstrated only fragments of such lean-tos on the south and west sides, themselves of different construction (timber to south, stone to north) suggesting different dates of building. What function the lean-tos originally proposed and actually built were to fulfil is unknown.

The defensive provisions of the outer courtyard are ostentatious but intended to meet only a low-grade requirement. The lesser defensive role of the outer courtyard is perhaps illustrated by the 1579 order and its results, for the courtyard towers were included in the demolition list, but they were in the event left standing.

The design of the main works of Craignethan became obsolescent with the widespread introduction of Italianate bastioned fortification to Scotland during the war of 1547–50,[32] yet later siege preparations and the demolition order of 1579 indicate that it was still a place of strength to be taken seriously. The brute mass of its west rampart belongs to a short-lived fashion in artillery defence shown also in the near-contemporary reconstruction of Tantallon and Blackness as major strongholds. The articulation of the west rampart with an exotic caponier make Craignethan the last private Scottish castle of major defensive capability built *de novo*—a unique experiment in the history of Scottish fortification.

ACKNOWLEDGEMENTS

I would like to acknowledge the help in preparing this paper given by many colleagues. Since I first became involved with Craignethan, so many members of the staff of the Ancient Monuments Branch and the Principal Photographer of the Department of the Environment for Scotland have helped elucidate its problems and illustrate its character that I can give only a general expression of thanks for their diligence and patience. I must, however, mention my especial debt to Neil Livingston and Tom Borthwick for all the work that has gone into the drawings.

The plates are Crown copyright reproduced by permission of the Department of the Environment. Fig.1 is based upon the Ordnance Survey map with the sanction of the controller of H.M. Stationery Office, Crown copyright reserved.

REFERENCES

1. See J. B. Greenshields, *Annals of the Parish of Lesmahagow* (Edinburgh, 1864), pp. 50–67.

2. *The Register of the Great Seal of Scotland* (*R.M.S.*), H.M. General Register House, Edinburgh, 1882-1914, III, No. 1885.

3. *dicto castrum per dictum Jac edificat.*

4. Iain MacIvor, 'Blackness Castle and the Dunbar Castle blockhouse', in *Proceedings of Society of Antiquaries of Scotland.* (*P.S.A.S.*: forthcoming).

5. Before 1531 Sir James's arms were the three cinquefoils of Hamilton debruised by a bend dexter (a baton); a grant dated 13 January 1530/1 bears that James V dispensed with the baton, the new difference being 'a single tressure near the circumference of the shield powdered with silver lilies placed contrariwise such as the King bears double' (*R.M.S.*,III, No. 983). I am indebted to Mr. W. N. Robertson for discussion and advice on this matter.

6. In June/July 1541 a carter was paid for the carriage of two double falcons and five smaller brass pieces from Draffan and Hamilton. *Accounts of the Lord High Treasurer of Scotland (Accts. L.H.T.)*, H.M. General Register House (Edinburgh, 1877–1916), VII, p. 497. A double falcon has an approx. bore of 2½ in.

7. *Accts. L.H.T.*, III, p. 422.

8. J. B. Greenshields, *op. cit.*, p. 58.

9. *Calendar of the State Papers relating to Scotland and Mary Queen of Scots, 1547–1603 (Scottish Papers)*, H.M. General Register House (Edinburgh, 1898), II, No. 1017, p. 630; III, No. 538, p. 404.

10. *Ibid.*, III, No. 250, p. 182.

11. *A Diurnal of Occurrents in Scotland 1513–1575*, Bannatyne Club (1833), p. 181; *Scottish Papers*, III, No. 402, pp. 195–6.

12. *Scottish Papers*, III, No. 404, p. 301.

13. *Ibid.*, III, No. 595, p. 454.

14. *The Register of the Privy Council of Scotland (R.P.C.)*, H.M. General Register House (Edinburgh, 1887), III, p.189.

15. W. Hamilton, *Description of the Sheriffdom of Lanark* (Maitland Club, 1831), p. 68.

16. D. MacGibbon and T. Ross, *The Castellated and Domestic Architecture of Scotland (Cast and Dom. Arch.)*, Edinburgh (1887–92), I, pp. 255–65.

17. *Transactions of the Glasgow Archaeological Society, N.S. XV*, Pt. II, pp. 34–45.

18. Rev. John M. Wilson, *Imperial Gazetteer of Scotland* (Edinburgh, 1857), p. 309, mentions only the supporters in the 'much effaced escutcheon'; *Cast and Dom. Arch.*, I, p. 255, mentions the arms themselves as (unspecifically) the Hamilton arms.

19. The spouts are now all broken off, but fragments were recovered during clearance round the towerhouse. Four of the beasts survive, damaged and displaced from their original sites; they are analogous to those remaining *in situ* on the 1540–42 Palace at Stirling Castle. The distinctive parapet is not closely datable stylistically: staggered double corbelling is found throughout the sixteenth century.

20. The stairs giving access to the caponier (and the traverse: p. 252 below) seem to have been open in the mid-nineteenth century: 'a deep moat . . . defended by two parallel vaults, which are still accessible, though deeply buried in the rubbish wherewith the moat is filled' (Rev. John M. Wilson, *op. et loc. cit*).

21. The parapet in the section given on Fig. 4 is based on the approximately contemporary Tantallon Castle parapet.

22. *Cast and Dom. Arch.*, III, pp. 430–2.

23. The highest surviving part of the castle, the south-east tower, stands 37 ft. 9 in. from ground level to corbelling; the volume of masonry debris excavated from the ditch suggests this as a maximum likely height for the west rampart.

24. The variations in those Craignethan gunloops with intact external and internal openings are:

(i)   Externally averaging 2 ft. 9 in. by 13½ in with internally either a 7 in. diameter circular throat set in a cupped recess or a simple 7-in. square chamfered throat.

(ii) Externally averaging 1 ft. 7 in. by $7\frac{7}{8}$ in. with a square internal opening as above. The smaller size is found uniformly on the caponier, but otherwise the distribution of the two follows no discernible pattern.

(iii) Externally as (i) above, with an $8\frac{5}{8}$ in. square throat, raking downwards below the parapet of the south-east tower as described p. 260 below.

The external openings of the displaced west rampart loops measure 2 ft. 11 in. by 1 ft. 6 in. The diameter of their throats is unknown.

25. Royal Commission on Ancient and Historical Monuments of Scotland: *Inventory of the Ancient and Historical Monuments and Constructions in East Lothian* (1924), pp. 61–67.

26. *A Collection of Inventories and other Records 1488–1606*, ed. Thomas Thomson (Edinburgh, 1815), e.g., p. 166 ff., Edinburgh Castle, 1566; Scottish Record Office, E96/1, munition and artillery at Tantallon Castle 1557, printed in *Tantallon Castle* (guidebook), H.M.S.O., 1937. The bore of cannon, properly so called, varied according to type between 9 in. and 6 in.; the bore of the largest culverins was about 5½ in., and of a double falcon about 2½ in.

27. The word *culverin* is confusingly applied to a piece of great artillery, as above, and to a handgun cognate with a hackbut. The general subject of these lesser pieces will be explored by David H. Caldwell, 'Lesser artillery in the defence of 15th–16th century castles in Scotland', in a forthcoming volume of *P.S.A.S.*

28. Martini, *Trattato di architettura*, ed. C. Promis (Torino 1841); Dürer, *Etliche underricht, zu Befestigung der Stett*, etc. (Nurenberg, 1527).

29. e.g. at Stirling Castle, where caponiers were built in 1711–14 to designs by Captain Talbot Edwards: P.R.O., WO55/345. The papers refer to them as 'coffers'.

30. M. R. de Montalembert, *La fortification perpendiculaire* (Paris, 1776–84); A. D. Saunders, 'Hampshire coastal defence since the introduction of artillery', *The Archaeological Journal*, CXXIII, p. 149, foll.

31. *v. supra*, p. 244.

32. Dr. Marcus H. Merriman, *The struggle for the marriage of Mary Queen of Scots; English and French intervention in Scotland 1543–50*, 1975, London University Ph.D. thesis, Chap. 7 and foll.

The Building of Upnor Castle, 1559-1601

by

A. D. SAUNDERS

THE REIGN of Queen Elizabeth I was not remarkable for the construction of new coastal defences, and one of the few exceptions is Upnor Castle, begun in 1559. The beginnings of the castle are to be found in the account of the Office of Treasurer of Marine Causes.[1]*'Also the saide Accountant is allowed for money by hym paide within the tyme of the Accompte to Thomas Devenyshe of Frinnesbury in the County of Kent, for certeyne grounde of hym boughte to the Queen's Majestie's use conteyning sixe acres or there-aboute, whereupon hir highnesse hathe ranged to be buylded hir Castell òf Upnor, whiche grounde was praysed by six indifferent persons on the behalf of hir Majestie'* . . . and purchased for £25. The purpose behind the building of this castle and the choice of the site at Upper Upnor on the north bank of the river Medway, three miles downstream from Rochester Bridge, was made abundantly clear in the contract of Richard Watts, Paymaster, Purveyor and clerk of the fortifications and building. It was *'for the Savegarde of our Navye'*.[2]

The upper reaches of the Medway (Fig. 1), below Rochester Bridge, had become increasingly valuable for laying-up Henry VIII's navy when 'in ordinary', or out of commission. Henry VIII established two new dockyards on the Thames, at Deptford and Woolwich.[3] These were mainly shipbuilding and repair yards and gradually the Medway was brought into use as an anchorage. In 1547 payment was made for the hire of a storehouse at Gillingham, and from these insignificant origins sprang the future Chatham Yard.[4] Although there was no dry-dock at Chatham until the reign of James I, shipbuilding and repair came to be established.

There were sound reasons for bringing the Medway into use for the Navy. The river had the advantage of slow-running water with a good rise and fall of the tide. The channel was free of rocks and lay between low-lying banks with shelter from the south-west winds provided by the surrounding hills. As there were no strong currents, ships could be grounded for repairs. Defensively, the existence of ten miles of sand and mudbanks between the mouth of the estuary and Gillingham Reach made the unpiloted navigation of a sailing-ship in any but a fair wind a hazardous operation. Strategically, the

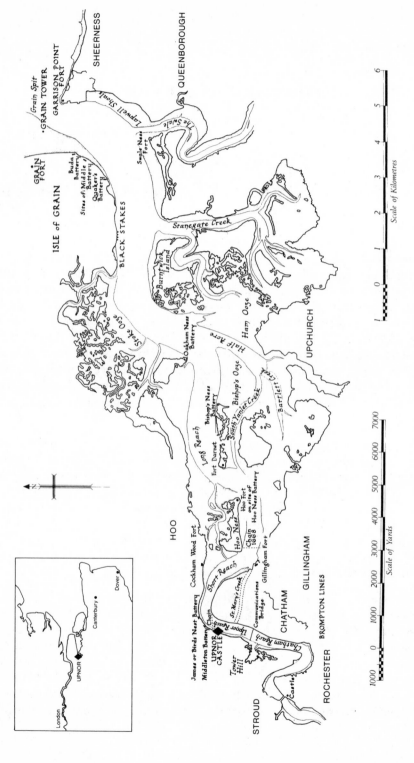

Fig. 1 The sixteenth to nineteenth century defences of the Medway Estuary.

Medway was well situated for the all-important centre of naval operations, offensive and defensive, in the eastern channel, the Thames Estuary, and the coasts of the Low Countries.

By 1564 twenty-three of the largest ships of the Queen's fleet, nearly the the whole of it, were moored below Rochester Bridge. It was understandable that some form of protection was required, as the ships, without sails and rigging, were vulnerable to a bold raid up-river. There had been no tradition of coastal defence here in medieval times. Rochester Castle guarded the bridge-crossing, while the fourteenth-century castles at Queenborough and Cooling protected Sheppey and the Isle of Grain respectively, rather than the approaches of the Medway estuary. Henry VIII's castle-building programme began before the full importance of the Medway for the Navy was appreciated. It was the Thames which was provided with five blockhouses, and on the Medway only one, at Sheerness.

For rather more than a century, until after the Dutch raid on the Medway of 1665, Upnor Castle was the chief defence of the anchorage and the naval establishments at Chatham. The defences were supplemented to two sconces or small batteries and a boom consisting of a chain which could be stretched across the river and fixed to timber structures on either bank. A boom was in existence in 1585 and claims for its effectiveness were made by William Bourne, while master-gunner at Upnor, in a memorandum on means of protecting the Navy.[6] A drawing of about this date shows the ships moored athwart the stream in three groups between Rochester Bridge and Upnor Castle, the largest vessel being near Upnor.[7] As the number of ships at anchor grew, and the size of warships increased, the position of the boom moved further and further downstream and away from the protection of the castle. In 1575 Swaleness Fort was erected opposite Queenborough, and the previous year St. Mary's Creek, Gillingham, was blocked with piles so that the Upnor anchorage could not be taken on the flank.[8] In the year of the Queen's death J. Linewraye, in a survey of ordnance, wrote of Upnor: *'The Castle of Upnor and two sconces there situate, for the guarding and defence of the same your most Royal Navy; wherein I have averre that no kinge in Europe is able to equall your excellant Majeste'*. It possessed a demi-cannon, seven culverins, five demi-culverins, a minion, a falcon, a saker, and four fowlers with two chambers apiece. Warham Sconce had two culverins and five demi-culverins; Bay Sconce had four demi-culverins. The garrison of Upnor consisted of a captain, a master-gunner, paid sixteen pence a day, seven gunners, at a shilling a day, and twenty soldiers at eightpence.[9]

The strategic position in 1665 had scarcely altered when the Dutch fleet under de Ruyter entered the Medway, burnt the new but unfinished fort at Sheerness and bore down on Chatham. Despite gunfire from Upnor and its associated batteries the Dutch were able to carry off the *Royal Charles* and burn a substantial number of ships. It was a notable disaster and was followed by a prodigious fortification programme for the protection of naval ports comparable with Henry VIII's castle building of 1539-40. Many of the new fortifications were designed by Charles II's chief engineer, Sir Bernard de Gomme. He was particularly concerned with the Medway. As well as defending the entrance to the estuary, forts were built on either side of the river; at Cockham Wood, about a mile below Upnor Castle and at Gillingham at the entrance to the former St. Mary's Creek. These defensive revisions completely changed the function of Upnor Castle. In 1668 it was ordered to be converted into 'a Place of Stores and Magazine'.[10]

The castle as it stands today (Fig. 2) carries the marks of its conversion, principally in its internal arrangements and its riverside elevation (Pl. XX a). But these changes are superficial and in its main elements the castle is still in its Elizabethan form. It consists of a large angle bastion projecting into the river and backed by a high wall along the river frontage carried up to a two-storey domestic block or barrack range on top of the river bank. North and south of the barracks are two square towers connected to it by a continuation of the wall revetting the river bank. The river elevation was heightened with false battlements after 1668. Much of the original fenestration was blocked and new windows in the form of roundels were substituted. The riverside elevation, 170 ft. long, is divided vertically by five thin projecting turrets. Apart from the central turret which contained the stairs connecting barracks and bastion, the other turrets were placed at either end of both the river wall and the barracks. To the rear of the barracks is a courtyard enclosed by a now filled ditch and a wall which linked the north and south towers with a square gatehouse sited centrally opposite the domestic range.

The castle has an appearance of structural unity which has led observers to suppose that it all belonged to the early years of Elizabeth.[11] Examination of the building in the light thrown by a considerable amount of surviving documentation shows that the castle has emerged from two distinct building periods separated by nearly fifty years.

Period I (1559-1567)

The building accounts run from 30 October 1559. Initially there are accounts covering the years 1559-1562[12] The documents relate to expenditure and control of the works. The organisation of the operation is set out in a patent of 26 March 1560.[13] This states that: '. . . *a certeyne Bulwark shoulde be made at Upnor . . . for the savegarde of our Navye . . . and by these lettres do gyve power and authoritie unto our well belovyd Subiecte, Richarde Wattes of Rochester, Paimaster, Purveyor and Clerke of the Workes of our saide fortifications, to prest, taike upp and provide for us, and in our name, in the counties of Essex, Kent and Surrey, as well within franchises and liberties as withoute, over and besides our speciall person alreadie appointed for*

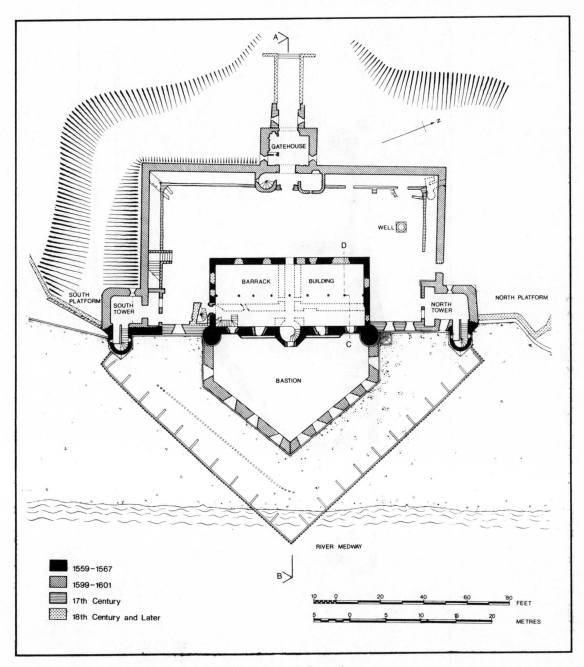

Fig. 2 Ground floor plan.

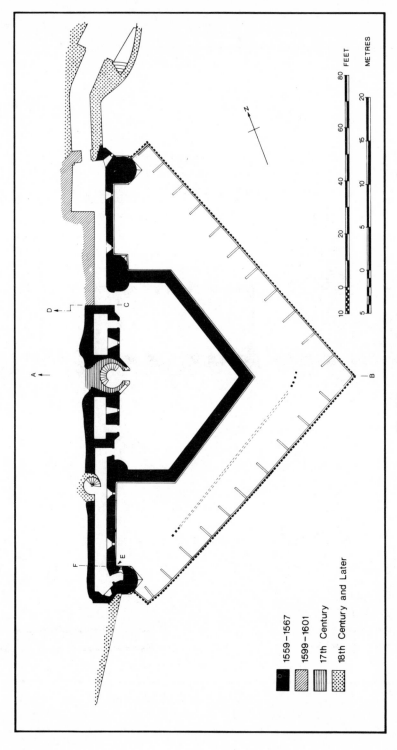

Fig. 3 Basement plan.

1559–1567
1599–1601
17th Century
18th Century and Later

*Surveyor and Chefe Carpenter and one Clerke, called Surveyor's Clerk, at wages
and prices reasonable. Further the number of Artificers and Laborers and
likewise further proportion of provisions as is contayned in a Schedule annexed
to this our Commission, with carriage by lande and water requisite for the
same. The wages of all which persons according to a rate signed with th'ande
of Sir Richard Lee, Kt. and also the charge of all manner of provisions and
carriages. Oure pleasure is shall be defrayed by th'ande of the saide Richarde
Wattes from suche of oure Treasure as he hath alredie and hereafter shall,
receive in prest for that purpose . . .'* Besides being fully accountable for the
expenditure on the works *'we gyve authoritie, power, and libertie unto the
saide Richarde Wattes that if he shall fynde or perfectlye understand anye
person or persons obstinate unreadye and refusing to serve us in our saide
fortifications whereby delaye or hindrance shall ensue to the same by further
obstinacye, unreadynes or refusall, that they he shall and maye, with th'
advise and assent of anye our Justices of Pax or Constables commytt them or
hym so offending to prison . . .'* *'And where we be gyvven to understand
that certain Tymbre remayneth privye at the place called Sherenesse of the
buildings of the late blockhouse that we have authorised . . . Richarde Wattes
to take the same . . .'* It was stipulated that besides paying wages Wattes was
expected to purchase *'. . . sondrye kindes of stone, Tymber, Leade, Iron,
coales, Bricks, Lyme, Sande, Shovells, spades, Mattoxe, Basketts, Sondrye
kindes of Artificers and Laborers—carriadge and diverse matters occupied
and Spente in the said fortifications. And the like employment of the same
Treasure in workes, carriage, workmen and Laborers woorkes in and uppon
the said fortifications, the lyme killes, the pulling downe and clearinge of
stone at diverse places, the squaringe and forminge of Tymbre and diverse
and sondry other workes belonging to the saide fortifications together with
sondrye other payments and allowances touching these same made, payde and
defrayde by the saide Accomptant within the tyme of this Accompte, as by
foure sondrye perticler bookes of his severall payments hereupon dulye prised,
noted, cast tiyed and examined at lardge maye appeare. Which bookes have
been subscribed with th'andes of Humfrey Locke, Surveyor of the said works
and . . . signed but with th'ande of the saide Richard Wattes, payeur there.
Of all which Receiptes and payements the saide Accomptant dothe yealde
Accompte from the last of October 1559 . . .'* until Michaelmas 1564.

The initial schedule of the labour force needs to be quoted in full: *'A note of
numbers of artificers and laborers and of provisions for the bulwark to be
made at Upnoure in Kent. Humfrye Lock to be Surveyor and Chief Carpenter,
2s. 6d. [a day]. The saide Surveyor's clerke 12d. Richard Watts to be Paymaster clerk of the Store and Purveyor 2s. Hardhewers and Layers, fowety,
carpenters eight, saweyers forre; Lymeburner, one, Laborers fortie. Pix axies
twentie, shovelles four dozen. Tymber one hundred tonne, sea cooles xxvii
chaulders. Yt is to be noted that at the fyst lettring out of this house thies
nombres of Artificers and provisions was thought suffycient, but afterwards*

the house was otherwise appoynted to be buylded by the suasion whereof the nombres as well of provisions as of Artificers were increased, as was thought were necessary by the Surveyor and Paymaster of the said workes'.

It is clear that Sir Richard Lee was the designer of the castle and Humfrey Locke was his nominee as surveyor. Apart from drawing the plan and recommending the composition of the labour force and the general lines the work should take, Lee has only a shadowy part in the building history. There seem to have been at least two designs before Lee's castle took shape.[14] Undoubtedly he was much occupied elsewhere with the construction of the defences of Berwick-upon-Tweed to pay Upnor much attention.[15] Humphrey Locke was the professional expert on site. Richard Watts, a prominent Rochester citizen, former mayor and benefactor to the town, had charge of the accounts and general administration.[16]

Building accounts in considerable detail cover the period between 21 November 1559 and 19 December 1562.[17] In all £3,621 13s. 1d. was spent. Building materials amounted to £685 2s. 8½d. Wages of craftsmen and labourers totalled £1,912 15s. 10½d., payments to the officials and supervising staff £329 13s. 10d., transport cost £620 7s. 11d., and hire of store buildings, wharfage, etc., £16 12s. 4d.

The quantities and cost of the various building materials were listed. Oak was the principal timber in use followed by elm, mainly cut for boards, and ash. Stone was divided into square ashlar, rough ashlar and large quantities of ragstone. There were besides purposely dressed stone purchased by the foot run: water-tabling, crests, vent stones, paving and channel stones. Iron was required for shoeing carts, binding betles, for hooks, staples, bars, lynch pins, doors, sledges, chalk axes, hammers, crow bars, etc. Nails of various kinds were needed and tools such as mattocks and pick axes. Coal came from Newcastle, and a little charcoal was needed. Lime was of course, much needed and most was burnt on site; 248,000 bricks were bought. Laths were bought ready cut in the beginning and were later made on site. Wheels were bought for tumbrells and handcarts. Wheelbarrows came by the pair. Shovels and spades came by the dozen and in addition there were *'11 great sholves to drawe mortar'*. Baskets of all sorts were much used, and sieves were needed to sift chalk. The coopers provided tubs, pails and a Malmeseye butt cut down for the lime kiln. Sackcloth was bought, cut and made into lime bags. There were numerous miscellaneous items like the base boxes for the scaffolding, loads of straw and rushes, books and money bags, lead for fixing the iron cramps in the stonework, wax, pitch, resin, scaffolding timber *'certeyne plancks for plateformes, the Quene's Armes, certain verses ingraven and other things'.*

Skilled craftsmen earned 10d., 11d. or 12d. a day. At the bottom rung labourers received 6d. The hourly rate would be 1d. an hour for craftsmen, and labourers ½d. There were masons, *'hardhewers and layers of stone',* bricklayers, carpenters and sawyers, wheelwrights, smiths, limeburners and choppers of chalk, thatchers mending the storehouses, paviours, painters, and the labourers who not only worked at the castle but also at *'Rochester Castle, Aylesford, Boxleye, and other places in pulling down and clearing of stone, transporting the same to and from the waterside, lading and unlading of shippes, Quayes, Cartes, with manye other woorks belonging to the said fortification'*.

It was necessary to hire store-houses, wharfs, and a storehouse at Rochester and two barns for the masons to work in, and a smith's forge with its equipment. Compensation was paid for *'foure acres of wheate sowen at Upnor by Elizabeth Devenis and there destroyed by reason of the fortifications and carriage to the same'*.

There is a further set of accounts *'for fynishing of the workes and fortifications of the said castell'* in the sum of £728 13s. 4d. which extends to Easter 1568.[18] The materials bought and the nature of the labour force follows the general pattern of the earlier accounts, but there are a number of items which show that the building was nearing completion. Stone for chimneys and windows appear and *'two loopes of stone'*. Larger quantities of coal were purchased and *'small coales to make blacke mortar for the chimneys'*. Paving tile and stone are there and 37,900 bricks were bought. Lathes, lime, hair and plaster were for the internal finishing, 169 ft. of glass and, most significant of all, £253 was spend on lead, more than the cost of all the other items put together. This clearly means the roofing of the main building. *'Smale pypes of leade for conveying the water from the well into the castell'*. *'Cockes of Brasse for the kytchen, the Butlerye, the upper Courte and the lower platforme'* demonstrate the business end of the water supply. The kitchen was paved with hard stone, also the north and south platforms and in *'the Courte aboute the Castell'*. Finally there was payment to the *'paynters for paynting the Lyon with the vane and handle of yeon, set upon the toppe of the steis with 16d. for one gallon of Oyle and with 9s. for haulfe a hundrethe of fyne golde'*.

Richard Watts was now completely in control. Perhaps Humfrey Locke had died in the interval, for he is only recorded as having made two journeys to this final stage of the works.

Period II (1599–1601)

In September 1599 following advice from the Lord Admiral that the defence of the navy at Chatham should be improved consideration was given to the condition of Upnor Castle.[19] Next month an estimate of £761 9s. 10d. for new work from Sir John Leveson was accepted and he was instructed to oversee the works with professional advice from an engineer, Arthur Gregory, who was to be continually in attendance.[20] Another engineer, an Italian called Baptist, made occasional visits and may have advised on design. A plan was sent indicating the position of a timber palisade which was urgently needed in front of the water bastion. The plan also showed an enclosing ditch with flankers to cover it and the water bastion, or great platform, was to be raised *'with a parapett of good height to be furnished with lopes for great ordnance'.* (Pl. XX b) Serviceable stone could be obtained by demolishing parts of Rochester Castle. One hundred and sixty trees were requisitioned in the hundred of Axstone and a furious complaint ensued because an enthusiastic official marked down 200 trees on land belonging to a Mr. Lovelace. *'I cannot well like of the indiscreet dealing herein'*, wrote the Lord Admiral's office to Sir John Leveson.

By 27 May 1600 the *'palisade is fynished, the ditches of 32 foote wide and 18 foote deepe surrounding the castle is cast, the great platforme over the castle is repaired and the defects of the walls thereof together with the covering of Ledd is fixed. The stone wall at each end of the drawbridge new made, the platforme over the gate covered with lead, the stone worke of the said gate with the square tower raised from the ground of new, the hewed stones for the great parapett of the platforme at the waterside are brought from Borton quarry and nowe in layeng and by the'end of time to be finished . . . There remayneth to be done towards the inclosinge the castle and perfecting the plott subscribed by yr Ldshps: The flancke at each end of the Ditch to be made of stone which being 7½ pearches of length and 20 foote deepe, at 24 the pearche will cost: £180. The Turfinge of the whole ditche on bothe sides will cost: £100. The tymber platformes on bothe sides the tower to be new made and covered with lead: £60; The repair of th'olde decayed walls and bringinge the water by lead to the Castle: £40. Total £380. The necessitie of this worke is suche as without which nether can the Palisade be assured, nor the Castle enclosed, nor the ditch stand . . .'.*[21]

The estimate was too low, however, and did not take into account the decayed state of the old walls of the castle. There followed on 15 September 1601 a further request for funds: *'. . . there was in February last £380 paid out of the receipt towards the perfecting of certeine workes to be don at Upnor Castle, according to an estimat made there of the said workes in which the decaies of the old walls of the said castell (for the repair of which there was only £70 allowed) have soe far surmounted the said estimat, as in a manner wee migght with as little charge have made new walls as repayred the old, and yeat besides the repayre of them, we have been forced to make a new wall of Ashlar stone 24 foote in height, 6 foote in thickness and 18 foote in lenght and have alsoe covered with new leade fower Turrettes of the said castell being so ruinous as the differing of those coverings thorow the fall of Rayne water would have been the decay of the said Castell in which extraordinary charge of wall and leading for which noe allowance was made, a great parte of the said £380 hath been exhausted and nothing ys remayning . . .'* A further hundred marks was requested.[22]

The accounts submitted by Sir John Leveson throw further light on the building history. They cover the period from 15 October 1599 to 3 September

1601.[23] Besides dealing with the major items already described they include *'makinge the drawbridge with yron chaines and an yngen to rayse it . . . new raysinge the stonework of the saide gate with the square tower from the grounde, makinge the flankes at eache end of the dyche of stone. Turfynge the whole dyche on bothe sydes, newe makinge and coveringe with leade the tymber plattforme on both sydes of the tower . . .'* Among the usual lists of materials, elm was needed *'to make curbes for the newe well . . .'*, *'corde for settinge out the trench line for the scaffolde'*, *'earthen potts to carry a synke'*, ironwork for the casemates. In addition to the wages paid to the various tradesmen and labourers directly employed there were several separate contracts. *'The same John Bannester as well for makinge the vaulte in the north flanke, being xxi foote in length xiii foote in bredth and xii foote in heighth, as also the Corten of the saide vaulte, newe vaulted being xxxvi foote longe, iiii foote wyde and viii foote iii inches highe and paved with free stone and the wall of the corten embattled and raysed three foote highe, findinge alle maner of stuff and workmanship lx.*[li] *And to him more for makinge the well three foote and a halfe ynch and vi fathome deepe, the digging drawinge and wallinge all at his own chardge . . . Nicholas White Joyner for repayringe the hall and dyninge chamber of the castle xxs . . . Thomas Andrewes for makinge a frame of tymber xxx foote longue and xiiii foote broad for the stable with a lodging over the same, a garrett and two payre of stayres'.*

Excavation (Fig. 2)

Limited excavation was undertaken within the Castle in 1964 in an endeavour to observe different constructional stages in the fabric. Two trenches were dug: (a) across the north end of the barracks C–D (Fig. 4) and (b) across the interior of the South Tower E–F (Fig. 5).

(a) *Barracks.* The ground floor of the barracks (Fig. 2) consists today of a single room without any sub-division. The only structural feature within the walls is a single row of nine wooden posts supporting the floor above, but originally the interior was divided into four compartments. (Pl. XXI). A longitudinal cross-wall parallel to the river frontage created a wide 'corridor' along that side. Behind this 'corridor' were two rooms 27 ft. by 17 ft. internally with a narrow lobby between them entered from a single doorway in the middle of the landward side.

A trench was cut 7 ft. from the north wall following the removal of part of the wood block floor (a survival from the Castle's days as a magazine) (Fig. 4). Below a concrete base were the hacked down remains of the longitudinal cross-wall and between it and the west wall of the main range was a compact layer of chalk and brick fragments which probably served as a base for the original floor. Between the chalk and brick and the natural sand into which the west wall foundations were dug, was a levelling up layer of mixed clay with a limited spread of chalk immediately on the natural. The demolished cross-wall was 7 ft. wide, its western side built upon the natural sand. The 'corridor' between it and the river wall had been vaulted over in brick. The bricks were a pinkish red and measured 2¼ in. by 4 in. by 8½ in. The north

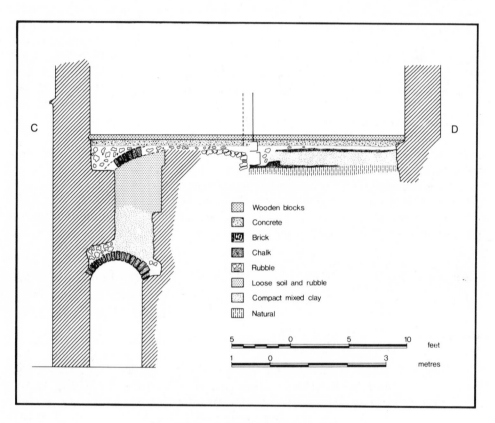

Fig. 4 Barrack building: Section C-D.

wall of the small room at bastion level (Fig. 3) immediately north of the stair turret had been brought up to ground-floor level and this in effect created a walled cell below the north-east corner of the barrack range. The brick vault, 9 in. thick, was sprung from a wide offset on the eastern wall but the junction with the cross-wall had been broken through. Below the vault was nearly 5 ft. of loose soil and rubble over compact mixed clay, which covered another brick vault, that over the north basement passage 9 ft. 6 in. below ground floor level. This vault was of secondary construction. The masonry on either side had been hacked back in order to obtain a seating for the vaulting and chalk and brick rubble were packed back into the space between the vault and the core of the walls. The soil and rubble filling above the lower vaulting contained a number of lead shot suitable for pistols or muskets and a sherd of sixteenth-century pottery.

The section C–D (Fig. 4) demonstrates the way the castle was built on and over the edge of the high river bank. The massively thick 'corridor' cross-wall

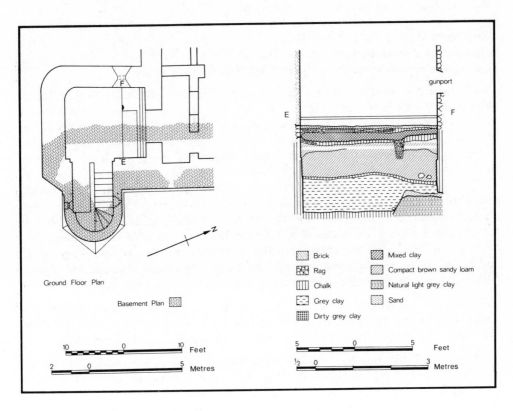

Fig. 5 South tower: plan and section E-F.

acted as a retaining wall against the bank. The river frontage was founded on the foreshore. Presumably for structural reasons the two walls were linked just below ground-floor level by the upper brick vault. The cell thus formed in the north-east corner of the building did not appear to have been put to any use and may always have been filled. It is tempting to see the breach of this vault and the insertion of the lower vaulting over the north basement passage as the work of John Banester in 1601 already quoted on p. 273. The basement passage as far as the gorge of the North Tower is 38 ft., its width is 4 ft., and its height is now 8 ft. 9 in. The dimensions tally so closely with the building accounts that there can be no doubt regarding the date and authorship of this feature of the Castle.

(b) *South Tower.* One of the chief problems at Upnor has been the difficulty in distinguishing the two sixteenth-century building periods within the North and South Towers. It is clear from the accounts that a ditch was dug round the landward sides in 1599 and 'flankers' built to command it. Both North and South Towers have the role of flankers and share common characteristics with the Gatehouse which is indisputedly the work of Period II: rounded angles and gunports of identical size and form. Yet the river front appears to belong to Period I at least at its lowest stage and a complication arises from the carved initials 'T.H.' with the figures '1596' cut into one of the voussoirs of the arched entrance into the ground floor flanker of the South Tower presumably antedating its construction by four years.

A trench E–F was cut across the interior of the South Tower in an attempt to elucidate this problem (Fig. 5). Below the present wooden floor was one of brick clearly related to the level of the entrance threshold. The bricks were bedded on chalk and clay and below were 6 in. to 9 in. of mixed clay covering a compact chalk and mortar foundation. Against the west wall of the tower there was a patch of brick flooring bedded on the chalk and mortar foundation. This earlier floor level had been cut by a stone-filled posthole. Underneath the floor were nearly 6 ft. of made-up material, compact brown sandy loam, separated from a heavy grey clay by a thin layer of chalk. The west wall of the tower was founded on natural loam streaked with reddish sand. Four feet to the east the loam fell away sharply. This was the top of the river bank, and between it and the west wall of the tower was a mass of chalk and mortar which covered the ceiling of the basement passage and its west wall.

There was a distinct constructional change in the tower walls. Below the lower floor level the walls were built with chalk blocks with flint galleting in the joints. Above the lower floor the walls were built in galleted ragstone.

Thus, the 1599 'flanker' was built on the same plan as an earlier structure. The posthole observed in the trench had a maximum diameter of 11 in. tapering to a depth of 1 ft. 8 in. It was 3 ft. 6 in. from the west wall and may represent the position of one of the scaffold poles for the Period II rebuilding. The floor level was raised when the walls of the tower were completely rebuilt or, on the east side, refaced internally.

This interpretation is reinforced by the appearance of the external south-west angle. At its lowest point the masonry is considerably offset from the face of the walling above. It has a very roughly finished squared angle unlike the well-built rounded corner above. This angle may be the foundation of the Period I structure which was exposed when the later ditch was dug. On the river frontage the masonry of the 1560s seems to survive up to the first string course. Above that, the facework appears to belong to the remodelling of the seventeenth century.

The differences in the masonry and the two floor levels bear out the building accounts which indicate that the North and South Towers are the 'flankers' being built in 1599–1601. But there is still the problem of the arch dated 1596 in the South Tower. The doorway clearly relates to the later floor level and is of one build with the rest of the masonry of Period II. It can only be assumed that the voussoir was a stone re-used from elsewhere, or that 'T.H.' antedated the stone for some unknowable reason.

Discussion (Figs. 2, 3 and 6)

The two sets of building accounts combined with limited excavation make it possible to isolate the 'bulwark' designed by Sir Richard Lee from the castle as it stands today.

Fundamentally Lee's castle consisted of a single large angle bastion, 70 ft. across, built on the foreshore and lapped by the river at full tide. (Pl. XX b: Fig. 3.) The faces of the bastion were 50 ft. long. The flanks, which were at right angles to the curtain wall, were 22 ft. long.

Across the gorge at bastion level were five doorways. The central door gave access to a newel stair to the barracks above and was contained in a slightly projecting half-octagonal turret. On either side of the turret were doorways leading into two small rooms, each lit by a small pointed arched window. These rooms may have served as expense magazines, but more probably as shelter for the gunners serving the cannon on the bastion. The outermost pair of doorways led into a narrow passage extending on either side of the bastion to the limits of the river front culminating in small D-shaped turrets on semi-hexagonal plinths. At the top of the river bank, about 35 ft. above river level was the rectangular two-storey barracks. (Pl. XX a: Fig. 6.) From the river the castle therefore had a lofty appearance standing 68 ft. above the water. Where the flanks of the bastion meet the limits of the barrack range are two round turrets, solid at basement and ground-floor level. These turrets, together with the central stair turret and those of the extreme ends of the castle must have presented an unusually old-fashioned and medieval aspect even in the 1560s.

The main range was both domestic and offensive in purpose. Originally the ground floor was arranged as two rooms divided by a central passage connecting the entrance with the stair on the river front. (Pl. XXI.) Along the river frontage was a wide 'passage' which was essentially a firing gallery and there is evidence today for single light windows or loops. This plan can be inferred from eighteenth-century plans and was confirmed by excavation. The upper floor was probably divided in a similar way. The north-south cross-wall was probably carried up to support the roof over the domestic rooms, and along the river front there could have been platforms for heavy guns at roof level for which there are strong suggestions in the 1601 accounts[24] (Fig. 6).

The greater part of the main range contained accommodation. A kitchen and a dining hall are mentioned in the accounts as being paved. Since the

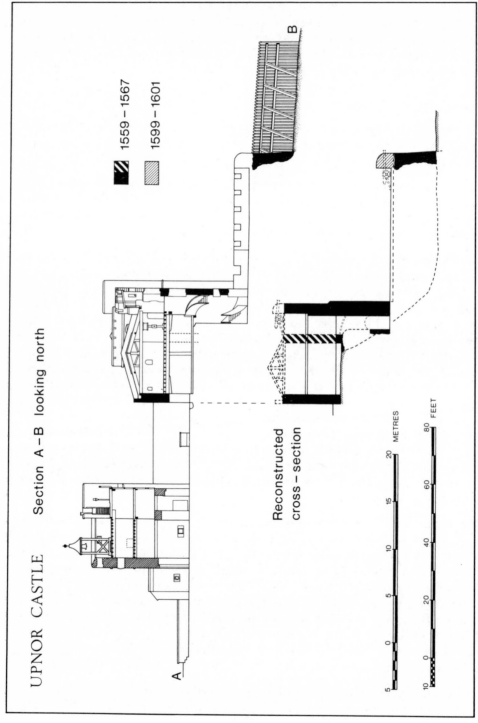

Fig. 6 Upnor Castle: Section A-B and conjectural reconstruction of the original design to show the disposition of the principal armament.

well lies to the north of the courtyard it is probable that the kitchen is the northerly of the two rooms. This bipartite arrangement whereby the main armament was mounted separately to the front with accommodation to the rear is paralleled in Henry VIII's blockhouses, and in later castles such as King Charles's Castle, Tresco, Isles of Scilly.[25] Of the 'house' mentioned in 1560 there are now no chimneys though a blocked fireplace can be seen on the first floor. Nor does any of the external ornament survive.

The form of the early North and South Towers is difficult to determine. Certainly the D-shaped turrets at either end of the castle belong to Period I and have archaic 'keyhole: and 'dumb-bell' pistol loops flanking the river front. At ground level the towers may have provided the basis for the north and south platforms which were paved in hard stone in 1567. The platforms were presumably square in plan since their lower walls appear to have determined the plan of the later 'flankers'.

Outside the main building was a paved court with a well and stables. There is a possible hint in the engineer Arthur Gregory's letter of 24 December 1599 of an enclosing wall, but the court may have been surrounded by nothing more than a timber palisade.[26]

In Phase II there was a significant change of emphasis in the defences. Previously the whole weight of the armament was directed towards the Medway, leaving the landward side extremely vulnerable. The castle was now to be provided with defences offering a fair degree of security. It is not certain whether the Period II courtyard repeated the plan of the earlier one. It is clear, however, that the ditch was an innovation as was the Gatehouse and the conversion of the north and south towers as 'flankers'. The gun ports in the ground floor of the three towers cover all three land sides, the ditch and the thin curtain wall behind it. The curtain wall is featureless except that under the later brick capping there are regular holes 4 in. by 4 in. set at an angle in the rubble core of the rounded parapet and suitable for storm poles.

The activity which was considered most urgent by contemporaries was the heightening of the bastion parapet and erecting a palisade in front of it. An horizontal straight joint indicates the degree of rebuilding. (Pl. XX b.) The new work stands 6½ ft. high and its curved top has the style of the first half of the sixteenth century. The palisade was presumably intended to keep ships far enough away from the bastion to prevent boarding parties leaping on to the platform and silencing the guns.

The three new towers of Period II all appear to have been open-backed or closed with timber. They were considerably altered in the seventeenth century and later, principally to improve them from the point of view of accommodation. Since these towers are referred to as platforms they were intended for high level guns and evidence of embrasures and gun ports remain.

The building work of 1599-1601 can be seen, therefore, not so much as a significant alteration of the castle, but rather complementing the original design; making good earlier deficiences. The internal arrangements are largely lost owing to the changes which affected the building later in the seventeenth century following its conversion into a magazine.

As a piece of fortification Upnor Castle has no parallels, and presents an unusual design for its date. At a time when low-profiled bastioned forts of the Italian school were the general rule, Upnor is something of a hybrid. There seems to be more of the Middle Ages than the Renaissance in the mind of its designer. Viewed in plan there is a resemblance to a number of Henry VIII's later castles. Sandsfoot, near Weymouth, Browneas, and Portland, to some extent, combine a distinct battery and a defensible barrack. This was repeated in the 1550s on Tresco, Isles of Scilly, with King Charles's Castle. The difference at Upnor is that instead of a rounded, rectangular or hexagonal battery there is an up-to-date angle bastion.

Sir Richard Lee had a brief to defend the fleet anchorage and was forced to take into account the difficulties of the site. To have constructed a conventional 'Italian' bastioned fort with correct geometrical proportions as he was doing at Berwick would not have answered the problem. The river bank is about 35 ft. above the level of the river, and in order to stop warships it was better to have a sizeable proportion of the heavy guns at the same level as the target. By placing a battery a few feet above water level and siting the barracks on top of the river bank the castle was therefore given a disproportionately great height.

Height, however, can be an advantage when dealing with shipping. It can enable plunging fire to be brought on to the decks, and men in the rigging and fighting tops can more readily be dealt with. In this respect the North and South Towers take on the aspect of fore and stern castles of a warship. The towers could provide good observation and no doubt in the sixteenth and seventeenth centuries could command long views down the Medway. This factor was appreciated by Sir Bernard de Gomme more than a century later when he built tall towers behind the main batteries at Cockham Wood and Gillingham Forts, a mile or so further downstream[27]

In using an angle bastion Lee was in the mainstream of military engineering in 1559, but perhaps, with hindsight, he was using the bastion without really understanding its proper purpose. It was a means of obtaining complete flanking cover, and bastions were normally used in conjunction with others in order to obtain effective cross-fire over every angle of the *enceinte*. At Upnor, Lee was using the bastion in an offensive roll against warships advancing up-river. By doing this he revealed the limitations of its plan when used in isolation. Only one face of the bastion (and when its parapet was heightened in 1600 it was provided with only five embrasures) could be directed against oncoming shipping. The other face of the bastion (with three embrasures) could only take the enemy in reverse. The flanks at right angles to the curtain were limited to defending the front of the castle against assault from the water. The flanks, if intended to defend the castle from a land sortie, are useless. The castle is, in a sense, back to front. A century later when de Gomme was faced with an identical problem at Cockham Wood and Gillingham he arranged powerful batteries in two tiers parallel with the river. Upnor would have had a more effective plan if the bastion had been made the dominant feature of the landward defences with a straight battery along the water's edge.

In order that his bastion should work at all Lee had to make its salient angle an obtuse 105 deg. This argues well for his adaptability, but in contemporary terms the plan was eccentric. Salient angles in the mid-sixteenth century were all acute, usually between 64 deg. and 74 deg.[28]

While it is clear that Humphrey Locke and Richard Watts attended to the actual building and might have adapted the plan in the course of construction, Lee was responsible for the initial plan and undoubtedly a feature so fundamental to the design must have been his idea.

There are a number of problems affecting forts which are built near the sea or to navigable rivers. A battery close to the water's edge with a parapet of insufficient height made it possible for the defenders to be at risk from the round top or the ship's rigging. Forts in this position are also sometimes left open at the rear and therefore liable to attack and capture by a landing party. Upnor suffered from both these defects and it was the attention paid to the castle in 1599–1601 which set about remedying them.

There was also the weakness of the exposed position of the main stair which occupied the central turret on its river elevation. This could easily have been wrecked under bombardment, thereby severing communications between the platforms on the barrack building, and the bastion. This was a mistake never made in Henry VIII's castles where stairs were always well protected, and in the larger castles communications were duplicated.

Such cricitisms of the design of a fort, which unlike most of its English fellows actually saw action and was thought to have acquitted itself adequately, may appear carping. However, it is as well to consider in some detail this particular design of Sir Richard Lee, who in his major work at Berwick is held to have contributed to the advance of military engineering in this country.[29]

REFERENCES

1. P.R.O. E 351/2204 m. 3 dorse. The accompte of Benjamin Gouson Esquire. Treasurer of Maryne Causes and affairs. 'Certeyne grounde whereupon the Castell of Upnor is buylded.'

2. P.R.O. E 351/3345. Authority for construction of the Castle, 26 March 1560, and contract of Richard Watts. See also B.M. Add. MS. 5752 ff. 371-2; Original documents relating to Naval and Military Affairs of England in sixteenth and seventeenth centuries. Presented by Sir William Musgrave. *Ibid.*, f. 373 Estimate of labour necessary for construction of the Castle, signed by Richard Lee.

3. *V.C.H., Kent*, II, p. 339.; Michael Lewis, *The History of the British Navy*, p. 42.

4. *V.C.H., Kent*, II, p. 340.

5. *Ibid.*, p. 341.

6. William Bourne, 'A Regiment for the Sea', and other writings on Navigation, *Hakluyt Society* Series II, Vol. cxxxi. A chain across the river would be a greater safeguard and he quotes from his *Inventions and Devices* (1578), stratagems that could be employed once the enemy was checked by the chain.

7. B. M. Cott, MS., Aug. Ii, 52.

8. *V.C.H., Kent*, II, p. 343. Acts P.C. 20 July and 19 August 1574; B.M. Lansdown MS., xviii, 77, P.R.O. Decl. Accts. 2210 and 2211.

9. J. Linewraye, *Survey of Ordnance*, 1603, B.M. Royal MS., 17A, xxxi.

10. P.R.O. SP 44/30, 34. 'And we having found fitt for the Good of Our Service to convert our saide Castle to the use of the office of our Ordnance as a place of stores and magazine.' P.R.O. WO 55/464, 31 July, 12 Charles II.

11. B. H. St. J. O'Neil and S. Evans, 'Upnor Castle, Kent', *Archaeologia Cantiana* (1952), LXV, I.; B. H. St. J. O'Neil and S. Evans, *Upnor, some notes on the castle and other things.*

12. P.R.O. E 351/3543. Accounts of Richard Watts, 21 November 1559–December 1562.; P.R.O. SP 12/24, 12. 'A new blockhouse at Upnor not yet perfected', 21 December 1561–20 August 1562; P.R.O. SP 12/26, 18. Charges of 'a newe blockhouse at Upnore', 21 December 1561–19 December 1562.

13. P.R.O. E 351/2204 and B.M. Add.MS.5752, ff. 370–88.

14. B.M. Add. MS. 5752. *'It is to be noted that at the fyrst lettring out of this house thies nombres of Artificers and provisions was thought suffycient, but afterwards the house was otherwise appoynted to be buylded by the suasion whereof the nombres as well as provisions as of Artificers were increased . . .'.*

15. Iain MacIvor, 'The Elizabethan Fortifications of Berwick-upon-Tweed', *Ant. J.* (1965), XLV, pt. 1, p. 64.

16. Richard Watts has a memorial in Rochester Cathedral and Watt's Charity 'for six poor travellers, not being rogues or proctors', still stands in the High Street.

17. P.R.O. 351/3543.

18. P.R.O. A.O.1 2513/535.

19. B.M. Add. MS. 5752, f. 374. *'After our verie hartie commendacion, Whereas her Majestie, by the advice of me, the Lord Admirall, and the rest of her Counsaile, hathe resolved that for the better defence and safe garde of her Navie at Chatham, some fortification shal be made at the Castle of Upnor . . .'.*

20. *Ibid.*, f. 373–79.

21. *Ibid.*, f. 385.

22. *Ibid.*, f. 387.

23. P.R.O. A.O.1 2513/536.

24. *Ibid.*, '... *repayringe the greate plattforme over the Castle and the wall thereof with the renewinge of leade* ...'.

25. T. J. Miles and A. D. Saunders, 'King Charles's Castle, Tresco, Scilly', *Post Med. Arch.* IV (1970), p. 1.

26. B.M. Add. MS. 5752, f. 380. '... *there issueth out springs both under the foundation of the Castle wall (which I take was the cause that the Wall did yeld and overhang) and out of the outsides of the ditches, which will turne all to quicke sande, the whole lower grounde being all quick. I dare pioneere no further till the Lds be advertised thereof* ...'. The Castle wall may be an enclosing wall round the court or the North and South Towers where exposed by the cutting of the ditch.

27. B.M. Kings MS. 43 f. 36-38 Survey of the Harbours and Dockyards, 1698.

28. Yarmouth Castle, Isle of Wight, one of the earliest surviving angle bastions in the country (*c.* 1547) has a salient of 72 deg. The abortive 'Italian' fort of Harry's Walls, St. Marys, Scilly, of 1551 is of 64 deg. Ridgway's citadel at Berwick-upon-Tweed is 62 deg., and Lee's own Brass Mount at Berwick is 74 deg.

29. MacIvor, 1965. See note 15.

Heath Old Hall, Yorkshire

by

O. J. WEAVER

ONE-AND-A-HALF MILES to the south-east of Wakefield, on a ridge of high land above the river Calder, is the village of Heath, an unusual and exciting

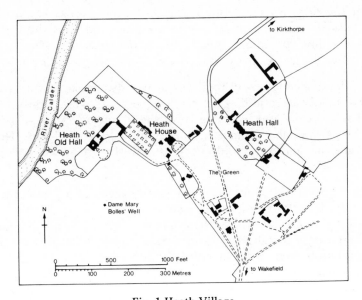

Fig. 1 Heath Village

cluster of buildings once described very aptly as a 'village of mansions'.[1] It is a scattered village (Fig. 1) with a large green, groups of cottages, and not one ut three large houses of outstanding quality.

Pride of place in the village must go to Heath Hall, a building of the mid-eighteenth century by John Carr, an imposing house with a central range flanked by pavilions and wings and a general air of magnificence that would do justice to a major estate. Across the green and less grandiose but with a grave and sober charm is Heath House, remodelled by James Paine a few years earlier than the Hall.[2] Finally, completing the trio, there was the Old Hall, not Georgian in date but Elizabethan.

This, the earliest member of this extraordinary group, is now a ruin, three-quarters demolished in 1961 after standing empty for several years. It was a building of considerable interest and importance, unusual in its design and remarkably complete, and above all it was a house of tremendous presence.[3]

History

It was built by John Kay and begun before 1584. This date, according to Ambler, was on the 'Jezebel' overmantel in the great chamber which had every appearance of being an original feature and, allowing a few years for the course of building, points to the house being started shortly after 1580.[4]

There was no evidence in the fabric of an earlier building on the site and no doubt John Kay chose the site for the same reason that Wollaton was built on top if its hill and Hardwick raised on its commanding height—for magnificence. From the ridge at Heath one looks across the river Calder towards the town of Wakefield and one can picture in pre-industrial days the broad sweep of a pleasant valley spread out below the house and, in reverse, the house rising in towered silhouette above the wooded slopes of the valley side.[5]

John Kay was descended from the Kays of Woodsome, near Huddersfield, an unspectacular family of middling gentry whose roots were firmly planted in the soil of south Yorkshire. He came from the younger branch of the family, of Dalton, his father, also John Kay, marrying a local girl, Jane Dodsworth of Shelley, and having two children, John (of Heath) and a younger sister Elizabeth.[6]

Of the younger John's career little is known except that he became deputy steward to the honour of Pontefract and so deputy to Sir Henry Savile, to whom he was bound by more than administrative duties. According to Whitaker, Sir Henry's daughter, Dorothy Savile, bore John Kay seven illegitimate children before eventually marrying him. Sir Henry had himself fathered a son by his wife's maid-servant, so Dorothy's conduct, Whitaker suggests with clerical displeasure, was scarcely surprising in view of 'the natural influence of such an example.'[7]

It is a lively story, repeated several times after Whitaker, but there are some doubts as to its accuracy. The pedigree of Kay taken in 1585 gives John Kay of Dalton and of 'ye Heath' married to Jane Storrs of Storrs Hall and having by her six children, of whom Robert, the second son, was heir.[8] This in itself does not contradict Whitaker, but besides suggesting that John Kay was remarkably prolific it does limit the period in which he could have married Dorothy Savile to the last nine years of his life and there is no clear evidence that in this period John Kay did indeed marry for a second time.[9]

Kay died in 1594 having enjoyed his new house for ten years. He was succeeded by his son Robert, who sold Heath before 1604 to Lady Mary Bolles of Ledston, wh lived at Heath and kept the property until her death in 1662. Thereafter it passed through a succession of owners, descendants of Mary Bolles, until it was purchased in 1809 by John Smyth, member of Parliament for Pontefract and owner of the Carr mansion across the green. Before Smyth acquired the house it had been let to a series of tenants one of whom, in the late 1770s, was John Wombwell, a retired nabob, and during Smyth's owner-ship, and subsequently through the nineteenth century, it was also in the hands of tenants. From 1811 to 1821 it was occupied by French Benedictine nuns and later it was used as a girls' school.[10] In 1865 it was leased to Edward Green who restored parts so that at the turn of the century it could appear as a handsome, well-groomed building in the pages of *Country Life* in July 1907.[11] It was lived in until the 1939/45 war, when it was put to military use, but not subsequently, and after the theft of lead from the roofs its condition rapidly deteriorated, leading to its demolition in 1961.

Description

A general impression of the exterior was that of a tall, compact, towered building, dark and forbidding and distinctly medieval in character (Pl. XXII a). A little of this sprang from its sombre colouring, but for the most part the impression was quite deliberately contrived. John Kay built for himself not a conventional West Riding manor house, but a square, keep-like structure, turretted and embattled, in effect a mock castle.

It was three storeys high with kitchen and offices in the basement, hall and chambers on the floor above (which I shall describe as the principal

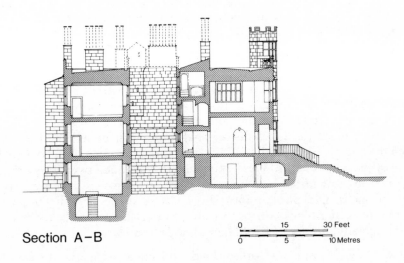

Section A–B

0   15   30 Feet

0   5   10 Metres

Fig. 2 Sections across Heath Old Hall.

floor) and, on the topmost floor, great chamber and long gallery. The basement was partly above ground at the front of the house and wholly so at the back where the ground at first gradually and then more steeply falls away to the river below (Fig. 2).

It was nearly square in plan, measuring 74 ft. across and 68 ft. in depth, excluding bay windows, and though apparently a solid mass when viewed externally it had a small internal court originally open to the sky. This measured 16 ft. by 17 ft. at its maximum extent but, as may be seen from the plans, at its upper levels it was an irregular shape with one angle cut off and with small projections corbelled out from its walls. Originally it was open from basement level upwards, but subsequently, probably at the time of extensive alterations by John Smyth, *c.* 1809–11, a floor was inserted at principal floor level, resting on a vault, which entirely altered the proportions and effect of this central area.[12]

The entrance front faced south-east and had a wide central porch and, on either side of this, not quite at the extremities of the façade, bay windows in the form of half octagons which were taken up above roof level to form battlemented turrets. In these were small chambers, little more than 8 ft. across, accessible only from the roof. It was a symmetrical façade save at principal floor level where for internal convenience an extra window was provided to the right of the entrance; this apart, bay answered bay and one part balanced another to an extent not attempted on the other façades. Two elevations, north-west and north-east, were very plainly treated; the fourth, facing south-west, had, like the entrance front, projecting bay windows, but here the bays were shallow and three-sided and both were at the western end of the façade, one of them rising through all three storeys and the other corbelled out above the principal floor to serve the upper floor only. (Pl. XXII b.) At this upper level was the great chamber. Both bays continued above the parapet and were embattled.[13]

The general appearance was severe. There was little ornament—no niches, medallions, or cartouches. No pilastered windows or columned entrance. No decoration other than an unusually elaborate balustrade and two carved stone plaques on the porch over the doorway, the lower one bearing the arms of Kay quartering Dodsworth and the initials J.K., and the higher one the royal arms. The balustrade had baluster shafts between panelled dies which rested on large bulging bases and, on top of the rail, a series of fan-shaped lunettes between panelled blocks. This arrangement continued over the porch, but here on the front rail instead of lunettes were two devices crudely carved in the form of shells. Old photographs show also a single heraldic beast sitting on one of the corner blocks of the entrance porch and probably there were several more originally, but by 1961 all had disappeared.[15]

Essentially it was a Gothic face enlivened with the merest touch of Renaissance detail. The fenestration was of traditional mullioned and transomed windows, plain chamfered and with hood moulds. String courses were used on the entrance front only, at cill level, and were stopped in an awkward fashion short of the corners.

As to the later changes, these were in the main the substitution of sash windows in place of the original mullions and transoms, but in addition the main entrance was altered and given an eighteenth-century surround, and a subsidiary entrance was formed on the garden front (south-west) with an external staircase. In modern times the corbelled bay window of the great chamber was removed and the opening built up flush with the wall. Generally, however, the exterior suffered remarkably few changes in the course of its four centuries.

Originally some of the window glass was decorated with the arms of 'the chief nobility of the reign of Elizabeth', but much of this had disappeared by 1788 and none survived to 1961.[16]

Flanking the house on its north-east side was a small courtyard entered through a carriageway in its north-east wall. It was simply a walled enclosure with two small buildings in its south-east corner, but one of these was raised up as a tower clearly with the intention of emphasising the medieval character of the house. Near the entrance to this courtyard was a carved shield bearing the arms of Witham of Ledston but this was a later embellishment and the courtyard itself was contemporary with the house.

On the same side as this courtyard were other detached buildings on the three sides of a larger enclosure. One, formerly a barn, had been converted to serve as a chapel, probably in the early nineteenth century by the Benedictine nuns, but all were later than the house.[17]

A pair of handsome eighteenth-century gate piers with pineapple finials marked the entrance to the grounds. Finally, some distance away from the house to the south-west there still survives a tall square brick tower which dates from the time of Lady Bolles and which, built over a spring, supplied water to a cistern in the courtyard next to the house.[18]

Interior

The changes to the interior were more extensive. Several rooms had been given Georgian dress and various alterations made to the plan. In particular the long gallery had been divided into three rooms (and was still so divided in 1961), its fireplace covered over, and the windows in its end walls blocked up.[19] However, prior to demolition, the original fireplace was found and also fragments of the original ceiling. Other original fireplaces were found elsewhere in the house during pre-demolition investigation, and the positions of these are given on the accompanying plans which show the house as originally planned, omitting later alterations.

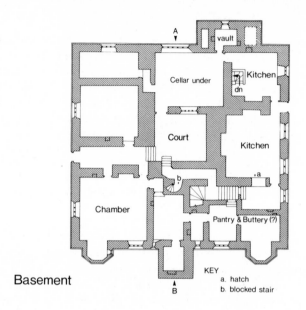

Basement

KEY
a. hatch
b. blocked stair

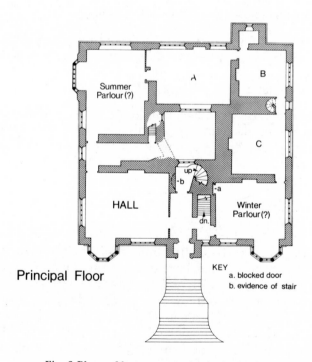

Principal Floor

KEY
a. blocked door
b. evidence of stair

Fig. 3 Plans of basement and principal floor.

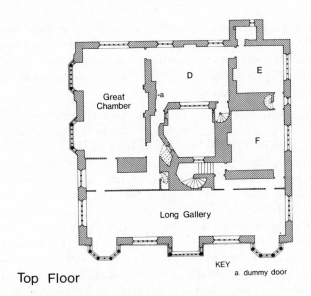

Top Floor

KEY

a. dummy door

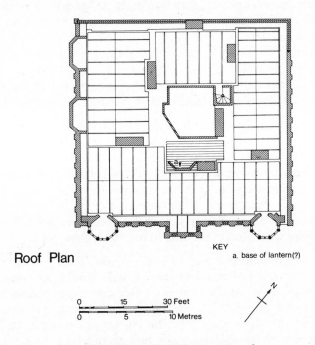

Roof Plan

KEY

a. base of lantern(?)

0   15   30 Feet

0   5   10 Metres

Fig. 4 Plans of top floor and roof.

As regards plan, Heath was a tightly organised, sophisticated building which had such orthodox elements as hall, great chamber and long gallery, but these and its other parts were combined in an unusually compact and ingenious form that extended vertically as well as horizontally so that for a thorough understanding a study of the plans of all three floors is essential. There is no known inventory of rooms, but some may be identified with certainty and others more tentatively from their relationship and by comparison with other buildings of the period.

Taking first *the principal floor* (Fig. 3), the entrance porch led to a lobby or vestigial 'screens passage' with the hall on the left-hand side and, on the right, beyond a flight of stairs to the offices in the basement, a chamber probably to be identified as the winter parlour. At the end of the 'screens passage', which was separated from the hall by a timber partition, was the principal staircase, a moderately large newel stair of timber which went to the upper floor only and primarily to the long gallery. However, diverging from the main staircase, about halfway up, was a side stair, not original in its final form but deliberately allowed for in the original plan and going in the direction of the great chamber. A later, corkscrew staircase inserted at the back of both the main staircase and its subsidiary branch confused the evidence, but of this intended dual access there can be no doubt.

It was not by any standard an impressive staircase being cramped and badly lit. Nor was it the first staircase attempted by the builders. Close to it there was evidence in the fabric of a newel stair in a different position which coincided with an unfinished staircase at basement level. Also there was an original doorway in the winter parlour that could not function with the staircase as built. The evidence, taken together, suggests a change of mind during the course of building, not a change of major significance but rather an uncertainty of touch on the part of the owner, or of his masons, when working out the details of an unfamiliar and intricate arrangement.

That the staircase as finally built was that of Kay's house is not in doubt. It was an integral part of the building and for comparison it closely resembled in form and in position the staircase at Barlborough Hall, Derbyshire, a building similar in plan and contemporary in date.[20] Whether it was originally top-lit like the one at Barlborough is uncertain; at Heath there survived at roof level part of the base of what might have been an octagonal lantern, but between this and the staircase, immediately under the roof, was a small chamber complete with fireplace which was certainly an early arrangement.

The hall was single-storeyed and of modest size. It had been transformed in the eighteenth century and none of its original character remained, but from the first it was evidently not the dominant element in the house, being equalled in size by the room adjacent to it ('summer parlour') and exceeded by the great chamber on the floor above. In the eighteenth century its windows had been given timber sashes and its walls and ceiling decorated with elaborate plasterwork of rococo-gothick style (Pl. XXVI). The walls were divided into panels containing ogee arches with trefoil and quatrefoil decoration and thick clusters of pendant flowers and foliage. The doors and the corners of the bay window were dressed with triple-shafted columns with small foliated capitals and the ceiling of the room had a large circular central motif within a rectangular panel enriched with ogee curves, scrollwork and foliage decoration similar to that of the walls. There was also a shallow coved cornice made up of a series of small trefoil arches. It was altogether a remarkable display, complete even to its timber chimneypiece carved with ogee arch and trefoil. Regrettably there is no known date for the work. For much of the eighteenth century the house was let to tenants and though at least one of them, John Wombwell, would have had the resources to undertake extensive re-decoration of this sort, stylistically the plasterwork looks more the work of the mid-century than of the late 1770s when he was in occupation.[21] No other room is so treated, but there is one isolated feature in the same style on the upper floor (p. 295).

All that survived of the hall's original fittings was part of its stone fireplace, a Tudor arch in a square, moulded surround, and part of the doorway from the 'screens passage'.[22]

Moving in a clockwise direction from the hall there was next a lobby which had in its north wall a doorway to a narrow flight of stone steps, later blocked. From the little that could be seen they appeared to ascend to the upper floor but despite careful examination there was no evidence of an exit on the floor above.[23] A later alteration gave the lobby an external staircase, converting the window into a doorway, but this was certainly not part of the original scheme.

Beyond the lobby was a chamber probably to be identified as the summer parlour. At the time of demolition its general dress was eighteenth century and unremarkable save for its timber chimneypiece which had acanthus capitals above tapering pilasters and fruit and flower carving in high relief, but behind this was the original stone fireplace in the form of a Tudor arch within a square surround similar to that in the hall. The walls and ceiling were plain but under layers of modern paper were fragments of a 'Chinese' wallpaper of eighteenth-century date.

There followed four chambers ('A', 'B', 'C', and 'winter parlour' on plan) in each of which some original plasterwork survived. In the first, that in the centre of the back range ('A'), only one small fragment of the original ceiling remained in one corner, but in the next chamber ('B') the entire ceiling was *in situ* and also its decorated freize. The ceiling had thin moulded ribs forming a geometric pattern of small circles, squares and hexagons with curved sides and with rosettes and short fat pendants in some of its panels (Pl. XXV a). The frieze had a candelabra motif with scrolled foliage, but its finer detail was obliterated by layers of whitewash, a good preservative but an impediment to appreciation. There was some small-scale panelling in this room but of doubtful provenance.

The ceiling of the next chamber ('C') was also complete. The pattern was again geometric and made up of thin moulded ribs with rosettes as ornament, but here the ribs formed large star-shaped patterns and circles within crosses. At intersections of the ribs were small flat bosses which were quite plain and appeared to be unaltered. There had been a decorated frieze of the same design as in chamber 'B' but only a small part survived.

Finally, in the chamber in the south-east corner, the winter parlour, there was yet a third ceiling design with the ribs forming star-shaped patterns within larger circles and half-circles; at intersections of the ribs were small pendant bosses and sprays of foliage and fleurs-de-lys. The frieze in this room had small human masks set in shell frames and embedded in scrollwork. The panelling was probably original but re-fixed. There was an original stone doorway, square-headed and with plain chamfers, in the north-east corner, and behind the eighteenth-century chimneypiece there was still the original stone fireplace similar in form to those in the hall and summer parlour.[24] In the north-west corner of this room was the blocked doorway described above (p. 292).

In the centre of the house was a small court enclosed by the high walls of the surrounding ranges. Originally open to the sky, it was later given a glazed roof and with its new raised floor treated as a communicating hall with openings forced through its lower walls to adjacent rooms. However, in the original arrangement the only access to this court was from the basement and in function it seems to have been little more than a light-well, serving the staircase and a few chambers. In the course of the later alterations the original parapets were removed, but a suggested reconstruction has been drawn on the section (Fig. 2).

Much of *the top floor* (Fig. 4) of the house was given up to two rooms, the long gallery and the great chamber. Both were spacious and impressive chambers, the long gallery measuring 67 ft. in length and 15 ft. wide. It had large mullioned and transomed windows at each end and in its long wall a total of six windows including a wide central bay (above the porch) and two smaller bays in the flanking turrets. There was a decorated ceiling of which a small part survived, geometric in pattern with cartouches and rosettes within the panels, and there was also a decorated frieze with cartouches and small masks, birds and foliage (Pl. XXV b). A part of the original stone fireplace was *in situ* though covered up and bisected by a later partition. It had the same simple four-centred arch of others in the house, but this in itself cannot have been the whole story. One imagines that originally it had also a timber overmantel carved and ornamented, not of the same splendour as the chimney-piece in the great chamber but of sufficient scale and richness to match the proportions of the room.

Access to the long gallery from the main staircase was through a narrow lobby formed by a timber partition, and there was a similar partition at the opposite end forming a rather wider lobby between the long gallery and great chamber. Generally access was from room to room along the outer walls of the house in the traditional way, but these two lobbies and a short inner corridor on this floor at the back of the great chamber show that some attempt was made in the original plan to avoid the inconvenience of the traditional room-to-room access. Heath did not have the ingenious solution of Barlborough where corridors were devised on all four sides of its central courtyard, giving separate and private access to each chamber, but the plan shows that the creator of Heath was seeking an answer along the same lines.[25]

In the lobby between long gallery and great chamber was an item similar in style to the eighteenth-century decoration in the hall—a pair of openings with surrounds enriched with rosettes and pseudo 'ball-flower' ornament and with glazed lights above filled with gothick tracery.

The other principal room on the top floor was the great chamber, measuring 36 ft. by 20 ft. with two large bay windows in its long wall giving this room at the top of the house a commanding view across the valley. It had a ribbed ceiling of geometric pattern similar to those elsewhere in the house, but here the ornament was heraldic. In small circles were griffins holding a key, which was the crest of John Kay, and in the rectangular panels the arms of Kay quartering Dodsworth supported by *putti* (Pl. XXVc). The frieze had serpents and foliage sinuously intertwined, and small human figures.

The dominant feature in the great chamber, however, was its large two-tiered chimney-piece of stone which rose to the underside of the cornice and occupied most of the inner wall of the room (Pl. XXIV). It had two orders of fluted columns, Ionic below and Corinthian above, with a moulded straight-headed fireplace in its lower half and above this a large stone panel carved in high relief. Both orders had narrow friezes enriched with delicately carved foliage and below the carved panel was a band of ornament composed of grotesque heads and swags of fruit. The panel itself was carved with a scene drawn from the Old Testament. It portrayed the death of Jezebel with the victorious army of Jehu on the left-hand side of the panel and on the right the figure of Jezebel falling to her death from an upper window of the palace, a building modelled in sixteenth-century form complete with gun-loops in its lower storey.[26]

The chimney-piece as a whole was a most accomplished piece of carving with the detail crisp and sharp and the formal ornament, the guilloche behind the columns, the swags and masks, and the surround of the panel, impeccably classical. It cannot have been the work of local craftsmen but where it was made and by whom is not known.[27]

There were three other chambers on the top floor none of which had original fittings save the one next to the great chamber ('D' on plan) which had a dummy door and doorcase carved in stone and situated to no apparent purpose immediately behind the fireplace in the great chamber. Two of the rooms had eighteenth-century bolection panelling, box cornices, and timber chimney-pieces, but it was not possible to establish if original fireplaces had survived. From 'D' a small stone newel staircase gave access to the roof and so across the leads to the rooms in the turrets. Another small staircase between 'E' and 'F' went to the floor below, but this was entirely modern.

At the back of the house was a tower-like projection rising from ground level to just below the parapet which contained a small vaulted chamber at basement level, and on the upper floors small closets leading from chambers 'B' and 'E'. The arrangement was similar to that of a medieval garderobe but there was no evidence that this was ever its function. At a later period it contained a staircase.

Finally *the basement*. Here were the kitchens and domestic offices arranged with economy and convenience, the kitchens being in the side range next to the outer courtyard, and pantry and buttery in a series of smaller chambers under the front range near the service stairs. One chamber, that in the south-west corner, may have provided living quarters, but the others on this side of the house were the ample larders and storerooms necessary to a sixteenth-century household. There was a direct entry to the kitchens from the outer courtyard on the north-east side, and an entry to the storerooms on the opposite side, the south-west.

Access from basement to the principal floor was by means of a staircase with straight flights of wide stone steps which began in a lobby next to the kitchens and emerged in the 'screens passage' next to the hall. A service hatch from the kitchens was provided in the lobby and from the lobby there was access also to pantry and buttery. There was evidence of another staircase in a different position, but it was incomplete and probably never finished (see above, p. 292).

Finally, under the basement in the centre of the back range was a lower cellar cut deep into the native rock which, splitting and opening as a result of mining subsidence, seemed to one observer in the dim light of a winter after-noon to open up passages into the bowels of the earth.

Discussion

Perhaps the most obvious feature of Heath is that it was designed to impress, to demonstrate to the world John Kay's success and importance. Such an ambition was not rare in Elizabethan England and several fortunes were lavished on raising a magnificent pile of masonry and then, with generous hospitality, on 'maintaining a port', even to the point of ruin.[28] Kay's resources were limited; his wealth came from a relatively small office, not to be compared with the great estates of a Talbot or the mine revenues of a Willoughby, but within his limits he built grandly and impressively. The site was chosen care-fully to achieve maximum effect, the style of building was bold and fashionable, and the interior was furnished with rooms of considerable state, a splendid great chamber and long gallery as well as a hall and all other necessary chambers and offices.

But, seeking a building of some splendour, it is curious that he should have adopted for his new house the form and trimmings of a medieval fortress. There was indeed a taste for mock castles in the Elizabethan period, but it was never widespread and of those that were actually built nearly all belong to the end of the century. In the early 1580s this was a novel form and particularly so for a family not previously given to experiment. The family's principal house, Woodsome Hall, near Huddersfield, is a sober building of traditional pattern where even the additions and embellishments made at the end of the sixteenth century were modest and traditional.[29] Nor, at first sight, does the Savile connection offer much architectural inspiration. Kay's patron, Sir Henry Savile, lived at Thornhill, near Wakefield, now an indecipherable ruin but from all accounts a fifteenth-century house on a moated site with no hint of later modernisation. Another branch of the family built at Methley, also near Wakefield, adding to an earlier house and remodelling the hall, but this was after 1588 and so several years after Heath had been completed. There is nothing in the Kay or Savile background that anticipates Heath; one must look therefore outside this circle for the source of its design, and since its style was unusual and not part of the common currency to a particular inspiration rather than to a general trend.

The Savile connection may not have offered much in the way of architectural stimulus, but it was crucial to John Kay for his general advancement. Through the Saviles as well as through his own office Kay would be in touch with other great families of the area. He would be well informed of local affairs, of land purchases, of family alliances, and of that particular mark of success, ambitious new building. If he did not have first-hand knowledge of Wollaton he would certainly know by report of this extravagant structure some fifty miles away, begun in 1580 by Sir Francis Willoughby with Robert Smythson as 'Architector and Survayor', a building whose central block rises keep-like above its outer ranges and whose mass and silhouette bring to mind the strength and power of a medieval castle. To contemporaries Wollaton must have been an overwhelming display of pomp and position; to some perhaps it gave a taste for pseudo-military splendour. One thing certainly, it brought to the district an architect of genius whose influence would reach beyond Wollaton and whose services would be available to others who had a desire to build.

Smythson was one key figure. Another was Francis Rodes of Staveley Woodthorpe, near Chesterfield. Rodes was from much the same sort of background as John Kay and, successful at law, had amassed an estate on the borders of Yorkshire, Nottingham and Derbyshire. A Serjeant-at-Law and later a Justice of the Common Pleas, he was also steward to the Earl of Shrewsbury on whose behalf he was active in south Yorkshire and the north

Midlands, and though there is no documentary evidence to prove that Kay and Rodes were acquainted it is difficult to believe that, with the one engaged on legal and estate business in the area and the other an official of the Duchy court, they were not known to each other and aware of each other's ambitions. Rodes had already built at Great Houghton, ten miles from Heath, and in the early 1580s began to build a new house at Barlborough in Derbyshire.

The significance of this is that Heath and Barlborough are virtually twin buildings, not identical but remarkably similar (Pl. XXIII). They are nearly the same size, their principal elevations are of the same pattern, and their plans are variants of the same uncommon theme. The similarities are so close that it is reasonable to suppose that the two buildings spring from the same design.

There are differences, of course. Of the two, Barlborough is the more assured. The plan is better organised, the façades more elegant and the detail more refined. Heath in places was uncertain. It lacked the unity and coherence of Barlborough. It had the air of things half-understood, of masons skilled in the vernacular coping with unfamiliar problems inadequately set out. For these reasons one believes that Barlborough was the primary building and Heath the secondary; that Kay, knowing Rodes and learning of his plans for Barlborough, determined to build in the same manner but, varying the plan to suit his own tastes and with less skilled supervision, he produced in consequence a slightly different and somewhat less accomplished building.[30]

There remains the question of the origin of the design. Dr. Girouard has stated elsewhere the case for attributing Barlborough to Robert Smythson and it is a convincing argument.[31] Accepting this it follows that Heath also is Smythson-inspired, but at one remove. In both cases there are the characteristic Smythsonian touches—the use of a high basement, the placing of principal chambers on the top floor, the sparing use of decoration, the compactness, height, and sense of drama. There is in addition the medievalism. Heath and Barlborough are Gothic, not in the sense of the enduring tradition of Tudor Gothic, but rather as new versions of an old model. They are tower-houses, a familiar building in the northern counties and here re-created to suit the tastes of Elizabethan gentry; an old theme brought up to date in a bold and imaginative way. To do this called for qualities of a special sort; it required a sympathy towards medieval architecture as well as the necessary skill to shape it to new uses, qualities that point very strongly to Smythson, who at Wardour and at Wollaton had displayed both.

To link Heath with Smythson is to rely heavily on circumstantial evidence, but the case I think is a strong one. There is no plan in the collection of Smythson drawings in the R.I.B.A. that can be identified with either Heath or Barlborough, but there are a number of the same type. They are an important element in the collection, fully developed and showing a strong family likeness.[32]

The mock castle is a fascinating part of the Elizabethan world. It was not a formula in frequent use but when employed it produced buildings eloquent of the period, of its people and of their fancies. This is certainly true of Heath and Barlborough. Barlborough survives and one may still view its soaring turrets and intricate patterns with excitement and delight. Heath regrettably is a heap of stones, tumbled and destroyed, whose presence one can now recall only from records.[33]

REFERENCES

1. By Hugh Honour in an article with this title in *Country Life,* Vol. CXVI, pp. 1084–6, (30 September 1954).

2. Paine's work at Heath House is dated to 1744–5, and Carr's Heath Hall to 'before 1760'; H. M. Colvin, *Dictionary of English Architects* (1954).

3. Before demolition the house was surveyed by the Ancient Monuments branch of what was then the Ministry of Public Building and Works, and this survey forms the basis of the plans accompanying this article. They have been re-drawn by Mr. J. C. Thorne to whom I am indebted. There are other measured drawings in the National Monuments Record together with photographs of various dates. For an early view of Heath, a painting by Henry Singleton of *c.* 1790, see *Country Life,* Vol. CXI, p. 728 (14 March 1952).

4. The only firm date for Heath is that given by Ambler for the 'Jezebel' chimney-piece which he states was dated 1584; L. Amber, *Old Halls and Manor Houses of Yorkshire* (1931), p. 51. At the time of demolition no such date was visible, but by then some of the stonework had crumbled away as a result of water seepage. It is true that elsewhere in his book Ambler dates the house to 'about 1564', but this general attribution is probably based on an earlier comment by Hunter (see Note 16), and stylistically such a date is not possible.

5. The present view is somewhat restricted by a massive power station and other industrial installations.

6. Glover's *Visitation of Yorkshire 1584–5,* ed. Foster (1875), p. 323.

7. T. D. Whitaker, *Loidis and Elmete* (1816), pp. 314–5.

8. Glover, *op. cit.*

9. Contemporary with John Kay of Dalton and Heath there was also a John Kay of Woodsome and Oakenshaw and some accounts link Dorothy Savile with this John Kay, but in neither case is the evidence conclusive.

10. Lady Green, *The Old Hall at Heath, 1568–1888* (1889), for the later history of Heath.

11. *Country Life,* Vol. XXII, pp. 90–6 (20 July 1907).

12. The inserted vault blocked an original window opening into the court from the back range, and there was some evidence of another blocked window in the front range (not shown on the plan).

13. Originally, as shown on early nineteenth-century views of the house, these bays were carried up above the parapet to the same height as the turrets on the front elevation, but they were reduced in height in 1866; Green, *op. cit.*

14. Kay of Dalton: argent, 2 bendlets sable, a martlet for difference of the last; Dodsworth: argent, 3 bugle horns stringed sable. The plaque also carried the Kay crest, a griffin's head holding a key, and had putti supporting the coat of arms.

15. Iron supports in two other blocks on the porch suggested more beasts or figures on this part at least.

16. J. Hunter, *Antiquarian Notices of Lupset, the Heath etc.* (1851), p. 54. Little of the original glazing survived, but one window looking into the inner court retained its original lattice pattern of small squares and hexagons which was complete.

17. The building used as a chapel had four large pointed windows in one elevation. There was no part of the house itself that could be identified as a chapel.

18. 'The water from the spring collected in a stone tank and from this descended on to a wheel 18 ft. in diameter fitted with buckets which forced it to another tank at the top of

the tower and thence it gravitated to the cistern', Green, *op. cit.*, p. 24. See also the will of Mary Bolles which contains a reference to the water tower 'which she lately built'.

19. At one time the great chamber was also divided into three rooms and its chimney-piece boarded over, but the original arrangement was restored in 1867, Green, *op. cit.*, p. 22.

20. M. Girouard, *Archaeological Journal*, Vol. CXVIII (1961), pp. 223-7.

21. The plasterwork is similar, in its rococo elements at least, to some of Paine's work at Nostell Priory and it is tempting to associate this decoration in the Old Hall with Paine's presence at Heath House in 1744-5. Mr. Peter Leach has also drawn my attention to Paine's fondness for tapering pilasters in his fireplace designs, a motif that appeared in the Old Hall in the summer parlour chimney-piece. As to the Gothic elements in the decoration, is this a deliberate response to the character of the building, a character recognised and appreciated in the eighteenth century?

22. This was square-headed and of timber, with a simple ovolo and cavetto moulding.

23. Possibly the staircase was never completed.

24. The eighteenth-century chimney-piece was of simple design with a projecting cornice and low relief carving of shells and foliage. The sixteenth-century fireplace, which was intact, had moulded jambs with high stops and a carved rosette above the stops. The spandrels in the head of the fireplace were carved with foliage. Several fireplaces in the house were of this stock pattern which was thoroughly vernacular.

25. For Barlborough see Girouard, *op. cit.*

26. Contemporary also were the matchlocks carried by the soldiers.

27. At the time of demolition the chimney-piece was taken from Heath to Hazlewood Castle where it is now happily installed in a room with a ceiling modelled on that of the great chamber at Heath. I am informed by Mr. J. H. Milne, agent of the estate, that the stone plaque with the royal arms, and other items, were taken to Wakefield Museum, and that various other pieces were salvaged and preserved locally.

28. H. R. Trevor-Roper, *The Gentry 1540-1640*, Economic History Review supplement, p. 6.

29. *Country Life*, Vol. XX (1906), pp. 906-14.

30. A comparison of detail is interesting. Heath had lunettes and panelled blocks on its balustrade while the turrets were battlemented. At Barlborough the same elements are reversed, with the turrets (and formerly the lantern also) having lunettes and blocks and the body of the house a battlemented parapet.

31. M. Girouard, *op. cit.* For a comprehensive account of Robert Smythson and his work see the same author's *Robert Smythson and the architecture of the Elizabethan era* (1961), on which I have drawn heavily for all matters Smythsonian.

32. M. Girouard, *Architectural History*, Vol. 5 (1962). See especially I/18, I/19, II/2, II/3.

33. Furniture designed by Thomas Jekyll in the late 1860s for Edward Green for use at the Old Hall is described and illustrated in *Country Life*, Vol. CXLII, pp. 1704-7 (28 December 1967). One of the pieces was a 'Jacobean' dresser.

The Lady Anne Clifford (1590-1676)

by

JOHN CHARLTON

Vixere fortes ante Agamemnona. Some two hundred and fifty years before
H.M. Office of Works began to repair and consolidate the great series of
Edwardian Welsh castles, which Arnold Taylor has made his particular study,
a sixty-year-old countess set about restoring the five castles of her northern
inheritance—restoring them not just as antiquities, but as part of the old way
of life which they represented. The castles were Appleby, Brough, Brougham,
Pendragon, and Skipton, and she was the Lady Anne Clifford, Countess
Dowager of Dorset, Pembroke and Montgomery, hereditary high sheriff of
the County of Westmorland, and Lady of the Honour of Skipton-in-Craven.
A staunch royalist and a devout member of the Church of England, she spent
most of the Commonwealth in restoring the castles and churches of the great
northern estates of the ancient family of Clifford of which she was the last
direct descendant.

Anne Clifford was born in the Yorkshire castle of Skipton-in-Craven on
30 January 1590. Her father was George, 13th baron Clifford and 3rd earl
of Cumberland. A considerable mathematician and a skilful navigator he was
also a typical Elizabethan adventurer; he sailed some nine times to the Spanish
Main, with varying success, and commanded the Queen's ship *Bonaventure*
against the Armada. He was moreover a favourite of Elizabeth I, who was
present at his marriage in 1587 to Margaret Russell, daughter of Francis,
2nd earl of Bedford. The Lady Anne thus combined in her blood, and was
to display her character, the turbulent courage of the ancient Clifford strain
with the ability and practical wisdom of the rising new aristocracy represented
by the Russells.

She was brought up by her mother with the aid of governesses and tutors,
but her childhood was not particularly secluded, for her parents were people
of consequence about both the Tudor and Stuart courts. She records in her
Diary[1] that she 'was much beloved by that Renowned Queene Elizabeth'
and she was soon to become a favourite of James I's consort, Anne of
Denmark. This Queen's greatest pleasure was in masques, which were the
chief entertainment of the early Stuart court, and Lady Anne performed in
several of them. Mention here must be limited to one: *Tethys Festival,* which
was written by her former tutor, Samuel Daniel (1562–1619), with dresses

and scenery by Inigo Jones, and performed at Whitehall in 1610. Tethys, Queen of Ocean, was played by the Queen herself, attended by thirteen ladies of the court representing English rivers and clad in 'sky-coloured taffetas all embroidered with maritime invention'. Lady Anne (newly-wed as Countess of Dorset) took the character of the river Aire in the West Riding—the river nearest to her birthplace.

Samuel Daniel, praised by Edmund Spenser and sneered at by Ben Jonson, seems to have formed Lady Anne's literary tastes (her favourite poems were those of Spenser) and secured her affectionate regard. And years later, after she succeeded to her northern estates and the revenues that went with them, she set up monuments to Spenser in Westminster Abbey (by Nicholas Stone), and to Daniel (perhaps by Joshua Marshall) at Beckington in Somerset.

She was married twice, both times unhappily, and to owners of great houses. In 1609 she married Richard Sackville, later 3rd earl of Dorset and master of Knole, by whom she had two daughters, Margaret (later countess of Thanet) and Isabella (later countess of Northampton). He died in 1624, and in 1630 in a 'triumph of hope over experience' she married Philip Herbert, 4th earl of Pembroke and Montgomery, friend of Inigo Jones and lord of Wilton. She was mistress of great households but unhappy: 'the marble pillars of Knolle in Kentt and Wilton in Wiltshire, were to me oftentimes but the gay Harbours of Anguish [wherefore] I gave myself wholly to Retiredness, as much as I could, in both those great families, and made good Bookes ... my companions'. Her favourite reading, sitting away from the rest on the leads at Knole, might have been. The Fairy Queen.

Her greatest troubles, however, were not matrimonial, but legal: the battle for her northern inheritance, which, aided for the first ten years by her mother, she was to fight for nearly forty years against a host of adversaries which included James I. The dispute hinged on the fact that the barony of Clifford passed to heirs general, but the earldom of Cumberland was limited to heirs male. Under the will of her father the original fourteenth-century entail of the barony was ignored and the estates passed with the earldom to his brother; but it also provided that should there be a failure of male heirs the estates should go back to Lady Anne and not to a later Cumberland daughter, in this case Lady Cork. It was to prevent this return of the northern estates that her uncle and cousin vainly endeavoured to get her to renounce her rights.

The issue was finally settled by the death in 1643 of the last earl of Cumberland without male heirs and the consequent return of the inheritance to Lady Anne: but she did not at once set out to claim it. The Civil War had broken out and, while she was an ardent royalist, her husband, though he had held the post of Lord Chamberlain from 1621 to 1641, was a prominent parliamentarian. (He still occupied his official lodgings in Whitehall, though Lady Anne herself lived during this period at Baynard's Castle in the City). Moreover, her castles, though not of prime military importance in the war, were apt to change hands with the varying fortunes of the two sides. So it was not till some five months after the execution of Charles I (on her fifty-ninth birthday) that she took formal leave of her husband in Whitehall, said goodbye to her daughters at Baynard's Castle and at last set her face towards the northern hills and her birthplace, Skipton Castle, never to return.

She found her estates sadly disordered after years of neglect. During this interregnum many of her tenants had behaved much as they pleased: rents were unpaid, agreements broken, and her courts ignored. She set about them with all the determination she had shown to her adversaries in London, and in like manner brought them, after many contests, eventually to book. This is why one of her first acts was to provide places at her castles where her manor courts could be held.

The castles themselves were in poor fettle. Skipton had been 'slighted', albeit moderately; Appleby, under orders from London, had not been despoiled by the Commonwealth troops, but still bore the marks of the Rising of 1569. Brougham, least harried in the Civil war, had suffered a generation's neglect as had Barden Tower, a fortified house near Skipton which she maintained (quite wrongly) to be her property under her father's will. The main living-quarters at Brough had been burnt in an accidental fire in 1521 and twenty years later Pendragon had been finally spoiled by the Scots. Her first task, therefore, was first-aid repairs, to be followed as circumstances (and money) permitted by complete restoration.

The main works took some twelve years. They began with a general survey of the castles, after which a programme seems to have been drawn up which gave priority to the most important cases: Appleby, Brougham and Skipton. Appleby was the assize town for Westmorland where at the castle the Cliffords had for centuries lodged the King's Justices; Lady Anne's mother, moreover, was buried in one of its churches. Brougham Castle, the best preserved, was associated with her mother's death and the scene of their last meeting; it was besides her father's birthplace—and she was noted for her filial piety. It was also, next to Appleby, the largest and most important Clifford stronghold in the county. Skipton was the centre of the lordship of Craven and had been partly demolished by the Parliamentarians six months earlier. Here urgent repairs and some rebuilding were put in hand shortly after her arrival from the south, as well as at Barden Tower; and eighteen months later the building team that had been assembled crossed the Pennines to Appleby and Brougham. Appleby was first completed, then Brougham; but work continued slowly at Skipton till 1650. Barden, Brough and Pendragon, all smaller and less important buildings, were restored between 1659 and 1662, in which latter year the service buildings at Brougham were rebuilt.

Lady Anne's work at her various castles may now be considered in greater detail, beginning with Appleby. In 1641 she had had the castle fortified for the king and placed under the command of her relative, Sir Philip Musgrave, who held out till after the battle of Marston Moor. It had, however, never really recovered from the damage done to it in 1569 during the Rising of the North when the roofs were removed, though Lady Anne was probably exaggerating when she claimed that there was 'no one chamber habitable'. After its final surrender in 1648 to the Parliamentary forces it was further, but not drastically, dismantled, except for the destruction of the gatehouse, which commanded the town.[2]

Lady Anne began work on 'Caesar's Tower', the twelfth-century keep, laying on 21 April 1651 the foundation-stone of a new cross-wall, seven feet thick, which rises to roof level.[3] This incidentally was at a time when, as she records, 'the warres was so hott in Scotland' that the judges could not get to Appleby to hold the assizes. The general character of the repairs to the keep albeit in a slightly different stone, generally accord well with its original medieval character, and the doors to the rebuilt turrets of the keep have shouldered arches which only their style of dressing robs of medieval authenticity. 'Gothic' fireplaces of later sixteenth- or early seventeenth-century pattern were inserted in the cross-wall in the two upper storeys, which were then used as guest-rooms, like some of the rooms in her other Norman keeps at Brougham and Brough.

The rebuilding by the 6th earl of Thanet of much of the rest of the castle in 1686–8, mostly with stone from Brough Castle, has removed a great deal of Lady Anne's work, but details of her movements, set out in various parts of her Diary, suggest that her unvaried route on entering or leaving the castle was by the great hall and past the chapel to the great chamber. Beyond were further stairs leading to the withdrawing-room, with Lady Anne's own room beyond. She seems to have contrived a similar sequence of rooms in all her castles.

Brougham Castle, where her father was born, her mother died, and she herself was one day to die also, was perhaps her favourite castle. Like Appleby and Brough it had a Norman keep (the 'Pagan Tower'), which, however, was embedded in a complex of later buildings. It communicated directly not only with the inner and outer gatehouses, of c. 1290 and c. 1300 respectively, but, by an earlier great chamber block, with the fourteenth-century hall at a lower level. It bore least scars of Scottish attacks of the various Clifford castles, for Lady Anne's uncle, the 4th earl of Cumberland, had entertained James I there for three nights in 1617, a visit marked by a musical entertainment, written and composed for the occasion and performed by singers from London; but it had, of course, suffered during the Civil War.

The state of the structure called for no drastic rebuilding, but later in 1662 the main offices were demolished and rebuilt against the western curtain-wall to give more room in the main courtyard. Internally the changes were limited to renewal of minor doorways, windows and partitions, and the insertion of fireplaces, all in her 'Gothic' style. The main work of restoration in the Brougham area relates to the two parish churches, both of which were rebuilt.

In the castle the sequence of the principal rooms can be identified from descriptions of her arrival there set out in Lady Anne's Diary. On leaving her entourage in the courtyard she went up the external stairs of the Great Hall, where she took leave of the principal members of her escort. She then passed upstairs to the Great Chamber, which in turn opened on to a withdrawing-room over the outer gatehouse and called the Painted Chamber. From this she went by a wall-passage to her own apartment on the top floor of the inner gatehouse. This was a long perambulation for a lady in her seventies and eighties, but she probably chose her own apartment for two reasons: it was consecrated in her mind by being the scene of her father's birth and her mother's death; and it gave direct access to the second floor of the keep. This was now divided by partitions and housed one or more of her personal attendants. It also gave access to the private chapel on the floor above and, while strength was with her, to the leads, where (as at Knole) she could sit and read; and see on the Appleby road, a thousand yards away, the pillar she had set up in 1656 'as a memorial of a last parting in this place with her good and pious mother' in 1616.[4]

Skipton Castle with its seven round towers had no keep. Mainly early fourteenth-century, its entrance flanked by massive drum-towers of Angevin date, it was extended in the grand manner by the 12th baron Clifford when his son married Eleanor Brandon, niece of Henry VIII in 1537. The 'slighting' of the castle at the end of the Civil War seems to have been limited to the throwing down of upper parts of, e.g., the great gateway and the removal of such of the lead or stone roofs as might form a platform for gunnery, for which latter reason Lady Anne was permitted in her restoration (during the Commonwealth) to use only slates for re-roofing. After emergency repairs in 1650 and much complaint about 'the smell and unwholesomeness of the new walls' the work was completed in 1657–9. The most striking work of restoration was the great gateway of which she rebuilt the upper half, crowning the whole with a balustrade which incorporates the family motto 'Desormais'. Of unusual interest is the survival of a great number of lead fittings, profusely decorated with the arms of the Vipont[5] and Clifford families and the crest and initials of the lady herself.

Lady Anne also repaired and enlarged Barden Tower, a fortified manor house some ten miles to the north-east of Skipton. Though she regarded this as her property it had some forty years earlier been quite legally excluded from the entailed estates for the benefit of the last earl and his rightful heirs and should have passed on his death in 1643 to his daughter, Lady Cork. The latter's husband, however, was at that time subject to sequestration and her claim could not be pursued. By the time that this was possible, Lady Anne had taken possession of the property and held it till her death. She took great pride in her restoration of it (in 1658–9) and added a chapel, planned like her other chapels, with chancel and nave in one, but lit by grander windows than the rest.

Brough had been gravely damaged in an accidental fire in 1521 and was so ruinous when Lady Anne surveyed it in August 1649 that work was put off for some ten years. Its principal features are the late twelfth-century keep (the 'Roman Tower') and a thirteenth-century and later three-storeyed, hall-block with a large thirteenth-century round tower ('Clifford's Tower') projecting from one angle. It was this block that was burnt out in 1521 and which first received most attention not only as living quarters but as providing accommodation for the Countess's courts, which were held in the hall. Clifford's Tower was virtually rebuilt, as were the staircase to the great hall and the great chamber, but much of this restoration work was swept away in 1695 and early 1763, when the place became a quarry, and only foundations survive of the kitchen, brewhouse and bakehouse, opposite the Hall, and the stables, near the gatehouse, which were erected in 1662.

The arrangement of the principal rooms shows an adaptation of Lady Anne's standard domestic plan to a rather restricted site. Her own room was on the top floor of Clifford's Tower (which would give her access to the leads) with a smaller, irregularly shaped ante-room and a kind of small withdrawing-room, between it and the great chamber, the latter being lit by tall windows now robbed of their stone dressings. This was above the first-floor hall, which in turn was approached by a grand staircase rising from courtyard level.

Though Lady Anne occasionally slept in the Roman Tower that building was generally used, like the other keeps, for guests, though the room on the second stage was reserved for her clerk of works, Gabriel Vincent, who died there on 12 February 1666.[6]

Brough is the best example of Lady Anne's restoration work as it was there that she had most to do and most survives despite later demolition. In the Norman keep the openings were given rounded arches, Norman in general character, though not always so in construction, and the windows restored to match the surviving original window on the south side. The south wall of the Great Chamber, which Buck's view shows as having had tall transomed windows which look like her work, was refaced with rubble matching the walling of the fourteenth-century hall beneath (Pl. XXXVII a). And a careful match was made in the extensive repairs to the missing ashlar walling of Clifford's Tower, lit by windows which combine practical effectiveness with traditional character (Pl. XXVII b).

Pendragon Castle,[7] guarding the remote valley of Mallerstang, Norman in origin but enlarged and strengthened by the Cliffords in the fourteenth century, had suffered severely during successive Scottish wars, the last time in 1641, since when it had lain ruinous. Here had lived one of Lady Anne's ancestors, the childless Idonea de Vipont, whose sister Isabella had married the first of the northern Cliffords in the time of Edward I, and whose lands by her death were joined to the Clifford barony. Its restoration had been one of Lady Anne's childhood dreams, and in 1660 she set about realising it. Today the castle is a faceless ruin and the extent of her work cannot be estimated, but she records she was put to great costs and charges. She enclosed it with a wall of 'lime and stone' and rebuilt the domestic offices. It was too small for the suite of rooms found at her larger castles, but could provide on a smaller scale the basic sequence, which included a great chamber. And when all was done here as elsewhere she rebuilt the parish church in the solid unostentatious style she favoured.

It may well be asked why this formidable lady of known royalist tendencies was allowed during the Commonwealth to reconstruct a series of castles in defiance of the new regime. They are several. First, the castles themselves were of only marginal strategic importance. Second, the Lady Anne had many friends even at the Commonwealth Court and Parliament. Third, she was persistent in claiming her rights under the laws of the land, which were not abrogated by the death of the sovereign. Lastly, she was recognised as a lady of great and determined character, best left alone.

The first point speaks for itself: the battles of the Civil War were not fought in the Eden valley or among the wastes of Mallerstang. Only Skipton castle, which had withstood a rather gentlemanly three-year siege during the First Civil War, was really 'slighted' and the prolongation of the defence by its royalist garrison may have been due to its being so far from the real seats of power that no one bothered about it till the rest of Yorkshire was safe for the Roundheads.

As to Lady Anne's friends at court or in parliament (of which she had a number), she had after all married as her second husband, however unhappily, that parliamentary earl of Pembroke who received Charles I from the Scots in 1647, while Colonel Fairfax,[8] her principal man of business and one of her trustees, was the uncle of General Fairfax. Even Lambert, who occupied Appleby briefly in 1647, was married to a relation of the Fairfax clan.

Third, her respect for law was as wholehearted as her religion, perhaps because it had eventually vindicated her claims to her northern estates. She had every confidence in the judiciary and from her first arrival in Westmorland till her death many years later she provided as hereditary high sheriff of Westmorland lodging in the castle for the judges when they held the assizes at Appleby. Indeed, if she should happen to be at Brougham on the occasion of the assizes, the judges were asked to dinner there on their way to Appleby. Again, when she had a law-suit in chancery with her tenants and Oliver Cromwell was inclined to intervene by appointing a commission to compose the differences between the two parties, she declared she would not refer her concerns to the 'protector or any one living, but leave it wholly to the discretion of the law, adding she had refused to submit to King James on the like account'.[9]

Finally, there was the Clifford spirit, tempered with Bedford discretion, which inspired her behaviour and had a remarkable impact on the men of her day. Her secretary, Sedgewick, tells us that when she decided to rebuild her castles her neighbours tried to dissuade her—the times after all were hardly propitious; but her reply, according to Sedgewick, was 'As long as I have money or credit I will repair my houses, though I were sure to have them thrown down next day'. This being reported to Oliver Cromwell—'Nay', says he, 'let her build what she will, she shall have no hindrance from me'.[10]

There can be little doubt that Lady Anne Clifford's style of life and choice of architecture was deliberate. Her years at court and at Knole and at Wilton must have made her perfectly familiar with the social and architectural fashions of the day, but she turned her back on them when she went to live on her ancestral estates in the north. There she stepped back in time to the great days of her Vipont and Clifford ancestors, whose arms she delighted in displaying. And, as if she was conscious that she was the last of the Cliffords, she created around her the kind of court life she may have believed they had lived, as strict in its way as that of medieval or Tudor royal households. Indeed lands in north Westmorland and the Honour of Skipton-in-Craven became during her reign almost extra-territorial to the rest of England; only the judges, whether Commonwealth or Royal, were received from the outer world as purveyors of uncorrupt justice; and but for the fact that the writ of law still ran and she did not strike her own coins, she behaved like a Countess Palatine.

Moreover her progresses from castle to castle, if not consciously modelled on, clearly echoed much of the ceremony attendant on a royal progress from palace to palace. Each castle (like each palace) contained only the bare essentials of life: its richness and comforts—silver, napery, dresses, even bedding —travelled from castle to castle. So, too, with her household. Each castle had its housekeeper and its attendant chaplain, the parson of the local church or chapel, but the officers of her Ladyship's household travelled with her as did the bulk of her servants, or family as she called them.

Her departure from one of her castles and her entry into another was a pageant in itself. Long before her departure her principal tenants would be gathered in the great hall, to be followed by her 'cousins', the heads of leading local families like the Musgraves and Lowthers who were related to the Cliffords. When all was ready—and punctually we may be sure—she came down from her private chamber, following always a prescribed route, to the castle hall to greet the company which was to attend her on her journey. Then, several hundred strong, they set out with her on her journey (performed at first on horseback, later in a horse-litter) through villages prepared to welcome her and cheer her on her way. Arrived at her destination she took leave of the company in the hall before retiring, again by a prescribed route, to her private chamber.

What then of her choice of architecture? That she had decided notions about architectural styles is confirmed by the various church monuments she erected. One of *c*. 1612, set up at Chenies to her childhood friend, Lady Frances Bouchier, is in the latest court style of Inigo Jones. That to Edmund Spenser in Westminster Abbey is so heavily restored as to make it difficult to judge, but it was made (twenty years after the poet's death) by Nicholas Stone, Inigo Jones's master mason, who received £40 for it from Lady Anne. Her monument to her tutor, Samuel Daniel (died 1619), set up in Beckington church some time after 1650, is again in the classical taste, with a bust of the poet wreathed and wearing a toga.[11]

Her northern tombs were very different. That to her mother (died 1616) placed in St. Laurence church, Appleby about 1617, echoes that in the Abbey to Elizabeth I, by Maximilian Colt, appropriately enough for one so closely associated with that sovereign's court. The monument to her father in Skipton, erected in 1654, nearly fifty years after his death, looks further back, however, to the table tombs of the Middle Ages: plain, of black marble, it is relieved by a grand display of heraldry. Both monuments were London work. Her own monument, devised some twenty years before her death, for the church where her mother lies, was in form the plainest of all: a simple table-tomb backed by a wall-piece with Doric pilasters, surmounted by a pediment, enclosing twenty-four shields-of-arms beginning with those of her thirteenth-century Vipont ancestors and ending with those of her married daughters: an idiosyncratic compromise between the old style and the new.

It may be appropriate here to consider very briefly her various enterprises in church architecture. For as her castle-rebuilding drew towards its close— and she herself reached her seventies— she turned to the renewal of the churches and chapels near her castles. In them she had continued throughout the Commonwealth to use the liturgy of the Church of England, despite threats of sequestration '—yet by means of her honourable friends and relations in both houses of parliament she always escaped it'.[12] Doubtless she regarded these structures as so many domestic chapels—the panel of the Royal arms in that at Mallerstang bears the initials AP, for Anne Pembroke, as well as CR for Charles II: and the local parson was of course expected to act as domestic chaplain whenever the Countess and her little court came to stay at the neighbouring castle. The larger churches, the two at Appleby and, to a lesser degree, the parish church of Skipton, had probably needed much external repair, but later restoration makes assessment difficult, though those parts which enclosed Clifford tombs must have received particular attention. The church and chapel at Brougham and the chapel at Mallerstang, however, were almost wholly rebuilt, Brougham church retaining to this day its original woodwork. The style is consistent throughout and is best described as a kind of semi-Gothic. The architectural detail is plain: windows have round-headed lights in square heads with simply moulded labels, doorways have hollow continuous mouldings with occasionally an ogive head, but the keynote is modesty, simplicity and good proportion.[13]

Finally, back to those castles which to her were the heart of the ancient medieval inheritance of the Cliffords—a sacred trust whose terms demanded that their aspect should where possible be created anew in their old image. This was not just an old woman's fancy to be brought into being without regard for the normal comforts and conventions of contemporary life—there were no central hearths or similar elements of medieval discomfort in her halls or great chambers, but ample fireplaces. Yet these chimney-pieces were not confections of pillared marble, but plain carved openings with four-centred heads looking back in style to the previous century. Similarly the kitchen quarters and stabling, unchanged for a century or more, were brought up to date as a practical measure. But the total effect of the restoration of the buildings was to restore, where possible and with due regard to its context, the main features of the Clifford castles (whether Norman, Edwardian or Tudor) in such a manner that time, in a sense, had stood still. It was not for nothing that, on the commemorative inscriptions which the Countess set up on each building she restored, she should, after setting forth her various styles and titles, refer the reader to Isaiah lviii, 12: 'And they that shall be of thee shall build the old waste places: thou shalt raise up the foundations of many generations; and thou shalt be called, The repairer of the breach, The restorer of paths to dwell in'.[14]

REFERENCES

1. This diary is the main source for the sequence of Lady Anne's works, the building accounts for which, with trifling exceptions, have not come to light. It is very much a personal document, recording the lady's movements and those of her family whenever they came north, but providing only limited direct evidence about her restoration work, though throwing light on the conduct of her household. It appears to be a summary of a series of day-to-day books, containing much detail, including costs of works. A version in the British Museum (Harleian 6177) was published by the Roxburgh Club in 1911 and there is another in the Cumbria Record Office at Kendal. An eighteenth-century transcript of an earlier diary, ending 1619 and now at Knole, was edited by Miss V. Sackville-West in 1923. The two biographies of the lady are G. C. Williamson, *Lady Anne Clifford* (1922), a voluminous but somewhat unreliable compilation, which contains a sketchy account of her building activities, and M. R. Holmes, *Proud Northern Lady* (1976), which gives a full and accurate account of her life, but does not pretend to deal with her buildings.

2. On 24 November 1648 the Committee of both Houses of Parliament ordered that a letter be written to the commander of the forces at Appleby to take care that no harm be done to the castle or the goods therein, and no spoil made on the country when they march out of it. (*Calendar of State Papers Domestic Series, Charles I [1648-1649]*, p. 332.)

3. This not only simplified the practical problems of restoration and gave greater stability to the structure, but increased the number of rooms available as lodging. See also M. R. Holmes, *Appleby Castle* (1974).

4. The diary also suggests how matters were ordered at dinner-time. The main body of servants ate in the hall, the upper servants and officials, which might include the chaplain (i.e., the local vicar) in the Painted Chamber or withdrawing-room, and the Countess and her intimates in her private chamber, to which after dinner the people in the Painted Chamber might be called.

5. The Cliffords (of Clifford in Hereford) acquired their northern estates through the marriage of Roger (d. 1282) to Isabel, daughter and co-heiress of Robert Vipont, hereditary high sheriff of Westmorland. Their son, Robert, the first baron, was granted Skipton Castle by Edward I and was killed at Bannockburn.

6. His tombstone in Brough church describes him as steward to Lady Anne and 'cheif director of her buildings in the North'.

7. The name appears to echo the antiquarian names given to the three Norman keeps at Appleby ('Caesar's Tower'), Brough ('Roman'), and Brougham ('Pagan'), the last two of which stand within Roman forts. It is found, however, in documents from the fourteenth century onwards. Other 'Arthurian' place-names in the Clifford country are King Arthur's Round Table, near Brougham, and the Round Table (otherwise Roper's Castle) in the hills above Brough. (A. R. Smith, *The Place-names of Westmorland*, 2, 13).

8. Charles Fairfax (1579-1673) of Denton, Yorks., married Mary Breary of Brenston, where Cromwell and his comrades held a conference just before Marston Moor. Much light is thrown on Lady Anne's relations with the Parliamentarians by Sedgwick, her amanuensis, in an account now lost, but published in part in J. Nicholson and R. Burn, *History of Cumberland and Westmorland*, 2 (1777), pp. 294-303.

9. Sedgwick, *loc. cit.*

10. Sedgwick, *loc. cit.*

11. Probably by Joshua Marshall (1629-78). See M. D. Whinney, *Sculpture in England 1530-1830* (1964), p. 241. Daniel is described on the monument as 'Tutor to the Lady

Anne Clifford in her youth . . . who in gratitude to him erected this . . . a long time after when she was Countess Dowager of Pembroke', etc.; so it was probably put up after the Restoration.

12. Sedgwick, *loc. cit.*

13. Her 'cousin', Sir Philip Musgrave, did the same for the church at Soulby, some four miles from Brough, in 1662.

14. 'Countess Dowager of Pembrook, Dorsett and Montgomery, Baroness Clifford, Westmorland and veseie, Ladie of the Honour of Skipton an Craven, and High Sheriffesse, by inheritance of the countie of Westmorland'. The fact that the Vescy title was restricted to heirs male she ignored and would doubtless have disputed.

The Seventeenth-century Buildings
at Tredegar House, Newport [1]

by

M. R. APTED

INTRODUCTION

TREDEGAR HOUSE as it stands today is built round the four sides of a rectangular courtyard. One side of this courtyard, the south-west, is occupied in part by a late-medieval hall; a second, the south-east, has been substantially rebuilt within the last hundred years or so; the remaining two were built in the seventeenth century, probably *c.* 1670, by the Sir William Morgan who owned Tredegar from 1664 to 1680. The nearby stable block is likely to have been added somewhat later.

There is no known plan of the medieval house at Tredegar other than that traced by Octavius Morgan from an original now lost.[2] Octavius (1802–88) was a brother of Viscount Tredegar and a noted antiquary with a personal interest in the history of the house, so that it is reasonable to assume that the plan he copied was authentic. The tracing is annotated 'Drawing from a rough plan of the ancient mansion and gardens at Tredegar as they were in the early half of the seventeenth century (probably in the time of Elizabeth) before the alterations to the building were made after the Restoration by William Morgan, in whose handwriting the notes on the plan seem to be'. The layout of house and grounds is similar to the present one, but with buildings round only three sides of the courtyard and the fourth enclosed by a wall with central entrance gate. The walled gardens include a bowling green, maze and flower garden, as well as a series of orchards. This layout in fact corresponds closely to that existing today so that the new arrangements perpetuate the old, although on a far more splendid scale.

THE SEVENTEENTH-CENTURY BUILDINGS

The principal façade of the new seventeenth-century buildings faced north-west on the line of the medieval access and consisted of two main storeys with cellars below and attics above (Pl. XXVIII a and XXXI a). The range is symmetrical, with the entrance from the forecourt at the centre on the site of the medieval gateway and with projecting pavilions at either end. The main fabric is of brick with rustic stone quoins and stone mullioned windows. The

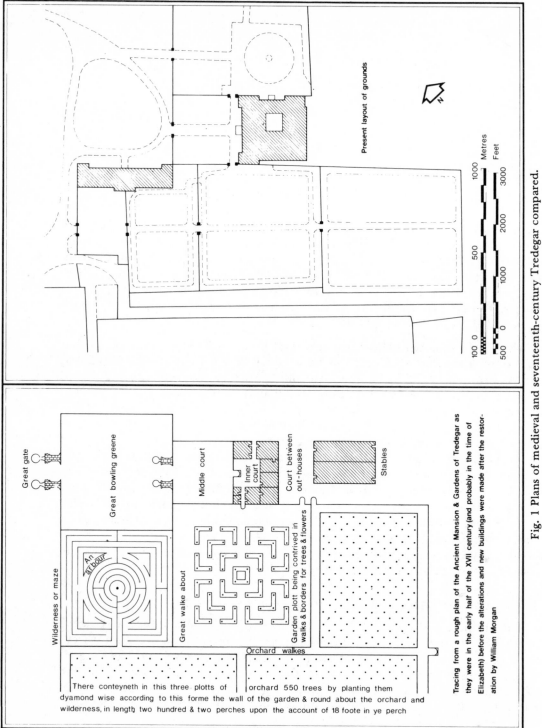

There conteyneth in this three plotts of | orchard 550 trees by planting them
dyamond wise according to this forme the wall of the garden & round about the orchard and
wilderness, in length two hundred & two perches upon the account of 18 foote in ye perch

Tracing from a rough plan of the Ancient Mansion & Gardens of Tredegar as
they were in the early half of the XVII century (and probably in the time of
Elizabeth) before the alterations and new buildings were made after the restoration by William Morgan

Fig. 1 Plans of medieval and seventeenth-century Tredegar compared.

sculptured decoration above and below the windows is also of stone and is connected above the windows by a continuous horizontal stone string course. The general effect produced by the adjacent north-east range is similar, but in fact the proportions are different, there being three windows side by side in each of the pavilions as against two, and only three windows in the façade between the pavilions instead of seven. The porch which projects from the north-east wing is a nineteenth-century addition to a doorway formed from what was originally a window. Thus it is from the north-west that the house is seen at its best.

Internally the original front doorway gives access directly to a large hall, referred to in the seventeenth-century inventories[3] as 'the New Hall', which is the key to circulation throughout the house (A). To the right lie the two principal public apartments now known as 'the Brown Drawing Room' (B), and 'the Gilt Room' (C), but called in the seventeenth century 'the Dining Room' and 'the Gilded Room' (Pl. XXVIII b). These have been decorated with a lavishness which explains why for a time the house was underrated—elaborate displays of carving and gilt work (highly esteemed in the seventeenth century) were regarded as vulgar in the eighteenth. David Williams, for example, writing in 1796 said of Tredegar 'The internal parts, now decaying, were too much decorated: large objects, to be grand, should be simple'.[4] These rooms are directly inter-connected in the medieval manner.

To the left of the entrance hall is 'the New Parlour' (D) (later to be Lord Tredegar's dining-room and then a chapel). Beyond that again is the modern entrance hall, called in the seventeenth century 'the drawing room that is hanged with gilt leather' (E). The rooms on this side of the house, i.e., in the north-east wing, are linked not only by intercommunicating doors as in the north-west range, but also by a corridor running the full length of the wing. Thus there is access from the New Hall to every room in either direction on the ground floor and (since the main stair ascends from it at a point opposite the entrance) to the rooms on the first floor also. At this higher level there is a corridor extending from the stair-head the full length of the wings in either direction, serving all the principal bedrooms (called in the inventories 'the Chambers'). The rooms at the east angle (F) form a suite of three and probably include one referred to as 'My Master's Room' in the contemporary inventories. The room now known as 'the Pink Room' was 'the Best Room' (G). The only room still to retain its seventeenth-century name is the 'Passing Room' which appears to have first so-called in 1689 (H).

The servants access to the attics may originally have been only by a back stair from the servant's hall (I)—the existing stair from ground to first floor at the east corner of the courtyard is at least in part an addition, as is the secondary stair from the main stair landing to the attics. The original arrangements for general circulation were nonetheless remarkably good and apart from the stairways already mentioned the only alteration deemed necessary

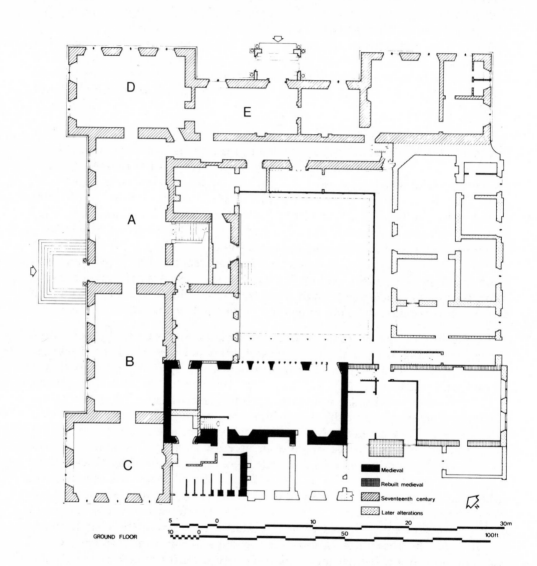

Fig. 2 Tredegar House: ground floor.

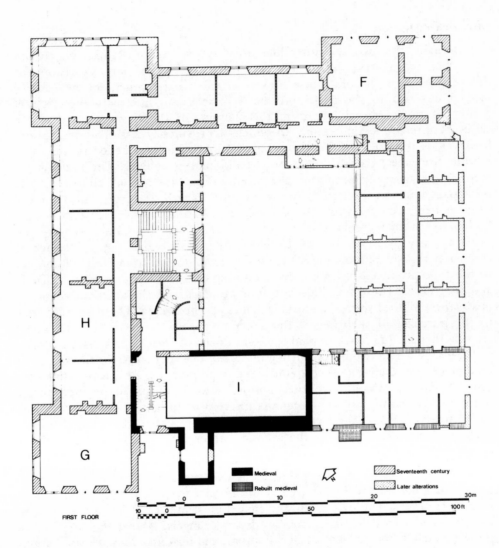

Fig. 3 Tredegar House: first floor.

in the nineteenth century was the addition of lean-to roofed passages in the courtyard to provide covered access all the way from the kitchens to the New Hall.

Interior Decoration

Externally the two seventeenth-century ranges are of Renaissance origin with their symmetry, decoration and total absence of any provision for defence. Whereas the old house looked inward to the court, the new house looked outward to the park and the fields beyond. Internally there is still a hint of the medieval layout in the planning of the New Hall and in the series of interconnecting rooms to which it provides access. The decoration, however, is typical of the seventeenth century with its panelled rooms, tiled marble fireplaces, painted overmantels and plaster ceilings. The panelling is seen at its most elaborate in the ground-floor rooms, but almost all the principal rooms on the first floor are panelled as well, the panels in a number of cases being covered with fabric. The marble fireplaces were probably bought in London from merchants who had imported them from Italy as were the contemporary examples bought by the Earl of Lauderdale for the Palace of Holyrood House, Edinburgh.[5] The tiles were imported from Holland and are of the type produced in large numbers during the seventeenth century at Delft and elsewhere.[6] These tiles illustrate four principal and characteristic themes— landscapes, biblical scenes, children's games and horsemen. There is a reference to the purchase of such tiles in the Tredegar papers, an entry of 1715 which records that £1 12s. 5d. was paid for eight dozen of Dutch tile at 4s. per dozen and package.[7] This would be sufficient to tile one, perhaps two fireplaces, or to replace tiles damaged over a considerable period. It is noticeable that even those fireplaces which have tiles almost entirely of one type incorporate 'intruders' which may be replacements inserted to fill gaps caused by damage. Unfortunately these tiles cannot be accurately dated, but the Tredegar examples certainly belong to the second, rather than to the first half of the seventeenth-century.

The subject-matter of the paintings above the fireplaces is again characteristic of a period which favoured symbolic pictures, bible stories and themes from the classics. The painting in the chapel illustrates Lot leaving Sodom with his wife and two daughters, escorted by two angels. Above the fireplace in the New Hall is 'the Judgement of Solomon', and upstairs, 'Mercury and Argus' in the Pink Room, 'Apollo pursuing Daphne' in the Passing Room, and 'Mercury and the daughters of Cecrops' in the King's Room. In the Gilt Room the original painting over the fireplace has been removed, but the panelling itself on three sides of the room has been painted, on one wall with landscapes and on the others with a series of symbolic figures representing the Cardinal Virtues (e.g., Temperance, Prudence and Justice) and the Seasons (Summer, Winter) as well as Venus and Cybele.

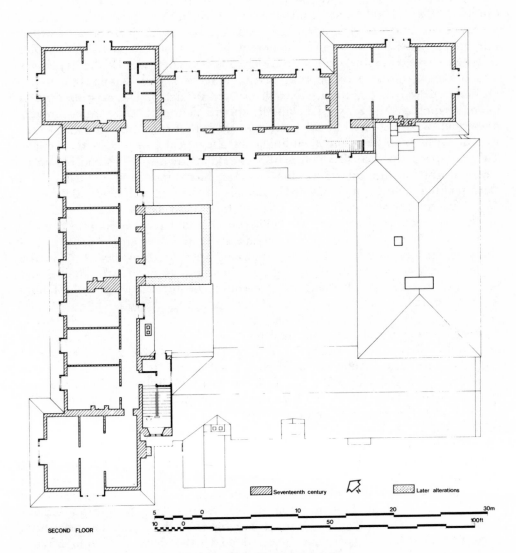

Seventeenth century   Later alterations

5   0   10   20   30m
10   0   50   100ft

SECOND FLOOR

Fig. 4 Tredegar House: the attics.

All the ceilings in the seventeenth-century range were plastered and some incorporated paintings as well. The most elaborate of the unpainted ceilings was in the New Hall; this fell in the 1950s, but fortunately was recorded by *Country Life* in 1908.[8] The ceiling area was divided into three, with a wreath of oak-leaves and cherries at the centre of the rectangular central area which was enclosed within a cornice decorated in the same manner. The smaller rectangular areas at either end were enriched with arabesques. Of the unpainted plaster ceilings still surviving that in the first-floor Pink Room is the best example, although somewhat clumsily restored in places. The existing ceilings in the chapel and the Brown Drawing Room are Victorian. The former replaces one which was decorated in the same manner as that still to be seen in the Gilt Room, with an oval frame containing an allegorical painting in the centre. This was partially recorded before it was taken down in 1848 and is said to have illustrated 'the tribute of the gods to Flora and Zephyr'.[9] There is a third painted ceiling, much restored, upstairs in the Cedar Room, which is one of the rooms forming part of the suite of three. In this instance the painting occupies the whole of the available ceiling space and depicts a group of cherubs disporting themselves with floral garlands in the heavens. Perspective is characteristically emphasised as one looks up into the blue sky through the frame of foliage bordering the painting. The room is filled with shelves and cupboards for the safe-keeping of documents or for the display of family treasures and curios.

Most, probably all, of the paintings were copied from contemporary engravings of work by notable artists. 'Lot's wife' and the 'Judgement of Solomon' are after Rubens, the first copied from an engraving by Lucas Vosterman and the second from one by Boethius a Bolswert. In the case of the Solomon it is worth noting that there are minor differences between the original and the engraving and that the Tredegar version follows (as one might expect) the engraving rather than the original. 'Mercury and Argus' in the Pink Room is based on a sculptured relief in the Town Hall at Amsterdam (now the Palace), while Prudence, Justice and Cybele are copies of sculptured figures in the same building. The Tredegar versions have all been copied from books of engravings published in Amsterdam in 1665 and 1668. The 'Venus' in the Gilt Room derives from a Prado version of Titian's 'Venus and the Organ-Player', although the figure of the organ-player has been omitted. Additional drapery has been added to the figure of Venus after it was painted, obliterating incidentally the dog at the bottom left-hand corner of the picture: its 'ghost' can, however, still be clearly seen. The painting on the ceiling in the Gilt Room (Pl. XXIX a) is copied from part of a ceiling by Pietro da Cortona in the Palazzo Barberini, Rome, and is taken from an engraving by C. Bloemaert dated 1647 (Pl. XXIXb). Even in the seventeenth century there was some doubt about the symbolism of this ceiling, but according to Tetius it represents 'Pope Urban's human wisdom, study of Philosophy and other disciplines fostered by Divine Aid, who shields the toiler and promises laurel to him who perseveres. Since Wisdom has nothing in common with Venus, Chastity attacks the luxurious and intemperate'. Octavius Morgan believed that this ceiling might have been painted by 'Isaac Fuller, an artist who painted wall and ceiling at the time and who died in 1692'.[10] There is no record of such a painter in the surviving Tredegar papers which relate, however, with only two exceptions, to painting work undertaken after 1701. The inventories list pictures, although normally without any indication as to what they portrayed or by whom they were painted. In 1688 for example, there was 'my Masters picture' in his bed-chamber, but apart from that '21 painted pictures, 60 French pictures and 1 map of America' in 'the Long Entry and in the Staircase'.

Pictures painted on the panelling, as in the Gilt Room, were the exception. Some idea of the more generally used schemes of decoration is given in a painter's account dated 12 November 1688 for painting the 'New Chamber at the head of the great stairs'[11]—presumably the room which was inventoried as 'the New Chamber' in 1688 and thereafter as 'the Passing Room'. According to this account the walls of this room were finished in 'grey noble marble' while a month later the walls of 'the empty chamber' (possibly the room next door) were painted in 'grey marble tortel shell'. In both cases the outsides of the doors were painted white. Windows, bars and casements were also painted. Confirmation that white paint was used is to be found in a note by Octavius Morgan on an account for timber, etc., dated 1766. The document is headed 'Mr Coles estimate of the Dutch Oak Floor in the Great Parlr at Tredegar' and is an account for laying the floor in the parlour (the present chapel); it includes 1,423½ ft. of wainscot at 6d. per ft., with haulage from the yard to the Tredegar sloop, at 3s., laying as per estimate £15 11s. 11d., plus a sum to be added for freight from Bristol to Newport.[12] At the bottom of the timber-merchant's account Octavius Morgan has written 'Flooring the dining parlour with oak—the room was most probably painted white according to the fashion of the time—the same white paint remained white without ever being renewed till the year 1856—and was then in as sound and perfect state as when done'.

Furnishings

The Tredegar inventories, which survive for the period 1688–1698, list the contents of the house room by room (including the stable and outhouses) in great detail. They show that the Gilt Room was empty in 1688 except for red curtains, but by 1689 there were in addition a green, silver-embroidered couch with twelve embroidered chairs to match. By 1698 the room was fully furnished, containing:

1 table and 2 stands covered with leather.
1 large looking glass.
1 'scritore', with gilt frame covered with leather.

2 large chairs.

1 tea table with 2 small stands all of Japan work.

6 elbow chairs.

1 squab and bolster cased with blue damask and gold tissue and covered with coloured linen.

2 blue damask cushions striped with gold ribbon.

2 low stools.

1 paper screen.

1 Dutch mat.

2 gilded sconces.

10 window curtains of striped muslin with knotted fringes and valences of the same.

The hearth was equipped with shovel and tongs, steel 'chimney hooks' with gilded tops, hearth brush and iron fireback.

In 1698 the furnishings of the bedchambers upstairs were equally elaborate. In the 'Best Chamber' were:

1 standing bedstead with feather bed and bolster, 2 large pillows, 2 lesser pillows, 3 blankets, 1 calico quilt, 4 green silk damask curtains flowered with gold and lined with white chequer silk with double valence, tester and quilt embroidered with silk fringes.

1 large Turkey carpet.

1 table and 2 stands.

1 large looking-glass with gilt frame.

1 dressing glass.

1 cabinet.

1 Indian screen.

6 elbow cane chairs.

1 large easy silk chair.

7 silk cushions the same as the bed.

2 large orange-coloured dust curtains, the covers of the chairs of the same.

4 window curtains of white damask trimmed with knotted fringes.

2 Dutch chairs.

1 Japan bowl.

3 white images.

2 white glass bottles.

2 china basins.

2 white glass tea-cups.

4 chocolate cups.

1 jar.

1 cedar close-stool box with white earthen pan.

Firebasket with brass shovel and tongs, iron back, pair of bellows with brass tops and handles, hearth brush.

The Date of the Seventeenth-century Buildings

Tredegar House with its Renaissance façades and rich interior decorations could be dated to quite a wide span of years in the seventeenth century. In practice, however, it is possible to be more precise, although, only two documents survive which could relate to the period of construction. The first is what may be a mason's account headed 'A memorandum for what the new windows and doors came to for the new building at Tredegar (1664–1674)'[13] and reads:

'For the windows with the frontispiece and ornaments £5 a window.
Windows without the frontispiece £4.
The cornice that goes between the windows, with the ornaments, 1s a foot.
The quoin stones 1/- a quoin foot.
The great door with all the ornaments £55.
The gate-piers with the two statues and ornaments in stone about £47 (Query—stables?).'

This is an unsatisfactory document for a number of reasons. In the first place it only survives as a transcript in the handwriting of Octavius Morgan in a collection of transcripts entitled 'Sundry curious notes extracted from various old pocket books and memorandum books' so it is impossible to check the original document—presumably the dates in brackets (possibly the entire heading) and the query about the stable were added by Octavius Morgan himself. The document he copied was apparently undated and gives no overall sum for the amount of money involved—indeed no statement that the account is actually for making the items listed. Nonetheless, the sums quoted seem about right, the language appropriate and the detail precisely related to the building so it seems likely that this is a document—more probably part of a document—contemporary with the building of the house. If so it is a unique survival, but there are other such unique survivals, e.g., the bread account for 1677 (no other seventeenth-century housekeeping accounts survive) which may have been preserved because it is endorsed by Elizabeth Dayrell, Sir William Morgan's second wife.[14]

The second document which may relate to the period of construction is a drawing of a door, without caption or date, which has been superinscribed by Octavius Morgan 'Design for one of the large doors in the oak drawing room at Tredegar. 18 century'.[15] This drawing is the product of two quite different techniques—the outlines have been carefully ruled in while the decoration appears to have been added by some mechanical process involving perhaps the super-imposition of a suitably prepared sheet of tracing paper. Since the drawing does not show the door as it actually is it could only be a preliminary design which was modified before the door came to be made. This drawing again may have survived by chance—not because of the interest of the drawing as such but because, written on the back, are the words 'Lord have mercy on me an in cline my hart to kep his law'.

Unfortunately these two documents, even if related to the period of construction, give no help with the dating of the house. The earliest document that does (albeit indirectly) is the inventory of 1674 (now lost) referred to in the *Country Life* account which is said to contain internal evidence that the house concerned was the one that exists today: if so the house must have been there by 1674. The building itself provides further evidence. The painted sun-dial in the Cedar Room, for example, is dated 1672, and the boards forming part of a door now lying in the cellar are inscribed 'Roger Lewis Butler 1674'. Note that Octavius Morgan's transcript of an inventory of silver-plate at Tredegar dated 1676 includes the heading 'In the buttery under the charge of Roger Lewis Butler'.[16] Less precise evidence is provided by the monogram WM concealed within a wreath intricately carved on the overmantel in the Gilt Room. This could refer to the Sir William Morgan who died in 1553 or to his grandson of the same name who owned the house from 1664–1680. The latter is inherently more likely and this may be supported by heraldic evidence, since the arms over the front door are believed to relate to the second Sir William who married Blanche Morgan of Therrew in 1661.[17] Blanche was the daughter of William Morgan of Therrew (known as Judge Morgan) who was the King's Attorney for South Wales and a wealthy man in his own right. Since Blanche inherited his estate her dowry may well have helped to finance the building of the new house. The fact that some of the paintings and the tiles date to the second half of the seventeenth century rather than the first is also significant—indeed, some at least of the pictures could not have been painted before 1668.

Such evidence as there is, therefore, suggests that the house was in existence by 1672 and unlikely to have been begun before 1664 at the earliest. The carved panelling in the Brown Drawing Room appears, however, to be at least a generation later. The elaborate, carved coat of arms over the fireplace in that room, with its twenty-four quarters, displays in the final quarter the arms of Vaughan of Trebarried. These arms are repeated, fully tinctured, in the painted glass windows in the chapel and would not be appropriate to any Morgan of Tredegar before the Sir William Morgan who inherited in 1719.

The Designer of the Buildings

No reference to the builder of the house has as yet been found amongst the Tredegar papers, so that it is impossible to name the man responsible for designing the building. The seventeenth century was in fact a period when the division between designer and builder was still indistinct and, with some exceptions, houses are often attributed to designer-craftsmen who both designed and built them, rather than to architects who designed them for other people to build. It is likely that Tredegar was such a house. The general design is not original. It was introduced to France at Ançy-le-Franc by the Italian architect, Serlio, in *c.* 1546: it was reproduced in brick with stone details at Rosny for the French statesman, Sully, *c.* 1599: it was used by

Roger Pratt at Clarendon House, Piccadilly, *c.* 1664 (Pl. XXXIb).[18] In each case there is the symmetrical layout, the emphasis on the central entrance, the projecting corner pavilions and the two storeys of almost equal height. The similarity between Tredegar and Clarendon House was originally even closer than it is now since early illustration show that at Tredegar, too, there was a lantern or cupola crowning the principal facade. This can be confirmed from the documents; in 1715, for example, there was a payment for twenty-two deal boards for the cupola and in 1725 the cupola was painted.[19] It was still in position in 1792 when there were payments for '3 days for Jacob at the cupola' and for '5 days for finishing plumbing the cupola and painting'[20] but it was removed fairly soon thereafter since it is now shown in Barber's engraving of 1826.[21]

The general style of building adopted at Tredegar was, therefore, not new—it is representative of a number of houses of which the earliest in Britain date to the period just before the Civil War. It is likely to have been the work of a member of the designer-craftsman school (dubbed 'Artisan Mannerism' by Sir John Summerson)[22] rather than one of the pupils of Inigo Jones—the brick build, the ornate external decoration, the use of the broken pediment are all characteristic of the school, although the stone mullions are a conservative feature which one would not expect to see so late in the seventeenth century,[23] while the 'barley-sugar' columns on either side of the entrance are as far as is known without domestic parallel in Britain (Pl. XXX b). Simpler versions of these columns were used to support Archbishop Laud's notorious porch at St. Mary's, Oxford (1635), and also appear inside Tredegar in the Gilt and Cedar Rooms.

The use of brick in Wales is rare since stone is normally readily available. The source of the brick used at Tredegar House has not been established, but it is on record that bricks were being produced on the estate early in the eighteenth century. There was a payment in 1703 'towards making bricks at the Rock' and another in 1722 'for making the clamp of bricks at the Rock'.[24] 'The Rock' is presumably the site marked as such just north of the Eboth bridge on a survey of the demesne of *c.* 1770.[25] There were also payments in 1703 'for raising 103 dozen coals to Tredegar brick-kiln' and another dated 1726 for 18 dozen 6 sacks 'to the brick kiln'. John Gilbert, the bricklayer, was paid £3 15s. 'in full of his bill' in 1723, and a further £5 17s. in 1725.[26]

The Iron Gates

The only features at Tredegar that can be precisely dated and firmly attributed are the wrought-iron gates of which the finest examples are currently under repair, but which were recorded by *Country Life*. There are also two side-gates and fences enclosing the sides of the forecourt in front of the main entrance (Pl. XXX c) and a larger but plainer gate somewhat concealed by growth at the north end of the north garden. At one time this was the access from garden to stable yard, although now blocked by a line of later buildings.

Octavius Morgan attributed the gates to the John Morgan who inherited Tredegar in 1700 and died in 1719. His arms, quartered with those of his wife Martha of Trebarried, were in fact to be seen on the head of the great gate.[27] Octavius adds that 'in the heads of the gates going into the garden and towards the shrubbery are, or were, the interlaced cyphers JMM for John and Martha Morgan'. These cyphers are not now to be seen.

Payments for the erection of gates at Tredegar are recorded in James Pratt's accounts on two occasions, the first in 1713/15 and the second in 1717/18.[28] The earlier series of entries reads:

		£	s.	d.
Aug. 14	Paid Mr Edney in part for the iron gates and palisades	100	00	00
	Paid Mr Adlington for lead towards the iron gates ..	6	05	00
	Paid Phil. Jones the stone carver 7 weeks @ 10/- ..	3	10	00
Nov. 20	Paid Mr Adlington in full for lead to the palisades etc.	5	13	00
Dec. 8	Paid Mr. Edney more in part for Ironwork	30	0	00
1714 Jan. 15	Paid Mr Edney (with £130 before) in full for the iron gates and palisades	420	00	00

The total amount paid to Mr Edney for this work was therefore £550.

The second series of entries follows in 1718:

		£	s.	d.
1718 Apr. 17	Paid Mr Townsend for stone and workmanship to the iron gates	9	06	00
18	Paid Simon Edney for 6 pair of candlesticks and carriage	1	16	00
	Paid ditto for 25,050 Li of iron gates and palisades to the Green Court at 5d	104	07 [sic]	06
1719 Feb. 3	Paid Mr Adlington for plumber in full		12	06
June 19	Paid Mr How for painting the iron gates & other work	10	11	00

The curious thing about this second series of accounts is the fact that while the gates were stated to have been paid at 5d. a pound—normal rate for good quality work of the period—they were entered in the cash columns at 1d. a pound. Mr. Edney thus apparently only received £104 7s. 6d. instead of the

£552 which was his due. Presumably this error was subsequently corrected, although no such correction has been identified in the accounts. Assuming the higher figure to be nonetheless correct the total cost of the second series of entries amounted to only £28 less than the first.

The fact that Simon Edney is specifically mentioned on the second occasion possibly implies that the smith employed on the first was his better-known brother William, who was made a burgess of Bristol in 1706 and paid £110 for the chancel gates in St. Mary's Church, Bristol, in 1710. No other work can be attributed to the Edneys on documentary evidence, apart, now, from the gates of Tredegar, but a number of examples of wrought-iron work at Bristol and elsewhere have been tentatively identified as theirs on stylistic grounds.[29]

The location of the gates referred to in the 1715/16 accounts is not specified but it is assumed that the references relate to the great gate and associated fences illustrated in *Country Life*. The 'green court' referred to in the second account recalls 'the bowling-green court' marked on the plan of the old house. However, the drawing of Tredegar on the *c.* 1770 survey, which bears every indication of being authentic, shows this outer court (i.e., the area in front of the existing stable) as enclosed within a wall and not a wrought-iron fence.[30] The references, therefore, presumably relate to the existing side-gates and fences.

The Stables

The stable building is modelled on the house—i.e., brick-built with projecting pavilions at either end of the principal façade, central entrance architecturally stressed and dormer windows matching those of the house itself (Pl. XXX c). On the other hand there are significant differences between the two buildings—the bricks are different, the bond is different, the unusual flat brick pilasters terminating in cupped acorns are without parallel at the house as is the series of oval windows. In addition the central archway surmounted by a bust flanked by suits of Gothic armour and cannon is perhaps somewhat more sophisticated than the doorway of the seventeenth-century house (Pl. XXX a). All this suggests that the stables were built after the house and possibly not until the eighteenth century.

Octavius Morgan believed that the stables were added in the time of the John Morgan who was responsible for the gates, and that the orangery and second small stable were added at the back by his successor, Sir William (1719-31). This is a reasonable assumption, but the records for this period, which appear relatively complete, do not account fully for a major building project such as the building of the great stable, even though there are references to a 'new' stable in 1726-27. The situation is further complicated by the fact that there were stables at Tredegar even before the seventeenth-century house was built and it is impossible to deduce from the documents prior to 1726 whether particular references relate to the old stable or the new.

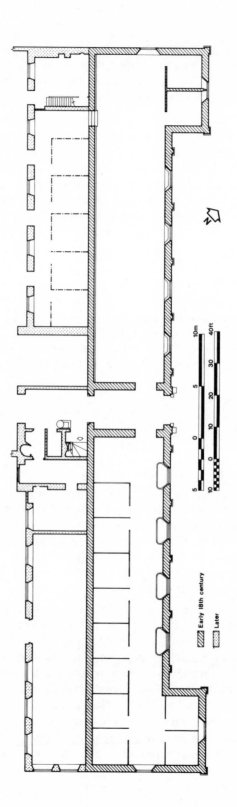

Fig. 5 Tredegar House: the stables

The old stable was sited at the back of the house and shown on the plan as a long rectangular block divided into two longitudinally with access to either half at each end. The surviving inventories refer to the stables in the same terms in every case—they all list two beds, one in the stable and the other in the stable chamber. This suggests that there was no significant change between 1688–1698.

A number of other documents refer to the stable or stable yard. In 1686 the painter was paid 'for cleaning, stopping and colouring the two pairs of bowls, cornices and bassos of the two pair of gates in the stable court'.[31] Possibly this is a reference to the '3 pair of iron gates' which were cleaned and coloured the year before.[32] Thereafter there are a number of brief references, e.g.:

1688: for painting and gilding 'the Harledg Diall' and figure over the stable.
1702: for tiling the stable court.
1710: for casting and exchanging the stable clock bell.
1715: for pitching 111 yards in the stable.
1724: for tiling Tredegar in house and stable.
1726: for mending the stable clock.

It is only in July 1726 and February 1727 that there are specific references to a 'new' stable, e.g., in October 1726 Mr. Adlington was paid £23 14s. 'for lead to the new stable', and in the following February Mr Tyndall was paid £41 10s. 'for stones and workmanship to the new stable'. There are other items at about the same time which could refer to the same operation, such as the payment for 55,000 bricks in September 1727, but the entries do not specify the use to which they were put. They could refer to the addition of stable and orangery at the back of the main stable as suggested by Octavius Morgan.[33] According to Octavius the great clock at the stable was put up in 1776. 'The earlier clock was said to have struck the quarters by boys like the old clock at St. Dunstans now at . . . villa in the Regent's Park'.[34]

Within the stables the left (south-east) half contained the stalls while the right (north-west) half was until recently a riding stable. There are no references to a coach-house in the accounts although there were certainly coaches at Tredegar. The codicil to Sir William Morgan's will dated 1679 includes the following bequest: 'I give unto my said wife [Dame Elizabeth Dayrel] the best of all my coaches as she shall choose, and six of my best coach horses and all those three nags and one more that are known by the name of her horses'. In 1686 there was a payment for 'gilding the four crests on the new coach',[35] in 1721 for a new chaise and other work, and later in the same year 'to Mr Dobson the coach painter in full of his work'.[36]

The earliest surviving inventory of horses is dated 1787. At that date there were at Tredegar eight black coach horses and a black coach colt, together with ponies for the small phaeton and twelve saddle horses, of which one belonged to the butler and another to the housekeeper. There was also a mule.[37]

ACKNOWLEDGEMENTS

The photograph reproduced at Plate XXIXb was provided by the Warburg Institute and is an engraving by C. Bloemaert after P. da Cortona, from G. Tetius, *Aedes Barberinae* (1647). Plate XXXIa is reproduced by courtesy of the London Library. The remaining photographs were taken by the staff of the Royal Commission on Ancient and Historic Monuments in Wales. Commission on Ancient and Historic Monuments in Wales and are reproduced by permission of the Comptroller of H.M.S.O.

The line drawings have been prepared by Mr. P. Humphries from the plan of Old Tredegar in the National Library for Wales, and from surveys provided by Messrs. E. R. Bates, Son and Price (the house) and the School of Architecture, U.W.I.S.T. (the stables).

The house was visited and recorded by kind permission of the Reverend Mother Superior of St. Joseph's Convent and of the Headmaster of St. Joseph's High School.

REFERENCES

1. O.S. 1 in. map sheet 155, ref. ST 288852. The house and park now belong to Newport Borough Council.

2. Preserved in the Tredegar Collection (TC 1079) in the National Library of Wales with the remainder of the Tredegar records. One hundred and forty-three boxes of documents are listed with brief details in the index volumes, and two further collections are summarised in the National Library of Wales Annual Reports (N.L.W.A.R.) for 1958–59 and 1961–62.

3. TC 1496. This is a bound volume containing inventories of the contents of the house for the period 1688–1698.

4. David Williams, *History of Monmouthshire* (1796).

5. R. Scott Mylne, *The Master Masons to the Crown of Scotland and their Works* (Edinburgh, 1893). Lord Lauderdale wrote about 'marble chimneys' in 1671: 'I came upon them by chance in an Italian merchant's hand.' (p. 167.) In 1675 there is payment in the Holyrood accounts 'for nine marble chimney pieces bought at London' and later the same year for 'seven chests of wrought marble chimneys imported from London'. The carving above one fireplace was the work of a Dutchman called Jan Vansantvoort.

6. C. H. de Jonge (trans. Falla), *Dutch Tiles* (1971).

7. TC 315–345. These are the steward's accounts of receipts and expenditure at Tredegar from 1700–1732.

8. Anon, 'Country Homes: Tredegar Park, Monmouthshire', *Country Life* (1908), pp. 792–801 and 838–845. This is a well-illustrated account of the house (interior and exterior) as it was in its heyday.

9. N.L.W.A.R., 1961–62, p. 57. 'Drawing of one quarter of the original ceiling in the oak dining room at Tredegar taken down in 1848'. This sketch outlines the plaster decoration but gives no more than the title of the allegorical painting. With the exception of this sketch I am indebted to the staff of the Warburg Institute for identifying the Tredegar paintings and their provenance. For the Amsterdam sculptures, see H. Quellinus, *Prima Pars Praecipuarum Efficierum* (Amsterdam, 1665) and *Secunda Pars* ditto (Amsterdam, 1668). See also K. Fremantle, *The Baroque Hall of Amsterdam* (1959). For the Palazzo Barberini see G. Tetius, *Aedes Barberinae* (Rome, 1647) and for a fuller account Rosichino, *Dichiartatione della pitture della sala de signori Barberinae* (Rome, 1640).

10. TC 1304.

11. TC 102/98.

12. TC 69/89.

13. TC 1303.

14. TC 102/111.

15. TC 69/94.

16. TC 1283.

17. The heraldic evidence at Tredegar requires further study and could be conclusive. The shield over the front entrance tentatively identified as that of Sir William Morgan, Second has sixteen quarterings which are repeated with a further eight quarterings in the elaborately carved shield over the fireplace in the Brown Drawing Room and in the painted window in the chapel. The majority of the latter appear on the memorial to Sir Charles Morgan in Bassaleg church and are identified in a drawing TC 105/239. There is also a useful note on the heraldic seal of John Morgan of Tredegar (1700–1719) in TC 105/115.

18. Anthony Blunt, *Art and Architecture in France 1599–1700*, second impression (1957), pp. 38–44, Pls. 28A and 78A and John Summerson, *Architecture in Britain 1530–1830*, fifth edn. (1969), pp. 89–98, both in the Pelican *History of Art* series.

19. TC 315–345.

20. TC 68/76.

21. Engraving by T. Barber after J. P. Neale in N.L.W.

22. Summerson, *op. cit.*

23. But see D.O.E. official guide, A. J. Taylor, *Monmouth Castle and Great Castle House* where the latter, which also has stone mullions, is dated 1673.

24. TC 315–345.

25. N.L.W.A.R., 1961–62, p. 57. Plan of Tredegar Park by Robert Snell, *c.* 1770.

26. TC 315–345.

27. TC 1303 and 1304.

28. TC 315–345.

29. See Ifor Edwards, 'William Edney, Gatesmith of Bristol', *Country Life*, 21 Sept. 1961.

30. N.L.W.A.R., 1961–62. Robert Snell's plan.

31. TC 102/97.

32. *Ibid.*

33. TC 1304.

34. N.L.W.A.R., 1958–59, p. 65. Typescript account of history of gardens at Tredegar to end of eighteenth century.

35. 102/97.

36. TC 315–345.

37. TC 68/65. For further information about everyday life at Tredegar see M. R. Apted, 'Social Conditions at Tredegar House, Newport, in the 17th and 18th centuries', *Monmouthshire Antiquary*, 111, Pt. 11, pp. 124–154.

Stott Park Bobbin Mill, Colton, Cumbria:
an historical outline, 1835-1971

by

P. R. WHITE

WHEN STOTT PARK BOBBIN MILL ceased production in October 1971 it was the end of an era, if not of an industry. The mill was the last complete example of its type to survive. It was driven out of business when its few remaining clients adopted bobbins made from synthetic materials; the limited demand which still exists for the wooden products continues to be met by one largely re-equipped mill at Staveley, near Kendal, a village which was once the centre of the industry.

Wood-turning, with bobbins and later reels, spools, and handles as the staple product, thrived in Furness and south Westmorland for about a century and a half, the first recorded mill being in Staveley in 1797.[1] During the 1830s a rapid expansion took place stimulated by the growth of the Lancashire textile trade, which of course the bobbin mills served, though with lesser dependence after the 1870s. It was not uncommon for a textile mill to need up to ten million bobbins to carry the yarn (Stockport 1843), and more besides. Clearly, therefore, at a time of expansion in textiles, trade would be brisk if not overwhelming for the bobbin makers, whereas a period of mild recession in the textile mills would be felt in much greater proportions by the bobbin men.[2]

The organisation of the Lakeland bobbin industry, identified either as a specialised branch, or as general wood-turning, seems to have differed from other areas where such work was carried on. All the textile areas needed bobbin manufacturers to service them, and generally the two trades operated side by side. So, in the West Riding the bobbins were made in shops close by the textile mills, if not actually in 'bobbin departments' of the same building.[3] The same applied to Northern Ireland around Belfast, and to Scotland, in Dundee, Paisley and Glasgow.[4] By contrast, in Lakeland the industry was quite identifiable in its own right and physically was many miles from its nearest major customers in South Lancashire. As a rural industry, however, it does not compare for example, with the wood-turning trade of the Chilterns, which was carried on predominantly for the manufacture of furniture. In that area perhaps with a kinder climate, the operatives worked singly in temporary shelters and wandered about the coppice woods using their own muscles to power their crude lathes.[5]

The Lakeland industry was organised quite formally, in mills, some purpose-built, many converted, and most using water power to drive thirty or more lathes, which were operated by a sufficient number of skilled men. Their siting was significant in two respects: there was a ready availability of water for power; many were surrounded by well-wooded slopes which had been coppiced for generations to provide the charcoal fuel for the local iron trade and which now provided the mills with their raw material. It was, of course, much easier to transport the finished product than poles of ash, alder, or birch to some distant spot, where their quality might have been found unsuitable for turning.

The mill at Stott Park was built specifically for bobbin-turning during the course of 1835, at a time when the trade was beginning to dominate the economy of the area. Indeed, it was built by an ironmaster, John Harrison, presumably to benefit from the shift in trade. It was put up for lease in December 1835, and again in February 1836, to 'be entered at May Day next'. An advertisement in the local press described it thus: 'This mill has been recently erected and is eligibly situated in Finsthwaite in the parish of Colton, Lancs., possessing sufficient convenience and power for thirty lathes [the earlier advertisement says twenty-four lathes; the increase may have been to make the mill appear a more attractive proposition] exclusive of all other appendages, together with a roomy and convenient dwelling house and an extensive garden and (if required by the taker) two or three cottages will be erected and be ready to be entered upon at the same time. (Fig. 1).[6]

It is likely that no takers were found by the first advertisement, but the place was certainly occupied by the time of the 1841 census,[7] and at least two of the cottages subsequently appeared. The mill was a two-storey structure built of the local rubble, with a lathe shop 40 ft. by 27 ft. Within an extension at the northern end was a water wheel (Fig. 2), probably high breast shot, and of about 32 ft. in diameter, supplied by a substantial pond immediately to the west. The stair for access to the first floor was housed in an extension to the south. Since maximum use had to be made of natural light, considerable attention was paid to the orientation of the building, which is on an axis north-west/south-east.[8] The lathe shop was then lit, characteristically, with a regular row of windows on each side (Fig. 4). The lathes themselves were located immediately against the cills, with the operatives facing outwards. These early machines were mounted on wooden beds, some of which survive (Fig. 4), fixed to the walls of the building. They were driven by belting from a line shaft in the roof ridge. The lower floor would probably have been used for blocking and cutting the timber, and for paint vats and grindstones (Fig. 3).[9]

The mill built by Harrison compares with another put up for lease by a neighbouring landed family, erected a few months later at Force Forge. It, too, had two floors, but was slightly larger, with dimensions of 64 ft. by

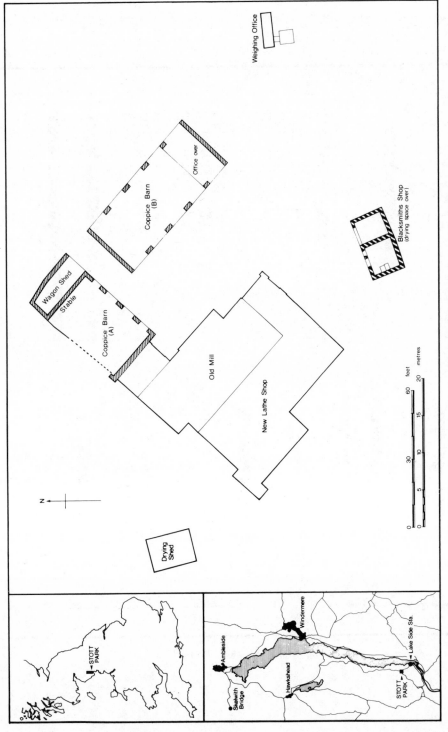

Fig. 1 Location map and general plan of Stott Park Bobbin Mill.

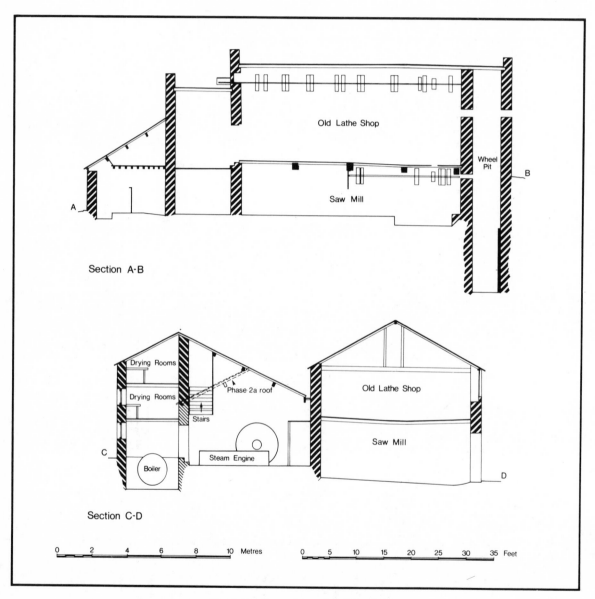

Fig. 2 Sections through mill buildings.

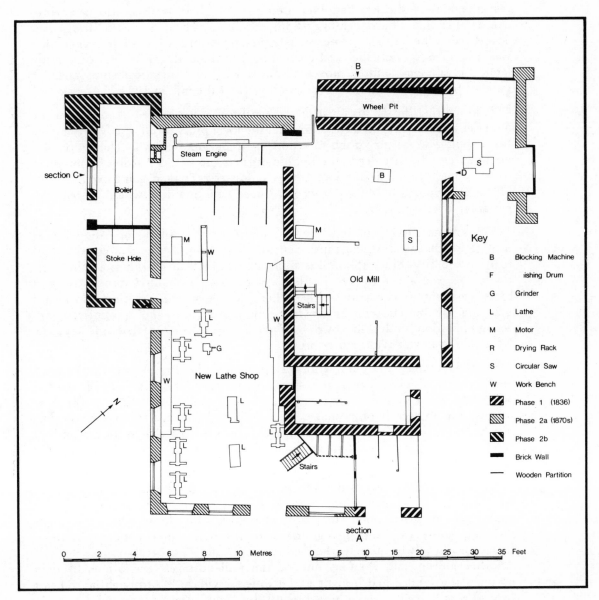

Fig. 3 Ground plan.

30 ft. on plan.[10] Many mills, however, were not purpose built. An advertisement describes a mill at Sedbergh, formerly a woollen mill, to be let as a corn mill (with stones extant) and for bobbin turning.[11] Another mill, with considerable significance for the later history of Stott Park also came into use at this time. In December 1836, a bobbin mill at Skelwith Bridge was advertised to be let. The owner was Jeremiah Coward, who, a few years earlier was described as 'victualler and corn miller' in a local directory.[12] A generation later, his son and widow moved to Stott Park and in partnership started a family business which ceased with the closure of the mill in 1971.[13]

Trade during the 1830s must have been prosperous indeed. Apart from the increasing number of premises available, the local press is full of advertisements for coppice wood or 'bobbin' wood as it became known. There are also numbers of advertisements for bobbin turners, and it is possible from them to get some idea of production. One is addressed: 'To men doing over 15 gross of 1¾ in. spinning bobbins per week'. Those who qualified would be paid 2d. per gross 'over Union price'.[14]

No records survive to indicate the intensity of activity, or otherwise, at Stott Park during the nineteenth century, but a number of sources do point to its prosperity. Since the mill is somewhat isolated from others in the same trade, the census returns are particularly valuable, as bobbin turners living at Stott Park almost certainly worked there. Moreover, its isolation also meant that the bobbin master was providing his journeymen and apprentices with accommodation under his own roof to a greater extent than in, say, the Kendal, Staveley or Windermere areas.

In 1841, James Bethom, who was probably the first lessee of the mill, employed four journeymen and six apprentices.[15] The first lease had been advertised for a period of seven or nine years,[16] and by the time of the next census, the master bobbin maker was William Wharton. He was employing eleven men, including two apprentices, and half a dozen boys, and at thirty-four was a year younger than his predecessor when visited by the enumerator.[17]

By 1871 William Coward, only aged twenty-eight himself, employed six apprentices, the youngest of whom was aged thirteen, and nine men. The apprentices all lived under his roof, at Bobbin Mill House (the 'convenient dwelling house of 1836'?) together with his wife, three children, mother, sister, brother (who also worked in the mill) and one of his journeymen![18] Another journeyman lived at one of the mill cottages, and others lived in cottages the family had bought at Finsthwaite village.[19] Although he did not own the mill itself, which was bought for four thousand pounds in 1921 by his son John,[20] it can be appreciated that he was the provider for a considerable community, which enjoyed some stability during relatively bad times from the investment and expansion at the mill premises. It is also interesting to note that the names which appear among his apprentices at

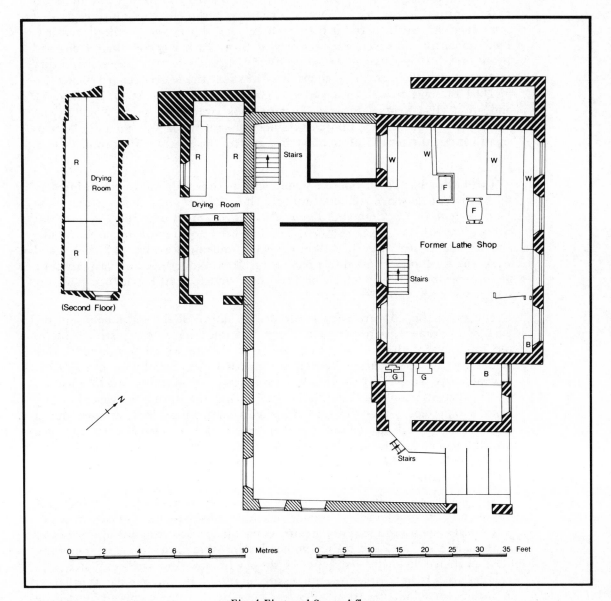

Fig. 4 First and Second floors.

this time appear again on the firm's books well into the twenties and thirties of the present century.

Bobbin turning does not seem to have led to longevity to judge by the Stott Park returns for the mid-nineteenth century, although it is quite clear that some men did work there for fifty or more years during the twentieth century. Predominantly, however, the workers at Stott Park were in their teens and twenties, with only two recorded up to 1871 in their forties. One contributory factor must have been the regularity with which the lease changed hands, for in 1861 the master was Thomas Eyers (who was not at home on census day), and about five years later the Cowards took over, with some workers who were little more than children, staying on to work for them.[21] Perhaps significantly, the period of stability began after the death of Harrison's widow, in 1867.

The health hazard in bobbin manufacturing must also have contributed to the apparent absence of continuity. The *'Report of Commissioners on Employment of Children and Young Persons in Trades and Manufactures not already regulated by Law'* (1863–7) examined the position of the bobbin trade, and its investigator, Mr. J. E. White, visited mills in the area, at Staveley and Windermere, though not, unhappily, Stott Park. Nonetheless, a very accurate picture of the conditions can be had, since much of the evidence is in the operatives' own words.[22]

The causes for concern were twofold: the nature of the machinery and the dust. With respect to the former, complaint must have been justified, for to the last days of the industry machines were in use which possessed neither guides for the pieces being worked nor guards to protect the operatives from moving parts (Pl. XXXII b). It is not surprising to read, therefore, 'My hand is tied up because the bobbin split in a knot and the boring bit went into my hand' (John Black, aged thirteen, Chadwick's Mill, Staveley); or 'one time I bored right through my elbow. Another time I split through the part between my thumb and hand; . . . [I was] about 10 . . . Never saw any one break a limb' (William Philipson, aged seventeen, Chadwick's Mill, Staveley). The investigator added 'Has a slight cough'.

The cough was indicative of the more insidious hazard, dust. A number of the operatives complained of coughs or chest pains and one who gave evidence was clearly consumptive. Poor health from this cause created a much greater impression on White, and his recommendations were clear: '. . . it is, therefore, of importance that the work places should be airy and well-ventilated . . . The nature of the work does not easily admit of it. But regular ventilation or means for admitting fresh air or carrying off the dust seems to meet little attention . . . appliances, such as fans, etc. . . . would be beneficial, ie if they could be adapted . . . but they do not appear to have been tried in this trade'.

The bobbin mills worked a long day, and sometimes into the night because of difficulties with the water supply, upon which most of them were dependent. White recorded that some mills worked for sixteen hours, which was considerably longer than the controlled textile mills.

The report found nothing scandalous or even unusual; it is a source of much useful information. Among other things, it gives a general description of the processes which the boys carried out. The early process was just changing at the time of the Commissioners' survey, and bobbins of composite form, with the ends glued on to the shank and then machined, were being replaced by those lathe-turned from one piece.[23] 'Some [boys] put on glue with a brush; others put in small pieces of wood, called "bushes" with a hammer, sort bobbins, carry away the pieces sawn . . . at the circular saws, &c. The first machine work done by them is boring (the hole through the centre of the bobbin), "rincing" [pronounced "rining"], or cleaning out the mouths of the holes bored, and "roughing" a kind of rough turning, all done at lathes worked by power'. The rough bobbins were then finished on lathes operated by the skilled men, and sometimes polished by rotating in a drum with a lump of beeswax.

This description of the process holds good for the duration of the industry's life, with one notable omission. After the coppice wood had been cut into cylinders, or 'blocked', it was seasoned in a kiln, or drying room. The fetching and carrying would undoubtedly have been boys' work. More importantly, at Stott Park, an increasing amount of space was given over to the drying process. Initially, the only provision could well have been the loft of the small smithy, which still stands a little apart from the main building, to cut down the risk of fire, a hazard which claimed many of the mills. Certainly it was provided with a 'fireproof' floor of cast iron joists and perforated iron plating. It is possible that drying was also done in the outshut at the south end of the lathe shop (Fig. 1).

The production of one-piece bobbins was made possible by improvements in machinery, and the Coward family, soon after their arrival at Stott Park must have set in train a series of improvements which transformed the mill into the complex which survives today. They leased the mill after 1867 from the trustees of Thomas Newby Wilson, Harrison's grandson. Before their arrival in 1858, a water turbine had been supplied by Williamson's of Kendal, presumably to supersede the waterwheel as power source.[24] The new turning and boring machines which were becoming available were also made locally, in the foundries of W. A. Fell, a family concerned in the trade for many years, who turned to machinery manufacture in 1859 at Troutbeck Bridge, Windermere, and at the works of the inventive Henry Braithwaite, at Crook.[25]

The machines were not only important because they simplified, and to some extent automated, the process of bobbin turning, but also because of the effect they had on the design of the mill buildings where they were installed. They were obviously heavier, partly because more complex, but largely because they were constructed almost entirely of cast iron, and were free standing. Unlike the old machines, with the iron parts bolted to fixed wooden beds (q.v.), the new machines needed a good strong floor, and the first floor lathe shop, with its timber floor was quite unsuitable.

At Stott Park the solution was to build a new lathe shop (Figs. 1 and 2) immediately adjacent to the existing mill, to the west. This is a single-storey building, and the lathes stand on the ground. Unlike its predecessor, however, it is rather dark, sandwiched between the dam for the pond to the west, and against the old, two-storey mill to the east. And, of course, its location only permitted of one row of windows, although almost certainly it would have had rooflights from the outset (Pl. XXXII a).[26]

The reason why it was not built on the other side of the old mill, where the ground was originally more open, was probably because the area was already occupied by at least one of the two coppice barns which had been built, giving a courtyard effect (Fig. 1). They were certainly not part of the original scheme, but they were erected before the turn of the century.[27] Of traditional design in the area, the barns simply comprise a roof supported on square rubble-built pillars, and were used to store and season the timber before use. Both are of the later pattern, earlier examples in the area having round, tapering pillars.[28]

The upshot of the Child Employment Commission had been the complementary Factory and Workshops' Regulation Acts of 1867, and these applied to the bobbin mills' activities. About a dozen mills closed over the next few years,[29] partly as a result of this restriction on child labour. An article in the *Saturday Review* in 1869 drew attention to the high wages in the north, and compared rural Lancashire and Cumberland with Devonshire, where workers were paid at only half the rate.[30] Stott Park seems rarely to have employed lads below the age of twelve, however. There were other causes of failure. The general depression, which set in from 1873, and lasted to the last years of the century, particularly affected profits. Furthermore, the bobbin trade had inevitably fluctuated for years with the American cotton harvest, the effects transmitted through Manchester. In the 'seventies, it further faced a shortage of its raw material in the coppices, and had to import from Scandinavia.[31] Before long it was facing competition from finished products originating from areas across the North Sea, which also possessed an abundance of timber and water power, and also the use by some textile mills of cheaper, paper cops.

Naturally every mill that went under gave more chance to those that could survive. From the only extant records of a mill at this period we can see that survival was ensured in at least two ways: by keeping regular customers satisfied, and by diversification.[32] The presence of a convenient railway station should not be underestimated either (Fig. 1). Until the 1960s sacks of bobbins and handles were regularly consigned by this form of transport.[33]

The extent of the diversification achieved by the Stott Park enterprise is manifest in the records of the business which survive from about 1908 onwards. Considerable quantities of bobbins and reels were still produced for firms in the midlands and north-west, though virtually none in Yorkshire, and clearly there were mills in places like Macclesfield and Stockport who were customers of the old type. However the firm was by now producing many gross of handles, for files and other small tools, and for shovels and picks. This production had led to links with toolmakers in Sheffield, and regular orders from them, though significantly not from the local Lakeland spade forges. Many ironmongers were also supplied, particularly in London, and pick handles were, from time to time, shipped to India. During the First World War, the Admiralty was a regular customer, both for tool handles and for toggles; a number of the major railway companies, the London General Omnibus Co., and the L.C.C. tram department were regularly supplied with pickaxe handles.[34]

No doubt all this trade was the product of assiduous promotion in trade journals and by able representatives suitably placed on the ground. It was not regular trade, however, and stock books which survive show that items were made to order rather than sold from stock, which would have needed considerable organisation in view of the infinite variety of shapes and sizes of bobbin, reel, handle or washer which could be produced.[35] Between the wars the numbers employed at the mill never fell below fifteen, and generally about twenty were kept in work. The mill survived, however, in a dwindling market, and benefitted from the closure of its competitors, its strong family foundation providing an incentive to continue as long as possible, until its closure in 1971, when it employed only eight men.[36]

As far as raw material was concerned, the Cowards had managed to acquire a considerable acreage of their own coppice, and the schedule of the 1921 sale alone totalled 325 acres. At the same time they also purchased their own water supply from High Dam about half a mile to the west on Finsthwaite Heights, which they had previously held by agreement. Considerable quantities of timber had always been bought in by many of the mills, but few were literally surrounded by such an abundant supply. Yet one of Stott Park's products in the early years of the present century, pick handles made from hickory, must have been entirely dependent upon imported timber, and certainly the purchase books show that from the 'thirties to the 'sixties a yearly total of between four and six hundred tons was bought from other concerns and landowners.[37]

The acquisition of a steam engine does not seem to have been an immediate consequence of the building of the new lathe shop. Water power was a major prime mover until well into the twentieth century, as elsewhere in the area, but the steam engine was almost certainly to give enhanced power rather than standby capacity in times of water shortage. Considerable quantities of shavings, sawdust, and offcuts would be available as fuel, although of course, they would burn very quickly. If coal had to be used (the railway had arrived at Lakeside, about half a mile away, in 1869)[38] the use of the engine would become relatively very expensive. However, it shows little evidence of wear through use, allowing for its age of a hundred years or so, as two further turbines were installed. The first replacement was by Gilkes of Kendal, *c.* 1890; the second, by Armfield's was purchased in 1931. They supplied power until electric motors were installed in 1941 (Fig. 3).[39] The engine room itself was partitioned off from the new lathe shop, and the boiler house, with its double tier of drying rooms above, is an addition.

The steam engine was not locally made. It is of a type which would be common in the 1880s in a small, relatively isolated concern. It was built by William Bradley and Sons, of Brighouse, near Halifax, and has a single cylinder, engine bed and flywheel of single castings, and a simple ejector condenser which needs no moving parts. Given sufficient steam pressure it would develop up to 20 h.p.[40] No details of its acquisition survive, and it could well have been bought secondhand, as business generally was in a state of depression for the last quarter of the nineteenth century, and plant of this nature could almost certainly be had from an ailing concern at a low price. But there is no mention of the engine in the sale documents of 1921. The description in the schedule reads: 'Mill and Yard including all sheds turbine and shafting and all pipes and races inbring thereto'. The boiler house is not shown on the revised Ordnance Survey maps of 1911–12, although the coppice barns clearly are (q.v.)[41] The exact date of its installation is therefore uncertain.

As it survives today, the mill is essentially late nineteenth century in its form and equipment. The old lathe shop did not go out of use entirely. Timber beds still survive there with parts of what are possibly early lathes. In the centre of the shop are two finishing drums which worked until the mill closed, and there are sorting racks (Fig. 4). Most of the lathes, all of which are still driven by line shafting, are hand-operated examples by Fell of Windermere, and were never superseded by Braithwaite's cumbersome automatics, possibly because they are more versatile.[42] There are two semi-automatic borers by the Crook engineer, however. The mill was purchased for preservation in this condition, as the men had left it on their last day of work. It is perhaps ironic that those men were really the component most essential for its interpretation.

REFERENCES

1. *Blackburn Mail*, 8 November 1797 (I am indebted to Dr. J. D. Marshall for this reference).

2. *Westmorland Gazette*, 29 October 1971; D. W. Jones, 'The End of a Bobbin Mill', *Country Life*, 18 May 1972, pp. 1234–5; J. D. Marshall and M. Davies-Shiel, *Industrial Archaeology of the Lake Counties* (1969), p. 60–75. Gives the most comprehensive description of the process and products.

3. *An Illustrated Account of Halifax Brighouse and District* (1895), *passim*.

4. *Fourth Report of the Childrens' Employment Commission (1863-7)*, British Parliamentary Papers, Vol. XX (1865), p. 246.

5. J. Geraint Jenkins, *Traditional Country Craftsmen* (1965), Chap. 2.

6. *Westmorland Gazette and Kendal Advertiser*, 5 December 1835; 27 February 1836.

7. Census of 1841, Enumerator's sheets for Colton parish, HO 107/528 (P.R.O.), Sheet 9.

8. Ordnance Survey (1846–8), 6 in., Lancashire Sheet VIII.

9. Marshall and Davies-Shiel, *I.A. of the Lake Counties*, p. 65.

10. *Westmorland Advertiser and Kendal Mercury*, 28 January 1837.

11. *West. Advertiser*, 27 August 1836.

12. *West. Advertiser*, 12 November 1836; W. Parson and W. White, *History, Directory and Gazetteer of Cumberland and Westmorland* (1829), p. 620.

13. Census of 1871, Enumerator's sheets for Colton Parish, Sheet 9 (P.R.O.).

14. *West. Advertiser*, 5 November 1836. (There is no other evidence for union activity at this time, according to Dr. Marshall.)

15. Census of 1841, Enumerator's Sheets for Colton parish, HO 107/528 (P.R.O.), Sheet 9.

16. *West. Gazette*, 27 February 1836.

17. Census of 1851, Enumerator's Sheets for Colton Parish (microfilmed at Lancaster University Library), Sheet 10.

18. Census of 1871, Enumerator's Sheets for Colton parish, Sheet 9.

19. Pedder papers, Lancs. Record Office, Dd. pd. 26/427; I am grateful to Mrs. J. Martin for bringing this reference to my notice.

20. Conveyance of 1921. D.O.E. Deeds Registry.

21. Census of 1861, Enumerator's Sheets for Colton parish HO RG 9/3166 (P.R.O.), Sheets 10 and 11.

22. *Children's Employment Commission*, pp. 246–53.

23. J. D. Marshall, *Old Lakeland* (1971), p. 147.

24. I am grateful to Mr. M. Davies-Shiel for this information. The maker's number of the turbine was *28*.

25. J. D. Marshall and M. Davies-Shiel, *The Lake District at Work* (1971), p. 48; correspondence with Messrs. W. A. Fell, Ltd., Windermere; J. Somervell, in *Transactions of the Newcomen Society*, Vol. XVIII (137-8), p. 242.

26. Marshall and Davies-Shiel, *I.A. of the Lake Counties*, p. 70.

27. Ordnance Survey (1911–12 revision), 6 in. Sheet VIII SE.

28. Marshall and Davies-Shiel, *Lake District at Work*, p. 47.

29. Marshall, *Old Lakeland*, p. 153.

30. *West. Gazette*, 11 December 1869.

31. J. Somervell, *Water Power Mills of South Westmorland*, (1930), p. 12.

32. Suggested by Dr. J. D. Marshall from his knowledge of the records of Horrax mill, Ambleside.

33. Purchase Books, Abbot Hall Museum, Kendal.

34. Sales Books, Abbot Hall Museum.

35. Stock Book, Abbot Hall Museum.

36. Wages Book, Abbot Hall Museum.

37. Purchase Books, Abbot Hall Museum.

38. Marshall and Davies-Shiel, *I.A. of the Lake Counties*, p. 74.

39. I am grateful to Mr. M. Davies-Shiel for this information.

40. Mr. George Watkins of Bath University kindly supplied me with technical information on the steam engine.

41. O.S. (1911–12); First schedule to conveyance of 1821, D.O.E. Deeds Registry.

42. A preserved example of an automatic Braithwaite bobbin turning machine is exhibited at Abbot Hall Museum, Kendal.

ACKNOWLEDGEMENTS

Dr. John Marshall and Mr. Michael Davies–Shiel first called my attention to the bobbin industry and have given me unstinting help and advice during the preparation of this paper. My thanks for help are also due to Mr. George Watkins, Mr. Paul Wilson and Mrs. Janet Martin; also to Miss Mary Burkett for putting a room at my disposal to examine the records deposited at Abbot Hall Museum, Kendal where my wife kindly worked through the detailed ledgers, and to Messrs. Plowman Craven and Associates for help with the base plans, which my colleague Mr. J. Thorn has so capably adapted for publication. I am also grateful for invaluable discussions with Mr. John Ivison, who managed the mill for many years until its closure.

The photographs were kindly supplied by Dr. Marshall (interior) and the *Westmorland Gazette*.

I a. Hadrian's Wall: Turret 26b (Low Brunton).

I b. The Rudge Cup.

II   a. St. Magnus Cathedral: the north side.

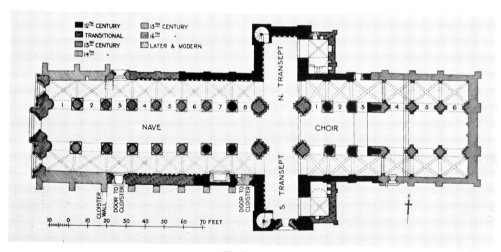

II   b. Plan.

III St. Magnus Cathedral: the Romanesque choir, *c*.1137–42.

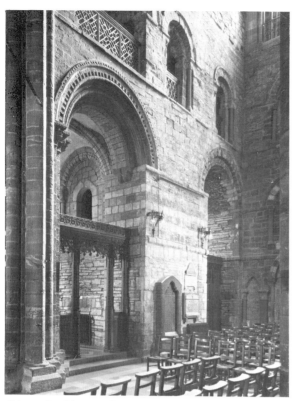

IV a. St. Magnus Cathedral: polychrome masonry in south transept.

IV b. Choir pier, north aisle.

IV c. East arch of choir: the cross-passage.

IV d. Romanesque window, first bay of nave aisle, first period style, *c*.1140.

V Usk Castle: general view from west in 1732 by Samuel and Nathaniel Buck. Left to right: North Tower, fourteenth-century hall range, Garrison Tower and twelfth-century keep.

VI a. Usk Castle: the twelfth-century keep from the east.

VI b. The Garrison Tower with present ground level now raised to original first floor level.

XI a. Wakefield Tower: exterior as excavated 1975, showing junction with Main Guard Wall.

XI b. Excavation of curtain wall, 1957, showing earlier abutment to east and culverts built prior to southward extension of defences.

XI c. Wakefield Tower: lower chamber as excavated, with ceiling restored. Lower part of a jamb and the steps of original entry are on the left: lower part of an original loop is visible in centre recess.

XI d. Upper chamber, looking north east, restored.

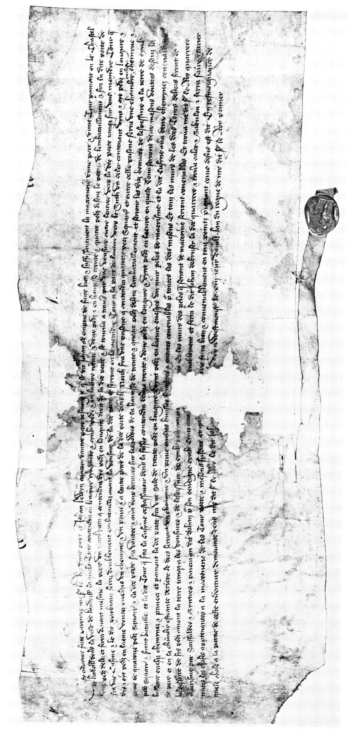

XII Carlisle Castle: indenture of 1378.

XIII   a. Carlisle Castle: De Ireby's Tower from the north. Photo: *Solway Studio*.

XIII   b. The tower from the south. Photo: *Solway Studio*.

XIV   a. Kenilworth Castle: Hall, Strong and Saint Lowe Towers — exterior view.

XIV   b. Interior view of the Hall.

XIX   a. Craignethan Castle: caponier from the north. Left: west rampart and spur wall beyond. Right: counterscarp wall.

XIX   b. West towers and curtains of outer courtyard. 'Buttress' projecting beyond curtain is contemporary with ranges of Andrew Hay's house.

XX a. Upnor Castle: aerial view from the east. Photo: *Aerofilms*.

XX b. Bastion with heightened parapet.

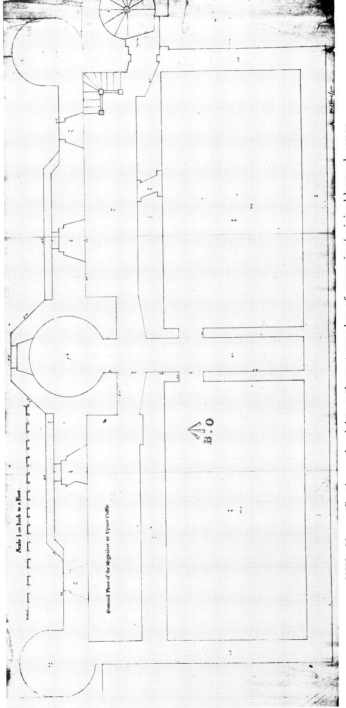

Scale ½ an inch to a Foot.

Ground Floor of the Magazine at Upnor Castle

B. O

XXI Upnor Castle: early eighteenth-century plan of magazine/original barrack range.

XXII a. Heath Old Hall: from the east.

XXII b. View from the south. Photo: *Country Life*.

XXIII   a. Barlborough Hall, Derbyshire: front elevation.

XXIII   b. Heath Old Hall: front elevation.

XXIV   Heath Old Hall: the 'Jezebel' chimneypiece. Photo: *Country Life*.

XXV a. Heath Old Hall: ceiling in chamber 'B'.

XXV b. Ceiling in the long gallery.

XXV c. Ceiling in the great chamber.

XXVI   a. Heath Old Hall: plasterwork in the Hall.

XXVI   b. The same.

XXVII   a. Brough Castle in 1739, from an engraving by Samuel and Nathaniel Buck.

XXVII   b. The castle today with (left to right) the Keep, the Hall block and Clifford's Tower.

XXVIII   a. Tredegar House: the north west range.

XXVIII   b. The Gilt Room. Painting 'Cybele' on rear wall copied from engraving (*c*.1668) of statue in Town Hall (now the Palace), Amsterdam.

XXIX   a.   Tredegar House: painted ceiling in Gilt Room.

XXIX   b.   Engraving (1647) of part of ceiling in the Barberini Palace, Rome.

XXX a. Tredegar House: entrance to stable
       yard.

XXX b. Front door.

XXX c. Side gates and stable block.

XXXI a. Tredegar House: front(north-west) elevation.

XXXI b. Clarendon House, Piccadilly (Roger Pratt, 1664–7, demolished 1683): front elevation.

XXXII a. Stott Park bobbin mill: exterior. Photo: *Westmorland Gazette*.

XXXII b. The new lathe shop: interior. Photo: *Dr. John Marshall*.

Bibliography of the Published Works of
Dr. A. J. Taylor

by

A. J. TAYLOR

1929

1 · The Diary of Henry Machyn. *Taylorian*, LI, pp. 150-3.
2 The Palace of Bridewell. *Ibid.*, pp. 252-4.
3 The Priory of St. John, Clerkenwell, and the Order of the Hospital of St. John of Jerusalem in England. *Merchant Taylors' School: Its Origin, History and Present Surroundings* (Oxford, B. H. Blackwell), pp. 143-57.

1930

4 Merchant Taylors' and the Great Fire. *Taylorian*, LII, pp. 171-3.
5 Review of *Hymns and Prayers for Use at Merchant Taylors' School. Taylorian*, LH, pp. 194-6.
6 School Prayer Books. *Ibid.*, pp. 231-3.

1931

7 A Great Old Merchant Taylor: Henry Longueville Mansel. *Taylorian*, LIV, pp. 17-20.

1933

8 A Medieval Roof in St. John's College, Oxford. *B.A.A. Journal*, New Series, 8, pp. 278-92.

1934

9 London before the Mayors. Letter in *The Times*, 16 January 1934.
10 Addenda to Sussex Place-Names. *Place-Names of Surrey*, (C.U.P. for English Place-Name Society), pp. xli-ii.

1935

11 The Ferry of Sefford. *Sussex Notes and Queries,* vol. V, pp. 237-42.
12 Keddle or Kettle? Letter in *The Times*, 11 July 1935.

1936

13 Review of *Merchant Taylors' School Register, 1561-1934. Taylorian*, LVII, pp. 220-2.
14 The Royal Visit to Oxford in 1636. *Oxoniensia*, I, pp. 151-8.

1937

15 The Alien Priory of Minster Lovell. *Oxoniensia*, II, pp. 103-17.

1939

16 The Buildings of St. Bernard's College. In Stevenson and Salter, *The Early History of St. John's College, Oxford* (Oxford Historical Society, N.S., vol. I), pp. 93-110.
17 Who was John of Hoveden? In F. J. E. Raby, *Poems of John of Hoveden* (Surtees Society, vol. CLIV), pp. 270-4.
18 *Minster Lovell Hall* (official guidebook), H.M. Stationery Office.

1940

19 *Records of the Barony and Honour of the Rape of Lewes*, ed., Sussex Record Society, vol. XLIV.

1942

20 Friends of the City Churches: Statement of Policy (pamphlet).

1946

21 *Basingwerk Abbey* (official guidebook), H.M. Stationery Office.

1947

22 *Minster Lovell Hall* (abridged edn.). H.M. Stationery Office.
23 Review of Marjorie Morgan, *English Lands of the Abbey of Bec. B.A.A. Journal*, 3rd Series, X, pp. 83-86.
24 Addresses to the Cambrian Archaeological Association at Rhuddlan Castle, Basingwerk Abbey, St. Winefred's Well, Flint Castle and Ewloe Castle. *Arch. Camb.*, XCIX, pp. 306-27.
25 Usk Castle and the Pipe Roll of 1188. *Ibid.*, pp. 249-55.
26 Montgomery Town Wall. *Ibid.*, pp. 281-3.

1948

27 Addresses to the Cambrian Archaeological Association at site of St. John's Priory, Carmarthen, Carmarthen Castle, Llanstephan Castle, Dynevor Castle, Talley Abbey and Kidwelly Castle. *Arch. Camb.*, pp. 123-50.

28 Annual Report on Activities of Ministry of Works Ancient Monuments Branch in Wales, *Ibid.*, pp. 56-60.

1949

29 *Rhuddlan Castle* (official guidebook), H.M. Stationery Office.
30 A Note on Walter of Hereford, builder of Caernarvon Castle. *Transactions of the Caernarvonshire Historical Society*, vol. IX (1948), pp. 16-19.
31 The Greater Monastic Houses. In *A Hundred Years of Welsh Archaeology* (Cambrian Archaeological Association), pp. 140-47.
32 The Cloister of Vale Royal Abbey. *Journal of the Chester and North Wales Architectural, Archaeological and Historical Society*, XXXVII, pp. 295-7.

1950

33 Thomas de Houghton: A Royal Carpenter of the Later Thirteenth Century. *Antiquaries Journal*, xxx, pp. 28-33.
34 *Raglan Castle* (official guidebook), H.M. Stationery Office.
35 A Bibliography of the Published Writings of Rose Graham, in *Medieval Studies presented to Rose Graham*, edited by Veronica Ruffer and A. J. Taylor (Oxford University Press), pp. 233-40.
36 Annual Report on Activities of Ministry of Works Ancient Monuments Branch in Wales, *Arch. Camb.*, C. pp. 267-70.
37 Harlech Castle, 'historical revision'. *Ibid.*, pp. 278-80.
38 The Birth of Edward of Caernarvon and the beginnings of Caernarvon Castle. *History*, XXXV, pp. 256-61 (Historical Revision No. CXVI).
39 Master James of St. George. *English Historical Review*, LXV, pp. 433-57.

1951

40 *Monmouth Castle and Great Castle House* (official guidebook), H.M. Stationery Office.
41 The North Wales Castles. *Archaeological News Letter*, vol. III, pp. 161-2.
42 Harlech Castle: the dating of the Outer Enclosure. *Journal of the Merioneth Historical and Record Society*. col. I, pp. 202-3.
43 Review of C. J. P. Cave, *Roof Bosses in Medieval Churches*. B.A.A. *Journal*, 3rd Series, XIII, pp. 51-2.
44 Review of D. H. S. Cranage, *Cathedrals and how they were built. Ibid.*, pp. 252-3.
45 Review of J. G. Edwards, *Edward I's Castle-Building in Wales. Antiquaries Journal*, XXXI, p. 224.
46 Annual Report on Activities of Ministry of Works Ancient Monuments Branch in Wales, *Arch. Camb.*, CI, pp. 77-82.

1952

47 The Date of Chirk Castle. Letter in *Country Life*, CXI, pp. 103-4.

48 The Date of Caernarvon Castle. *Antiquity*, vol. XXVI, No. 101, pp. 25-34.

49 Review of William Rees, *A History of the Order of St. John of Jerusalem in Wales and on the Welsh Border. B.A.A. Journal*, 3rd Series, XIV, pp. 65-6.

50 Review of A. D. R. Caroe, *Old Churches and Modern Craftsmanship. Ibid.*, pp. 67-8.

51 Annual Report on Activities of Ministry of Works Ancient Monuments Branch in Wales, *Arch. Camb.*, CI, pp. 113-7.

52 Addresses to the Cambrian Archaeological Association at Christ College, Brecon, Brecon Castle, Bronllys Castle, Hay Castle, Builth Castle and Carreg Cennen Castle, *Ibid.*, pp. 172-5.

53 A Note on The Berries, Crick, Monmouthshire. *Ibid.*, pp. 163-5.

54 Building at Caerphilly in 1326. *Bulletin of the Board of Celtic Studies*, XIV, pp. 299-300.

55 The Earliest Canal. Letter in *Country Life*, CXII, pp. 1495.

1953

56 Building at Caernarvon and Beaumaris in 1295-6. *Bulletin of the Board of Celtic Studies*, XV, pp. 61-6.

57 A Letter from Lewis of Savoy to Edward I. *English Historical Review*, LXVIII, pp. 56-62.

58 The Events of Palm Sunday, 1282. *Flintshire Historical Society Publications*, XIII, pp. 51-2.

59 The Castle of St. Georges-d'Espéranche. *Antiquaries Journal.* XXXIII, pp. 33-47.

60 The Land of Castles: Saving the Ancient Monuments of Wales. Article in *The Times*, 7 July 1953.

61 *Caernarvon Castle and Town Wall* (official guidebook), H.M. Stationery Office.

62 The Date of Bramshill. Letter in *Country Life*, CXIII, p. 1818.

63 A Famous View in Peril. Note in *Country Life*, CXIV, pp. 30-31.

64 Review of Sidney Toy, *The Castles of Great Britain. Antiquaries Journal*, XXXIV, pp. 103-4.

1954

65 The Death of Llywelyn ap Gruffydd. *Bulletin of the Board of Celtic Studies*, XV, pp. 207-9.

66 Bryan Hugh St. John O'Neil. *Taylorian*, LXVI, pp. 138-9.

1955

67 English Builders in Scotland during the War of Independence: A Record of 1304. *Scottish Historical Review*, XXXIV, pp. 44-6.

68 Offa's Dyke: the Northern Termination. Being pp. 14-20 of Sir Cyril Fox's *Offa's Dyke* (O.U.P., for British Academy, 1955).

69 Rhuddlan Cathedral: a 'Might-have-been' of Flintshire History. *Flintshire Historical Society Publications*, XV, pp. 43-51.

70 The Date of Clifford's Tower, York. *Archaeological Journal*, CXI, pp. 153-9.

71 Review of R. Allen Brown, *English Medieval Castles. Ibid.*, pp. 238-9.

72 Review of W. Douglas Simpson, *Dundarg Castle. Ibid.*, p. 239.

1956

73 *The Jewel Tower, Westminster* (official guidebook), H.M. Stationery Office.

74 *Conway Castle and Town Walls* (official guidebook), H.M. Stationery Office.

1957

75 The building of Flint: a postscript. *Flintshire Hist. Soc. Pubns.*, XVII, pp. 34-41.

1959

76 Kingston Bridge (a note on the medieval bridge at Kingston-upon-Thames, in *Kingston Tower*, the Parish Magazine of All Saints Church, Kingston-upon-Thames, Surrey).

1960

77 The identity of Hen Blas, Coleshill Fawr. *Flintshire Hist. Soc. Publications*, XVIII, pp. 37-40.

78 Samuel Robinson, 1559-1625 (M.T.S. 1569-157?). *Taylorian*, LXIX, pp. 80-82.

1961

79 Castle-building in Wales in the later thirteenth century: the prelude to construction, in *Studies in Building History: essays in recognition of the work of B. H. St. J. O'Neil* (London, Odhams Press, Ltd.), pp. 104-133.

80 White Castle in the Thirteenth Century: a reconsideration. *Medieval Archaeology*, V, pp. 169-75.

1963

81 The King's Works in Wales, 1277-1330, in *The History of the King's Works*, ed. H. M. Colvin (London, H.M. Stationery Office), I, pp. 293-408; II, pp. 1027-40.

82 Some notes on the Savoyards in North Wales, 1277-1300, with special reference to the Savoyard element in the construction of Harlech Castle. *Genava*, n.s., tome XI (Mélanges d'histoire et d'archéologie offerts en hommage à M. Louis Blondel), pp. 289-315.

1966

85 The earliest reference to works at Hope Castle. *Flintshire Hist. Soc. Publications*, XXII, pp. 76-7.
86 The rehabilitation of castles in the country districts in England and Wales. *Bulletin de l'Institut International des Châteaux Historiques*, No. 22, pp. 71-4.
87 Foreword to Horatia Durant's *Raglan Castle* (Pontypool, 1966).

1967

88 An incident at Montgomery Castle on New Year's Day, 1288. *Archaeologia Cambrensis*, CXIV, pp. 159-64.

1969

89 Caernarvon Castle: a Picture Book (HMSO). Text by AJT, photographs and illustrations by Lord Snowdon, John Piper et al.
90 Review of D. F. Renn, Norman Castles in Britain. *Antiquaries Journal*, XLIX, pp. 428-9.

1970

91 Ed. *Château Gaillard III*: European Castles Studies (Phillimore & Co.).
92 Evidence for a pre-Conquest origin for the chapels in Hastings and Pevensey Castles (*Ibid.*, pp. 144-51).
93 The Walls of Conway (Presidential Address to Cambrian Archaeological Association, Bangor, 1969). *Archaeologia Cambrensis*, CXIX, pp. 1-9.

1971

94 The Master Builders: 6—Conway. *Sunday Times Magazine*, 5 September 1971, pp. 20-30.

1973

95 Review of W. Douglas Simpson, Castles in England and Wales. *Welsh History Review*, VI, pp. 474-5.

1974

96 The King's Works in Wales, 1277-1330, reprinted from *The History of the King's Works* (1963).
97 John Stow and his Monument (Address delivered in St. Andrew Undershaft at the Annual John Stow Commemoration Service, 24 April 1974). *Transactions of the London & Middlesex Archaeological Society*, 25, pp. 316-21.

98 Castles and castle-building in the Middle Ages. *Transactions of the Architectural and Archaeological Society of Durham and Northumberland*, III, pp. 39-46.

99 An addition to the Welsh Rolls. *Bulletin of the Board of Celtic Studies*, XXVI, pp. 78-81.

1975

100 Review of *Prisca Munimenta: Studies in Archival and Administrative History presented to Dr. A. E. J. Hollaender*, ed. Felicity Ranger. *Antiquaries Journal*, LV, p. 157.

101 Three early castle sites in Sicily: Motta Camastra, Petralia Soprana and Sperlinga. *Château Gaillard, Études de Castellologie médiévale*, VIII, *Actes du Colloque International tenu à Blois 1-7 Septembre 1974* (Caen, 1975), pp. 209-14.

102 Review of *Welsh Entries in the Memoranda Rolls*, ed. Natalie Fryde, Cardiff, 1974). *Antiquaries Jorunal*, LV, pp. 435-61.

1976

103 Who was 'John Pennardd, leader of the men of Gwynedd'? *English Historical Review*, XC, pp. 79-97

104 Anniversary Address, 1976, *Antiquaries Journal*, LVI, pp. 1-10.   ]

105 Royal Alms and Oblations in the later 13th Century, in *Tribute to an Antiquary, Essays presented to Marc Fitch by some of his friends* (Leopard's Head Press), pp. 93-125.

INDEX

Note: *Reference numbers in bold type indicate a page*
on which a line illustration appears.

Abinger Roman villa (Surrey): 75.

Acoustic survey (bosing): 76.

Adlington, Mr., plumber at Tredegar: 331.

Aerial photograph of Stonehenge: 76.

Aesica, see Great Chesters.

Aigues Mortes (France): 151.

Aix-la-Chapelle (Aachen, Germany): 94, 95.

Alballava, see Burgh-by-Sands.

Alexander II, king of Scots: 191.

Alexander, Bishop: 124.

Alexandria (Egypt): 94.

Alnwick Castle (Northumbs.): 204.

Amesbury (Wilts.), Woodhenge excavation: 3.

Amiens patera: 14, 48, 49.

Analysis of: animal remains, 72, 76, 78; artifacts, 80; bronze, 74, 76; copper, 76; glass, 73; grain, 76; metal implements, metals, 75, 76; mineral, heavy, 78; mortar, 73; pigment, 73; pollen, 79; rain, 76; sediment (varve), 74; skeletal remains, 76; soil, 72.

Anau (Turkestan), excavations: 76, 78.

Ancient Agriculture Committee, 82.

Ancient Fields Research Committee, 82.

Ancient Monuments, Inspectorate of, *Intro.,* xv–xix, 80.
  Laboratory, *Intro.,* xviii, 44, 70, 80, 81.

Ançy-le-Franc (France), 17c. house design: 326.

Andenne (Belgium), kiln site: 223.

Andover (Hants.), Balkesbury Camp excavation: 9.

Andrew, saint, skull stolen: 94.

Andrewes, Thomas, work at Upnor: 273.

Animal remains: analysis of, 72, 76, 78; Neolithic, 4; Roman, 18. 19.

Anne of Denmark: 303.

Anselm, Abbot, Bury St. Edmunds: 117.

Antler picks: 4.

Anthée Roman villa (Belgium), enamelworking: 42.

Antiquaries (London), Society of: 72, 76, 79.

Antonine Newstead, brooches, 44.

Antonine Wall: 19.

Appleby (Westmorland), assize town: 306, 309.

Appleby Castle (Westmorland), The Lady Ann Clifford, 1590–1676: 303, 305, 306.

Appleby (Westmorland), St. Laurence, George Clifford tomb: 311.

Archaeology, Institute of: 78, 79.

Archaeometry: 80.

Architecture, Romanesque: 88, 91, **90, 92,** Pls. III, IVc.
  See also Base-mouldings, Romanesque.

Ards, Donnerupland: 82.

Armada (Spanish): 303.

Arms, heraldic: Craignethan Castle, 245; Elizabeth I, 157, 270; Langewehe ware, 221; Vipont and Clifford, 307, 310, 311.

Arran, earls of, *see* Hamilton.

Artillery, at: Carlisle Castle, 204; Craignethan Castle, 239 ff.; Upnor Castle, 265, 272, 277, 279, 280, **278,** Pl. XXb.

Assizes, see Appleby (Westm.).

Astronomy at Stonehenge: 75.

Atkinson, Professor R. J. C.: 75, 76.

Atomic Energy Research Establishment, Harwell: 81.

Avebury (Wilts.): embanked enclosures: 4; stone circles, 3.

Avenues of stones: 3; of posts, 3.

Babbage, Charles, tree-ring dating: 74.

Baillie Reynolds, P. K.: 211.

Balkesbury Camp hill-fort: 9, 10; excavation, 11.

Bamps, Anatole, pottery examination: 78.

Banester, John, work at Upnor Castle: 273, 275.

Banks East Roman turret: 18.

Banna, see Bewcastle.

Baptist, engineer: 271.

Barden Tower, near Skipton (N. Yorks.), restoration, chapel built by Lady Anne Clifford: 305, 307.

Baring-Gould, S., relics of St. Magnus: 94.

Barlborough Hall (Derbys.): 292, 295, 298, 299, Pl. XXIII.

Barn, Roman at Witcombe R. villa: 29, 36, 37.

Barrows (long, round): 1, 6.

Base-mouldings, Romanesque: 99 ff.; Definitions, 105, **105;** stones used for details, 100; tooling in Romanesque masonry, 101.

Base-mouldings (references in text):
  Castles: Bishops Waltham Palace, 123,

Base-mouldings—*Castles*—continued—
128, 153, 206; Castle Rising, 119, 120, 123, 129; Colchester, 110, 15; Dover, 129, 216; Farnham, 128, 210; Hedingham, 123; Norwich, 124, 176; Oakham, 129, 222; Richmond, 130; Rochester, 113, 117, 124, 87, 177; Sherborne, 122, 137, 138; Tower of London, White Tower, 119, 120, 101, 127, 128; Weeting, 120; Wolvesey, 123.

Collegiate churches and ancient minsters: Caen (France), St. Nicholas, 108; Chester, St. John, 100, 104; Chichester cathedral, 102, 108, 110, 113, 116, 119, 122, 47, 48, 77, 107, 112, 136; Dover, St. Martin-le-Grand, 117, 85; Etampes (France), 108; Gournay (France), St. Mary, 128, 129, 203; Lincoln cathedral, 111; London, Old St. Pauls, 116, 124, 73; North Elmham cathedral, 113, 116, 120, 40, 44, 130; Old Sarum cathedral, 110, 124, 171, 172; Repton Minster, 108; Rouen cathedral (France), 110; Sens cathedral (France), 128; Steyning, St. Andrew, 116, 70; Stow, 124; Wimborne Minster, 116, 119, 122, 123, 69, 108, 111.

Conventual structures: Bardney Abbey, 110, 128, 18; Bath Abbey, 116, 120, 64; Battle Abbey, 110; Binham Priory, 108, 119, 120, 129, 115, 119, 120, 215; Blackmore Priory, 127, 191; Blyth Priory, 120, 133; Bordesley Abbey, 124, 181; Bourne Abbey, 124, 180; Boxgrove Priory, 116, 129; Bury St. Edmunds Abbey, 111, 114, 116, 117, 29, 30, 31, 56, 89; Caen Abbey (France), 108; Canterbury, Christ Church cathedral, 108, 110, 111, 113, 116, 117, 119, 123, 124, 128, 13, 14, 24, 25, 49, 75, 113, 159; Canterbury, St. Augustine, 101, 110, 113, 114, 122, 9, 11, 12, 38, 52; Carrow Priory, 108, 110, 120, 2, 7, 122; Castle Acre Priory, 116, 120, 128, 66, 79, 134, 199; Cerisy-la-Forêt Abbey (France), 108, 3; Chepstow Priory, 113; Christchurch Priory, 122, 124, 144, 179; Colchester, St. Botolph Priory, 117, 88; Crowland Abbey, 126; Denny Priory, 126, 127, 188, 194; Dover Priory, 120, 124, 129, 125; Dunstable Priory, 117, 128, 129, 197; Ely cathedral, 116, 119, 123, 126, 65, 78, 149; Evesham Abbey, 113, 123, 46,

Conventual structures—continued—
51, 163; Fécamp Abbey (France), 110, 127, 10, 196; Gloucester cathedral, 114, 116, 119, 120, 123, 124, 53, 57, 67, 68, 102, 132, 152; Goring Priory, 123, 164; Horsham, St. Faith Priory, 108; Isleham Priory, 113, 43; Jumièges Abbey (France), 110; Lastingham Abbey, 130; Leiston Abbey, 128; Leonard Stanley Priory, 111, 122, 33, 141; Lesnes Abbey, 129, 215; Lessay Abbey (France), 110; Lewes Priory, 119, 120, 95; Lilleshall Abbey, 124, 182; London, New Temple, 128; London, St. Bartholomew Priory, 117, 124, 93, 178; Malmesbury Abbey, 122, 123, 154, 155, 156, 157; Mont St. Michel (France), 110, 8; Neufmarché-en-Bray (France), 120, 123, 158; Norwich cathedral, 116, 120, 123, 128, 80, 129, 148; Oxford cathedral, 128, 129, 204, 205; Penmon Priory, 100; Pershore Abbey, 113, 119, 45, 99, 100; Peterborough cathedral, 101, 103, 120, 124, 128, 129, 167, 168, 169, 209, 219; Portchester Priory, 122, 123, 127, 143, 146, 195; Ramsey Abbey, 123; Reading Abbey, 117, 90; Rochester Cathedral, 113, 126, 36, 37; Romsey Abbey, 116, 119, 123; Sherborne Abbey, 124, 174; Southwark cathedral, 128, 207, 208; Stamford Priory, 123, 129, 220, 223; Stoneleigh Abbey, 127, 192; Tewkesbury Abbey, 100, 114, 116, 119, 120, 61, 62, 63, 133; Thetford Priory, 108, 120, 122, 124, 165, 166; Thorney Abbey, 116, 119, 81, 82, 83, 99; Twineham, Christ Church Priory, 117, 123, 124; Waltham Abbey, 117, 124, 92, 179; Westminster Abbey, 110, 8; Winchester cathedral, 110, 111, 114, 116, 119, 16, 17, 31, 58, 59, 60, 69, 76, 106, 110; Wymondham Priory, 120, 121.

Hospitals: Bury St. Edmunds Infirmary, 128, 200; Cirencester, St. John's, 110, 6; Huntingdon, St. John's, 124, 184, 185; Westminster, St. Catherine's, 124; Winchester, Magdalen, 128; Winchester, St. Cross, 129, 218.

Houses: Bury St. Edmunds, Moyses Hall, 129, 224; Canterbury, Guildhall, 127, 190; Malling, Priest's House, 126; Minster, St. Augustine Grange, 123; Norwich, Music House, 128, 208; Southampton, King John's House,

Houses--continued--
126, 187; Trie Château house (France), 129; Warnford Hall, 128.

Parish churches: Ampney Crucis, 129, 225; Authie (France), 110, 19; Avening, 124; Bargham, 116; Bibury, 108, 129, 3, 225; Bishops Sutton, 122, 123, 142; Braunston, 124; Brize Norton, 110, 20; Broughton, 110; Bury, 123, 162; Castle Rising, 120, 117, 123, 129; Castor, 103, 116, 71, 72; Clapham (Beds.), 111; Compton (Sy.), 129, 226; Darenth, 129, 227; Devizes, St. John, 123, 124, 173; Dinton, 126; Dover, St. James, 117; St. Margaret-at-Cliffe, 129; Druggelde (Westf.), 113; Duxford, 114, 126, 55; East Meon, 120, 126; Egleton, 111; Elkstone, 117; Elsenham 111; Ely church, 126; Essendine, 119, 104; Everton, 127, 129; Eynsford, 108; Falaise (France), St. Gervais, 110; Folkworth, 113, 50; Framlingham, 129, 217; Gt. Canfield, 119, 109; Gt. Dunham, 116, 74; Gt. Paxton, 111; Gt. Wymondley, 108; Haddiscoe, 108, 1; Hadstock, 108, 110, 5; Hales, 120, 116; Heckingham, 113, 39, 41; Hemel Hempstead, 126, 189; Ickleton, 111, 123, 32, 161; Iffley, 117, 124, 126, 86, 176; Ilketshall, 113, 42; Kensworth, 116, 73; King's Lynn, 129, 228; Lakenheath, 123, 150; Langford, 108, 4; Leeds (Kent), 117, 91; Lincoln, St. Peter at Gowts, 108; Little Saxham, 113; Little Snoring, 129, 221; London, St. Bride's, 128, St. Mary-le-Bow, 119, 105; Lower Swell, 116; Marton, 108; Mettingham, 120, 118; Milborne, 113; Nately Scures, 108; New Shoreham, 128; Northampton, St. Peter, 119, 120, 124, 96, 97; North Elmham, 113, 120, 40, 44, 130; North Leigh, 127, 193; North Ockenden, 113, 34; Netheravon, 111, 22; Old Shoreham, 122, 140; Orford, 128, 201, 202; Oxford, St. Peter-in-the-East, 124, 145, 175; Oxhill, 128,198; Patrixbourne, 119, 94; Petersfield, 120, 131; Polstead, 108, 123, 151; Poslingford, 113, 35; Preston, 124; Reed, 113; St. Margarets (Kent), 124, 183; St. Marguerite-de-la-Mer (France), 110, 19; Selham, 119, 114; Shalfleet, 108; Smeeth, 111, 28; Sompting, 108; South Lopham, 116, 84; Southoe, 108;

Parish churches—continued—
Stewkley, 124, 186; Stopham, 111; Stoughton (Sx.), 111, 23; Sutton (Sx.), 111, 21; Tickencote, 126; Trie Château (France), 129, 212, 213; Wallingford, 119, 103; Walmer, 117; Wareham. 108; Water Stratford, 114, 54; Wickham, 122; Witley (Sy.), 111, 26; Yaverland, 122, 123, 139, 147.

Stave churches: Norway, 111.

Basingstoke (Hants.), Iron Age settlement, excavation: 9.

Baynards Castle (London): 304, 305.

Beadlam (Yorks.), bronze bowl: 48, **48**.

Beaker people: 1.

Beaulieu Abbey (Hants.): 75.

Becquerel, Henri, radio-activity: 76.

Beeston Castle (Ches.), built by Ralph de Blundeville: 152.

Belfast (N. Ireland), bobbin shops: 335; University, radio-carbon dating: 81.

Bellarmine masks, Langewehe: 221.

Benedict, Abbot: 110, 128.

Benedictine nuns, at Heath: 287, 289.

Bergen (Norway), Christ Church cathedral, wall burials: 95; King Haaken: 96.

Bersu, Dr., excavation at Little Woodbury: 7.

Berwick Castle (Northumbs.), defences: 270, 280, 281.

Bethom, James, of Stott Mill: 340.

Bewcastle (*Banna*) (Cumbria): 14.

Biek, L.: 70.

Bignor Roman villa (Sx.): 73.

Birdoswald (*Camboglanna*) (Cumbria); 13, 21.

Birmingham University, radio-carbon dating: 81.

Birsay (Orkney): 86; bishop, *see* Wm. the Old; episcopal see removed: 87.

Blackcarts Roman turret, 22, 24, **15**.

Blackness Castle (W. Lothian), 241; artillery defence: 250, 257, 258.

Blundeville, Ralph de, earl of Chester, castle-building Beeston, Bolingbroke, Chartley, 152, 174.

Bobbin Mill House (Cumbria): 340.

Bobbin Mill industry, 335 ff., buildings and machinery, 338, 339, 341; Health of Employees in Industry: 342.

Bolingbroke Castle (Lincs.): 152.

Bolles, Lady Mary, at Heath Old Hall: 286.

Bolton Castle (N. Yorks.), work by Lewyn: 204, 208.

'Bonaventure': 303.

Bond, F.: 104.

Bones, human: 72, 76, *cf.* Relics.

Bones, animal *see* Animal remains.

Bosing, *see* Acoustic survey.

Bothwell Castle (Lanarks.): 174.

Boulogne (France), castle compared with Usk: 148.

Bourne, William, master gunner: 265.

Bowness on Solway (*Maia*) (Cumbria)- 13.

Brading Roman villa (Kent): 75.

Braithwaite, Henry, machinery manufacture: 343, 346.

Brakspear, Harold: 102, 110.

Brandon, Eleanor, niece of Henry VIII: 307.

Braose, Reginald de: 152.

Bristol (Avon), St. Mary, work by Simon Edney: 329.

British Association for the Advancement of Science: 77, 82.

British Museum (London): 77; Natural History: 78; Research Laboratory: 77; radio-carbon dating: 81.

Broadchalke (Wilts), ploughing experiment: 82.

Bronze, analysis: 76; artifacts: 74; Roman: 41, 43, 44, 49; -smith workshop: 9; working sites, Roman: 19, 43.

Brooches, from Roman sites: 19, 43, 44, 51–64, 52, 53, 55, 57, 61, 63.

Brough Castle (N. Yorks.), the Lady Anne Clifford: 303, 305, 306; restoration (Buck's view): 308, Pl. XXXVIIa; Clifford's Tower: Pl. XXVIIb.

Brougham (Cumbria), bronze vessel, enamelled: 45, 47.

Brougham Castle (Cumbria), the Lady Anne Clifford: 303, 305; Norman keep: 306; repairs: 306, 307.

Parish Church, rebuilt: 307.

Brownsea Castle (Dorset): 280.

Brunssum/Schinveld (Netherlands), kiln, pottery: 223, 224, 225, 227, 219.

Brunton Roman turret: 22, 24.

Buckman, Professor James: 73.

Burgh-by-Sands (*Aballava*) (Cumbria): 13.

Burgh, Elizabeth de: 147–148: Hubert de, work at Grosmont, Montgomery, Skenfrith: 151, 152.

Burrium, site of: 139.

Bury Hill (Hants.) Iron Age hill fort: 11.

Bute, 3rd Marquess of: 94.

C14 dating, *see* Radio-carbon dating.

Cadzow Castle (Lanarks.), 241, 243.

Caerphilly Castle (Glam.), comparison with Usk: 144, 146, 147.

Caldicot Castle (Gwent), hourd beam holes: 143.

Caley, E. E., archaeological chemistry: 72–74.

caldarium at Witcombe R. villa: 31.

Camboglanna, see Birdoswald.

Cambridge University, radio-carbon dating, 81.

Canterbury (Kent), Christ Church cathedral, Gervase: 88, 89; Lanfranc: 101; *see also* Base-mouldings (references); St. Augustine's Abbey, Abbot Scotland: 101; *see also* Base-mouldings (references).

Carberry Tower (Midlothian): 250.

Cardigan Castle (Dyfed), granted to Wm. Marshall: 151.

Carlisle Castle (Cumbria): 191 ff, **193**; de Ireby Tower gatehouse: 193, **194**; Constable: 207; domestic buildings: 205–207, **206**; fireplaces 14c.–16c.: 192, 196–200; Hall Range: 193, **195**, **196**, Pl. XIIIb; Indenture of 1378: 200 ff. **201**, Pl. XII; Kitchen Tower: 192, 193, 196–8, 202; Military buildings: 204–205, **201**, Pl. XIIIa; 18c. musket loops: 195; portcullis: 195, 197; prisons: 192, 202, 205, 207; 14c. rebuilding: 207.

Carmarthen Castle (Dyfed), granted to Wm. Marshall: 151.

Carr, John, architect of Heath Hall: 287.

Carvoran Roman fort, *see Magna*.

Castles, *see*: Aigues Mortes, Alnwick, Appleby, Barden Tower, Baynards, Beeston, Berwick, Bishops Waltham, Blackness, Bolingbroke, Bolton, Bothwell, Boulogne, Brough, Brougham, Brownsea, Cadzow, Caerphilly, Caldicot, Carberry Tower, Cardigan, Carlisle, Carmarthen, Castle Rising, Chartley, Chepstow, Chilham, Chinon, Cockham Wood fort, Colchester, Conisbrough, Conway, Cooling, Corfe, Coucy, Craignethan, Dirleton, Dourdan, Dover, Dumbarton, Dunbar, Edinburgh, Farnham, Gisors, Goodrich, Gower, Falaise, Grosmont, Haverfordwest, Hedingham, Kenilworth, Kidwelly, Kildrummy, King Charles's Castle, Laval, Llangybi, Lochmaben, London, Tower of, Longtown, Maiden, Montgomery, Newark, Norwich, Oakham, Odiham, Portland, Pendragon, Queenborough (Sheppey), Raglan, Richmond, Rochester, Rouen, Roxburgh, Sandal, Sandsfoot, Scarborough, Sherborne, Skenfrith, Skipton, Stirling, Swaleness fort, Tantallon, Tickhill, *Tillietudlem*, Threaves, Tynemouth, Upnor, Usk, Villeneuve-sur-Yonne, Warkworth, Warwick, Weeting, White, Wolvesey.

Castor (Cambs.), St. Kyneburga: 103; *see also* Base-mouldings (references).

Cawfields Roman turret, 20, 21.

C.B.A., *see* Council for British Archaeology.

Ceilings, ornamental: 289, 292-5, 322.

Cemetery, Iron Age, *see* Owslebury.

Cereal grains, analysis: 76; pottery: 79-80.

Champlevé enamelwork: 41.

Charcoal study: 78.

Charles IV, Emperor, bequeathed relics to Prague: 95.

Chartley Castle (Staffs.). building by Ralph de Blundeville: 152; by Ralph, earl of Chester: 174.

Châtelherault, Duke of, *see* Hamilton, 3rd Lord.

Chatham (Kent), naval establishments: 263, 265.

Chedworth Roman villa (Glos.): 31, 75.

Chemical analysis: 73.

Chenies, monument at: 311.

Chepstow Castle (Gwent), work of the Marshalls: 142, 144, 146, 151.

Chester (Ches.), St. John, dating: 100, 104; *see also* Base-mouldings (references).

Chesters (*Cilurnum*) Roman turret (Northumbs.): 13, 21, 24.

Chicago University, radio-carbon dating, 81.

Chichester cathedral (W. Sx.), rebuilt by Ralph Luffa: 102; *see also* Base-mouldings (references).

Children and Young Persons, Commission on Employment: 342, 344.

Chilham Castle (Kent) tower: 151; *cf.* Usk.

Chilterns, furniture manufacture: 335.

Chimneypiece, Clifford castles: 312; Heath Old Hall: 295; Tredegar House: 320.

Chinon (France), Tour de Coudray: 174.

Christ Church cathedral, *see* Bergen, Birsay, Canterbury.

Church, A. H.: 74.

Cilurnum, see Chesters.

Circles of stones: 3; of wood, *see* Ringposts.

Cirencester, Roman: 73.

Clapham, Sir Alfred W.: 79, 102, 103, 104.

Clare, Gilbert de, 9th earl of Clare, Caerphilly and Usk castles: 144, 146, 147; Gilbert de, 10th earl of Clare (killed 1314): 147; Isabel de, m. Wm. Marshal: 140; Richard FitzGilbert de, earl of Pembroke (died 1176): 139; Richard de, 8th earl of Clare (died 1262): 146; Walter de, Lordship of Struguil (*alias* Chepstow), 139.

Clarendon House (London): 327, Pl.XXXIb.

Clark, G. T., account of work at Tower of London: 155-171 *passim*.

Clay figurines, Roman, at Nornour: 44.

Clifford, Mrs. E. M., excavations at Witcombe R. villa: 27, 34.

Clifford, 12th Baron, at Skipton Castle: 307; George, 13th Baron, earl of Cumberland: 303; The Lady Anne, Countess Dowager of Dorset, Pembroke and Montgomery, high sheriff of the county of Westmorland, Lady of the Honour of Skipton-in-Craven: 303 ff.; church-building: 311; *see* castles of Appleby, Brough, Brougham, Pendragon, Skipton and Bardney Tower.

Clinton, de Witt, tree-ring dating: 74.

Cockham Wood fort (Kent): 266, 280, 281.

Coghlan, H. H.: 75.

Coins, Roman, from Bartlow: 45; Hadrian's Wall: 19, 22; Nornour: 44.

Collingwood, R. G., enamel study: 41, 42.

Cologne (Germany), pottery: 200, 223, 233, 219.

Colton (Lancs.), Bobbin Mill: 335, 336.

Congress of Archaeological Societies: 79.

Conisborough Castle (Yorks.): 211.

Conservation, *Intro.*, xvi ff., 77, 79.; Department, Institute of Archaeology: 79.

Contract of 1347, Kenilworth: 213.

Conway Castle (Gwynedd); 209.

Cooling Castle (Isle of Grain): 265.

Copper, analysis: 76.

Corfe Castle (Dorset), gateway: 144.

Corrosion in metals: 73.

Costrels, *see under* Pottery, medieval.

Coward family, at Stott Park Bobbin Mill: 340, 343, 345.

Commissioners on Employment of Children and Young Persons: 342, 344.

Cowen, J. D.: 41, 48.

Couçy (France), circular keep: 151.

Council for British Archaeology (C.B.A.): 11, 79, 80.

Craignethan Castle (Lanarks.), seat of the Hamiltons: 239 ff., Pls. XVI, XVII, 240, 242; build of Hamilton of Finnart: 240; caponiers: 239, 247, 251, 256-258, 248, 252, Pl. XIXa; description: 244-255; excavation 1971: 255; historical background: 239-244; house of Andrew Hay: 244, 256; plaques: 256; programme of work: 256; slighting 1579: 243, 244; Towers, N.E. demolished: 254; N.W.: 254; S.E.: 253, 254; Towerhouse: 239, 244 ff., 242, 246, Pls. XVIIIa, b, c; *see also* Artillery.

Cranborne Chase (Dorset), Iron Age settlement site: 6.

Cromwell, Oliver (mention); 309, 310.

Crook (Durham), machinery manufacture: 343.

Crown Jewels, *see* London, Tower of, Wakefield Tower.

Crusade, undertaken by earl Ronald: 88.

Cunnington, Mrs. M. E., excavations: 3.

Curwen, Dr. C.: 78.

Curwen, Dr. E.: 78.

Cuthbert, saint, shrine: 93.

Cutthrottis, firearms: 257.

Danebury (Hants), Iron Age settlement: 9.

Daniel, Samuel, masque author; 303, 304, 311.

Darnley, Henry Stuart, Lord: 241.

Darwin, Charles R., effect of earthworms: 72, 74, 75.

Davison, B. K.: 158.

Davy, Sir Humphrey: 73.

Davy, John: 73.

De Ireby Tower, *see* Carlisle Castle.

De la Mare, Sir Peter, Seneschal of Lande: 213.

Delft (Holland), tiles: 320.

Dendrochronology: 74.

Denton Roman turret: 22, 24.

Department of the Environment: (Foreword) xiii,, 80, 222; *see also* Ancient Monuments, Inspectorate of.

Department of Human Environment: 79.

Department of Scientific Industrial Research: 77.

Deptford dockyard (G.L.C.): 263.

Deshoulières, F., Romanesque bases: 104, 126.

Despenser, Hugh le, the Younger: 147, 148.

Devenyshe, Thomas, of Frinnesbury: 263.

Dirleton castle (E. Lothian): 174.

Dimbleby, Professor G. W.: 79.

Documents, stored in Wakefield Tower: 157, 165, 174.

Dobson, coach-painter at Tredegar: 331.

Dodsworth, Jane, m. John Kay, *senior*: 286, 288, 295.

Dorchester, Roman: 6.

Douglas, Dr. A. E., astronomer: 75.

Dourdan (France), circular keep: 151.

Dover Castle (Kent): 204; Constables Tower: 207; *see also under* Basemouldings (references).

Draffan (Lanarks.), lands of: 239.

Drawbridge at Upnor: 273.

Drury, Sir William, Governor of Berwick; 243.

Dumbarton Castle (Dunbartonshire): 241, 243.

Dumnonii, tribal levy: 21.

Dunbar Castle (Dunbartonshire): 257.

Dundee (Angus), bobbin shops: 335.

Dunfermline Abbey: 88, 90.

Dürer, Albrecht, caponier design: 257.

Durham cathedral, masons: 88; shrine of St. Cuthbert: 93.

Durrington Walls (Wilts.), embanked enclosure: 3, 6, **2, 5**; excavation: 3; pottery: 3, 4; radio-carbon date: 3.

Dutch fleet: 265; tiles: 320, 326.

Eadmer, chronicler: 102.

Earthworms: 72, 74, 75.

Edinburgh (Lanarks.), pottery: 222.

Edinburgh Castle, taken by English: 243; David's tower: 257.

Edney, Simon, smith: 328, 329; William, smith, burgess of Bristol: 329.

Edward I, 13c. work at Tower of London: 156–174 *passim*.

Egilsay (Orkney), Earl Magnus slain: 86.

Elizabeth I, arms at Tower of London: 157; building of Upnor: 263; masques at Court: 303, 304; tomb: 311.

Elizabethan England: 296.

Enamel residues: 70.

Enamel-working sites: Anthée Roman villa: 42; Garranes: 42; Mt. Beuvray: 42; Traprain Law: 43: Wilderspool: 42.

Enamelled articles, Roman, 41 ff.; *see* Brooches, Tables and stands, Vessels.

Enclosures: with antennae ditches: 7; causewayed (henges): 3, 4, **5**; embanked: 3, 4, **5**; kite-shaped: 6, 7; Little-Woodbury type, 7, 9, **8**.

Environmental archaeology: 79.

Erlendur, Icelandic bishop: 95.

Ernulf, prior of Canterbury, abbot of Peterborough and bishop of Rochester: 116, 120, 126.

Evans, Sir Arthur, archaeologist: 77.

Evans, Sir John, archaeologist: 72, 77.

Evans, Dr. J. G., archaeologist: 3.

Ewell (Surrey), Roman pottery: 73.

Excavations: *see* Anau, Balksbury Camp, Basingstoke, Craignethan Castle, Cranborne Chase, Danebury, Durrington Walls, Gussage All Saints, Hadrian's Wall, Little Woodbury, London, Tower of, Marden, Mount Pleasant, Nornour, Owslebury, Portway, Thundersbarrow, Upnor Castle, Walesland Rath, Witcombe Roman villa, Woodhenge.

Eyers, Thomas, of Stott Mill: 342.

Factory Acts, 1867: 344.

Fairfax, Colonel: 309; General: 309.

Falaise (France), tower: 174.

Farmsteads, Iron Age: see Cranborne Chase, Little Woodbury, Walesland Rath.

Faraday, Michael: 73.

Faro Islands: 95.

Fell, W. A., machinery manufacturer: 343, 346.

Felstead (ffelstead), Richard of, master carpenter: 213-215, 217.

Fenland Research Committee: 78.

Finsthwaite (Lancs.): 336.

Finsthwaite Heights High Dam: 345.

Fireplaces: at Appleby Castle: 306; Brougham Castle: 307; Carlisle Castle: 192, 196-200; Heath Old Hall: 289, 293, 295, Pl. XXIV; Holyrood House: 320; Tower of London (Henry III): 160, 179; Tredegar House: 320, 326; Usk Castle: 150.

FitzOsbern, Roger, son of William: 139; William, earl of Hereford, subdual of Gwent: 139.

FitzRolf, Thurstin, in Domesday Survey of Usk: 139.

Flambard, Ranulf, associated with building period: 103.

Flint implements: 4, 72.

Force Forge Bobbin Mill (Cumbria): 336.

Frechen (Germany) medieval kiln: 219, 220, 219.

Frigidarium at Witcombe Roman villa: 31.

Frontier, Antonine: 16, 19; cf. Antonine Wall; Severan: 18, 19, 20; Trajanic: 14.

Fuller, Isaac, artist (1692): 323.

Furness (Lancs.), wood-turning: 335.

Furnishings 17c. at Tredegar House: 323–324.

Gadebridge Park Roman villa (Herts.): bath-house: 31; brooch found: 60; comparison with Witcombe: 38; courtyard: 39.

Garranes (Eire), enamel-working site: 42.

Garthside turret: 13.

Geer, Baron G. de: 74.

Geological Society: 75.

Geophysical survey: 76, 81.

Gervase of Canterbury: 89, 92.

Gibbes, Dr., chemist: 72.

Gilbert, John, bricklayer: 327.

Gillalees Beacon, Hadrian's Wall: 14.

Gillingham (Kent): 263; Fort: 266, 280, 281; St. Mary's Creek, naval defences: 265, 266.

Gisors Castle (France): 151, 174.

Glasgow (Lanarks.), bobbin shops: 335.

Glass, analysis: 73.

Goldcliff Priory (Gwent), prior abducted: 148, 149.

Gommes, Sir Bernard de, engineer: 266, 280, 281.

Goodrich castle (Herefs.), gatehouse: 204.

Gower castle (Glam.), granted to Wm. Marshall: 151.

Gowland, Professor William: 75, 76.

Grays Thurrock (Essex), hoard: 76.

Great Chesters (Aesica) (Northumbs.): 21, 22.

Green, Edward, Heath Old Hall: 287.

Greenfield, E., excavation Witcombe Roman villa: 27–38 passim.

Gregory, Arthur, engineer: 271, 279.

Grosmont castle (Gwent): 151, 152.

Guild of Potters: 220, 221.

Gundulf, bishop of Rochester: 113.

Gussage All Saints (Dorset), Iron Age settlement, antennae ditches: 7; bronze-smith's workshop: 9; excavation: 7, 8; phases of settlement: 9.

Gynewell, John, bishop of Lincoln: 213.

Haakon IV: 96.

Hadrian's Wall: 13 ff.; coins: 19, 22; enamelled vessels: 43; Military Way: 21; pottery: 19, 20, 22; turf wall: 13, 14, 15, 16; turrets: construction, 15, 19, 15; dating, 19; demolition, 20, 23; excavations, 20, 21, 22; function, 14, 22–23; garrison, 22; Guardianship (schedule), 24; inscription of 6th Legion, 16; interior, 16 ff., Pl. Ia, 17; mortarium, 22; occupation, 19; reconstruction, 18; schedule of turrets, 24.

Hakon, Earl, of Orkney: 86.

Haltonchesters turret (Onnum): 23.

Haltwhistle Burn, Roman fort: 14.

Hamilton, Anne, duchess of: 244; Lord Claud: 241, 243; James, 1st Lord Hamilton: 239; James, 2nd Lord Hamilton, 1st earl of Arran: 240; James, 3rd Lord Hamilton, 2nd earl of Arran, Duke of Châtelherault: 241; James, 4th Lord Hamilton, 3rd earl of Arran (insane): 243.

Hamilton of Finnart, Sir James (illeg. son of 2nd Lord Hamilton): 240, 241; work at Craignethan attributed: 244.

Hamilton, Lord John: 243; John, archbishop of St. Andrews (illeg. son of 2nd Lord Hamilton): 243.

Hammerbeams at Kenilworth: 213, 215.

Harrison, John, built Stott Mill: 336.

Hartley, Richard A.: 151.

Harwell, Atomic Energy Research Establishment: 81.

Hastings, battle of: 139.

Hatchett, C., chemist: 72.

Haverfordwest Castle (Dyfed), granted to Wm. Marshal: 151.

Hawkes, Professor C. F. C.: 82.

Hawley, Lt.-Col. W., excavation at Stonehenge: 78.

Hay, Andrew, of Craignethan: 244, 256.

Healing, miraculous: 86, 96.

Health of employees in industry: 342.

Heath Hall (W. Yorks.): 285, **285**.

Heath House (W. Yorks.): 285, **285**.

Heath Old Hall (W. Yorks.): 285 ff., **285**; exterior: 287-289, Pls. XXIIa, XXIIb, XXIIIb, **287**; fireplaces: 293-295, Pl. XXIV; Great Chamber: Pl. XXVc; hall/courtyard: 294, **287**; interior, 289-296, **290**, **291**; plasterwork, decorated, 292-293, Pls. XXVIa, b.

Heavy mineral analysis: 78.

Heer: 72.

Heidsteikis; 257.

Henge monuments, *see* Enclosures, Stonehenge, Woodhenge.

Henry, Mlle. Françoise: 41.

Henry III, siege of Usk: 144; Montgomery Castle: 152; Tower of London defences: 156, 158, 159, 162; Wakefield Tower camera: 171.

Henry IV, imprisoned earl of March: 149.

Henry VIII, blockhouses: 279; castle-building: 265, 266, 280, 281; dockyards: 263; Usk Castle: 150.

Henry of Blois: 103, 120, 122, 123, 129.

Henry of Oxford: 122.

Herbert, Philip, 4th earl of Pembroke, 1st earl of Montgomery: 304, 309; Sir Thomas, of Tintern (17c.): 150; William earl of Pembroke (executed 1469), son of William ap Thomas: 150; Sir William (16c.): 150.

H.M. Office of Works: 27, 80, 191, 303.

H.M. Ministry of Works: 80, 191: *see also* Ministry of Public Building and Works.

High Wycombe Roman villa (Bucks.), bathhouse: 31, 33.

Hill forts, Iron Age, *see* Balksbury Camp, Bury Hill, Danebury, Maiden Castle.

Hirsel, Lord Home of the, *see* Home, 12th earl.

Historic Buildings Council, *Intro.*, xviii.

Hoards, copper and bronze: 76.

Hoare, Sir Richard Colt: 71, 72.

Hockwold-cum-Wilton (Norfolk), plate brooches: 54, 60, **55**, **61**.

Holy Land, crusade: 88.

Holyrood House, Edinburgh, fireplaces: 320.

Home, earl of: 239; 12th earl of, repairs to Craignethan castle: 244.

Honorius of Autun: 91.

Housesteads (*Vercovicum*), Roman fort: 13, 24.

Housesteads Milecastle: 22.

Humphries, R. H. S., Seigneur of Usk: 154.

Iceland: 96; Bishop Thorlacius of: 95.

Implements of flint: 4, 72; of bronze: 7, 41, 43, 44, 49.

Indenture for Carlisle Castle: 192, 207, 208; Kenilworth: 213, 217.

Industry, *see* Lakeland, Stott Park Bobbin Mill.

Innocent IV, papal bull: 174, **174**.

Inspectorate of Ancient Monuments: *Intro.*, xv, xvii, 80; *see also* Ancient Monuments Laboratory.

Institute for Quarternary Research: 79.

Institute of Archaeology: 78, 79.

Inventory of Tredegar House, 17c.: 323, 326, 331; and horses 18c.: 331.

Iodine, identification of: 73.

Ireby, William de: 191.

Iron-working, Roman: 19.

Jackson, Dr. J. W.: 78.

James I: 304, 306.

James III, of Scotland, earl of Orkney: 96.

James V of Scotland: 241, 256.

James VI of Scotland, boy king: 241.

Jewel House, *see* Crown Jewels *under* London, Tower of.

John, work at Corfe castle: 144; affairs with Wm. Marshal: 151; work at Tower of London: 159, 173; de Ireby, tenant-in-chief: 191.

John of Gaunt, duke of Lancaster: 216.

John, bishop of Oxford: 128.

John of Séez: 101.

Jones, Inigo, masque at Whitehall: 304; work at Chenies: 311.

Jülich (Germany): 219; Duchy of: 219, 220.

Kappeskrug, *see* Pottery, medieval.

Kay, John (senior): 286; John (his son), built Heath Old Hall, *c.* 1580: 286-298 *passim*.
    Robert (his son): 286.

Kelso Abbey (Roxburghshire), 239.

Kenilworth Castle (Warwicks.): 211 ff. **212**; contract (Lendenture): 213, 217; Hall 14c.: 211 ff.: hammerbeams: 213, Pl. XVa; keep 12c.: 211; Leicester block: 211; phases of reconstruction: 214–215; Saint Lowe Tower: 213; Strong Tower: 213, Pl. XIVa; undercroft: 211, 213, Pl. XVb.

Kennard, A. S.: 78.

Kidwelly Castle (Dyfed): 207.

Kildrummy Castle (Aberdeenshire), tower: 174.

Kinch, Professor E.: 76.

King Charles Castle (Tresco): 279, 280.

Kirkby Lathorpe (Lincs.), enamel vessel from: 45, 48, **46**.

Kirkjubøur (Faro I.), Magnus cathedral: 95; relics: 96.

Kirkwall (Orkney I.): Bishop's see transferred: 87; Palace, 96; odal land rights: 88; St. Magnus cathedral: 85 ff.; building phases, 88–91; collapse of tower, 90; dedication, 88, 89; E. end demolished, 91; founding, 85, 87, 88; mural interments, 94, 95; Orkneyinga Saga, 85; Romanesque work, 88, 91, **90**, **92**, Pls. III, IVc; St. Magnus shrine, 87, 91, 92, 96, **94**.

Knole (Kent): 304, 310.

Kol, father of earl Ronald: 85.

Kolson, earl Ronald, *see* Ronald, earl.

Kreissparkasse (Langwehe, Germany), kiln; 222, 226, 227, 229.

Kuckertz-Renner family, potters: 221.

Laboratories, *see* Ancient Monuments, Belfast University, British Museum Research, Cambridge University, Chicago University, National Physical, Oxford Research.

Lake dwellings, Swiss: 72.

Lakeland Industry (Cumbria): 335–336.

Lancashire textile trade: 335.

Lancaster, Duchy of, contract, *see* Kenilworth Castle.

Lancaster, Henry, earl and 1st duke of: 213.

Land rights, odal: 88.

Lanfranc, Archbishop of Canterbury: 101, 108; building period: 103.

Langbroek (Netherlands), Van Beuningen collection: 226.

Langewehe (Germany), medieval kiln: 219 ff., **219**; historical evidence: 220–221; trade route, plan: **219**; *see also* Pottery, medieval.

Largs, battle of: 96.

Lathe shops, *see* Stott Park Bobbin Mill.

Lauderdale, earl of, at Holyrood House; 320.

Laurence, abbot: 124.

Laval (France), hourd at castle: 143.

Layard, Sir Austen H.: 74.

Lead glaze: 73.

Lee, Sir Richard, designer of Upnor castle; 269, 270, 277, 280, 281.

Legions, Roman: 16;

Leicester, earl of: 211.

Leicester, disc brooch: 51, **52**.

Lendenture, Kenilworth castle: 213, 217.

Lennox, Earl of, Regent of Scotland: 243.

Leveson, Sir John, at Upnor castle: 271, 272.

Lewyn, John, mason: 192, 203, 208, 209.

Libby, Professor W., radio-carbon dating: 81.

Limestone Bank Roman turret: 21.

Linlithgow Palace (W. Lothian): 241.

Little Woodbury (Wilts.), Iron Age farmstead: 7, 9; antennae ditches: 7; excavation: 7; -type: 7, 9.

Llangybi castle (Gwent): 147.

Lochmaben castle (Dumfriesshire), siege of: 241.

Locke, Humphrey, surveyor and carpenter: 269-272, 281.

Lockleys Roman villa (Herts.): 38; *cf.* Witcombe R. villa.

Lockyer, J. N.: 75.

London, Langewehe ware found: 222.

London, New Temple Church, inscription; 103; *see also* Base-mouldings (references).

London, Tower of: 155 ff.; Beauchamp Tower: 159; Bell Tower: 159; Bloody Tower gateway: 159, 162-3, 173; Blundeville Tower, *see* Wakefield Tower; Broad Arrow Tower: 162; Coldharbour Gate: 157, 161, 173, 174; excavation, 158; dating, Edward I: 177; drains: 162, 163; Edward I fortifications: 163, 168; *enceinte*, pre-Henry III: 159.

excavations:
E. of Wakefield Tower, and postern, 157; IXa, b; Coldharbour gatehouse Main Guard, 158; W. of Wakefield Tower, 158; Water Lane, 158, IXc, IXd; Wakefield Tower grd. flr., 158, **Xa, b, c, XIa, 160, 178**; Roman building found, 158; Bloody Tower, 158, 159.

Garden Tower: 161; Great Hall: 156, 173, 174; Guardroom: 159, 161, **160**; Hall Tower, *alias* Wakefield Tower; Lanthorn Tower: 173; Main Guard: 157, 171-174, Pl. XIa, **166**; Old Treasury House: 157, 158, VIIIa; Palace, medieval,

London, Tower of, continued—
155, 171, 173, Pl. XId; Palace Ward: 156; Portcullis: 159, 161; Record Tower, *alias* Wakefield Tower; Roman wall: 159, 173; St. Thomas Tower watergate: 155, 157, 163, 168, 170, 171, *passim*; Salt Tower: 157, 162.
Wakefield Tower: 155 ff., **156**, Pl. VIIId; Clark account, 155-171, *passim*; Crown Jewels, vault, 155, 157, 158, **Xa, b, c,** 165, **VIIIc;** floor reinstatement, 155, 165, **167;** Guardroom, 159, **160;** king's chamber, 174; loops, 161, 166, **160,** Pl. XIc; masons' marks, 165, 172, **172;** oratory, 170; other names of: Hall Tower, 155; Record Tower, 157; Blundeville Tower, 175; papal bulla, 174, **174;** pottery, 165, 177-188, **178, 180, 182, 186,** *cf.* 160; record store, 157, 174; timber lacing, 168, **169;** -props, **160c.**
Wardrobe Tower: 159; Well: 162; White Tower: 159, 161, 163, 174.
Long barrows, 6, **5.**
Longtown castle (Herefs.): 140, 150, 151.
Losinga, Herbert: 113.
Lucia, saint, day of: 87.
Luffa, Ralph, Chichester cathedral: 102.
Lullingstone Roman villa (Kent): 38, 40.
Lyell, Sir Charles, tree-ring dating: 74.
Lyre Abbey (France); 139.
Lysons, S., excavations Witcombe R.v.: 27-38, *passim*.

Maby, J. C.: 78.
Macclesfield (Ches.), bobbin mills: 345.
Magna fort (Carvoran): 14, 21.
Magnetic surveying: 80.
Magnus, saint, the earl: 85 ff.; *cf.* Kirkwall; canonisation: 86, 87; cathedral founded: 85, 88; relics: 85-87, 91, 94-96; Sagas: 85, 86, 88, 95; shrines (reliquary): 86, 87, 91, 92, visit by King Haakon: 96; vision: 86.
Maia, see Bowness on Solway.
Maiden castle hill fort: 6.
Maid of Norway: 95.
Mains Rigg Roman signal tower: 14.
Malmesbury Abbey (Wilts.), sculptures: 102; *see also under* Base-mouldings (references).
Malmesbury, William of: 88, 102.
Manchester, cotton trade: 344.
Mar, earl of, Regent of Scotland: 243.

March, earl of, *see* Mortimer.
Marden (Wilts.), embanked enclosure: 3, 5; excavation: 4; pottery: 4; radio-carbon date: 4; ring-posts: 4, 6.
Margaret, queen: 95.
Marietta (Ohio), Ohio mounds: 74.
Marine Causes, Treasurer of: 263.
Mark, saint, body stolen: 94.
Marshal(l), Anselm, titular earl of Pembroke and Striguil: 146; Richard, earl of Pembroke and Striguil: 144; William (the Elder), earl of Pembroke and Striguil: 140; castles of Cardigan, Carmarthen, Gower, Haverfordwest, 151; Chepstow, 140, 142, 144, 151; Usk, 141, 151; died 1219, 152; m. Isobel de Clare, 140.
Marshall, Joshua, sculptor: 304.
Marston Moor, battle of: 306.
Martini, Francesco di Giorgio, caponier design: 257.
Mary of Lorraine, Regent of Scotland: 241.
Mary Stuart, Queen of Scots, at Craignethan and Cadzow castles: 241.
Maskelyne, N. S.: 74.
Masonry, re-use of, in Carlisle castle: 197; in St. Magnus cathedral: 90; polychrome: 88, 90, Pls. III, IVa.
Masons marks: 162, 172.
Masques at Stuart court: 303.
Medway, r. (Kent), naval defences: 263, 265; Dutch fleet: 265, **264.**
Metallurgical analysis: 75, 80.
Ministry of Public Building and Works (Ministry of Works): 3, 80, 239.
Mollusca study: 78, 80.
Montalembert, M. R. de: 257.
Mont Beuvray (France), enamel-working site: 42.
Montgomery castle (Powys), twin-towered gatehouse: 151, 152.
Moray, Earl of, Regent of Scotland: 241, 243.
Morgan, Octavius, antiquary, of Tredegar: 315-331, *passim*; John, of Tredegar (1700-1719): 329; Sir William, of Tredegar (1603-1653): 326; Sir William, of Tredegar (1664-1680): 315, 325, 331; Sir William, of Tredegar (1719-31) (son of John): 329.
Mortar, Roman, analysis: 73.
Mortarium, Hadrian's Wall: 22.
Mortimer, Edmund, 5th Earl of March, work at Usk: 148-149.
Morton, earl of, Regent of Scotland: 243.
Mount Grace (N. Yorks.), pottery: 222.

Mount Pleasant (Dorset), embanked enclosure, excavation: 3, 4, 2; pottery: 4; radio-carbon date: 4; ring-posts: 4.
Mucklebank Roman turret: 22.
Musgrave, Sir Philip, at Appleby castle: 305.

Napoleon (Bonaparte): 73.
National Physical Laboratory: 81.
Nauthane fortalice (Lanarks.): 240.
Naval defence, see Upnor castle.
Nether Denton Roman fort (Cumbria): 14.
Newark castle (Selkirkshire): 245.
Newcastle-upon-Tyne, Black Gate, pottery: 222; (*Pons Aelius*) Roman Turrets: 13.
Newmarch, C.H.: 73.
Newstead (Border), brooches: 44.
Nornour (I. of Sc.). prehistoric and Roman site excavation: 43, 44; group of bronze objects: 43–44, 54, 56, 58, 59, 60, 57; *cf.* Brooches, enamelled.
Norsemen: 88, 96.
Norway, Maid of: 95.
Norway: 85; king of: 88, 96.
Norwich cathedral (Norfolk), Romanesque bases: 101 *q.v.*
Nymphaeum at Witcombe R. villa: 36.

Oakley, Kenneth P.: 78.
Odal land rights, Orkney: 88.
Odiham castle (Hants.): 151.
Old Hall, see Heath Old Hall.
Old Winteringham (Humberside), brooch: 62, 63.
Olympia (Greece), excavation 1875: 73.
O'Neil, B. H. St. J.: *Intro.*, xviii, 151.
Onnum, see Haltonchesters.
Ordnance, see Artillery.
Orkney: 85, 88, 91; Egilsay: 86; Birsay: 86; James III, earl of: 96; see also Kirkwall.
Orkneyinga Saga: 85 ff.
Osteology: 71, 72, 75, 76, 78.
Owslebury (Hants.), Iron Age settlement, excavation: 9.
Overton Down (Wilts.), artificial earthwork: 82.
Oxford Research Laboratory: 80.

Paine, James, architect: 285.
Paisley (Renfrews.): 335.
Palaeo-ecological studies: 80.
Palaeo-magnetic dating: 80.
Palisades at Mt. Pleasant: 6.
Papal Bulla found in Tower of London: 174, 174.
Park Street Roman villa (Herts), bathhouse: 31.

Patent for bulwark at Upnor: 266.
Pathology: 72.
Paul, earl of Birsay: 85, 86, 87, 91.
Pavement, Roman, at Witcombe R. villa: 29, 31.
Pearson, Dr. G.: 73.
Peel Crag Roman Turret: 21.
Peers, Sir Charles: 78.
Pembroke, earls of, *see* Herbert.
Pembroke castle (Dyfed), hourd: 143.
Pendragon castle (Mallerstang, Westm.), The Lady Anne Clifford: 303, 305, 308–309; Parish Church, rebuilt: 309.
Penmon Priory (Anglesey): 100.
Penrose, F. C.: 75.
Penshurst Place (Kent), 14c. roofing: 216.
Peterborough (Cambs.), John of Séez: 101, 103; *see also* Base-mouldings (references).
Petriana, see Stanwix.
Petrology: 74, 78, 80.
Philippe Auguste, of France, towers: 151, 174.
Photography, archaeological recording: 75, 76.
Piggott, Professor Stuart: 3.
Pigments, analysis: 73.
Pike Hill Roman tower: 13, 14, 15, 22.
Pitt Rivers, General A.: *Intro.*, xv, 71–72, 75, 76, 78, 83.
Plaster, Roman: 73.
Plasterwork, decorative: 292–293, 320, 322.
Pollen analysis: 79.
Poltross Burn Roman turret: 22.
Pompeii: 73.
Pons Aelius, see Newcastle-upon-Tyne.
Portcullis, *see under* Carlisle castle, Tower of London.
Porter, Kingsley: 102.
Portland castle (Dorset): 280.
Portway (Hants.), excavation: 9.
Postholes, Ringposts: 3–11, 2.
Potters, Guild of: 221: emblem of: 220; marks of: 221.
Pottery:
    Neolithic: Durrington Walls, 3, 4; Marden, 4; Mount Pleasant, 4.
    Iron Age: Balksbury Camp, 9, 11.
    Roman: Ewell (Sy.), 73; Hadrian's Wall, 18, 19, 20, 21, 22.
    Medieval: Bellarmine, 221; Cistercian, 226; Tudor Green, 224, 226; Langewehe: British finds, 221, 222; chimney pots, 221; costrels, 233–234, 235; cups, 234, 235; English arms, 221; fabric and forms, 223–224;

Pottery—Medieval—Langewehe—continued— floor tiles, 221; history, 220–221; horns, 234, 235; jugs, 224–233, 236, **227, 228, 230, 232,** 235; *kappeskrug*, 221; kiln sites, 219; museum, 220; Pingsdorf type, 220, 224; pipkins, 235, **235**; roofing tiles, 221; water pipes, 221.

Pottery glaze analysis: 73, 78; manufacture study: 80, 82.

Prague, St. Vitus Church, relics: 94.

Pratt, James, steward at Tredegar: 328.

Pratt, Roger, architect of Clarendon House: 327.

Preservation of monuments: *Intro.*, xv ff, Industrial: 346; *cf.*, Conservation.

Prestwich, J.: 72.

Queensborough Castle (Kent): 265.

Querns from Hadrian's Wall: 19.

Radio-activity discovered: 76.

Radio-carbon dating (C.14): 76, 79; installations: 81; Durrington Walls: 3; Marden: 4; Mt. Pleasant: 4; Sanctuary: 4; Woodhenge: 3.

Raeren (Belgium), kilns, pottery: 220, 221, 223, 224, **219**.

Raeren Neudorf, kiln, pottery: 224, 232, 233.

Raglan castle (Gwent): 139, 150.

Rain analysis: 76.

Rath, *see* Walesland Rath.

Reconstruction, Hadrian's Wall turret: 18; Witcombe R. villa: 27, 39, **32, 33,** 35, 37.

Redman, Matthew, warden of Carlisle castle: 208.

Regalia, *see* Crown Jewels *under* London, Tower of

Reginald, abbot of Evesham: 113.

Relics, medieval cult, *see* Magnus, saint; Ronald, saint; Thorlacius, bishop; William the Old; *cf.* Kirkwall, St. Magnus cathedral shrines.

Remigius, bishop of Lincoln: 111.

Renn, Derek F.: 151.

Resistivity survey: 76.

Richard II, Carlisle castle: 192.

Richard of Ilchester, bishop of Winchester: 103, 128.

Richmond, Professor I. A.: 41, 48.

Richmond castle (Yorks.): 204.

Ring-posts and post-holes: 3–11, **2**.

Rochester castle (Kent), coast protection: 265; as quarry: 271, 272.

Rodes, Francis, steward to earl of Shrewsbury: 297.

Roger, bishop of Salisbury, building periods attributed to, 102, 103, 104, 119, 122, 123, 124.

Romanesque bases, *see* Base-mouldings, Romanesque.

Rome: 73; skull stolen: 94.

Ronald, saint, the earl, canonised: 94; crusade to Holy Land: 88; founded St. Magnus cathedral, Kirkwall: 87; in saga: 86; relics in pier: 94, 95, Pl. IVb, **94**.

Röntgen, W. K.: 76.

Rosny (France), house of Sully: 326.

Rouen (France), keep: 151.

Rounds: 7.

Roxburgh Castle, commission of enquiry: 203.

Royal Academy of Arts: 74.

Royal Agricultural College, Cirencester: 73, 75.

Royal Archaeological Institute: 71, 75.

'The Royal Charles': 265.

Royal Institution: 81.

Royal School of Mines: 76.

Royal Society: 72, 76, 77.

Rudchester (*Vindovala*): 22.

Rudge Cup: 14, 41, 43, 48, 49, Pl. Ib.

Rudston (Humberside), trumpet brooch: 60, **61**.

Ruetimeyer: 72.

Ruprich-Robert: 103, 104.

Ruyter, Admiral M. A. de: 265.

Sackville, Richard, 3rd Earl of Dorset: 304.

Sagas: Orkneyinga, 85, 86, 88, 95; Sturlunga, 95; Sverri's, 96.

St. Albans (Herts.), disc brooch: 51, 52, **52**.

St. Magnus, *see* Magnus, saint, the earl.

St. Magnus cathedral, *see* Kirkwall.

Saints, power of: 85.

Salvin, Anthony, work at Tower of London: 155.

Salzman, Dr. L. F.: 213, 217.

Sanctuary, the (Wilts.), Neolithic henge settlement, excavation: 3, 4; pottery: 3; rings of post-holes: 3, 4, 2; stone circles: 3.

Sandal castle (Yorks.), Langewehe ware: 222.

Sandsfoot castle (Dorset), defences; 280.

Savile, Dorothy, m. John Kay: 286; Sir Henry: 286, 297.

Saxl, Friedrich (Fritz): 102.

Scandinavia, wood importation: 344.

Scapa Flow (Orkney): 96.

Scarborough castle (N. Yorks.), Constable's Tower: 207.

Schedule B, military building: 191.

Schedule of labour and material, Upnor: 269.

Schwarz, Josef, pottery collection: 220.

Sconces, at Upnor: 265.

Scotland, Abbot of St. Augustine's: 101, 103.

Scott, Dr. Alexander: 77.

Scott, Sir Walter, visit to Craignethan: 244.

Scrope, Sir Richard le, Lord of Bolton: 204, 208.

Sedbergh (Cumbria), woollen/corn mill: 340.

Sediments, analysis (varve); 74.

Segedunum, see Wallsend-on-Tyne.

Semphill, Lord, prisoner at Craignethan: 243.

Serlio, Sebastiano, architect: 326.

Sewingshields Roman turret: 20.

Sheerness, blockhouse, burnt by Dutch: 265.

Sheffield (S. Yorks), toolmakers: 345.

Shetland Islands, *see* Unst.

Siegburg (Germany), kiln, pottery: 220, 221, 223, 225, 233, 219.

Sigurdsson, King Sverre, relics: 95.

Silchester Roman town: 75.

Simpson, Dr. D. D. A.: 1.

Silvester, pope, saint, skull stolen: 94.

Skalholt cathedral (Iceland), relics of St. Magnus: 95.

Skelwith Bridge (N. Lancs.), bobbin mill; 340.

Skenfrith castle (Gwent): 151, 152.

Skipton castle (N. Yorks.), the Lady Anne Clifford born at: .303, 305; Craven, lordship of: 305; description: 307.

Skipton Parish Church (N. Yorks), rebuilding work, George Clifford tomb: 311.

slangis (firearms): 257.

Smyth, John, M.P., bought Heath Old Hall: 287, 288.

Smythson, Robert, architect: 297, 298.

Society of Antiquaries of London: 27, 76, 79.

Society of Chemical Industry: 77.

Soil analysis: 72.

Southall (Mddx.), hoards of bronze and copper: 76.

Southampton (Hants.) pottery: 222, 229.

South-Western Group of Museums and Art Galleries: 78, 80.

Spenser, Edmund, poet: 304; monument in Westminster Abbey: 311.

Spynie Palace (Moray): 245.

Stanwix (*Petriana*) (Cumbria); 13, 24.

Stapleton, William, sheriff of Cumberland: 208.

Staveley (Derbys.), centre of bobbin industry: 335, 342.

Staveley Woodthorpe, see Rodes, Francis.

Steelrigg Roman turret: 21.

Stirling (Lanarks.), Archbishop Hamilton hanged: 243; castle, heraldic beasts: 260; *cf.* Pl. XVIIIb.

Stockport (Gt. Manchester), textile mill: 335, 345.

Stonar (Kent), pottery: 222.

Stone, Dr. J. F. S.: 78.

Stone, Nicholas, master mason: 304, 311.

Stone, composition of: 72.

Stonehenge: aerial photograph: 76; astronomy: 75; earthworms: 76; excavations: 76; petrology: 74.

Stones, standing, *see* Avebury, Sanctuary, the, West Kennet.

Stoneware, *see* Pottery.

Storrs, Jane, m. John Kay: 286.

Stott Park Bobbin Mill (Cumbria): 335 ff., Pl. XXXIIa, 337; built by Harrison: 336; business started by Cowards: 340; lathe shops: 336, 343, new shop: 344, Pl. XXXIIa, 337, 338, old shop, 341; machinery: 343, 344, Pl. XXXIIb, 345-346, 341; production: 340; water wheel, 336, 336.

Sturlunga saga: 95.

Survey, acoustic: 76; geophysical; 76; magnetic: 80; metallurgical: 80; resistivity: 76; Sverri's saga: 96.

Swaleness Fort (Kent): 265.

Swiss Lake dwellings: 72.

Tables and stands, enamelled: 49, 51, 50.

Tantallon castle (E. Lothian): 256, 258.

Taxes, building, in Orkney: 88.

Taylor, Dr. A. J.: 139, 146, *Frontis.*

tepidarium, at Witcombe R. villa: 31.

Tethys Festival: 303; *cf.* Masques.

Tewkesbury Abbey (Glos.), mouldings: 100; *see also under* Base-mouldings (references).

Thermoluminescent dating: 80.

Thistleton (Leics.), enamel brooches: 53, 62, 64, 53, 63.

Thomas, H. H, Stonehenge petrology: 74.

Thorlacius, saint, bishop: 95.

Thorney Church (Cambs.), dedication date: 102, 103; *see also under* Base-mouldings (references).

Thorny Doors Roman turret: 21.
Threave castle (Kirkcudbrightshire): 245.
Throp Roman fortlet (Cumbria): 14.
Thundersbarrow Hill (Sx.): 78.
Tickhill castle (S. Yorks.): 151.
Tiles, Dutch 17c.: 320, 326.
Tillietudlem castle: 244.
Timberwork accounts, 17c.: 323.
Tower of London, *see* London, Tower of.
Trajan's Column, watchtower depicted: 14;
    Danube Frontier: 14.
Traprain Law (E. Lothian), enamelling site:
    43.
Treasurer of Marine Causes: 263.
Tredegar House (Gwent): 315 ff.; accounts:
    bread, 325; bricks, 327; coach-painting,
    331; gates, 218; masons, 325; timber-
    work, 323; barley-sugar columns: 327,
    Pl. XXXb; 17c. buildings, 315-320, Pl.
    XXVIIIa, XXXIa, XXVIIIb; ceilings: 320,
    322, Pls. XXIXa, b; dating: 325; fire-
    places 17c.: 320; furnishings: 323-324;
    iron gates: 328, Pl. XXXc; plans, 316,
    318, 319, 321; stables: 329-331, Pls.
    XXXa, XXXc, 330; survey of 1770: 329;
    tiles: 320, 326.
Tredegar, 1st Viscount: 315.
Tree-ring dating: 74.
Tresco (I.o.Sc.), King Charles castle: 280.
triclinium at Witcombe R. villa: 35, 39.
Tudor Green pottery: 224, 226.
Tyndall, Mr. work at Tredegar: 331.
Tynemouth castle (Tyne and Wear): 204.

Uhlhaus pottery, Langewehe (Germany):
    221.
Unst (Shetland), pilgrims to St. Magnus
    shrine: 92.
Upnor Castle (Kent): 263 ff., Pl. XXa, 267;
    accounts: 266, 270, 271, 273, 277; build-
    ing period 1 (Lee): 266-271, 277, 279,
    Pls. XXa, XXb, XXI, 268, 278; building
    building period 2 (Leveson): 271-273,
    279-280, Pl. XXb; drawbridge: 273;
    excavations: 273-276, Pl. XXI, 267, 268,
    274, 275.; garrison: 265; ordnance: 265,
    272, 279, 280; patent: 266, 269-270;
    Warham Sconce: 265.
Uranium: 76.
Usk castle (Gwent); 139 ff., Pl. V., 141;
    building of Wm. Marshall: 141-146,
    Pl. VIb, 141, 143, 145, 152; building of
    de Clare: 144, 146-147, Pl. VIa.; building
    of de Burgh, and Earls of March: 147-
    149, Pl. VIIb; chapel excavation: 148;
    garrison: 139; hourd: 143; Norman

Usk castle—continued—
    keep: 139, 140, 145, Pl. VIa, 141, 143,
    145; portcullis: 144.

Valens, coin of: 22.
Van Beuningen, H. J. E., pottery collection:
    222, 226, 229, 236.
Vaughan of Trebarried, arms of: 326.
Vercovicum, see Housesteads.
Vessels, enamelled: 45-49; Beadlam (Yorks.),
    bowl: 48, 48; Brougham (Cumbria),
    bowl: 45, 47; Kirkby Lathorpe (Lincs.),
    skillet: 45, 46.
Veteripont, Idonea de, *alias* Vipont: 308-
    309, 310.
Vézelay Abbey (France): 91.
Victoria and Albert Museum: 77.
Victorinus, coin of: 22.
Villeneuve-sur-Yonne (France), keep: 151.
Vincent, Gabriel, Clerk of Works at Brough
    castle: 308.
Vindovala, see Rudchester.
Vindolanda Trust, reconstruction: 18.
Vitreous deposit analysis: 70.
Vitruvius: 99, 100.
Voelker, John: 73.

Wakefield (Yorks.): 285.
Wakefield Tower, *see* London, Tower of.
Walesland Rath (Dyfed), excavation of
    embanked settlement: 7.
Wall, *see* Antonine, Hadrian's.
Wall paintings, Roman: 34, 73.
Wallsend-on-Tyne (Tyne and Wear), turret:
    13.
Walltown Crags turret: 13, 14, 21.
Walter of Cérisy, at Evesham: 113.
Walwick Bank milecastle: 21.
Wanborough (Wilts.), brooches, Roman:
    51, 56, 52, 55.
Warkworth castle (Northumbs.): 148, 209.
Warwick castle: 204.
Water Newton (Cambs.); bronze articles,
    miniature stand: 49, 50; brooch: 54, 55.
Water Wheel, at Stott Park Mill: 336, 338.
Watts, Richard, Paymaster at Upnor castle:
    263, 266, 270, 271, 281.
West Kennet Avenue (Wilts.): 3.
Westminster Abbey (London), apse: 93;
    monument to Spenser: 304; *see also*
    Base-mouldings (references).
Westminster Hall, roof: 215, 216.
Westmorland wood turning: 335.
West Riding bobbin shops: 335.
Wharton, William, master bobbin-maker:
    340.

Wheeler, Sir Mortimer: 78.

White, Nicholas, joiner at Upnor castle: 273.

White castle (Gwent): 140, 152.

Wibert, prior of Canterbury: 103, 117, 119, 124, 127.

Wilderspool (Lancs.), Roman enamel-working site: 42.

William, the Conqueror: 158.

William the Old, bishop of Orkney, blinded: 86, 91; bones in pier: 94; crusade to Holy Land: 88; episcopal see at Birsay: 86; removed to Kirkwell; 87; farmer's vision: 86; in Norway: 87; in Saga: 86; St. Magnus relics: 86, 87.

William of Malmesbury: 88, 102.

William of Sens: 89.

William ap Thomas, Sir: 149, 150; *see also* Herbert.

William de Ireby, *see* Carlisle castle.

Willoughby, Sir Francis, of Wollaton: 297.

Willowford Roman turret: 22.

Wilton (Wilts.): 304, 310.

Wiltshire Archaeological Society: 71.

Wimborne Minster (Dorset), crossing-bases: 104; *see also under* Base-mouldings (references).

Winchester cathedral (Hants.), base-mouldings: 101, 103: *see also under* Base-mouldings (references).

Windermere (Cumbria), mill machinery: 342, 343.

Winterton (Humberside), head-stud brooch: 62, 63.

Witcombe Roman villa (Glos.): 27 ff.; bathhouse: 29, 31, 33, 34, 33; barn: 29, 36, 37, 37; *caldarium*: 31; floor-levels: 29–31, 30; *frigidarium*: 31; *Nymphaeum*: 36; pavements: 29, 31: *tepidarium*: 31; *triclinium*: 35, 39.

Wolf, Tilman, master potter: 220.

Wollaton Hall (Notts.): 297, 298.

Wombwell, John, tenant of Heath Old Hall: 287, 293.

Woodbury Culture, Iron Age: 7.

Woodhenge (Wilts.), Neolithic site, buildings: 3; excavation: 3; pottery: 3; radio-carbon dating: 3; ring-posts: 3, 2.

Woodsome Hall (Yorks.): 297.

Woolwich dockyard (G.L.C.): 263.

Wor Barrow (Dorset), excavation by Gen. Pitt Rivers: 75.

Wotton, Sir Peter de, Receiver General, Duchy of Lancaster: 213.

Wroxeter Roman Town: 75; saw-fish brooch: 59.

X-rays: 76; Fluorescence spectroscopy: 80.

Zeuner, Professor F. E.: 79.